Social Work with Elders

A Biopsychosocial Approach to Assessment and Intervention

Kathleen McInnis-Dittrich

Boston College

D0206839

Allyn and Bacon

Boston • London • Toronto • Sydney • Tokyo • Singapore

Series Editor: *Pat Quinlin*
Editor in Chief, Social Sciences: *Karen Hanson*
Editorial Assistant: *Alyssa Pratt*
Marketing Manager: *Jacqueline Aaron*
Editorial-Production Administrator: *Annette Joseph*
Editorial-Production Coordinator: *Holly Crawford*
Editorial-Production Service: *Lynda Griffiths, TKM Productions*
Composition Buyer: *Linda Cox*
Artist: *Asterisk, Inc.*
Electronic Composition: *Peggy Cabot, Cabot Computer Services*
Manufacturing Buyer: *Suzanne Lareau*
Cover Designer: *Kristina Mose-Libon*

Copyright © 2002 by Allyn & Bacon
A Pearson Education Company
75 Arlington St., Ste. 300
Boston, MA 02116

Internet: www.ablongman.com

All rights reserved. No part of the material protected by this copyright notice may be
reproduced or utilized in any form or by any means, electronic or mechanical, including
photocopying, recording, or by any information storage and retrieval system, without
written permission from the copyright owner.

Between the time Website information is gathered and then published, it is not unusual
for some sites to have closed. Also, the transcription of URLs can result in unintended
typographical errors. The publisher would appreciate notification where these occur so
that they may be corrected in subsequent editions. Thank you.

Library of Congress Cataloging-in-Publication Data

McInnis-Dittrich, Kathleen.
   Social work with elders : a biopsychosocial approach to assessment and
intervention / Kathleen McInnis-Dittrich.
      p.   cm.
   Includes bibliographical references and indexes.
   ISBN 0-321-04947-0
      1. Social work with the aged—United States.   2. Aged—Services for—United
States.   3. Aging—United States.   I. Title.

HV1461 .M384 2001
362.6'0973—dc21   00-051088

Printed in the United States of America

10 9 8 7 6 5 4 3 2 1   06 05 04 03 02 01

To my mother, Mary McCarty McInnis,

and in memory of my grandmother, Gertrude Timm McCarty

Contents

Preface

There is little doubt that social work with elders is one of the "hottest" areas of social work practice in this new millennium. As the baby boomer generation moves from middle age to old age, the sheer size of this population and its birth cohort's experience of promoting rapid social change will force the profession to develop new and innovative approaches to practice. No social institution has remained unchanged as this population has moved through the life cycle. Education, health care, the workplace, and family life have all been transformed by the needs and interests of this generation. Likewise, social workers and other helping professionals can expect this group to forge new models of what constitutes "successful aging." This is a very exciting time to be studying gerontological social work!

Over the years, I have been fortunate to have worked with an extraordinary group of elders in both personal and professional contexts. My maternal grandmother presented such a vivacious and delightful picture of the joys of being an elder that it was not until much later in my life that I truly realized that aging has its challenges as well as its joys. She had such a positive, enthusiastic attitude about life, even in the face of much personal sorrow, that I learned to cherish the idea of growing older long before I saw any reason to fear it. In my professional life, I have seen the remarkable personal strength of elders—from elders living in the Central City Housing Project in New Orleans to the elders living in the Appalachian Mountains in Kentucky to elders living on the American Indian reservations of Wisconsin. The fortitude that helped these elders survive the bleakest poverty and greatest social oppression has helped them move through old age as true survivors. I have learned over a cup of coffee as much about aging from these elders—with whom I have shared the deep pain of the loss of a loved one to Alzheimer's disease, the joys of grandparenthood, or the challenges of learning to balance a checkbook for the first time—as I have learned from any professional literature.

This book presents a comprehensive overview of the field of gerontological social work, from the basics of the biopsychosocial changes associated with the aging process through the assessment of strengths and challenges to the design and execution of problem-solving interventions. *Social Work with Elders* is written for both undergraduate and graduate students in courses addressing social work practice with elders, focusing on interventions with individual elders, elders' support systems, and groups of elders. It is intended to cover topics as basic as encouraging elders to exercise to those as complex as the process of differential assessment and diagnosis of depression, dementia, or delirium. The topics covered throughout the book are relevant to practitioners working in social service agencies, nursing homes, congregate and assisted-living centers, and adult day care.

Unlike many other texts on gerontological social work, this text includes a comprehensive array of topics within a single text. It discusses the important consideration of human behavior in the social environment context as a foundation for undertaking a comprehensive assessment of elders and designing interventions. *Social Work with Elders* includes the protocols for both traditional and nontraditional interventions, recognizing the amazing heterogeneity of the aging population. In many respects, it can be considered as "one-stop shopping" for content on gerontological social work. Content on diversity of gender, race, ethnicity, and sexual orientation is integrated into each chapter as it is relevant to the topic rather than being isolated in a separate chapter. This approach helps students to incorporate the importance of cultural sensitivity as an issue is being discussed rather than doing so retrospectively.

The Plan of the Book

Chapter 1 begins with a demographic overview of the population of elders as they look in the early twenty-first century and as they will look 20 years from now as baby boomers move into old age. This chapter describes the variety of social and medical settings in which gerontological social work is practiced. A substantial portion of the chapter is devoted to the personal and professional challenges of working with this population. Chapter 2 presents an in-depth look at the physical changes that accompany the normal aging process as well as full descriptions of the unique challenges presented to elders faced with incontinence or HIV/AIDS. This chapter also presents the findings of the MacArthur Study, the largest set of individual research studies ever designed to identify those factors associated with "successful" aging. Chapter 3 addresses psychosocial patterns of adjustment observed in elders including those factors that contribute to delaying cognitive and intellectual losses and preventing social isolation.

Chapter 4 moves the student into the mechanics of the assessment process, building on the didactic and theoretical content of the previous chapter, including determining the purpose of an assessment, the components of a comprehensive assessment, tools for assessing cognitive and socioemotional characteristics, and the special adaptations necessary in working with elders. Differential assessment and diagnosis of the most common socioemotional and cognitive problems associated with aging, including depression, dementia, delirium, and anxiety, are presented in Chapter 5. Case studies are presented to help students sharpen their assessment skills in differentiating among these conditions. Traditional treatment approaches, such as cognitive-behavioral therapy, validation therapy, reminiscence, and life review, are explored in Chapter 6. Alternative approaches for work with both high- and low-functioning elders—using music, art, drama, and pets—are explored in Chapter 7.

Alcohol and drug abuse among elders is covered in Chapter 8 with specific attention to designing interventions that recognize the experiences of both life-long and late-onset addiction problems. This chapter also addresses the alarming problem of high suicide rates among elders who suffer from both untreated depression and long-standing addiction problems. Chapter 9 introduces the use of groups in work with elders experiencing a broad range of problems, including depression, social isolation, grief and bereavement, and the need for developing new social activities.

Chapter 10 is devoted entirely to the importance of spirituality and religion in the lives of elders and describes incorporating assessment and intervention techniques, such as the spiritual genogram and time line, into traditional practice approaches. This chapter includes the importance of the social work practitioner's developing awareness of his or her own spirituality. Chapter 11 examines the problem of elder abuse and neglect and the social worker's role in assessing abuse. A consideration of how elders' support systems can be mobilized in designing interventions follows in Chapter 12. Chapter 13 discusses dying, bereavement, and the issue of advance directives, a new and controversial attempt to empower persons of all ages to be more active in making end-of-life decisions.

Acknowledgments

I would like to thank those who reviewed earlier drafts of the book, including Marian A. Aguilar, University of Texas at Austin; Marla Berg-Weger, Saint Louis University; Patricia Kolar, University of Pittsburgh; and Elizabeth Kramer, University of Wisconsin–Madison. I am also grateful to Karen Hanson, Alyssa Pratt, and Annette Joseph of Allyn and Bacon; Lynda Griffiths of TKM Productions; and freelancer Holly Crawford for their help throughout production.

Special thanks to my graduate assistants, Tricia Beares and Lori Austin, who spent long and arduous hours in the library and on the internet helping with the tedious legwork involved in writing a text. After reading various drafts of the chapters, they know this material almost as well as I do. I am also grateful to Liz Kelner and Jack Casey of Elder Protective Services in Central and Western Massachusetts, who provided expert feedback on Chapter 11 from their vast experience. Thanks to Dr. Susan J. Coe, who has been one of my best cheerleaders in my career. She was living the challenges of caregiving for an aging parent as I was writing this book and brought me back into the real world on many an occasion.

My deepest gratitude goes to my husband, Bill Dittrich, who provided "expert review" for Chapter 10 on spirituality and aging and whose encouragement and support turned an idea into a book. Your love is and always will be the anchor in my life.

K. M.-D.

1

The Context of Social Work Practice with Elders

Aging in the Twenty-First Century

One of the greatest challenges of the twenty-first century will be the tremendous increase in the number of persons over the age of 65, a group referred to in this book as *elders.* Due to both the graying of the baby boomer generation (those persons born between 1946 and 1963) and improvements in health and medical care, the sheer numbers of persons entering "the third age" will be staggering. Social institutions, including the health care system, education, income maintenance and social insurance programs, the workplace, and particularly social services, are bound to be radically transformed. Current and future generations of elders will undoubtedly forge new approaches to the aging process itself and demand services that reflect positive and productive approaches to this time in their lives. As major providers of service to elders and their families, social workers need a wide variety of skills and resources to meet these demands. This book is intended to provide a solid knowledge base about aging as a process and to introduce practitioners to a wide range of assessment and intervention techniques.

Diversity within the Elderly Population

Recognizing and accommodating the diversity between the current and future cohorts of elders is an important component of gerontological social work. How elders adapt to the myriad biopsychosocial changes that accompany aging is as unique as elders themselves. For example, while physical changes inherent in the aging process follow a definite pattern, how biological changes affect each elder varies based on differences in genetic makeup, lifestyle choices, and even personal attitudes toward the aging process. While some elders face chronic pain due to crippling arthritis or heart disease, others live healthy, active lives well into their 90s. The psychological and cognitive challenges facing all elders may be similar but not every elder will face loneliness, depression, or intellectual decline.

For example, once free of the responsibilities of raising a family or nurturing a career, elders may pursue long-delayed interests in creative writing, painting, or music. While elders share universal concerns in redefining relationships with life partners, family, and friends, the social support system available to each elder will differ dramatically. Elders may maximize new social activities offered by senior centers or elder hostels to forge new friendships to complement or replace friends from earlier in their lives. Others will use volunteer work in the community as a means to remain active and feel useful. Culture, ethnic group membership, gender, sexual orientation, and socioeconomic status likewise add to the uniqueness of the aging experience for each elder.

The differences within the older population present a unique set of challenges to the social work profession. The needs of newly retired and healthy elders to continue active and productive lifestyles are appreciably different from the needs of frail elders forced into special living situations due to failing health. Somewhere in between the newly retired and frail elders are the largest group of elders, those who remain independent and function well in most areas of their lives but need specific social or mental health services to maintain and maximize that independence.

Elders' needs for social services fall along a broad continuum. Likewise, social workers' roles range from traditional assistance as broker, advocate, case manager, or therapist to nontraditional roles such as exercise coach, social support coordinator, or pastoral counselor. This is an exciting time to be studying gerontological social work because new and nontraditional models of service delivery are entering mainstream social work services. The future role of the profession in gerontological social work is limited only by the practitioner's imagination and initiative.

The Focus of This Chapter

This chapter is designed to introduce the reader to the demographic characteristics of elders in the United States and to explore the significance of birth cohort and aging from a life course perspective. People age in a context deeply influenced by when they were born and what life events they have experienced. Social workers come into contact with elders in a variety of gerontological settings that include community social service agencies, congregate housing, assisted-living facilities, adult day health centers, nursing homes, and hospitals. The chapter will help social workers begin to think about some of the unique challenges that make this line of work both rewarding and challenging.

The Demography of Aging

The Growth of the Older Population

As of 1997, one in eight Americans was over the age of 65, or 13 percent of the general population. By 2030, when the last of the baby boomer cohort reaches age

65, elders will comprise over 20 percent of Americans (Centers for Disease Control and Prevention, 1999; U.S. Bureau of the Census, 1996a). See Figure 1.1. The most dramatic growth in the older population will be among elders of color, who will constitute 25 percent of the elder population by 2030 as compared to 15 percent in 1995 (Cohen & Van Nostrand, 1994; U.S. Bureau of the Census, 1993). See Figure 1.2. This growth is due to improvements in childhood health care—increasing the likelihood that persons of color will even reach age 65—and improvements in the control and treatment of infectious diseases throughout the life cycle. Yet, the consequences of a lifetime of economic challenge combined with a greater probability of developing chronic health problems will follow these elders into this longer life expectancy. For elders of color, living longer does not directly translate into living better. The special problems and challenges of growing older as a person of color are recurrent themes throughout this book.

Life Expectancy and Marital Status

A child born in 1996 can expect to live to 76.1 years of age compared to a life expectancy of 49 years for a child born at the beginning of the twentieth century (U.S. Bureau of the Census, 1990). Women have a life expectancy of 79 years compared to 72 years for men. It was once assumed that men's life expectancies were shorter than women's because of the stresses of employment in which men were often performing intense physical labor. However, even in the first year of life,

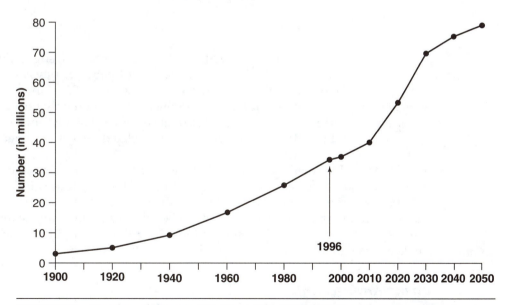

FIGURE 1.1 *Number of Persons 65+ Years Old, 1900–2050 (numbers in millions)*

Sources: U.S. Bureau of the Census, *Population Projections of the United States by Age, Sex, Race and Hispanic Origin, 1992–2050,* table entitled "Sixty-Five Plus in America," Current Population Reports, P25-1104, 1993; Census data 1900–1990.

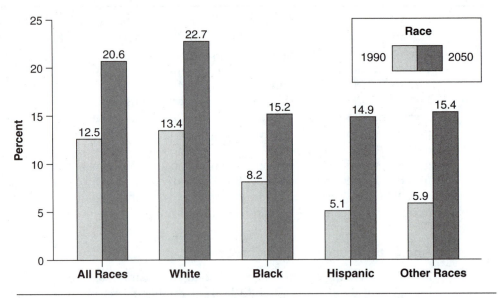

FIGURE 1.2   *Percent of Population over 65 Years: By Race and Hispanic Origin, 1990 and 2050*

Sources: Data for 1990 are from the U.S. Bureau of the Census, *Modified and Actual Age, Sex, Race and Hispanic Origin Data. 1990 Census of Population and Housing,* CPH-L-74, 1990; data for 2050 are from the U.S. Bureau of the Census, *Population Projections of the United States by Age, Sex, Race and Hispanic Origin, 1993–2050,* Current Population Reports, P25-1104, 1993.

girl babies have a lower infant mortality rate than boy babies, suggesting that a stronger biological constitution helps females adapt better to physical and psychological changes throughout the life cycle (Legato, 1997). Since the 1960s, women have entered the labor force as lifetime workers and only now are showing some of the same stress-related consequences of work. Only time will isolate the influence of biological advantage and work-related factors on longer female life expectancy.

In 1995, older men were more likely to be married than were older women, 76 percent and 43 percent, respectively, reflecting the differences in life expectancy between the genders (U.S. Bureau of the Census, 1991a). While those men and women not married are most likely to be widowed, the dramatic increase in divorced and never-married persons in the late 1990s suggests that the number of single elders will increase as well into the twenty-first century.

Living Arrangements

One-third of noninstitutionalized elders lived alone in 1997 compared with two-thirds who lived in a family setting, defined as living with a spouse, partner, or other relatives (Centers for Disease Control and Prevention, 1999). In 1996, 52 percent of elders lived in just nine states: California, New York, Florida, Texas, Pennsylvania, Ohio, Illinois, Michigan, and New Jersey. Thirty percent of elders lived in areas considered "central cities," with 45 percent living in suburban areas. The remaining one-quarter of elders lived in small cities and rural areas (U.S. Bureau of the Census, 1996a).

Although 90 percent of nursing residents are over the age of 65, they represent only 4 percent of the older population according to the Centers for Disease Control and Prevention (1999). This small percentage challenges the common perception that large numbers of elders end up in nursing homes due to failing health. Women comprise 72 percent of the nursing home population, another reflection of their longer life expectancy (National Center for Health Statistics, 1997).

Poverty

The change from Old Age Assistance to Supplemental Security Income in 1972, the establishment of minimum benefit levels in Social Security, and the expansion of government-funded health care programs for elders have reduced the overall poverty of elders since the 1960s when 30 percent of persons over the age of 65 had incomes below the poverty line (Schiller, 1998). Regardless, in 1996, nearly one-fifth of elders still had incomes that categorized them as poor or near poor. While 11 percent of 65–74-year-olds have incomes below the poverty line, this figure increases to 16 percent for those aged 75 and older (U.S. Bureau of the Census, 1996b).

A closer look at the poverty statistics indicates that individuals who have low incomes throughout their working lives are those most likely to continue to have low incomes or drop into poverty in their later years. For older women, poverty rates hover around 16 percent, while only 9 percent of older men live in poverty (Dalaker & Naifeh, 1998). Older women are more likely to be widowed or living alone than are their male counterparts—thus relying on one, rather than two, fixed incomes. However, poverty is not a new experience for many women. Women experience higher poverty rates throughout their lives whether due to the financial demands of raising children as a single mother, disrupted labor market histories, or low-wage occupational choices (Smolensky, Danziger, & Gottschalk, 1988).

There are disproportionately high poverty rates among elders of color with 33 percent of African American elders showing incomes below the poverty line. Hispanic and American Indian, Eskimo, and Aleut elders have poverty rates of 22 percent and 29.2 percent, respectively (U.S. Bureau of the Census, 1991b). The low lifetime earnings of both women and persons of color are reflected in lower Social Security benefits after retirement. Limited incomes do not enable individuals to accumulate assets, such as property or personal savings accounts, and low-wage jobs rarely have pension plans. When a low-wage worker retires, he or she simply does not have the financial resources to ensure an income much above the poverty line. On the other hand, high-wage workers have higher Social Security payments, have greater asset accumulation, and are more likely to have private pensions. Elders' retirement incomes mirror their lifetime earnings.

Employment

About 12 percent of the older population remains in the workforce past the age of 65, over half working part time either out of financial necessity or a continued interest in employment (Fullerton, 1995). This figure includes only those officially considered in the labor force and may mask the numbers of elders participating in what is known as the underground economy. That is, some elders work off the books for cash and do not report the earnings to avoid reductions in pensions or Social Security. The numbers of elders who remain in the labor force will likely increase in the twenty-first century. Changes in the retirement age under Social Security and private pensions, accompanying changes in eligibility for Medicare, and a trend toward a decrease in personal savings for retirement suggest that aging baby boomers will remain working for more years than the current cohort of retirees.

Health Status and Disability

By age 85, over half of elders need some assistance with mobility, bathing, preparing meals, or some other activity of daily living (Centers for Disease Control and Prevention, 1999). However, in 1992, three-quarters of persons between 65 and 74 and two-thirds of persons over age 75 self-rated their health as good or very good (National Aging Information Center, 1996) despite a high incidence of chronic health conditions within this population. Heart disease, cancer, cerebrovascular disease, chronic obstructive pulmonary disease, and diabetes are the most frequent chronic health conditions found in persons over the age of 65 (Anderson, Kochanek, & Murphy, 1997). Elders are more likely than their non-aged counterparts to visit a physician or enter a hospital, which is consistent with the prevalence of chronic health care problems.

Economic well-being and health status are intricately linked in the population. Chronic poverty restricts access to quality medical care, contributes to malnutrition, and creates psychological stress, all of which influence an individual's health status. For low-income elders of color, late life becomes the manifestation of a lifetime of going without adequate medical care. Chronic conditions become more disabling. Prescriptions cannot be filled or glasses purchased because of limited financial resources. Poor elders may have to choose between food and medicine.

The economic burden of an acute or chronic illness can devastate middle-class elders' financial resources, quickly moving them from economic security to poverty. Much of this is due to the mechanics of financing health care for elders. Medicaid, the health insurance program for low-income persons, is available to those elders who qualify on the basis of low income and limited assets. Many low-income elders combine Medicaid coverage with Medicare, the federal health insurance program that covers 96 percent of persons over age 65 and does not have a means test. With the combination of both programs, most major health care costs are covered, although accessibility may still be a problem for low-income elders (Cohen, Bloom, Simpson, & Parsons, 1997). For middle- and upper-income elders, Medicare is frequently supplemented with what are known as medigap policies—private insurance that covers what Medicare does not. Medicare covers only a portion of health care costs for elders and is not sufficient in and of itself to provide adequate coverage.

For those elders who do not qualify for Medicaid and cannot afford supplemental policies, a significant gap in coverage exists. The National Center for Health Statistics estimates that almost 10 percent of elders, most of whom are poor, female, and of color, have unmet health care needs due in part to the gaps in the Medicare system (Cohen, Bloom, Simpson, & Parsons, 1997). This population is least likely to have routine physical exams, get immunized against the flu and pneumonia, have early screening for diabetes and hypertension, or take medications that prevent the development of more serious medical conditions. Therefore, when illness occurs, it is more likely to be serious. Prevention costs less than treatment for most chronic conditions, but a portion of the older population cannot afford preventative measures.

This overview of the demographics of aging shows a population of persons over the age of 65 that is growing and will continue to grow rapidly into the twenty-first century. Despite a higher incidence of chronic health problems, most elders are not sick, not poor, and not living in nursing homes. The vast majority of elders struggle with occasional health problems but continue to be active, involved, and productive members of society, defying the stereotype of sick, isolated, and miserable old people. The economic picture, however, is bleakest for elders of color, women, and the oldest of the old in the United States. The inequalities of elders' earlier lives will be mirrored in their later years. If trends continue, elders will continue to live longer but not necessarily healthier lives unless chronic poverty and health care inadequacies are addressed.

The Life Course Perspective on Aging

The Life Course as Stages in Development

This book approaches aging as the last stage in a series of life stages that comprise the life course. Each stage of the life course is comprised of biological developments and social tasks all of which are embedded in a larger sociocultural context. The human body develops from infancy through childhood, adolescence, young and middle adulthood through old age. While during any of these stages an individual's biological development may differ due to genetic makeup or the presence of disease or disability, there are universal physical changes that occur in each of the stages in all humans. Old age is the final stage in the biological life course of the human body and is profoundly affected by all physical changes that have occurred prior to old age.

Each stage in life has a set of social tasks normally associated with that life stage. Adolescents must deal with the establishment of their own identity and turn from their families of origin to peer groups as their primary frame of socialization. Young adults need to make occupational choices and decide about choosing a life partner. During young and middle adulthood, individuals usually focus their concerns on raising families or building careers and begin to look for social and financial stability. For elders of all ages, enjoying adult children and grandchildren, retiring from the demands of employment, and turning to personal enjoyment of social and recreational activities of their own choosing are common social tasks of the later years. The expectations that these are the appropriate and logical tasks of each of the stages of the life course are deeply embedded in a sociocultural context. This is what American society expects individuals to be doing during each of the life stages. As part of the process of socialization, individuals internalize these expectations as a blueprint for planning their lives.

The Life Course as a Fluid Process

In reality, the life course is not that predictable. Everyone can identify an individual in one of the life stages that is not engaged in the expected activities of that age. To truly understand the concept of life course, one must view each elder as an individual who has progressed through predictable biological stages but has a unique life course deeply affected by social tasks that do not fit the stereotype. Rather than view the life course as a longitudinal set of stages, a more accurate perspective is to view the life course as a fluid process (Jendrek, 1994). The length and intensity of each of the life stages varies with the individual. For example, some women become mothers in their teens and are finished with child rearing in their early 40s. Other women become mothers in their 40s and are still raising children at the same time they are considering retirement. Other women never have children by choice or chance and do not spend any of their young or middle adult years raising a family. Other women return to parenting responsibilities when circumstances find them raising their own grandchildren.

The life course is an individual experience that shapes each person in a unique way. This totality of experience is the frame of reference for every elder. As a result, there is more diversity among the elder population than among the population at any other of the life stages. To view elders as simply having "arrived" in old age is to miss the dynamic nature of human development across the life span.

Life Stage Variations within Old Age

It is important at this point to make distinctions within the general life stage of old age. Age 65 is generally agreed on as the beginning of old age only because it has been the traditional retirement age and not because there is a specific social or biological reason for this choice. The population between 65 and 74 years is generally referred to as the young-old. The young-old may still be working or newly retired, have few if any health problems, and remain actively engaged in the social activities of life. Many young-old do not consider themselves to be old and experience few if any of the psychosocial problems discussed in this book. The middle group of elders, aged 75 to 85, the middle-old, may experience health problems, face some mobility restrictions, and openly identify as elders. In this age group, elders are often widowed and completely out of the workforce. There is usually a greater need for support among this group. It is among the oldest-old, those over 85 years of age, that the greatest needs exist. Oldest-old elders are more likely to have serious health restrictions and need assistance in more than one personal care area, such as bathing, eating, dressing, toileting, or walking.

Consistent with the previous discussion about the uniqueness of the life course, it is important to restate that plenty of elders totally defy these general categories and enjoy a functional age that is quite different from their chronological age. There are people in their 50s who already have severe health problems and are homebound while the occasional 98-year-old is still skydiving. The 50- and the 98-year-old reflect their own unique life course experiences.

The Importance of Birth Cohort

Another aspect of the concept of life course is the importance of viewing elders as products of a unique birth cohort. *Birth cohort* is defined as a group of individuals born and raised during a specified time in history. Most people, of all ages, are familiar with the baby boomer birth cohort born between 1946 and 1963. Their sheer numbers have affected education, employment, politics, and the economy. Their shared experience of the war in Vietnam, the advent of rock music, the civil rights movement, the sexual revolution, and changing roles for women have had a deep effect on their lives not only as young adults but as middle-agers as well. This common historical frame of reference will also affect their experiences as elders. Divorce rates have been higher and families smaller among this generation. The result will be a smaller family support network available to baby boomers as they become elders. Two-wage households have become accustomed to a higher standard of living than any previous generation. With the uncertain future of the Social Security system and a wildly unpredictable stock market, economic security for this generation in retirement is uncertain. These sociopolitical realities will shape their experience of being elders.

The influence of birth cohort is particularly significant for elders of color and gay or lesbian elders. The current generation of elders of color all remember a time when their civil rights were not protected by law, when it was legal and common to be denied housing, employment, or education simply on the basis of skin color or ethnic group membership. They and their children were denied quality education and therefore access to well-paying jobs. This experience limited their access to the financial rewards that could help them build sound economic futures. Chronic poverty and substandard housing have affected their health and the health of their families. If they make it to old age, they are more likely to continue to be poor and experience chronic health problems on the basis of their birth cohort experience. Today's generation of gay and lesbian elders grew up in a time when their sexual orientation was not accepted. Homosexuality was seen, even by the social work profession, as a psychopathology that could be cured (Dorfman, Walters, Burke, Hardin, Karanik, Raphael, & Silverstein, 1995). Even today there is limited social and legal recognition of gay and lesbian partners as family members. In many states, their civil rights are not guaranteed simply due to their sexual orientation.

This, of course, does not apply to all elders of color or of a different sexual orientation. A portion of these elders functions solidly in the middle- and upper-middle class. However, the psychological scars of a second-class citizenship continue to affect this population in old age. Even if it does not affect them economically, it has an insidious effect on their psychological well-being. Understanding the significance of an elder's birth cohort combined with the ability to view an elder as the product of a unique life course are essential skills in sound gerontological social work. Elders, in many ways, are ordinary people who have led their own extraordinary lives.

Settings for Gerontological Social Work

Gerontological social workers can be found in a wide variety of practice settings. The role of the social worker is often unique in these settings as social work's primary focus is the psychosocial well-being of the elder. Nursing homes and hospitals are often seen as the most familiar settings for gerontological practice but with only 4 percent of the elder population living in nursing homes, more practitioners can be found in community settings. Social service agencies, home health agencies, congregate housing, adult day health facilities, and assisted-living centers are the settings in which the vast majority of gerontological social work is practiced.

Social Service Agencies

Social work roles in social service agencies are intimately tied to the function of the parent agency. In large communities, social service agencies offer a wide range of counseling, advocacy, case management, and protective services specifically designed for elders. These services may be housed in the local Council on Aging, Area Agency on Aging, or Department of Social Services or may be provided by sectarian agencies, such as Catholic Social Services, Lutheran Social Services, Jewish Family Services, and so forth. Elders or their families may feel more confident working with agencies that reflect their own religious affiliation. In small communities or rural areas, services to elders may be contained within an agency serving other populations that has a social worker with particular expertise in working with elders.

Contact with a social worker at a social service agency is frequently initiated by a concerned family member who is unsure about how to begin the process of obtaining services for a family member. In addition to conducting the assessment process to determine what services might be helpful to an elder, social workers can play an important role in initiating and coordinating services from a variety of agencies in a care management role. In some cases, the family of a frail elder becomes the client. While families can successfully provide caregiving, they may feel the strain of this responsibility and benefit from a support or educational group and respite services. For many elders and their families, the challenges of aging present the first time they come into contact with the social service system. As the contact is often precipitated by a crisis, families and elders may need reassurance and support as well as solid information to stabilize a chaotic situation.

Home Health Care Agencies

Home health care agencies, such as the Visiting Nurses Association, often have gerontological social workers on staff as part of a team approach to providing services to elders. While the primary focus of home health care is to provide health-related services, such as checking blood pressure, changing dressings following surgery, or monitoring blood sugar levels for diabetic elders, social workers can play an important role in addressing elder's psychosocial needs. An elder who has suffered a stroke may need medication and blood pressure monitoring from a health care provider but may also need help with housekeeping, meal preparation, or transportation. The social worker can arrange for these support services and coordinate the total care plan. Elders who are essentially homebound due to chronic health problems often experience intense isolation and may benefit from regular phone calls from an elder call service or friendly visitor volunteer. Gerontological social workers who work in home health care often provide supportive or psychotherapeutic counseling services or arrange for those services from another agency in the community.

Social workers also play an important role in helping elders work out the financial arrangements for home health care. Advocating for the elders to receive the care they are entitled to under private insurance, Medicare, or Medical Assistance can involve myriad phone calls and personal contacts that are difficult for an ill elder to handle. When elders are not eligible for needed services under existing insurance coverage, creativity is often needed to obtain additional financial resources, including working with elders' families or identifying low-cost community services that elders can afford. If an elder's illness becomes more debilitating, the social worker may need to work with the elder to identify care arrangements that offer greater support, such as assisted-living services or geriatric day health care. It is the social worker's knowledge of community services and financial aid programs that makes him or her a valuable asset to home health care.

Congregate Living Centers

Specialized independent living centers for elders in the community, such as low- or moderate-income housing, frequently have social workers on staff to provide a wide variety of services. Helping elders secure transportation to appointments or shopping centers, arranging opportunities for social activities such as plays and concerts, and promoting on-site activities are frequently under the auspices of a social worker in a congregate living center. On-site activities may include financial management workshops, yoga or tai chi classes, or shared interest groups such as book clubs, citizenship classes for immigrant elders, or creative writing groups. A social worker may serve as a liaison to the elder's family when appropriate or advocate on behalf of elders with physicians or other health care providers. Social workers in congregate living centers are often the first to notice when an elder's functioning is beginning to decline as evidenced by poor housekeeping or increasing isolation or disability. The community atmosphere that develops at most congregate living centers facilitates a social worker's familiarity with the residents, and elders may be more willing to seek assistance from someone they know.

Adult Day Health Care

A setting for elder care that falls between independent living and skilled nursing care is adult day health care. Adult day health care can provide individually designed programs of medical and social services for frail elders who need structured care for some portion of the day. Elders who live with their families or other caretakers or even live in semi-independent living situations and have some physical, cognitive, emotional, or social disability are typical users of adult day health care. These elders do not need full-time nursing care or even full-time supervision but do require assistance with some of the activities of daily living. This type of care provides a valuable role as respite care for caretakers as well. Adult children may be willing and able to have elders live with them if they can obtain supplementary care during the day while they work or for occasional respite.

Most adult day health centers only take elders who are able to be active participants in the development of their own service plans and consent to placement in the adult day health center. This type of care focuses on maximizing an elder's sense of choice and control in their own care. A smaller number of centers work exclusively with elders who suffer from dementia, including Alzheimer's disease, who may be less able to be full participants in the decision-making process.

Social workers are involved with an elder from the extensive preplacement process through the execution of a service plan. Social workers and elders explore the elder's needs and interests together and select from a variety of rehabilitative and recreational services available at the adult day health center. An elder may need physical or occupational therapy to compensate for losses due to a stroke or heart attack. Others may need supervision to take medication. The social worker in adult day health care is instrumental in coordinating all of the physical needs frail elders require during the day. In this setting, social workers may serve as care managers.

Group work is an essential role for social workers in adult day health centers. In most centers, elders belong to a specific group that meets on a regular basis to talk about the issues they face. This may involve problems with families and caretakers, concerns about friends and members of the group, or more structured topics such as nutrition, foot care, or arthritis. The group becomes a focal point for elders in the adult day health setting. It gives them an opportunity to maintain social skills or renew them if they have been socially isolated. The group is helpful in making new elders feel welcome and teaching them how the center operates.

In addition to running a therapeutic group and a variety of social and recreational activities, the social worker meets individually with each elder for counseling, advocacy, or problem solving. This individual attention plays an important role in maintaining the dignity of the elder in what is predominately a group setting and in helping the worker monitor the elder's mental and physical health status. At times, elders may be reluctant to share deeply personal issues such as family problems, depression, and incontinence with members of their group and benefit more from a private discussion with the social worker.

When elders are not meeting with their group or social worker, they are usually involved in a wide variety of activity groups geared to their special interests. Physical fitness, music, education, current events, arts and crafts, and creative writing are among the types of groups found in adult day health centers.

Assisted-Living Centers and Continuum of Care Facilities

One of the newest additions to the range of services available to elders in the community is the assisted-living center. *Assisted living* is defined as a residential, long-term arrangement designed to promote maximum independent functioning among frail elders while providing in-home support services. The assisted-living model fits in between completely independent living in congregate housing and the intensive care provided in a skilled nursing home. Some assisted-living facilities are part of a larger complex known as a *continuum of care facility*. Elders may purchase or rent an apartment while they are still completely independent. As their health changes, necessitating increasing levels of support, they move within the same complex to semi-independent living and perhaps eventually into an adjacent skilled nursing facility.

The focus in assisted living is on as much self-maintenance as possible for each resident. Residents live in individual apartments, complete with kitchen and bath, that are part of a larger complex. The monthly fees for these apartments include rent, utilities, a meal plan, and housekeeping services. Other services such as laundry, personal care services, or transportation are provided on an individual basis as part of a total care plan. Assisted living is expensive (usually between $1800 and $3500 a month) and currently caters only to middle- and upper-income elders, but shows great promise as an alternative to institutional-ization (Regnier, Hamilton, & Yatabe, 1995).

Assisted-living centers are committed to the development of a therapeutic milieu. That is, the purpose of assisted living is to help elders maintain and improve their psychosocial functioning through a variety of activities that maxi-mize choice and control. Social workers conduct intake assessments to review the medical, functional, and psychological strengths and weaknesses of incoming residents. These assessments play an important role in identifying those areas in which an elder may need supplementary services, such as chore services, assis-tance with bathing or dressing, or social activities to ease isolation.

Families and residents may need both information and support to make a successful transition to the center. The decision to leave one's own home, even to move into the privacy of an apartment, is a traumatic experience for elders and may require professional support to work through the grief and depression. Assisted-living centers can offer a variety of challenging social and recreational activities that help elders make the center their new home. Helping a resident find the right balance between private time and social activities is another important role for a social worker in this setting. In assisted-living centers, social workers often function as part of a multidisciplinary team composed of nurses and occu-pational, physical, and recreational therapists.

The obvious drawback to assisted-living centers is the cost, which eliminates them as a choice for many low-income elders. Currently, most assisted-living cen-ters are private pay and are not subsidized by Medicare or Medicaid. One of the continuing challenges for the social work profession is to find ways to offer high-quality, multiservice options to low-income elders with the hope of preventing the development of a two-tiered service system to older adults.

Hospitals

One-quarter of hospital admissions are persons over the age of 65, and one-half of these persons will be readmitted in the next 12 months (American Hospital Asso-ciation, 1989). At least 80 percent of elders suffer from at least one chronic health problem, which is often compounded by financial, legal, emotional, familial, or ethical issues (Centers for Disease Control and Prevention, 1999). The complexi-ties of chronic health problems make hospital social work with elders an essential part of the recovery process. Hospital social workers provide a wide variety of services, including crisis intervention, patient advocacy, patient education, family liaison work, care management, and discharge planning.

Hospitalization is a crisis for anyone of any age but with elders there is al-ways the fear that the hospital is the gateway to either a nursing home or the grave. Elders may be anxious about upcoming surgery or be lost in the maze of medical jargon they hear. They may be concerned about what happens to them during the recovery process when they return home by themselves. Families may be concerned that their loved ones will receive too little care or be hooked up to life-sustaining equipment against their wills. In sum, the hospital setting can be a very chaotic environment for elders and their families. Crisis counseling in a hospital setting involves helping the elder and the family re-establish an emotional equilibrium, begin to understand the medical condition, prioritize tasks, and develop a short-term action plan. The primary focus of the social worker is to help with the psychosocial needs of the elder in the hospital setting while medical personnel attend to physical health (Dhooper, 1997).

Patient advocacy is another appropriate role for hospital social work with elders. Elders may find the cold, impersonal atmosphere of the hospital frightening and confusing. They may need help in making their needs known or advocating on their own behalf. For example, a Chinese woman may need a translator, a special diet, or wish to meet with an herbal healer. Social workers can work with other health care professionals to find the best match between what the client wants and what the health care system can tolerate. A part of patient advocacy is patient education, working with elders and their families to better understand the presenting illness and its course of treatment. Patient education is aimed at empowerment of the elder. The more elders know and understand about their illness, the better their own sense of control. When they feel they are part of the treatment process, they are more likely to be active participants in their own healing.

Social workers may also serve as family liaisons for the hospitalized elder. The elder's family needs to understand what is happening to the elder, the prognosis for the illness, and what plans need to be made following the hospitalization. For many families, contact with a hospital social worker is the first contact they have had with the social services system. Up until that point, they may have struggled to provide care on their own, unaware of the range of community services available to them. The process of discharge planning, another important hospital social work role, involves developing and coordinating the support services for posthospitalization. Meals-on-Wheels, home nursing care, chore services, and homemaking services can be very effective in helping elders to maintain their independence while providing invaluable support. The trend away from nursing home care to home-based care has expanded the importance of gerontological social work. Elders and their families may need help confronting the financial and emotional consequences of a debilitating illness. When all of these roles are combined, hospital social workers may function as care managers coordinating the total care plan for the elder with the variety of medical practitioners involved in the case.

Social workers also play an important role in helping elders and their families make difficult end-of-life decisions. Helping elders make choices about what circumstances warrant being connected to life-support machinery, whether they want to be resuscitated after a heart attack, or who should make those choices when they are unable to is a sensitive process. Facilitating the discussion between an elder and the family about these issues may be the most difficult job of all. No one wants to have to make difficult end-of-life decisions but someone will have to. These decisions are called *advance directives* and are discussed in detail in Chapter 13.

Nursing Homes

One of the greatest fears of elders is that they will end up living in a nursing home. This fear explains why elders fight so hard to maintain their independence. Nursing homes are seen as a place older adults are sent to die, neglected and forgotten by their families. While this fear may be legitimate for some elders, nursing homes serve an important role in the continuum of care for frail older adults. When independent living becomes impossible and more structured nursing care is needed, a nursing home may be the only appropriate service.

With a growing older population, it would be expected that the number of nursing homes would be increasing proportionately. However, between 1985 and 1995, the actual number of nursing homes decreased by 13 percent. The number of beds has increased by 9 percent, meaning that today's nursing home is likely to be bigger than in previous years and that nursing home care is available in fewer locations (National Center for Health Care Statistics, 1997). The decrease in the overall number of nursing homes reflects the improvement in choices available to elders for health care. Older adults are opting to stay in their own homes longer with the help of less costly home-based alternatives to skilled nursing care.

The primary role of the social worker in a nursing home is to serve in both a supportive and educational role to elders and their families. Social workers begin to work with elders and their families prior to admission to a nursing home—arranging preadmission visits, doing a preliminary assessment of what kinds of services will best meet the needs of the elder once admitted, and working out financial arrangements. Nursing home care can cost more than $3000 a month and is not routinely covered by private insurance or Medicare. Some elders will spend only a few months in a skilled nursing facility—for instance, recovering from an acute illness or surgery—so the social worker's job may include discharge planning as well.

Once an elder is placed, the social worker helps the elder to adjust to the more structured life within the nursing home. Sharing a room after years of living in one's own home, adjusting to the lack of privacy frequently experienced in an institution, and coping with a more regimented lifestyle are major adjustments for an elder. The social worker can help the elder connect to activities within the nursing home. These may include pet therapy, music, or exercise classes depending on the elder's health. New residents often experience a deep depression after moving into a nursing home as they grieve the loss of their independence and miss family and friends. The social worker can be instrumental in helping elders improve their mental as well as physical health.

Nursing home social workers also play an important role in their work with the friends and families of residents. Placing a family member in a nursing home frequently generates guilt and anxiety among family members. They may feel they are abandoning their elders despite the fact that less drastic measures have already failed. Maintaining the relationship with the resident, identifying resources for handling the financial demands of placement, and processing the uncomfortable feelings that accompany placement are common responsibilities for nursing home social workers (LaBrake, 1996).

Personal and Professional Issues in Work with Elders

While deeply rewarding both personally and professionally, work with elders requires a high level of self-awareness on the part of the social worker. In all intervention efforts, workers bring their own emotional baggage to the helping process. However, in gerontological work, the issues are more complex. Unlike social work practice in the areas of alcoholism, drug abuse, family dysfunction, or domestic violence—social problem areas that may or may not personally affect the worker—everyone must eventually face the experience of aging and death for themselves and their families. The universality of the aging experience influences work with elders on both a conscious and subconscious level. Among the most significant issues workers will face are the subtle influences of lifelong messages about ageism, countertransference of feelings toward elders, fears of death and loss, the devaluation of work with elders, and conflicting issues surrounding independence versus dependence.

Ageism

The term *ageism* refers to the prejudices and stereotypes attributed to older persons based solely on their age (Butler, 1989). These stereotypes are usually negative and convey an attitude that older adults are less valuable as human beings, thus justifying inferior or unequal treatment. These attitudes develop early in life as children observe parental, media, and social attitudes toward elders. Parents may unintentionally send the message that aging parents and grandparents are a nuisance to care for, demanding, needy, or unpleasant. Even simple comments, such as "I hope I never get like Grandma" or "put me to sleep if I ever get senile," may be interpreted literally by children. Every time parents refer to aches and pains as "I must be getting old," the subtle message becomes clear that aging is destined to be painful and debilitating.

If the only time children and adolescents interact with elders is during a forced visit to a nursing home or seeing a physically disabled elder sitting on a park bench, they will have difficulty developing positive attitudes toward aging as a process and elders as people. Commercial television and other media emphasize the importance of being young and staying young as one of the major indicators of the quality of life.

Butler, Lewis, and Sunderland (1998) contended that while ageism is an attitude that hinders everyone's ability to adjust to the normal changes of aging, it also serves a more destructive social justification. Ageism rationalizes pushing people out of the labor market in the name of maintaining productivity without much thought to what happens to people when their lives are no longer centered on work as an organizing principle. Ageism justifies segregated living arrangements, substandard medical care, and generally derogatory attitudes toward elders. While blatantly racist or sexist comments and openly discriminatory activities would not be tolerated in today's business and social arenas, ageist attitudes and comments are rarely challenged.

Countertransference

When ageist attitudes are internalized by a social worker, countertransference may pose a serious threat to the integrity of the professional relationship. *Countertransference* is defined as the presence of unrealistic and often inappropriate feelings toward the client that distort the helping relationship (Greene, 1986; Woods & Hollis, 1990). The worker displaces feelings, attitudes, or reactions on to the client based on a past relationship rather than on the real attributes of the client. Unfortunately, a social worker may not even be aware of countertransference until it surfaces and has already damaged the relationship. These attitudes may be negative, reflecting a deep dislike for older persons. Such negative feelings restrict the worker's willingness (consciously or unconsciously) to invest in a professional relationship or result in impatience with or intolerance of the elder client.

Countertransference issues may also surface as inappropriate benevolent or caregiving attitudes toward the elder. The worker's need to "save" an elder may rob the elder unintentionally of his or her self-respect and personal dignity. Sympathy can be destructive in therapeutic work when it prematurely usurps an elder's ability to maximize independence.

Sprung (1989) identified what she calls "The Messiah Complex" in professionals and paraprofessionals working with elders. While elders face a multitude of biopsychosocial losses, helping professionals may feel self-induced pressure to "do good" and "make things better" (Sprung, 1989, p. 601). When the helping professional fails to alleviate many of the inevitable losses elders face, compassion is transformed to pity and the helping effort becomes counterproductive. The worker's efforts to save the older person from distress fail. The frustration with a failed effort may be transformed into anger with and hostility toward the older person.

Death Anxiety

Working with elders is a constant reminder to the social worker of the logical progression of the life cycle—from youth to aging and death. Facing mortality, regardless of one's age, can precipitate a variety of responses (Greene, 1986). Death anxiety is a highly agitated emotional response, invoked by reference to or discussion of death and dying (Greene, 1986). American society does not deal well with death or any discussion of death. Children are shielded from any talk of the inevitability of death of loved ones and pets. Most people go to extreme measures to avoid even talking about death and dying. Consider all the phrases used to avoid saying the word "death," such as "passed on," "expired," "gone on to the next world," and many others not quite so polite. No matter how sincerely these phrases are used, they reflect a very cynical and avoidant attitude toward death that hides the real pain the loss of human life causes family and friends. In other words, society is so uncomfortable with death, people have difficulty even saying the word.

Facing a variety of situations surrounding death is an inevitable part of work with elders. Many older adults will admit that death does not frighten them as much when they are older as it did when they were younger. They see friends and family members dying. Throughout their lives, they have thought about what death means to them, whether they believe there is an afterlife, and what their lives have been all about. If they have escaped the discomfort of chronic medical problems, they consider themselves lucky. If they live with a disabling or painful condition, they may welcome an end to the physical discomfort. Elders often want to talk about funeral arrangements or make plans for disposing of their personal possessions. While elders' families may cling to denial as a means of warding off a critically ill elder's death, hospital policy may simultaneously ask the family to make difficult end-of-life decisions. All of these issues are examples of how social work with elders requires some level of comfort on the part of the social worker in acknowledging and processing death not only with clients but in one's own work in self-awareness.

Death anxiety can surface as a number of different reactions by the social worker. One classic response is to simply avoid the entire client population or individual clients who have a stronger likelihood of dying. This fear of losing a client during intervention combined with generally uncomfortable feelings about the proximity of death surrounding elders accounts for some social workers simply avoiding work with elders. Even social workers drawn to gerontological social work may be troubled with unconscious issues in death anxiety. For example, a phone call or home visit to a dying client never gets made. Contacts with dying clients may decrease as the person moves closer to death. These actions may be ways to avoid the inevitable contact with a client because the reality of death is too painful for the worker to confront. At a time when elders and their families most need the support of the social worker, the social worker may be least able to give it.

Devaluation of Gerontological Social Work as a Career Choice

While social work with elders is one of the fastest growing areas of professional practice, it is rarely seen as having the glamor of a private clinical social work practice, the intensity of domestic violence, or the prestige of family therapy. "I could never work with old people" is a frequent response to a colleague's expression of interest in working with elders. In a youth-oriented society where the aging process is feared and elders are devalued, working with the elder population may be devalued by the profession itself.

The National Association of Social Workers (NASW) routinely gathers data from its members about their field of practice. While elders constitute nearly 13 percent of the population, less than 6 percent of social workers who belong to

NASW identify gerontological social work as their primary or secondary area of practice as compared to 30 percent for mental health (Gibelman & Schernish, 1997). This small number of social workers found in the field of aging suggests that despite a rapidly growing population of elders, the supply of social workers in this area of practice is woefully inadequate. The National Institute on Aging projects a need for 40,000 to 50,000 gerontological social workers in the early twenty-first century. Less than 10 percent of that number will be available (O'Neill, 1999).

Working with elders may seem to be primarily palliative care. Although it may be considered "noble" to be attracted to work with elders, it may not be seen as either prestigious or requiring high levels of skill (Kermis, 1986). These beliefs and attitudes may be internalized by social workers, a process similar to the internalization of negative social attitudes by oppressed populations (Pinderhughes, 1989). In other words, social workers may begin to believe the destructive social messages they hear about gerontological social work. The frustrations of a devalued self-worth may be acted out in rage, dislike, or ill-treatment of the elder.

One of the purposes of this book is to challenge the perception that gerontological social work is a "second best" professional career choice. Work with elders involves a high level of skills in interacting with all age groups including the adult children of elders, grandchildren, and friends who may be important parts of developing a case plan. Carefully preserving an elder's self-determination while recognizing the significance of the family in decision making is a very complex process requiring the most highly developed intervention and family work skills. Integrating alternative interventions, such as music or art therapies, requires a very broad knowledge base. The gerontological social worker must be both a specialist and an advanced generalist. Gerontological social work requires more, not fewer, skills than many of the more popular fields of practice.

The Independence/Dependence Struggle

One of the most frequently stated goals elders voice is their desire to maintain their independence as long as possible. This desire coincides with the social work profession's commitment to promote self-determination and preserve the dignity of the individual. On the surface, there appears to be no conflict. In reality, as elders require more and more support services and experience increasing difficulties in maintaining independent living, tensions between elders' desires and families' and social workers' perceptions of need are inevitable. A worker can appreciate the desperate efforts on the part of an elder to stay in his or her own home. Yet when struggling with stairs, a deteriorating neighborhood, and difficulties in completing the simple activities of daily living challenge the feasibility of that effort, professional and personal dilemmas abound. Who ultimately must make a decision about an elder's ability to stay in his or her own home? Who decides that an elder is showing poor judgment about financial decisions? When does protective services step in to remove an elder from a family member's home due to neglect or abuse despite the elder's objections? When do the wishes of the family supersede the wishes of the elder? These are difficult questions for which there are no simple answers.

While functioning an entire lifetime as an independent adult, a single illness can reduce an elder to dependency more quickly than he or she can emotionally process. In an effort to counteract a diminished sense of self-esteem, elders may fight dependency to the point they put themselves in physical jeopardy rather than risk relying on others (Gropper, 1986). They may act out, show extreme anger, or make excessive demands on both social workers and family members that cannot be met (Lerer, 1995). Maintaining independence should be a critical goal of all gerontological social work, and throughout this book, different ways of promoting independence, even among the most disabled elders, will be consistently addressed. Reaching this simple and straightforward goal is sometimes a complex process.

Other elders react by assuming dependent roles sooner than they need to and become more passive and resistant than their physical condition warrants. Rather than fighting for their own independence, they give up and willingly relinquish the decision-making issues in their own care. Although giving up their own rights to decision making may make case planning easier for workers and families, this situation lends itself to the development of other, more subtle problems. One of the fundamental concepts of social work practice is the importance of clients' choice of goals for intervention and their personal commitment to work on those goals. For example, a social worker may decide an elder needs to attend a senior center program to decrease personal isolation. Even though the elder may agree so as not to offend the social worker and out of gratefulness for all the worker has done for the elder, the elder will not go to the senior center and participate if he or she does not want to go. The elder may not blatantly refuse to go, but rather will make appropriate excuses for nonattendance. Although well-intentioned, the social worker has decided on a goal for the elder that is the social worker's goal, not the client's. It is not surprising that family and workers become frustrated when elders find ways to avoid doing something that is not their goal in the first place!

The process of relinquishing independence is the beginning of a very dangerous process even among those elders who are sincerely willing to let others make decisions for them. Elders become reactors rather than actors in their lives. Perceiving that they have little control over their lives, elders may fall into a deep depression and relinquish their will to live along with their independence. Families and caregivers who perceive that elders have given up, even when they are capable of some independent activities, may react with anger and hostility. The independence versus dependence continuum of care in work with elders is a delicate and sensitive area.

Self-Awareness and Supervision

While the challenges of working in a devalued field of practice within a societal context of ageist attitudes—which contribute to deeply seated fears about one's own aging and death—may seem a bit overwhelming at this point in the book, there are resources for resolving these issues. Through developing self-awareness with professional supervision, social workers can effectively work through these issues. They are discussed early in the text because they should be clearly present in your mind as you study this field of practice. Developing self-awareness is a process that takes time and continues to challenge professionals well into their own professional careers. It may take a lifetime of working with elders (and one's own relatives) to learn what are your own personal triggers for problematic feelings.

Workers need to take a critical look at any concurrent challenges they are facing in their own lives that could contribute to professional problems. A social worker who is also balancing the demands of an aging spouse, parents, or grand-parents may feel such excessive demands on his or her own resources that work-ing effectively with elders is not possible. While such experiences may be helpful to the worker in developing compassion for an elder's family, it may be counter-productive in the intervention process.

The ability to keep feelings at a conscious level is one of the most important parts of the process of developing self-awareness in working with elders. One's personal feelings toward a client, family members, and the quality of the profes-sional relationship are important clues to the worker about his or her own emo-tional issues. Supervisors can be helpful in diversifying tasks for the worker in an effort to defuse the emotions generated by intense cases and can address issues and a devalued sense of the job. Working exclusively with highly dependent el-ders or those with Alzheimer's disease can tax even the most well-adjusted, expe-rienced workers. The development of support and psychoeducational groups for social workers can help in dealing with unusually difficult cases.

Most gerontological social workers, including this author, would emphasize that working with elders has tremendous rewards. It is a professional and per-sonal joy to work with elders who have lived through the most interesting of times and delight in retelling their life stories. Seeing the power of the human spirit in elders who have survived and thrived through raising families, strug-gling with careers inside and outside the home, and reframing the meaning and purpose of their lives during the later years is a very positive and revitalizing ex-perience for any professional. Elders can be delightfully humorous, frustratingly stubborn, amazingly persistent, but always the most powerful reminder of the re-siliency of the individual to grow and flourish throughout the life span.

Summary

One of the greatest challenges to society and the profession of social work will be the dramatic increase in the number of persons over age 65 in the twenty-first century. While the baby boomer generation will no doubt forge new ways to meet the demands of the "third age," quality health care, a productive postretirement lifestyle, and adequate financial resources pose challenges to today's and tomorrow's elders. For some older women and elders of color, the devastating effects of a lifetime of poverty and substandard health care will follow them into old age. These groups are the most vulnerable elders.

Aging as a social phenomenon is best understood as a stage in the life course. As such, elders face a set of physical, psychological, and social tasks associated with the last stage in human development. The quality of the aging experience is inherently determined by the sum of the opportunities throughout the life course, membership in historical birth cohorts, and personal attitudes about growing older.

The future of gerontological social work is bright not only because of the growing demand for specially trained practitioners but also because of the variety of settings in which social workers will be needed. In addition to traditional settings, such as hospitals and nursing homes, social workers will be found in community settings and specialized housing arrangements, which are just in the beginning of their development. These settings will demand a high level of skill in specific practice techniques and a willingness to engage in the self-awareness necessary for professional work with elders. Working with elders can trigger powerful feelings about death, the aging of family members, and one's own attitudes about helping this vulnerable population.

Check Out These Websites!

1. www.aoa.dhhs.gov This Administration on Aging site offers a wide variety of statistical and demographic information on aging taken from the U.S. Bureau of the Census and *Current Population Reports.* The site has helpful links to topics of particular interest and offers valuable tips in defining an internet search and locating list servers geared to aging.

2. www.aoa.dhhs.gov/naic The National Aging Information Service is a service of the Administration on Aging that specializes in assisting professionals in the field of elder services in bibliographic searches for current research findings and service options. A calendar of events of professional meetings and national events of interest to professionals in the field is maintained.

3. www.alfa.org The Assisted Living Federation of America is a trade organization focused on the special concerns of both providers and consumers of assisted-living services described in this chapter. The website provides a description of assisted living as an option for elders, a consumer checklist for elders considering a specific center, and a list of assisted-living facilities throughout the country. The site also provides assistance to those looking for employment in the assisted-living field.

4. www.elderweb.com Elderweb is an online sourcebook that offers links to resources for specific topics, such as physical health, living arrangements, legal concerns, and financial resources. The strength of this site is its ability to provide links to specific state resources for both elders and professionals serving this population.

5. www.aahsa.org   The American Association for Homes and Services for the Aging is a national nonprofit organization representing nonprofit nursing homes, continuing care retirement communities, assisted-living residences, senior housing facilities, and community service organizations. It offers helpful resources for locating any of these facilities throughout the country and offers suggestions for those professionals considering a career in long-term and senior housing facilities.

6. www.naswdc.org/PRAC/standards   The website for the National Association of Social Workers contains the professional standards for social work practice in nursing homes, long-term care facilities, and case management settings. These professional standards give an in-depth description of social work with elders in these settings as well as providing the criteria that social work in these setting should meet to be considered "professional practice."

References

American Hospital Association. (1989). *Hospitals and older adults: Meeting the challenge.* Chicago: American Hospital Association.

Anderson, R. N., Kochanek, K. D., & Murphy, S. L. (1997). Report of final mortality statistics, 1995. *Monthly Vital Statistics Report, 45*(11, Supplement 2). Hyattsville, MD: National Center for Health Statistics.

Butler, R. N. (1989). Dispelling ageism: The cross-cutting intervention. In M. W. Riley & J. W. Riley, Jr. (Eds.), *The quality of aging: Strategies for interventions. Annals of the American Academy of Political and Social Science, 503,* 163–175.

Butler, R. N., Lewis, M. I., & Sunderland, T. (1998). *Aging and mental health: Positive psychosocial and biomedical approaches* (5th ed.). Boston: Allyn and Bacon.

Centers for Disease Control and Prevention. (1999). *Health, United States, 1999, Table 28.* Washington, DC: U.S. Government Printing Office, National Center for Health Statistics, National Vital Statistics System.

Cohen, R. A., Bloom, B., Simpson, G., & Parsons, P. E. (1997). Access to health care, Part 3: Older adults. *Vital Health Statistics, 10*(198). Washington, DC: U.S. Department of Health and Human Services, Centers for Disease Control and Prevention, National Center for Health Statistics.

Cohen, R. A., & Van Nostrand, J. F. (1994). Trends in the health of older Americans: United States, 1994. *Vital and Health Statistics, 3*(30). Washington, DC: U.S. Department of Health and Human Services, Centers for Disease Control and Prevention, National Center for Health Statistics.

Dalaker, J., & Naifeh, M. (1998). *Poverty in the United States, 1997.* Current Population Reports, P60-201. Washington, DC: U.S. Government Printing Office, U.S. Bureau of the Census.

Dhooper, S. S. (1997). *Social work in health care in the 21st century.* Thousand Oaks, CA: Sage.

Dorfman, R., Walters, K., Burke, P., Hardin, L., Karanik, T., Raphael, J., & Silverstein, E. (1995). Old, sad, and alone: The myth of the aging homosexual. *Journal of Gerontological Social Work, 24*(1/2), 29–44.

Fullerton, H. N., Jr. (1995). The 2005 labor force: Growing but slowly. *Monthly Labor Review, 118*(11), 29–44.

Gibelman, J., & Schernish, P. H. (1997). *Who we are: A second look.* Washington, DC: NASW Press.

Greene, R. R. (1986). Countertransference issues in social work with the aged. *Journal of Gerontological Social Work, 9*(3), 79–88.

Gropper, R. (1986). Strategic oneupmanship: A technique for managing the uncooperative client. *The Clinical Gerontologist, 6*(2), 25–27.

Jendrek, J. P. (1994). Grandparents who parent their grandchildren: Circumstances and decisions. *The Gerontologist, 34*(2), 206–211.

Kermis, M. D. (1986). *Mental health in late life: The adaptive process.* Boston: Jones & Bartlett.

LaBrake, T. (1996). *How to get families more involved in the nursing home: Four programs that work and why.* Binghamton, NY: Haworth Press.

Legato, M. L. (1997). *Gender specific aspects of human biology for the practicing physician.* Armonk, NY: Futura.

Lerer, G. (1995). Helping the irascible patient in long term care: Towards a theoretical and practice design. *Journal of Gerontological Social Work, 24*(1/2), 169–184.

National Aging Information Center. (1996). *Older persons with mobility and self-care limitations: 1990.* Washington, DC: U.S. Department of Health and Human Services, Administration on Aging.

National Center for Health Care Statistics. (1997). *An overview of nursing homes and their current residents: Data from the 1995 National Nursing Home Survey* (PHS 97-1250). Washington, DC: U.S. Government Printing Office.

O'Neill, J. (1999, February). Aging express: Can social work keep up? *NASW News, 44*(2), 3.

Pinderhughes, E. (1989). *Understanding race, ethnicity, and power.* New York: Free Press.

Regnier, V., Hamilton, J., & Yatabe, S. (1995). *Assisted living for the aged and frail: Innovations in design, management, and financing.* New York: Columbia University Press.

Schiller, B. (1998). *The economics of poverty and discrimination* (7th ed.). Upper Saddle River, NJ: Prentice-Hall.

Smolensky, E., Danziger, S., & Gottschalk, P. (1988). The declining significance of age in the United States: Trends in the well-being of children and elderly since 1939. In J. L. Palmer, T. Smeeding, & B. B. Torrey (Eds.), *The vulnerable* (pp. 29–52). Washington, DC: The Urban Institute.

Sprung, G. M. (1989). Transferential issues in working with older adults. *Social Casework: The Journal of Contemporary Social Work, 70*(10), 597–602.

U.S. Bureau of the Census. (1990). *1990 Census of Population and Housing.* Series CPH-L-74. Washington, DC: U.S. Government Printing Office.

U.S. Bureau of the Census. (1991a). *Marital status and living arrangements: March 1990,* by Arlene Saluter. Current Population Reports, P-20, No. 450. Washington, DC: U.S. Government Printing Office.

U.S. Bureau of the Census. (1991b). *Poverty in the United States: 1990.* Current Population Reports, P-60, No. 175. Washington, DC: U.S. Government Printing Office.

U.S. Bureau of the Census. (1993). *Population Projections of the United States by age, sex, race and Hispanic origin, 1993–2050.* Current Population Reports, P25-1104. Washington, DC: U.S. Government Printing Office.

U.S. Bureau of the Census. (1996a). *Projections of the number of households and families in the United States: 1995 to 2010,* by Jennifer C. Day. Current Population Reports, P25-1129. Washington, DC: U.S. Government Printing Office.

U.S. Bureau of the Census. (1996b). *Income, poverty and valuation of noncash benefits: 1994.* Current Population Reports, P60-189. Washington, DC: U.S. Government Printing Office.

Woods, M. E., & Hollis, F. (1990). *Casework: A psychosocial therapy.* New York: McGraw-Hill.

2

Biological Changes and the Physical Well-Being of Elders

Biological changes associated with the natural aging process are often the first overt signals to adults that they are moving from middle age to old age. While inevitable changes in the body occur in all aging people, the extent to which these changes precipitate chronic illness or impair functioning varies dramatically. Many elders remain physically active well into their 80s experiencing only minor inconveniences caused by sight, hearing, or joint changes. Others struggle with debilitating chronic illnesses beginning in their 60s and become increasingly frail in their 70s. These differences are due to a variety of factors including genetic predisposition to certain physical ailments, general lifetime health status, and most important, the influence of lifestyle choices, including nutrition and exercise.

This chapter will explore the normal and abnormal biological changes associated with the aging process, including the discussion of theories about why aging occurs and the cellular level changes that affect all of the physiological systems of the human body. Special consideration is given to the problem of urinary incontinence, a life-changing development that challenges the capability for independent living for some elders. A growing concern for gerontological social workers and health care providers is the increasing incidence of HIV/AIDS among elders, which is discussed as well. The chapter concludes with a discussion of the influence of nutrition and exercise on an elder's health and well-being, factors that have substantial influence on the quality of physical health for elders regardless of genetic predisposition to the development of disease or the natural changes that accompany the aging process.

Why Does the Body Age?

Before looking at the biological changes that accompany the aging process, it is important to explore why scientists believe biological aging occurs. If the cause of aging can be scientifically determined, can the process be stopped? Would it be desirable to significantly lengthen people's lives? These are some social questions that derive from the interest in knowing why the human body ages. The biological questions center more on ways to slow the process of aging to both minimize the development of disease and to improve the quality of life for elders as their bodies grow older. The scientific community does not agree on what initiates the biological aging process, but the primary theories currently espoused fall into three categories: genetic programming, cross-linked cells and free radicals, and changes in the immunological system. These categories do not exhaust all current theories of aging but represent the major areas of scientific inquiry under serious scrutiny.

Genetic Programming

Proponents of the "wear and tear" theory of aging suggest that the body simply wears out, reflecting a preprogrammed process determined by genetic makeup. Under this theory, the human body has a maximum life span and major physiological systems deteriorate at a relatively set rate (Finch, 1991; Hayflick, 1994; McCormick & Campisi, 1991; Wilson, 1974). Cells in all major systems lose the ability to repair damage with time. This deterioration is hastened by environmental and lifestyle factors but is genetically predetermined. The development of age-related disease, such as glaucoma, Alzheimer's disease, and late-onset diabetes, may be determined by genetic markers. Genetic markers for certain diseases would explain why certain conditions run in families. There is strong evidence that longevity (without disease) runs in families by a combination of sheer genetic luck and healthy living. However, the genetic programming theory of aging is not universally accepted as the only explanation of the biological changes associated with aging.

Cross-Links and Free Radicals

Cellular biologists propose that aging begins with adverse reactions within the structure of cells and molecules, but those changes are not necessarily initiated by a genetic program. According to this theory, molecules in the body develop cross-links within themselves and with other molecules that create subtle changes in the physical and chemical functioning of the cell (Martin & Baker, 1993). Cells accumulate collagen, a gelatinous substance present in connective tissues, which reduces the elasticity of tissue. The accumulation occurs because the body is not efficient in recognizing and eliminating cross-linked cells. This accumulation is observable in cartilage, blood vessel, and skin cells (Lee & Cerami, 1990). Cartilage becomes less flexible, leading to the joint stiffness associated with aging; blood vessels harden and skin wrinkles.

Another molecular-level explanation for aging is the free radical theory (Harman, 1956; Martin & Baker, 1993). Free radicals are unstable oxygen molecules produced when cells metabolize oxygen. These molecules attach to proteins in the body, impairing the functioning of healthy cells. The damage to the body occurs when cross-links and free radicals accumulate, damaging cellular structures. Free radicals are believed to impair the body's ability to fight cancer, repair skin cell damage, and prevent low-density fat cells from clinging to artery walls. The current interest in adding antioxidants to multivitamins represents an effort to stabilize free radicals and thus slow the process of cell damage and promote healing. (See Figure 2.1 for more information on antioxidants.)

Deterioration of the Immune System

The body's immune system is responsible for fighting disease and ridding the body of foreign substances. To accomplish that function, the immune system produces antibodies that attack viruses, bacteria, and aberrant cells, such as those produced by cancer. The immunological theory of aging proposes that the immune system's ability to recognize and fight disease is compromised with age (Miller, 1990). Abnormal cells are more likely to grow unchecked, causing chronic disease states that eventually lead to impaired functioning in major physiological systems. Other theories within this school of thought propose that immunological inefficiency results in an autoimmune response by the body. The body slowly rejects its own cells and produces antibodies that destroy even normal cells. Arthritis and diabetes are given as examples of the body's autoimmune reaction (Miller, 1990).

None of these theories is accepted as the "true" cause of aging in the human body but each approach offers some future promise for understanding what happens in the process. All three theories suggest that the process of aging begins on the cellular level and those changes accumulate throughout a person's lifetime, resulting in the physical changes observed in elders. The next section of this

---

FIGURE 2.1   *What Are Antioxidants?*

Antioxidants are vitamins and nutrients that have been identified as substances with chemical properties that stabilize free radical oxygen cells, thus slowing the damaging effects of deterioration on the cellular level. The three most common antioxidants are beta carotene, Vitamin C, and Vitamin E, all of which occur abundantly in familiar fruits and vegetables.

Antioxidant	Food Sources
Beta carotene	Yellow, orange, and red vegetables and fruit (such as squash, carrots, pumpkins, kale, spinach, peaches, oranges, and tomatoes)
Vitamin C	Citrus fruits, strawberries, cantaloupe, pineapple, brussels sprouts, tomatoes, spinach, kale, cabbage, and turnips
Vitamin E	Vegetable oil, wheat germ, whole grains, and nuts

Source: American Academy of Nutritional Research, 1997.

chapter explores specifically what changes accompany the process of normal aging and identifies what disease states may develop in each of the major physiological systems of the body.

Biological Changes That Accompany Aging

The normal process of biological changes in the human body over time is known as senescence. Aging of the physical body is not considered pathology nor is normal aging considered a disease. Certain biological changes that occur during this life stage may predispose elders to the development of illness and disease. However, physical changes in the human body that occur during senescence do not necessarily portend poor health in the elderly. This section of the chapter will explore the kinds of biological changes that define aging in all of the major physiological systems. Individual bodies actually age at different rates but the process of physical changes that denote aging follow an observable pattern.

Skin, Hair, and Nails

The dermatological system of the body includes the skin, hair, and nails. The most obvious physical change that accompanies the aging process is wrinkling of the skin, caused by a loss of subcutaneous fat and water beneath the skin's surface. This process is compounded by the loss of the elastic fibers within skin cells. Skin becomes thinner and less flexible as the body ages (Spirduso, 1995). Sun exposure is also the primary cause of intense pigmentation on the hands and face, known as "liver spots." Ethnicity, lifetime skin care, and physical health contribute to the rate at which these changes in the skin occur. Persons who have had excessive exposure to the sun may begin to show wrinkling of the skin as early as the 30s. African American elders, on the contrary, may be well into their 50s and 60s before any wrinkling occurs. This is due to a difference in oil content in their skin.

Between age 30 and age 70, the process in which skin cells are replaced as a normal part of the body's maintenance process slows by 50 percent (Richey, Richey, & Fenske, 1988). Skin is more delicate in elders, and skin replacement occurs more slowly. This combination explains why elders bruise more easily than younger adults. Bumps and falls may result in much more severe bruising than would seem warranted from the injury, especially for the very old. Blood circulation to the skin's surface slows as the body ages as part of a general decline in the efficiency of the circulatory system and contributes to a slower healing process when skin is injured. Elders need 50 percent more time to heal from wounds than younger persons (Richey et al., 1988).

Impaired blood circulation to the skin's surface is often responsible for elders' sensitivity to both cold and heat. Elders are less likely to shiver to generate body heat or to sweat to dissipate body heat. As a result, aging bodies are less efficient at regulating body temperature in general. Rooms may need to be three to five degrees warmer for elders to feel comfortable (Hooyman & Kiyak, 1999).

The potential problem created by an elder's inability to properly regulate body temperature is a serious issue (Cunningham & Brookbank, 1988). Hypothermia—low body temperature caused by prolonged exposure to the cold—can eventually lead to stroke, brain damage, and death. Hyperthermia, high body temperature caused by prolonged exposure to excessive heat, can cause heat stroke, which if left untreated can be fatal. Therefore, weather variations of both hot and cold are particularly dangerous for elders who may experience the effects of extreme temperatures long before younger persons. When elders fail to use fans or air conditioning in the summer or keep their thermostats turned low in the winter to conserve energy, they place themselves in physical danger.

These normal changes associated with an aging dermatological system may present a more serious issue in terms of an elder's self-esteem and self-concept than any inherent pathology. How one feels about one's self may be highly dependent on physical appearance, and these changes are usually the first to be noticed by self and others. A plethora of cosmetic solutions to minimize wrinkles and coloring gray hair can help people cope with these changes if they find them particularly bothersome.

While normal age-related changes in the skin are not considered pathology, two-thirds of persons over the age of 70 have skin disorders that require treatment—evidence that the skin takes severe punishment throughout life (Klingman, Grove, & Balin, 1985). A lifetime of exposure to the sun and a diminished ability to heal wounds put some elders at greater risk for skin cancer. Lesions, moles, and pigmented spots need to be carefully monitored. While skin cancer is treatable if detected early enough, it is still one of the most deadly forms of cancer. The best cancer prevention efforts for skin cancer should be directed to people long before they accumulate a lifetime of skin damage.

Graying of the hair is another common feature of normal aging although for some individuals this process commences long before old age. Graying occurs when hair follicles lose melanin, the pigment present in hair and skin. This process occurs gradually so that some elders are completely white while others retain varying amounts of their natural hair color throughout life. Hair becomes thinner, beginning in the 40s, due to the body's decreased production of estrogen and testosterone combined with the scalp's decreased efficiency in replacing lost hair. Men may become partially bald, a phenomenon more determined by genetic factors than the aging process. While hair on the head becomes thinner, hair growth may actually increase on other parts of the body in both men and women. Greater hair growth in the nose, ears, and eyebrows suggests that these hormonal deficiencies affect parts of the body in different ways (Hayflick, 1994). While hair becomes thinner as the body ages, finger and toe nails become thicker and drier, which may present a hygiene problem as reaching one's feet becomes more difficult.

The Neurological System

The changes in the neurological system associated with normal aging affect all of the other physiological systems in the human body. The neurological system consists of the brain and the supporting network of nerves in the body. While brain weight is reduced by 10 percent by age 75 due to loss of fluid, this change in itself does not cause a loss of brain functioning (Cunningham & Brookbank, 1988). The human brain has a phenomenal capacity to compensate for changes in its physical structure by rerouting functions to different parts of the brain, particularly those that control intelligence and cognitive operations. The actual amount of brain damage due to organic disorders or injuries can not always predict what, if any, functions will be affected.

The most notable changes associated with aging come from a decline in the efficiency of neurotransmitters, the chemicals that transmit signals within the brain and from the brain to corresponding parts of the body The synapses, the points at which electrical impulses pass between nerve cells, conduct impulses more slowly as the body ages (Ebersole & Hess, 1998). It takes a longer time for the neurological system to send a message to the brain, process a response, and return the message. That is why elders may have a longer reaction time to certain stimuli. For example, if an elder touches a hot surface, he or she may take longer to process the brain's message to remove a hand from the source of heat. Or, while driving, elders may take longer to react to a car darting into traffic or to the need to stop suddenly. An elder's cognitive functioning may be intact but require just moments longer to retrieve and process knowledge. The decreased efficiency of the neurological system is in part responsible for problems with hypo- and hyperthermia discussed earlier in this chapter.

Changes in sleep patterns are considered part of the neurological changes associated with normal aging. Elders experience less "efficient" sleep, meaning they spend less time in the deeper stages of restorative sleep and feel less rested when they wake up. This is due to changes in brain wave activity and changes in circadian rhythms, the normal pattern of sleep and waking (Richardson, 1990). A younger adult usually sleeps for seven or eight hours and is awake for the remaining sixteen hours of the day. Elders may need only six hours of sleep but fall into a pattern of napping during the day—a circadian rhythm that more closely resembles an infant's pattern rather than that of an adult. That is why it is common for elders to go to bed very early but be wide awake in the middle of the night. When elders nap during the day to compensate for fatigue or use sleeping aids to promote longer nighttime sleep, the problem is compounded. A later bedtime may help elders to stabilize their own circadian rhythms and restore better quality sleep.

Two sleep disorders deserve mention in the discussion about neurological disorders. Sleep apnea, the cessation of breathing during sleep for 10 to 15 seconds, can cause insufficient blood flow to the heart. Over time, this can contribute to or exacerbate heart disease. This condition is often treated by raising the head of an elder's bed or by using plastic breathing strips (the kind used by professional athletes) to open nasal airways. Other elders experience nocturnal myoclonus, a neurological disorder characterized by involuntary leg jerking in one's sleep (Hayflick, 1994). While this is not a serious condition, it often disrupts sleep.

Stroke and Parkinson's disease are two other conditions that are found disproportionately in elders. A stroke is caused by a lack of blood flow to the brain due to clotting or bleeding in the brain as a result of a damaged blood vessel. Eighty-five percent of all cerebrovascular disease occurs in persons over the age of 65 (Horvath & Davis, 1990). While some strokes are fatal, others leave elders with seriously diminished physical, cognitive, or communicative abilities. Most strokes are preceded by a series of transient ischemic attacks (TIAs), which are actually mini-strokes. During a TIA, the person experiences a short-term loss of speech, weakness on one side of the body, altered vision, or memory loss (Ebersole & Hess, 1998). The impairment lasts only a short time, and the individual usually recovers these lost functions promptly. However, TIAs are warnings of an impending stroke. TIAs can be treated, thus avoiding a stroke and its devastating damage. Parkinson's disease is a second serious neurological disease diagnosed more commonly in elders than younger persons. Parkinson's disease is a movement disorder characterized by tremors of the fingers, feet, lips, and head with progressive rigidity of the facial and trunk muscles (Horvath & Davis, 1990). Elders with the disease may have difficulty swallowing or shuffle when they walk because of attenuated ability to control their extremities. If detected early, the disease responds well to medication.

The Cardiovascular System

The cardiovascular system—the heart and blood vessels—becomes less efficient as the body ages. Increased amounts of fat and collagen are deposited in the heart muscles, reducing cardiac output. The valves of the heart become more rigid, making the heart work harder. This restricted blood flow accounts for why elders may tire more easily when doing physical activities or have reduced muscle strength. When elders most need more efficient circulation, their bodies are less able to provide it for them.

All major blood vessels have some degree of atherosclerosis—deposits of fat—that accumulate over a lifetime. These deposits make it more difficult for the heart to pump the blood efficiently throughout the body and to use oxygen efficiently (Lakatta, 1990). These fatty deposits reduce the size and elasticity of the large arteries that pump blood to large organs, such as the stomach, liver, and brain. With reduced blood flow, these organs function less effectively. The cardiovascular system, more than any other system in the human body, is positively affected by exercise. Even a minimal amount of exercise by elders can improve cardiovascular functioning. For elders who have been athletic throughout their lives, the heart can continue to function as efficiently as that of a much younger person. While the propensity to develop heart disease is strongly affected by genetic and lifestyle factors, exercise is an equally important determinant of how well the heart ages (Hayflick, 1994).

Two primary types of cardiovascular disease contribute to making heart disease the number one killer of older adults (Lakatta, 1990). The first is coronary artery disease, which develops in the form of arteriosclerosis—hardening of the arteries or atherosclerosis. Coronary heart disease can restrict blood flow to the heart, resulting in heart muscle damage known as a myocardial infarction or a heart attack. Elders have more diffuse symptoms of a heart attack than younger persons and complain more about a generalized discomfort and fatigue rather than an intense, heavy pain in the chest. Congestive heart failure occurs when the heart fails to pump enough blood throughout the body. Elders may complain about chronic fatigue, weakness, or edema—the accumulation of fluid in the joints. The discomfort associated with edema often causes elders to become sedentary, further exacerbating the circulation problem and making elders prone to other conditions such as pneumonia.

A second serious cardiovascular disease, not restricted to the elderly, is hypertension or high blood pressure. Hypertension is twice as common among African American elders as it is among their white counterparts (Ebersole & Hess, 1998; Lakatta, 1990). High blood pressure has no symptoms and is often referred to as "the silent killer" although it is easily diagnosed through simple blood pressure screening. High blood pressure damages the arteries predisposing people to the development of a blood clot, which is a common cause of stroke. It can be treated effectively with medication if the medication is taken consistently and the condition is diagnosed before the hypertension causes extensive damage to the arterial system.

The Musculoskeletal System

As people grow older, they actually become shorter due to the compression of the vertebrae in the spine. While both men and women lose some body height, women may become up to three inches shorter due to skeletal changes associated with the loss of estrogen following menopause (Cunningham & Brookbank, 1988). The spine may become more curved contributing to the illusion that elders are chronically slouching. Aging is accompanied by a general loss of muscle strength and endurance due to atrophy of muscle cells, loss of lean muscle mass, and loss of elastic fibers in the muscle tissue. Yet, research has shown that when elders begin to exercise these muscles on a regular basis, a moderate degree of muscle strength returns suggesting that disuse may hasten the deterioration of muscle strength (Hayflick, 1994).

The combination of a curved spine and loss of muscle strength contribute to a tendency for elders to have difficulties in maintaining their balance. They may have a decreased ability to orient their bodies by making subtle changes in the muscles that help them center their bodies over their feet. If elders feel less stable on their feet, they are likely to move more slowly to maintain control over balance. Some elders limit physical activity in general, which accelerates the deterioration of muscle strength and coordination.

The teeth and supporting jaw structure, considered part of the musculoskeletal system, may or may not deteriorate as an individual ages. Elders who have not had access to lifetime preventative dental care or flourinated water are usually at greater risk for losing their teeth prior to or during their later years. The most common cause of tooth loss for persons over the age of 65 years is periodontal disease—infections of the gums and bone structure of the jaw that hold teeth in place (Administration on Aging, 1999). These infections are usually caused by dental plaque, which can be removed with regular brushing and routine cleaning of the teeth. Once elders have lost their natural teeth and wear dentures, the structure of the jaw may change. Dentures may no longer fit and the mouth may actually "shrink." When dentures fit poorly, elders tend to avoid wearing them, hastening the process of shrinkage. This cyclical process may make chewing very difficult and even painful.

The most familiar musculoskeletal disease associated with aging is arthritis. It is rare for persons over the age of 75 not to have at least some minor osteoarthritis in joints. This condition is caused by deterioration of cartilage accompanied by the development of bone spurs on the joint surface (Ettinger & Davis, 1990). Deterioration of cartilage occurs naturally as the result of a lifetime of using joints or as a consequence of joint injury. Athletes often develop arthritis earlier in their lives due to excessive wear and tear on their joints. While it may be painful for elders to move their hands or knees, regular exercise of arthritic joints can actually improve the condition. A more severe form of arthritis—rheumatoid arthritis—is not associated with aging but rather is an autoimmune disease affecting persons of all ages.

Women face one of the most damaging effects of aging on the musculoskeletal system, osteoporosis—the thinning and deterioration of bone integrity. Postmenopausal osteoporosis affects women and is caused by the lack of estrogen in the body following menopause. Not all women will develop osteoporosis. Figure 2.2 describes the personal characteristics that predispose women to the development of the condition.

FIGURE 2.2   *Osteoporosis: Are You at Risk?*

High-Risk Factors That Are Genetically Determined

- Being female
- Having a family history of osteoporosis
- Being of Northern European or Asian ancestry
- Being small-boned or very thin
- Having fair coloring, such as blonde or red hair and fair skin or freckles
- Early menopause
- Inability to digest milk or milk products

Other High-Risk Lifestyle or Medical Factors

- Having had a pregnancy during teen years
- A medical history that includes loss of the ovaries or long periods of immobilization
- Eating disorders, chronic diarrhea, and kidney or liver disease
- Lack of exercise or excessive exercise
- High alcohol intake, low-calcium diets, or a Vitamin D deficiency
- High caffeine intake and smoking

Source: Adapted from the Massachusetts Department of Public Health, 1999.

Senile osteoporosis affects both men and women and is defined as the general deterioration of bone density associated with very advanced age. Hip and wrist fractures are more likely when bones are thin and brittle. While it is often assumed that an elder's hip breaks as a result of a fall, more recent research indicates that a hip can spontaneously fracture causing the fall (Ebersole & Hess, 1998). Some women develop kyphosis, a hump on the spine, also known as "dowager's hump." Others develop deformities of the vertebrae known as scoliosis. These conditions may be painful and severely limit mobility. Once these conditions develop in elders, modern medicine can do little to reverse them. However, calcium supplements and regular exercise for postmenopausal women can help stabilize bone loss and are the best preventative measures.

The Gastrointestinal System

The gastrointestinal system of the human body includes the esophagus, stomach, liver, and small and large intestines. While some people begin to experience the symptoms of an aging digestive system early in middle age, other elders notice little difference other than some diminished appetite due more to sensory losses in taste and smell than to actual changes in the digestive system. A loss of teeth or skeletal changes in the shape and strength of the jaw may contribute to difficulties in chewing, the first step in the long process of digestion. Food that is poorly chewed is more difficult for the entire digestive system to process. As the body ages, the esophagus—the digestive tube going from the mouth to the stomach—may narrow or become less elastic (Ebersole & Hess, 1998). As a result, it may take more time for food to pass into the stomach. It is common for elders to feel "full" after eating only a small amount. The stomach secretes fewer digestive juices so that elders may experience chronic inflammation of the stomach, known as *atrophic gastritis.* The symptoms of this may be as benign as occasional heartburn or as serious as the development of gastric ulcers. The small and large intestines decrease in weight due to the general loss of water in the body that accompanies age. This may be one of the contributing factors to more frequent constipation among elders.

Serious weight loss may become a problem for elders who have little appetite or experience digestive problems. They are less likely to eat if the process of digestion and elimination is uncomfortable. Poor dietary habits, smoking, and genetic predisposition are contributing factors in the higher incidence of stomach and colon cancer among elders. Both of these types of cancer are difficult to diagnose in their early stages and may not even become symptomatic until late in the progression of the disease.

The Respiratory System

As in the heart, the exact progression of aging in the respiratory system is the function of a lifetime of both lifestyle and environmental factors. In fact, it is difficult to distinguish between those changes in the respiratory system that are due to pollutants and toxins and those due to the normal process of aging. In general, the muscles that operate the lungs lose elasticity and strength. The loss of strength impairs elders' ability to breathe deeply, cough, and clear the lungs of mucus and fluids. The number of cilia—the hairlike structures in the lungs—are reduced, making lungs less efficient in obtaining oxygen (Tockman, 1995). As the body ages, the lungs have decreased functional reserve capacity, resulting in much slower, shallower breathing. Less efficient breathing may result in insufficient oxygen intake for the rest of the body.

While these changes are quite dramatic, if other lung disease is not present, elders may experience normal breathing while at rest. It is when their bodies demand more oxygen during activity that the changes become most apparent. Given the opportunity to rest during activity or to perform physical tasks at a slower rate, elders may function with no apparent dysfunction of the respiratory system.

Chronic oxygen insufficiency, however, can impair the function of the circulatory system and damage the heart. The inability to cough properly to expel foreign matter from the lungs can result in a greater tendency among elders to develop emphysema, chronic bronchitis, or pneumonia (Tockman, 1995). Pneumonia is the fifth leading cause of death among elders (Anderson, Kochanek, & Murphy, 1997). Many of the diseases of the lung that develop among elders are the result of cigarette smoking or environmental pollution.

The Urinary Tract System

For some elders, the changes in the urinary system—comprised of the kidney, ureters, and bladder—are the most bothersome. The kidneys serve two primary functions in the body. Kidneys filter water and waste material from the blood and dispel those wastes in the form of urine. The kidneys also are crucial in restoring the balance of ions and minerals to the filtered blood before it is returned to the bloodstream. The ability of the kidneys to perform both of these functions diminishes by as much as 50 percent as the body ages (Ebersole & Hess, 1998; Hooyman & Kiyak, 1999). Certain drugs, including antibiotics, become more potent in an elder's system because less of the drug is naturally filtered out by the kidneys. Kidneys may lose the ability to absorb glucose, thereby contributing to a great tendency among elders to become seriously dehydrated.

Both the ureters—the tubes leading from the kidney to the bladder—and the bladder tend to lose muscle tone, which may result in incomplete emptying of the bladder. When the bladder is not emptied during urination, elders are more likely to suffer from urinary tract infections. Elders may need to urinate more frequently, due to diminished bladder capacity. This is most likely during the night and may disrupt sleep. Despite frequency of urination, elders may experience a delayed sensation of needing to empty the bladder due, in part, to the less efficient operation of the body's neurological system. Incontinence may be the result of this combination of decreased bladder capacity and delayed sensation of urge.

The problem is more prevalent in women as a result of the relaxation of the pelvic floor muscles following childbirth.

For men, urinary tract problems may be exacerbated by problems associated with the prostate, a doughnut-shaped gland that encircles the urethra and produces most of the fluid in semen. Enlargement of the prostate may result in problems with starting and stopping urine flow, incomplete bladder emptying, or frequent urges to urinate. Prostate enlargement is not necessarily considered a disease unless the urinary tract system backs up and causes an infection or the prostate becomes cancerous. The risk of developing cancer of the prostate increases with advanced age and a family history of the disease.

If elders worry they will not have access to bathroom facilities when they are away from their homes, they may restrict fluids to reduce the need to urinate. However, the dangers of dehydration for elders and the frequency of bladder infections make this a poor solution to the problem.

The Endocrine and Reproductive Systems

The human body functions on the basis of a complex, carefully regulated system of hormones produced by the endocrine system. Hormones regulate reproduction, growth, energy production, and the general homeostatic condition of the body. The two primary hormonal changes that occur in aging that will be discussed in this section are changes in insulin levels regulated by the pancreas and the reduction of estrogen and testosterone levels in both men and women.

Insulin is produced by the pancreas to regulate glucose levels in the bloodstream. Glucose is one of the sugars in food that is metabolized to produce energy. For some elders, the pancreatic production of insulin becomes less efficient and glucose is not metabolized. As a result, blood sugar levels become elevated. Adult-onset diabetes may develop when the body's insulin levels are chronically insufficient. Elders may not exhibit the usual symptom of fatigue, increased appetite, weakness, slow healing, and frequent urination associated with diabetes. Diabetes may not even be detected in elders until found in blood tests conducted for other medical reasons. Untreated diabetes leads to frequent infections, kidney failure, and heart and blood vessel damage. Older African American women are particularly susceptible to diabetes due, in part, to what appears to be a genetic tendency combined with poor diet, physical inactivity, and a greater prevalence of other age-related disease (Cohen, Bloom, Simpson, & Parsons, 1997).

The universal change in the endocrine system for women occurs following menopause—the cessation of the menstrual cycle—that occurs for most women in the late 40s and 50s. As the ovaries cease to function, they reduce the production of estrogen and progesterone. Estrogen not only is associated with reproductive capacity but also plays an important function in protecting women from heart disease and Alzheimer's disease. The protective function of estrogen helps to explain why women are at lower risk for heart disease than men until their 50s when the incidence evens out.

Estrogen loss combined with other normal biological changes associated with aging leads to some degree of urogenital atrophy in women. That is, the vaginal walls become thinner and drier, which may cause pain for women during sexual intercourse. This discomfort can be alleviated with artificial lubricants and should not be interpreted as a woman's inability to enjoy sex.

The normal reproductive changes that occur in aging men happen more gradually than those observed in women. Menopause in women is an observable series of events resulting in loss of reproductive capacity while men may continue their reproductive abilities well into old age. Men may experience some reduction in testosterone levels, which diminishes sex drive, but this is not a universal phenomenon. Men require more direct stimulation and more time as they age to achieve an erection. There is usually a longer refractory period between erections as well. However, men's sexual desire and performance are more likely to be affected by the presence of prostate problems and other health problems than by hormonal insufficiency.

The Sensory System

All of the sensory systems show some change by age 70. Most elders lose some sensory acuity in their sight, hearing, taste, and smell and develop a higher sensory threshold in their sense of touch. In the absence of disease, these changes occur gradually, and most elders learn to compensate for losses.

Touch. Due to the diminished efficiency of neurotransmitters discussed earlier in this chapter, most elders have a higher threshold for pain (Timaris, 1988). They simply do not experience pain with the same intensity as when they were younger. Pain from serious conditions such as heart attacks may be experienced as a chronic but vague discomfort rather than the intense crushing pain experienced by younger persons (Legato, 1997). Elders may be less likely to complain about pain from burns or skin lesions, which are even more serious for elders in view of delayed healing. This loss of sensory threshold can also result in what appears to be increased clumsiness. Elders may not be able to feel the fine distinctions needed to grasp objects firmly. They may have more difficulty establishing their sense of balance because the neurological system takes longer to send messages to the muscles to work together to maintain balance.

Vision. Changes in vision begin as early as the late 30s when people begin to experience presyopia, the inability to change the focus of the lens for near vision. Phone books, newspapers, and other small print become increasingly difficult to read at close range. These changes in sight are due to changes in the shape of the eye. The lens of the eye becomes less elastic and therefore less able to adjust to the rapid change necessary when going from distance vision to close vision. The pupil of the eye is smaller, more fixed, and less responsive to changes in light. As a result, elders need more light to actually see. The pupil cannot automatically dilate to let in more light. Likewise, the pupil cannot constrict to limit the amount of light coming into the eye and therefore elders may have more problem with the glare. Shiny surfaces, especially floors, present a significant danger to elders, who are literally blinded by the glare. Elders may also gradually lose their peripheral vision even if their central vision remains. Sensitivity to glare and a decrease in peripheral vision create very serious problems for some elderly drivers (Kline, Kline, Fozard, Kosnik, Schieber, & Sekular, 1992).

The lens of the eye yellows, reducing an elder's color sensitivity. Blues, violets, and greens become the most difficult to distinguish although the human eye retains its sensitivity to red, yellow, and orange well into old age (Ebersole & Hess, 1998). This diminished ability to distinguish between colors contributes to the loss of depth perception and creates an additional risk to older drivers.

While these changes in vision may be inconvenient and annoying for elders, they are considered normal age-related changes in vision. A cataract—a film that clouds the lens of the eye—is not part of normal changes in the eye. When cataracts develop, it is often necessary to replace the clouded lens with a removable or permanent contact lens to restore clear vision. Cataracts are found more frequently in African Americans (Kupfer, 1995). The development of cataracts is strongly connected to a lack of antioxidants such as vitamins A, C, and E, which are frequently missing in a high fat, high carbohydrate diet. A more serious eye condition that frequently leads to blindness is glaucoma—the presence of excessive or insufficient fluid in the eye, which produces abnormal pressure. Untreated, it leads to tunnel vision. Glaucoma is the leading cause of blindness in African Americans. It is easily detected by a simple test given by optometrists and opthamalogists and can be treated effectively with medication. A third eye disease seen more frequently in elders than in younger people is macular degeneration, a slow progressive loss of central vision. Elders with this condition retain some of their peripheral vision but lose the ability to see straight ahead.

Hearing.   While normal changes are associated with hearing as the body ages, hearing damage may occur at an early age for some persons. Exposure to loud working environments, such as construction sites, factories, and drilling operations, may cause premature hearing loss as early as the 20s. Another leading cause of non-age-related changes is exposure to loud music at concerts and through personal stereo devices. The ear can repair nerve damage from occasional exposure to damaging sound levels but constant exposure will result in hearing loss that the body cannot repair. With the increasing number of such devices, the number of elders with significant hearing loss in the future will no doubt increase.

The progressive loss of hearing and the inability to distinguish between different frequencies of sound is known as presbycusis. These are due to age-related changes in the bones that conduct sound in the inner ear along with loss of cells in the cranial nerve (Gulya, 1995; Hayflick, 1994). Hearing loss may not be so much an issue of whether sounds are loud enough for a person to hear but whether they are able to distinguish between those sounds. Conversations may sound muffled or jumbled because certain frequencies of the human voice cannot be distinguished. A person with a hearing loss may have decreased ability to filter voices through other background noise. Amplifying the sound may exacerbate the problem. Volume may not be the issue but rather the ability to distinguish between sounds so as to give them meaning. This is especially true of human speech. Some hearing loss is due to a buildup of wax in the ear canal.

Taste and Smell.   These two senses are included together because they have such a strong interconnection. The body routinely loses taste buds regardless of age but even among the very old, these taste buds are regenerated. Despite the replacement of taste buds, however, elders often report a decreased taste threshold (Bartoshuk & Weiffenbach, 1990). Elders are likely to prefer more highly seasoned foods so that they can taste them or to be attracted to foods that are high in sugar or salt. However, loss of smell in elders may actually be the culprit in elders' loss of their sense of taste. The number of olfactory receptors diminishes with age despite the process of replacement. Receptors are not replaced at the same rate they are damaged. The inability to smell food decreases the power of taste, therefore diminishing the enjoyment derived from eating. The inability to enjoy food through taste or smell often contributes to a serious loss of appetite among elders. The inability to smell can be dangerous when elders do not smell natural gas, smoke and fire, or spoiled food.

Every major physiological system experiences some changes in the aging process, although these changes should not be equated with disease or disability. Some of these changes occur slowly and are hardly noticed by an individual, such as changes in taste or smell. Other changes, such as reduced efficiency of the heart and lungs, present significant challenges to elders in daily functioning. A summary of the major biological changes associated with the aging process is presented in Table 2.1.

Implications of Age-Related Biological Changes for Social Work Practice with Elders

This extensive review of the biological changes associated with aging is provided to help you understand the normal physiological changes associated with the aging process as well as begin to identify those changes that may not be normal and may require medical attention. However, a basic knowledge about the physiology does not substitute for a medical assessment by a physician, and social workers should never assume the role of medical expert. An elder's health should be carefully monitored by qualified medical personnel. It should be clear that many of the changes associated with aging are influenced by genetic makeup and the accumulative effects of environmental stressors, such as sun exposure, lifestyle choices about smoking and diet, and access to preventative health care. Yet, elders' diminished physical abilities and heightened tendencies to develop troublesome chronic diseases has important implications for gerontological social work.

TABLE 2.1 *Summary of Aged-Related Biological Changes*

System	Age-Related Changes
Dermatological System (Skin, Hair, Nails)	Skin wrinkles, hair thins and may turn gray. Finger and toe nails thicken. Elder may be more susceptible to hyper- or hypothermia. Injuries may take 50 percent longer to heal.
Neurological System (Brain, Nervous System)	Response time to stimuli is slowed. Sleep patterns are less efficient. Elders are more likely to experience cardiovascular disease with small or major strokes.
Cardiovascular System	Heart may become less efficient if arteriosclerosis or atherosclerosis is present. More likely to have hypertension.
Musculoskeletal System	Elders may become shorter and lose muscle strength and mass. Arthritis is more likely to develop in joints. Women may develop osteoporosis resulting in fractures, dowager's hump, or scoliosis.
Respiratory System	Functional capacity of lungs is diminished. Elders become more easily winded when exerting themselves. May become more susceptible to pneumonia.
Urinary Tract System	Kidneys are less efficient in screening toxins and restoring ionic balance to blood. Bladder loses tone and is more likely to develop asymptomatic infections. Some elders develop incontinence.
Endocrine/Reproductive System	Some elders are less efficient at metabolizing glucose and may develop late-onset diabetes. Estrogen loss after menopause may exacerbate osteoporosis.
Sensory System	
Touch	Elder may develop higher threshold for pain, greater tendency to develop hypo- or hyperthermia. Balance problems may develop.
Vision	Presyopia is common. Eye needs more light to focus and is sensitive to glare. Elder may experience reduced ability to distinguish between colors. Some elders develop cataracts, glaucoma, or macular degeneration.
Hearing	Hearing acuity may be reduced up to 50 percent with difficulties in distinguishing between sounds.
Taste/Smell	Sense of smell may be seriously impaired due to lifetime environmental damage. Taste is affected by lack of smell. Elder may not smell gas, smoke, or spoiled food.

Elders' Physical Health as a Social Barometer

For elders suffering from physical limitations and chronic illness, their day-to-day health status becomes the organizing principle in their lives. How they feel physically is the barometer for their willingness to leave their homes, participate in social activities, and interact with others. Some elders may feel their bodies have become prisons. As much as they might want to be more active, their physical well-being, rather than personal motivation, dictates what is possible. This is important in both the assessment and intervention phases of social work practice. It is difficult to accurately assess an elder who does not feel well, and it is advised that the assessment be delayed until a time when the elder can be a more active participant in the assessment process. Even when the assessment has been completed, it may be difficult to concretize any intervention activities if physical health is a consideration. Elders may be evasive about participating in future activities. Although willing, they may feel it is more practical to say, "Well, I'll see how I feel on that day." This should not be interpreted as resistance but rather a very practical way to handle the uncertainties of fragile health.

Too many elders simply assume that nothing can be done about the aches and pains they associate with aging. They may resolve themselves to suffer silently. The aging process should not be synonymous with pain. An important premise of gerontological social work is that elders have the right to maximum physical and emotional comfort whenever possible. It is paramount that social workers encourage elders to seek medical attention when they experience pain and to be assertive when dealing with their physicians. Social workers can play an important role in empowering elders to help physicians and other health care providers to be more responsive to their needs.

Private Functions Become Public Business

Discussing physical health problems with a social worker may be particularly uncomfortable for elders. For an elderly woman who has been very modest about personal matters such as bladder and bowel functions, discussing these topics with a relative stranger may be awkward. The same is true for an elderly man who does not feel his difficulties with maintaining an erection or urinating are a social worker's business. What have been private functions for elders all of their lives tend to become public business when social workers and other helping professionals get involved. While a solid understanding of an elder's health problems is essential to the development of an intervention plan, it is important to be sensitive to the deeply personal nature of this discussion.

Environmental Adaptation Is Necessary

With a strong knowledge base in the physical changes associated with aging, social workers can be helpful to institutions and families in designing environmental adaptations to accommodate these changes. Handrails can help the unsteady elder manage stairs or negotiate hallways. Using bright colors to distinguish individual steps and nonglare surfaces on floors can help the sight-impaired elder avoid falls. Large-print signs and color-coded doors can help elders reorient themselves in unfamiliar environments. Avoiding background music in senior centers and nursing homes helps elders to be able to concentrate on conversations without having to filter out distracting noises. Anticipating the kinds of environmental changes necessary for elders with sensory and physical limitations can be helpful in avoiding accidents and making elders feel more confident in both home and public settings.

Incontinence

One of the significant aspects of physical health in maintaining independent living is the elder's ability to manage basic bowel and bladder functions with minimal assistance. This section addresses urinary incontinence—the involuntary loss of control over the elimination of urine from the body. While incontinence was once assumed to be an inevitable part of the aging process, the medical community now knows that this is simply not so. The biological changes associated with aging may put elders at higher risk for the development of incontinence, but the aging process itself is not the cause.

The Prevalence of Incontinence

It is estimated that between 8 percent and 34 percent of community-dwelling elders experience incontinence at some time in their lives (Herzog & Fultz, 1990; Umlauf & Sherman, 1996). This broad estimate reflects the difficulty of accurately assessing the prevalence of incontinence. Incontinence is difficult to measure in surveys, a common research methodology for estimating the prevalence of a particular health problem. The slow onset of incontinence, its episodic nature, and the personal embarrassment elders feel about admitting to others they have the condition contribute to both a serious underestimate of its impact on elders and its underdiagnosis by health care providers (Fultz & Herzog, 1993). Health care providers may not even be aware of the problem among their patients nor initiate a conversation about it with their elderly patients. Umlauf and Sherman (1996) found that less than 25 percent of elderly patients seen by a physician are asked about incontinence. The embarrassment of losing bladder control combined with the fear of losing independence and being sent to a nursing home relegate many elders to suffer in silence. Elders' concerns about premature institutionalization are legitimate. Incontinence is one of the most frequently cited reasons for long-term institutional placement (Ouslander, 1983; Pinkston, Howe, & Blackman, 1987; Portnoi, 1981; Umlauf & Sherman, 1996). It is estimated that 50 percent of elders in the institutionalized setting suffer from incontinence adding $3.3 billion a year to health care costs in institutional settings (Hu, 1990).

Unfortunately, too many elders and their families feel that little can be done for incontinence. If elders report their incontinence to health care providers, it may be "managed" by special voiding schedules or protective garments. However, managing incontinence is different from using more aggressive methods to determine the underlying cause of the incontinence and curing it. Two-thirds of all cases of incontinence among elders respond to treatment. Even if treatment does not eliminate incontinence, it does substantially improve the quality of life for these elders (Palmer, 1996; Swenson & Siegal, 1994).

Types of Incontinence

When elders have experienced many years of incontinence accompanied by serious deterioration of their general health status and/or cognitive functioning, they may suffer from established incontinence. Only 20 percent of incontinence among elders is considered established incontinence and is primarily due to serious physical pathology, such as advanced muscle deterioration found in advanced cases of Parkinson's disease, multiple sclerosis, or bladder and bowel cancer (Brandeis, Bauman, Hossain, Morris, & Resnick, 1997). For some elders with advanced Alzheimer's disease or other organic brain disorders, the cognitive functioning needed to be alert to the need to void and the actual physical act of voiding may not be possible. Established incontinence requires more intensive intervention, such as surgery, and does not respond to treatment as well as other kinds of incontinence.

A more common form of incontinence is transient incontinence—short-term or temporary loss of bladder control. Women experience incontinence throughout their lives at twice the rate of men due to the unique design of the female urinary tract system and the physiological changes women experience during pregnancy, childbirth, and menopause (Herzog & Fultz, 1990; Swenson & Siegal, 1994). Male problems with incontinence are frequently due to an enlarged or diseased prostate that constricts the urethra and impairs normal bladder functioning. About 80 percent of transient incontinence can be treated and two-thirds of cases can eventually be cured (Brandeis et al., 1997). The onset of transient incontinence can usually be traced to a specific bout of illness, changes in either prescription or over-the-counter medications, changes in diet, severe constipation, or the onset of psychological stressors. This form of incontinence usually appears as one of four major types: stress, urge, overflow, or functional.

Stress Incontinence.   Stress incontinence is characterized by a loss of urine during a sudden activity that increases the pressure on the abdomen or bladder. Sneezing, coughing, laughing, swinging a golf club or tennis racket, or running are activities that may precipitate a loss of urine (Swenson & Siegal, 1994). This type of incontinence is caused by the inability to control the sphincter and urethral muscles. The pressure exerted by a full bladder exceeds the pressure of the bladder neck muscles to maintain bladder control causing an involuntary release of urine. It is more common in women than in men and may appear earlier in women's lives than old age. During childbirth, the vaginal muscles are required to expand and stretch to accommodate the movement of a baby through the birth canal, placing stress on the urethral and pelvic floor muscles. While vaginal muscles return to normal after birth, muscle tone in this area of the body may experience the effects of a birth long after the delivery. Loss of estrogen following menopause causes thinning of the walls of both the vagina and urethra. The generalized weakened condition of these muscles combined with sedentary lifestyles for some women help to explain the greater incidence of stress incontinence among women.

Urge Incontinence. Urge incontinence is characterized by a sudden and extremely strong need or urge to urinate with little prior warning that the bladder is full. There is not the normal lead time for a person to become gradually aware of a vague sensation of needing to urinate to the actual urgency to urinate. The urge is so strong that individuals may not make it to the toilet in time to void. Losing urine during sleep or after ingesting even small amounts of liquid are common in cases of urge incontinence. Elders experiencing urge incontinence report frequent urination, strong suggestibility to urinate when they hear water running, or when waiting in line at public toilets (Palmer, 1996). While urge incontinence is more common in men than stress incontinence, women over age 65 tend to suffer from a combination of stress and urge incontinence.

Dysfunction in the bladder muscle during the filling phase is the primary explanation for this type of incontinence. Inappropriate bladder contractions or nerve damage create an unstable or spastic bladder. Sometimes this type of incontinence is also referred to as "reflex incontinence." Overactive nerves in the bladder cause frequent bladder contractions. This involuntary action of the bladder can occur in persons who have had spinal cord or brain injuries, who suffer from multiple sclerosis, Parkinson's disease, or Alzheimer's disease, or who have suffered nerve damage during abdominal or urological surgery.

Overflow Incontinence. Overflow incontinence occurs when the bladder is full and leaks urine when an individual shifts positions or gets up from a sitting position. When the bladder is not completely emptied upon urination, it fills up quickly and an elder may not be aware of the need to void. Diabetes and other diseases may contribute to weak bladder muscles. Bladder stones, tumors, or prostate problems can block the urethra so that the bladder does not empty during normal voiding and subsequently leaks small amounts of urine on a regular basis. Some overflow incontinence is due to fecal impaction—severe constipation—which places pressure on the bladder.

Functional Incontinence. Functional incontinence is not due to any physiological problems but occurs when an elder is unable to access toileting facilities when they need to void. Functional incontinence may develop as a result of any impairment in ADLs, specifically the ability to transfer, walk, dress, or toilet (Brandeis et al., 1997). Wheelchair-bound elders may require assistance in getting to and using the toilet. If no caregiver is present to help them, an episode of incontinence may occur. Other elders may have difficulties communicating the need to void due to damage from a stroke, a movement disorder such as Parkinson's disease, or Alzheimer's disease. Functional incontinence can also occur in cases of severe depression where elders appear to not have the interest in or energy to get to toileting facilities. Functional incontinence is occasionally linked to cases of extreme hostility against caregivers, especially in institutional settings, but it is rarely the primary cause of functional incontinence (Palmer, 1996).

Treatment of Urinary Incontinence

Once the type of incontinence has been identified, health care providers may recommend one of many different types of treatment. The purpose of discussing treatments in this section of the chapter is to educate the social worker to act as an advocate in helping the elder understand the variety of approaches available to treat incontinence. Too often elders and their families assume that the only

TABLE 2.2   *Summary of Treatment Options for Urinary Incontinence*

Type of Incontinence	Treatment Options
Stress	Do Kegel exercises Practice biofeedback Use hormone replacement therapy Regulate intake of fluids Eliminate caffeine and alcohol Wear protective garments
Urge	Check for bladder stones or tumors Adjust medication Schedule, prompt voiding of bladder Improve ability to reach toilet Remove obstacles Use topical estrogen (women)
Overflow	Obtain medical evaluation for diabetes or spinal cord lesions Adjust medications Check for fecal impaction
Functional	Adjust medications Avoid use of caffeine or alcohol Eliminate obstacles to toilet access or provide commode or urinal Make clothing easier to remove for toileting Address sensory limitations Adjust restraints, if necessary Devise signals to caregivers regarding need to void

approach to treating incontinence involves surgery, which health care providers agree should be a last resort. Knowing what treatment options exist helps the gerontological social worker empower the elder client to explore less drastic measures. Sometimes simple adjustments in lifestyle and behavior can result in an immediate improvement in the condition. Treatment options for each of the kinds of incontinence are listed in Table 2.2.

HIV/AIDS and Elders

A growing concern among gerontological social workers and health care providers is the rising number of middle-aged and older adults who are being affected by the HIV/AIDS epidemic in the United States. Efforts to prevent, diagnose, and treat HIV (human immunodeficiency virus) and AIDS (acquired immune deficiency syndrome) have focused primarily on the younger population in this country since the early 1980s when the disease was first brought to the attention of the public health community (Crisologo, Campbell, & Forte, 1996; Linsk, 1994). It took years for the medical community to shift its attention from HIV/AIDS as a "gay man's disease" (Shilts, 1987) to the present awareness that the condition threatens all people regardless of sexual orientation, IV drug use, or age.

HIV/AIDS is transmitted by a number of what are considered high-risk behaviors including unprotected homosexual or heterosexual contact, sharing of needles with a person already infected with HIV/AIDS, or blood transfusions or organ transplants from persons with HIV/AIDS (Bachus, 1998; Gallo, 1994). HIV is a blood-borne pathogen—meaning that the exchange of bodily fluids, primarily blood and semen, is responsible for the spread of the virus, not casual contact with an infected person. AIDS is the end stage of the viral infection during which the body loses its ability to resist infection of any kind. Death is due to tuberculosis, opportunist infections, or kinds of cancer associated with HIV/AIDS. With new medical advances in both early detection and aggressive treatment of HIV/AIDS, the disease rarely has the immediate death sentence it once had for younger persons. With the use of AZT (azidothymidine), younger persons with HIV/AIDS are living longer and better lives. For many, HIV/AIDS has moved from being an acute infectious disease to a chronic medical condition (Bachus, 1998).

Currently, 11 percent of all reported cases of HIV/AIDS occur in persons over the age of 50 years with the number rising to 15 percent in areas such as Florida, which has large concentrations of older adults (Centers for Disease Control, 1997; National Institute on Aging, 1999). The Centers for Disease Control (1997) estimated that 78 percent of cases of HIV/AIDS among adults over 65 years of age reported between 1981 and 1993 were due to infected blood received through transfusions or tissue donations prior to the safeguards instituted in 1985 to screen the blood supply. With greater precautions in place to screen blood and organ donors, the risk of contracting the disease through transfusions or organ transplants has dropped significantly to 1 in 420,000 (Centers for Disease Control,

1997). The "graying" of HIV/AIDS, therefore, is due in part to the presence of elders with HIV/AIDS who are surviving into old age after having contracted the disease earlier in life either through these methods, from shared use of drug paraphernalia, or from unprotected male-to-male sexual intercourse. However, the numbers of adults over age 50 with HIV/AIDS has continued to rise since 1993, and the fastest growing source of HIV/AIDS infection for adults over 50 years of age is heterosexual contact.

Why Elders May Be More Vulnerable to Contracting HIV/AIDS

Lack of HIV/AIDS Education.   Once epidemiologists and public health officials were able to link HIV/AIDS with high-risk behaviors rather than membership in high-risk populations, such as gay males or IV drug users, an aggressive public education program targeted younger populations who were or were likely to become sexually active or exposed to IV drug use (Strombeck & Levy, 1998). HIV/AIDS education can be found in middle schools, high schools, colleges and universities, and community health clinics. Despite the good intentions of HIV/AIDS educators, little focus was placed on the education of older adults outside of the gay community. Limited resources, the popular demand for HIV/AIDS education among younger age groups, and a subtle ageist attitude about the unlikelihood of older adults engaging in high-risk behavior all contributed to this oversight and resulted in a lack of knowledge among older adults about HIV/AIDS (Nazon & Levine-Perkell, 1996; Solomon, 1996). Elders are at high risk for contracting the disease because many have little, if any, accurate information about high-risk behaviors, the mechanics of safe sex, or resources for early detection of the disease. It is only recently that organizations that serve older adults have taken aggressive measures to introduce HIV/AIDS education to the elder population.

Social Attitudes.   A lack of accurate information about HIV/AIDS among elders has contributed to the social attitude that "it cannot happen to me." Elders may assume that if they are not having sex with an openly gay or bisexual male or self-professed IV drug user, there is absolutely no way they can contract the disease (Solomon, 1996). Elders may become sexually involved with others they have known for a long time and may make dangerous assumptions about their partners' sexual or drug history. Elders who are widowed after having been in monogamous relationships for their entire adult lives may not consider that their social acquaintances may have engaged in extramarital affairs or frequented prostitutes in the past.

Data from the National AIDS Behavioral Study suggest at-risk elders (those exhibiting at least one high-risk behavior) are one-sixth as likely to use condoms as high-risk persons in their 20s (Stall & Catania, 1994). Elders may feel uncomfortable using one or asking their partner to use one. Bachus (1998) referred to this as a lack of "condom negotiation" skills, specific approaches often targeted by

HIV/AIDS education programs. Without preventative education, elders may lack both the awareness of the importance of using a condom and the motivation to demand that a partner use one.

The Biological Vulnerability of Elders to HIV/AIDS

Elders are not only socially more vulnerable to engaging in unprotected sex, thus contracting HIV/AIDS, but also the biological changes associated with aging make elders more vulnerable to contracting the disease. They succumb more quickly to the devastating effects of the disease and fail to be accurately diagnosed.

Changes Associated with Menopause. The loss of estrogen in an older woman's body following menopause causes thinning in the vaginal walls (as discussed earlier in this chapter). This thinning makes the vaginal walls more susceptible to small tears providing a greater opportunity for the virus to enter the body (Bachus, 1998). For those older women utilizing hormone replacement therapy to ease the symptoms of menopause, the additional hormones may actually make them more susceptible to contracting HIV. These hormones, estrogen and progestin, have been identified as immunodepressive—agents that compromise the efficiency of the body's natural immune system.

Changes in the Immune System. Due to changes in the efficiency of the immune system in the aging body, the presence of HIV has been found to progress more quickly into full-blown AIDS in elders than in younger persons who contract the disease (Aupperle, 1996; Nokes, 1996). Even without HIV infection, elders are more likely to develop pneumonia, some cancers, and a range of opportunistic infections. An already compromised immune system deteriorates more quickly in the presence of HIV. The latency period for the general population—the time from which HIV develops into AIDS—is about 10 years (Schmidt, 1989). For elders this period is much shorter. Among elders over the age of 80 years, 37 percent died within one month of the diagnosis of HIV/AIDS (Catania, Turner, Kegeles, Stall, Pollack, & Coates, 1989; Zelenetz & Epstein, 1998).

HIV/AIDS Symptoms and Age-Related Changes. Some of the first symptoms of HIV/AIDS are nonspecific and include fatigue, loss of appetite, weight loss, chronic pain, respiratory problems, skin rashes, decreased physical strength, and some loss of cognitive abilities (Kendig & Adler, 1990; Linsk, 1994; Wallace, Paauw, & Spach, 1993). A health care provider may consider asking a younger patient presenting with these symptoms about high-risk behaviors and suggest testing for the presence of HIV. However, these same symptoms are common complaints among elders who may have other chronic conditions, including diabetes, cardiovascular disease, digestive disorders, or even the early stages of dementia (Aupperele, 1996; Bachus, 1998; Strombeck & Levy, 1998). Age-related conditions are more likely to be considered by health care providers than looking specifically at HIV/AIDS. The combination of an elder's denial about the possibility of having contracted HIV/AIDS combined with a health care provider's inability or unwillingness to consider the presence of the disease in an elder can be a deadly combination. By the time HIV/AIDS is accurately diagnosed in some elders, it is no longer responsive to drug therapy.

HIV/AIDS among Elders of Color

African American males account for 30.8 percent and Hispanic males for 15.1 percent of all cases of HIV/AIDS in the population over 50 years of age. This number is far above their proportional representation in the population (Brown & Sankar, 1998; Centers for Disease Control, 1997). The Centers for Disease Control (1997) attributed the high rate of HIV/AIDS in these populations to male-to-male sexual contact and disproportionate incidence of IV drug use. These numbers represent a tragic demolition of the older male population of color, a group already compromised by higher mortality rates than their white counterparts. However, two-thirds of new cases of HIV/AIDS in the past 10 years among persons over the age of 50 are women of color—an alarming increase (Centers for Disease Control, 1997). The Centers for Disease Control attributed this increase to greater incidence of unprotected heterosexual sex and the sharing of drug paraphernalia between women of color and persons with HIV/AIDS. Without significant changes in these infection rates, HIV/AIDS may decimate the older population of color.

Socioeconomic Status and Health.   Elders of color are more likely to have low socioeconomic status than their white counterparts. A lifetime of low income contributes to inadequate heath care and a greater vulnerability to illness and disease. Chronic health problems combined with the increased susceptibility to diseases that accompany an aging immune system may make the elder of color particularly vulnerable to contracting HIV/AIDS (Brown & Sankar, 1998). Once an elder of color is HIV positive, he or she may be less likely to seek treatment for health problems due in part to difficulty in accessing health care services and a general distrust of the white medical establishment (Brown, 1997).

The Stigma Associated with HIV/AIDS.   Despite the alarming numbers of persons of color over age 50 with HIV/AIDS, the condition remains deeply stigmatized in this population, primarily because of its strong association with male homosexuality (Brown & Sankar, 1998). Among African Americans, homosexuality remains more stigmatized than it is in the white population due to cultural messages about male virility and the cultural influences of traditional black churches that continue to see homosexuality as sinful. The same is true for Hispanics who fear bringing shame to their families because of the association of HIV/AIDS to male homosexuality. Disclosing one's HIV/AIDS status may be particularly risky in both African American and Hispanic populations as family and friends may reject, rather than support, persons with the disease (Mueller, 1997).

Implications for Social Work Practice

Improving Preventative Education.   Social workers play an important role in arranging and encouraging a comprehensive HIV/AIDS education program aimed at older adults, particularly in areas with large number of elders. To date, efforts aimed at elders who are not members of the gay community have been inadequate due to an erroneous assumption about how much elders actually know about the disease and the belief that high-risk behaviors are uncommon among elders (Solomon, 1996). Senior centers, area agencies on aging, and community health care centers are excellent venues for educational presentations on HIV/AIDS focused on the needs and interests of elders. Rose (1996) found that elders responded most positively to educational programs that focused on the myths surrounding the transmission of HIV/AIDS and presented a frank, forthright discussion about the importance of using safe sex practices to avoid infection. It was as important for elders to dispel their own concerns about contracting the disease from casual contact with persons infected with HIV/AIDS as it was to heighten their awareness of the ways in which the disease is transmitted (Rose, 1996). Presenting HIV/AIDS education within a climate that stresses how important accurate knowledge is not only encourages safe sex practices among elders but also helps elders better understand how the disease affects others, such as adult children, grandchildren, and social acquaintances. Disseminating accurate knowledge about the disease as well as encouraging a compassionate response on the part of elders to those who are HIV positive are essential parts of the preventative education process (Rodgers-Farmer, 1998).

Timely Diagnosis and Treatment.   For elders who have engaged in high-risk behaviors or have a history of blood or organ transfusions, early screening and treatment are imperative. The nonspecific symptoms associated with the early stages of the disease and the tendency of health care providers to attribute these symptoms to other age-related conditions endanger high-risk elders with missed or inaccurate diagnoses. In the context of the biopsychosocial assessment process, as part of care management, or in his or her role as an advocate for elders in the health care system, a social worker needs to make elders aware of the high-risk factors for and symptoms of HIV/AIDS (Crisologo, Campbell, & Forte, 1996; Strombeck & Levy, 1998). Elders who are made aware of their own high-risk behaviors are in a better position to work with their health care providers to consider HIV/AIDS screening as a first line of defense in identifying the cause of health problems rather than as a last resort when all other possible causes have been exhausted. Denial about the possibility of having contracted HIV/AIDS can be a deadly mistake for anyone but it is even more significant for elders whose aging bodies may be less resilient in fighting the infection.

Expanding Social Networks for Elders with HIV/AIDS.   Elders who have contracted HIV/AIDS may need different support systems to cope with the disease than younger populations due to the special social and psychological challenges facing older adults. Elders with HIV/AIDS may feel very "different" from other persons with the disease particularly if they have always associated the condition with gay or bisexual men or IV drug users (Solomon, 1996). Elders may fear the stigma still associated with HIV/AIDS and be hesitant to seek out professional services early in the course of the disease. The guilt and shame they experience may prevent them from disclosing the diagnosis to family and friends until the very end when death is imminent. For older gay men who have not disclosed their sexual orientation to family and friends or for elders who have engaged in sex with prostitutes or had extramarital affairs, revealing the presence of HIV/AIDS late in life may be seen as particularly risky. They may fear total rejection by family and friends at a time in their lives when social support is most crucial (Johnson, Haight, & Benedict, 1998). Being alienated from a spouse, partner, children, or grandchildren can be as psychologically devastating as the disease itself.

The families and friends of elders with HIV/AIDS may need special support and the opportunity to process conflicting feelings in order to prevent the rejection of the elder. Support groups for families and friends of elders with HIV/AIDS may be helpful in educating, encouraging, and empowering these groups to maintain important social connections with these elders. Elders who have no support system or have lost support systems upon disclosing their HIV status may need a social worker's assistance in identifying and arranging support services in the community. While elders need time to grieve the loss of the support of family and friends, they most urgently need ongoing medical treatment, assistance with activities of daily living as the disease progresses, and financial and social support for treatment.

The MacArthur Study and "Successful" Physical Aging

While physical aging of the body is inevitable as persons grow older, disability and illness are not. Since the early 1980s, gerontology and medicine have turned their research focus to learning about how people can age "successfully"—that is, how elders can minimize the potentially debilitating results of the physical effects of the aging process and maintain and even enhance their physical and mental health. In 1984, the John D. and Catherine T. MacArthur Foundation brought together a group of scholars from assorted disciplines concerned with the aging process to design a long-term research project to study the positive aspects of the aging process and those elders who were considered to be aging successfully. The combined effort of dozens of research projects conducted by physicians, biologists, geneticists, psychologists, sociologists, and others has come to be known as the MacArthur Study. It is the most comprehensive attempt to date to ascertain what constitutes successful aging and what individuals of all ages can do to promote good physical and psychological health in the later years (Rowe & Kahn, 1998).

Based on two important findings, the MacArthur Study has challenged both society's and medicine's assumptions that old age is a time of inevitable decline and disability (Rowe & Kahn, 1998). First, elders are taking better care of themselves than ever before in history, through adjustments in diet and exercise. Second, the medical community is taking better care of elders as it learns more about how to treat acute conditions, such as pneumonia and other infections, and how to help elders minimize the debilitating effects of chronic conditions, such as arthritis, heart disease, and age-related losses in visual and auditory acuity. The study found that although a genetic predisposition to developing certain diseases, such as hypertension and heart disease, did affect an elder's health, the influence of genetic predisposition becomes less important than lifestyle choices as an individual ages (Rowe & Kahn, 1998). In other words, genetic proclivity may put an elder at risk for heart disease in his or her 60s, but diet, exercise, and other choices actually determine the course and disabling nature of the condition.

The Influence of Diet

As people age, their metabolic rate slows down due to loss of lean muscle, meaning they burn fewer calories to perform the same activity. If elders consume the same amount of food they did when they were younger without additional physical activity, weight gain is inevitable. The dangerous combination of poor nutrition and inactivity in elders clearly not only exacerbates existing health conditions but also promotes the development of cardiovascular problems that are genetically determined. The tendency to eat more than one's body needs may be the result of a lifetime of poor eating habits or the tendency to eat when one is bored rather than hungry.

The MacArthur Study found that elders need a balanced diet of low fat, high carbohydrate, and high protein to maintain good physical health (Rowe & Kahn, 1998). While this finding is consistent with what nutritionists know about a healthy diet, elders are at high risk for not eating enough of the right kinds of food to maintain health. Elders may consume too many processed carbohydrates, such as those found in white bread, bakery, or candy, and not enough of the complex carbohydrates found in peas, beans, and lentils. Complex carbohydrates can be helpful in promoting good bowel health and avoiding the tendency among elders to experience constipation or other gastrointestinal problems. Elders need more protein—as found in meats, fish, poultry, eggs, or dairy products—than younger people. Elders are less likely to consume enough protein because it is one of the more expensive foods and because they may have difficulty chewing or swallowing meat. Vitamin and mineral supplements can be helpful in promoting good health among elders who, unlike their younger counterparts, may not be getting sufficient vitamins in their daily diet. Antioxidants, discussed earlier in this chapter, are particularly important to an aging body to help cells fight the damaging effects of oxygen free radicals and to repair cellular damage caused by some diseases.

These findings suggest that elders who make an active effort to eat a vitamin-rich diet high in protein and complex carbohydrates can prevent age-related physical changes from deteriorating into debilitating impairments. What is most encouraging is that even if elders have had a poor diet throughout their lives and resign themselves to the belief that the damage is done, the human body begins to respond very quickly to changes in diet. Health and general well-being can be improved within a very short time with improved nutrition. Social workers can play an important role in working with nutritionists to provide nutrition education and counseling to older adults not only before but also after a serious health condition develops. These findings also suggest that congregate meal sites and mobile meals program need to pay more attention to developing lower fat, higher protein selections for elders rather than those that contain too many processed carbohydrates—a less expensive and more filling, but potentially damaging, dietary choice.

Exercise and Physical Activity

The MacArthur Study also confirmed the importance of physical activity and exercise for elders, regardless of current health or mental health status. As the body ages, muscles weaken and become smaller, thereby affecting physical strength, sense of balance, and mobility. Developing and maintaining physical fitness is not about taking up basketball at age 70 for most elders. Rather it is about maintaining the ability to walk comfortably and safely, to negotiate stairs, to reach up to shelves and cupboards, and to perform daily activities without becoming winded or injured. Unfortunately, as many elders experience some loss of strength or endurance, they tend to engage in less physical activity and in that way promote a downward spiral in physical fitness. The phrase "use it or lose it" is a powerful adage!

Physical exercise is perhaps most helpful in its ability to cut the rate of coronary heart disease and diminish the risk of developing high blood pressure, two of the most dangerous physical problems elders experience. Increased physical exercise protects against colon cancer, Type 2 diabetes, and osteoporosis when included as a component in a regime of diet and medication. Even though some people believe that strenuous exercise causes arthritis, the MacArthur Study found that moderate regular exercise actually relieves arthritis pain and disability by promoting joint flexibility and general physical health. The MacArthur Study identified two forms of physical exercise that have shown dramatic results in slowing the physical deterioration of the aging body and promoting a general sense among elders of feeling healthier and stronger.

Aerobic Exercise.   Rapid walking, calisthenics, jogging, dancing, or working out on some exercise equipment is considered to be aerobic exercise, which is specifically aimed at increasing the heart rate for a certain amount of time to strengthen heart muscles. A stronger heart is more efficient and enjoys improved circulation and greater endurance. The MacArthur Study found that elders who regularly participate in aerobic exercise can be in better physical shape than sedentary middle-aged adults (Rowe & Kahn, 1998). If designed with the special needs of the elder in mind, aerobic exercise can be very safe for elders with little chance of serious injury or physical damage. Researchers found that even once sedentary elders can double their endurance within less than a year by participating in activities as simple as walking 45 minutes several times a week (Rowe & Kahn, 1998).

Strength Training.   Weight training has become increasingly popular among all age groups and has shown great promise in helping elders regain lost muscle strength. The MacArthur Study found that even the frailest of the oldest-old will respond to resistance training on weight machines or free weights. Strengthening muscles through weight training can help an elder lose weight by increasing an elder's metabolic rate. More efficient muscles not only burn more calories but also improve an elder's sense of balance, thereby decreasing the likelihood of devastating falls. One of the side effects not anticipated by researchers in the MacArthur Study was the positive influence of weight training on elder's mental health. Those involved in weight training were less likely to become or remain depressed than elders who were not involved in this kind of exercise.

The importance of physical exercise and physical activity in minimizing the debilitating effects of physical aging are very encouraging to both social workers and others who develop intervention efforts for elders. Any intervention should include opportunities for elders to begin (or continue) some form of physical activity that appeals to them. This is one of those situations where social workers can play an important role in taking on the role of coach! Connecting elders to physical activities that give them the opportunity to push their own physical abilities as well as to have fun doing it with other elders promises both physical and psychological benefits.

Summary

The job of a gerontological social worker is to view every elder within a complex biopsychosocial context. This chapter has addressed the biological changes associated with the aging process, some of which are universal to all aging persons and others that are considered pathological. All of the vital physiological systems are affected by the aging process as the body becomes less efficient in replacing worn and damaged cells. Age-related changes in vision, the neurological system, the gastrointestinal system, and the urinary tract depend on general health and genetic endowment while cardiovascular, dermatological, respiratory, and hearing changes may be hastened by the accumulative effects of lifelong personal habits.

Urinary incontinence is not a normal part of the aging process, but elders experience the problem more frequently than do their younger counterparts. Left untreated, incontinence may lead to social isolation, medical complications, and loss of independence—all issues of vital concern to a gerontological social worker.

As the majority of cases of incontinence can be effectively treated, it is important for social work professionals to recognize the significance of incontinence as a problem for some elders and to encourage them to seek aggressive treatment for the condition.

The growing incidence of new cases of HIV/AIDS among the aging population suggests social work will play an increasingly important role in promoting preventative education to elders. Dispelling prejudicial myths about the infection through preventative education, encouraging early diagnosis and treatment, and developing age-specific community support systems for HIV-positive elders are compassionate and effective ways to respond to the HIV/AIDS crisis in the elder population.

The most encouraging news about the biological process of aging and ways in which to minimize the debilitating effects of physical changes comes from the MacArthur Study, an ongoing research effort to identify those factors that contribute to successful aging. Through a program of diet and exercise, elders can not only prevent but also reverse physical impairment caused by age-related conditions. Social work plays a significant role in incorporating nutrition counseling and physical activity as part of any intervention plan for elders.

Check Out These Websites!

1. www.cis.nci.nih.gov   This website is maintained by the Cancer Information Services, a patient and professional resource sponsored by the National Cancer Institute. The site offers information about specific kinds of cancer, how to order educational materials for individual and group presentations, and how to obtain technical assistance for training in this area.

2. www.aad.org   This site is sponsored by the American Academy of Dermatology and is especially helpful in locating free skin cancer screening services for elders. These are provided by volunteer dermatologists throughout the United States. Educational materials about skin cancer and other skin conditions common among elders are available for downloading from the site.

3. www.nof.org   The National Osteoporosis Foundation offers extensive information on the prevention, detection, and treatment of osteoporosis on this website. Materials are offered in both English and Spanish. The site offers links to other resources for persons who have osteoporosis and includes support groups, specially adapted fashions, fall prevention, and clinical trials of new treatments currently in progress throughout the country.

4. www.noah.cuny.edu/aging   NOAH is an acronym for the New York Online Access to Health, a joint information access project sponsored by the City University of New York, the Metropolitan New York Library Council, the New York Academy of Medicine, and the New York Public Library. The site offers excellent material on all aspects of biological aging with exceptionally good resources on Alzheimer's disease, prostate cancer, vision problems, and hearing loss.

5. www.nih.gov/health/chip/nia/aging   The National Institutes of Health and the National Institute on Aging have compiled a comprehensive report on current theories about aging and the cause of biological aging, which is available at this website. The report "In Search of the Secrets of Aging" outlines in detail all current theories of aging, including theories about the use of hormones and caloric restrictions to slow the aging process—two of the most recent and controversial approaches being explored.

References

Administration on Aging. (1999). *National Institute on Aging age page: Taking care of your teeth and mouth.* Washington, DC: Author. Retrived August 2, 1999 from the World Wide Web: http://www.aoa.dhhs.gov/aoa/age/agepages/teemou.html

American Academy of Nutritional Research. (1997). *Antioxidants provide anti-aging benefits.* Washington, DC: Author. Retrieved July 23, 1999 from the World Wide Web: http://www.antiox4life.com/aging.html

Anderson, R. N., Kochanek, K. D., & Murphy, S. L. (1997). Report of final mortality statistics, 1995. *Monthly Vital Statistics Report 4*(1), #2.

Aupperle, P. (1996). Medical issues. In K. M. Nokes (Ed.), *HIV/AIDS and the older adult* (pp. 25–32). Washington, DC: Taylor & Francis.

Bachus, M. A. (1998). HIV and the older adult. *Journal of Gerontological Nursing, 24*(11), 41–46.

Bartoshuk, L. M., & Weiffenbach, J. M. (1990). Chemical senses and aging. In E. L. Schneider & J. W. Rowe (Eds.), *Handbook of the biology of aging* (pp. 429–443). San Diego, CA: Academic Press.

Brandeis, G. H., Bauman, M. M., Hossain, M., Morris, J. N., & Resnick, N. M. (1997). The prevalence of potentially remediable urinary incontinence in frail older people: A study using the Minimum Data Set. *Journal of the American Geriatric Society, 45,* 179–184.

Brown, D. R. (1997). *Cultural mistrust among African Americans: Results from the AIDS Awareness and Behavior Survey.* Detroit, MI: Wayne State University, Center for Urban Studies.

Brown, D. R., & Sankar, A. (1998). HIV/AIDS and aging minority populations. *Research on Aging, 20*(6), 865–885.

Catania, J. A., Turner, J., Kegeles, S. M., Stall, R., Pollack, L., & Coates, T. (1989). Older Americans and AIDS: Transmission risks and primary prevention research needs. *Gerontologist, 29*(3), 373–381.

Centers for Disease Control and Prevention (CDC). (1997). *Surveillance report.* Washington, DC: Author.

Cohen, R. A., Bloom, B., Simpson, G., & Parsons, P. E. (1997). Access to health care. Part 3: Older adults. National Center for Health Care Statistics. *Vital Health Statistics, 10*(198).

Crisologo, S., Campbell, M. H., & Forte, J. A. (1996). Social work, AIDS, and the elderly: Current knowledge and practice. *Journal of Gerontological Social Work, 26*(1/2), 49–70.

Cunningham, W. R., & Brookbank, J. W. (1988). *Gerontology: The psychology, biology, and sociology of aging.* New York: Harper and Row.

Ebersole, P., & Hess, P. (1998). *Toward healthy aging: Human needs and nursing response* (5th ed.). St. Louis, MO: Mosby.

Ettinger, W., & Davis, M. (1990). Osteoarthritis. In W. R. Hazzard, R. Anders, E. Bierman, & J. Blass (Eds.), *Principles of geriatric medicine and gerontology* (pp. 880–888). New York: McGraw-Hill.

Finch, C. E. (1991). *Longevity: Senescence and the genome*. Chicago, IL: University of Chicago Press.

Fultz, N. H., & Herzog, A. R. (1993). Measuring urinary incontinence in surveys. *The Gerontologist, 33*(6), 708–713.

Gallo, R. (1994). Acquired Immune Deficiency Syndrome. *Encarta*, 1994 ed., Macintosh CD-ROM, Microsoft Corporation, USA.

Gulya, A. J. (1995). Ear disorders. In W. B. Abrams, M. H. Beers, & R. Berkow (Eds.), *The Merck manual of geriatrics* (2nd ed., pp. 1315–1342). Whitehouse Station, NJ: Merck Research Laboratories.

Harman, D. (1956). A theory based on free radical and radiation chemistry. *Journal of Gerontology, 11*, 298.

Hayflick, L. (1994). *How and why we age*. New York: Ballantine Books.

Herzog, A. R., & Fultz, N. H. (1990). Prevalence and incidence of urinary incontinence in community-dwelling populations. *Journal of the American Geriatrics Society, 38*, 273–281.

Hooyman, N., & Kiyak, H. A. (1999). *Social gerontology* (5th ed.). Boston: Allyn and Bacon.

Horvath, T. P., & Davis, K. L. (1990). Nervous system disorders in aging. In E. L. Schneider & J. W. Rowe (Eds.), *Handbook of the biology of aging* (3rd ed., pp. 309–336). San Diego, CA: Academic Press.

Hu, T. (1990). Impact of urinary incontinence on health care costs. *Journal of the American Geriatrics Society, 38*, 292–295.

Johnson, M., Haight, B. K., & Benedict, S. (1998). AIDS and older people: A literature review for clinical nursing research and practice. *Journal of Gerontological Nursing, 24*(4), 8–13.

Kendig, N., & Adler, W. (1990). The implications of the acquired immunodeficiency syndrome for gerontology research and geriatric medicine. *Journal of Gerontology, 45*(3), 77–81.

Kline, D. W., Kline, T. J. B., Fozard, J. L., Kosnik, W., Schieber, F., & Sekular, R. (1992). Vision, aging, and driving: The problems of older drivers. *Journals of Gerontology, 47*, M27–34.

Klingman, A. M., Grove, G. L., & Balin, A. (1985). Aging of the human skin. In C. E. Finch & E. L. Schneider (Eds.), *Handbook of the biology of aging* (pp. 820–841). New York: Van Nostrand.

Kupfer, C. (1995). Opthamologic disorders. In W. B. Abrams, M. H. Beers, & R. Berkow (Eds.), *The Merck manual of geriatrics* (2nd ed., pp. 1289–1314). Whitehouse Station, NJ: Merck Research Laboratories.

Lakatta, E. (1990). Heart and circulation. In E. L. Schneider & J. W. Rowe (Eds.), *Handbook of the biology of aging* (3rd ed., pp. 181–209). San Diego, CA: Academic Press.

Lee, A. T., & Cerami, A. (1990). Modifications of proteins and nucleic acid by reducing sugars: Possible role in aging. In E. L. Schneider & J. W. Rowe (Eds.), *Handbook of the biology of aging* (3rd ed., pp. 116–130). San Diego, CA: Academic Press.

Legato, M. L. (1997). *Gender specific aspects of human biology for the practicing physician*. Armonk, NY: Futura.

Linsk, L. N. (1994). HIV and the elderly. *Families in Society: The Journal of Contemporary Human Services, 75*, 362–371.

Martin, G. R., & Baker, G. T. (1993). Aging and the aged: Theories of aging and life extension. *Encyclopedia of bioethics*. New York: Macmillan.

Massachusetts Department of Public Health. (1999). *Osteoporosis: Are you at risk?* Boston: Author.

McCormick, A. M., & Campisi, J. (1991). Cellular aging and senescence. *Current Opinion in Cell Biology, 3*, 230–234.

Miller, R. A. (1990). Aging and the immune response. In E. L. Schneider & J. W. Rowe (Eds.), *Handbook of the biology of aging* (3rd ed., pp. 157–180). San Diego, CA: Academic Press.

Mueller, M. (1997). Social barriers to recognizing HIV/AIDS in older adults. *Journal of Gerontological Nursing, 23*(11), 17–21.

National Institute on Aging. (1999). *HIV/AIDS and older adults*. Washington, DC: Department of Health and Human Services. Available at http://www.thebody.com/hhs/older_adults.html

Nazon, M., & Levine-Perkell, J. (1996). AIDS and aging. *Journal of Gerontological Social Work, 25*(1/2), 21–31.

Nokes, K. M. (1996). Health care needs. In K. M. Nokes (Ed.), *HIV/AIDS and the older adult* (pp. 1–8). Washington, DC: Taylor & Francis.

Ouslander, J. G. (1983). Incontinence and nursing homes: Epidemiology and management. *The Gerontologist, 23*, 257.

Palmer, M. H. (1996). *Urinary continence: Assessment and promotion.* Gaithersburg, MD: Aspen.

Pinkston, E. M., Howe, M. W., & Blackman, D. K. (1987). Medical social work management of urinary incontinence in the elderly: A behavioral approach. *Journal of Social Service Research, 10*(2/3/4), 179–194.

Portnoi, V. A. (1981). Urinary incontinence in the elderly. *American Family Physician, 23*, 151–154.

Richardson, G. S. (1990). Circadian rhythms and aging. In E. L. Schneider & J. W. Rowe (Eds.), *Handbook of the biology of aging* (3rd ed., pp. 275–305). San Diego, CA: Academic Press.

Richey, M. L., Richey, H. K., & Fenske, N. A. (1988). Age-related skin changes: Development and clinical meaning. *Geriatrics, 43*, 49.

Rodgers-Farmer, A. Y. (1998). HIV risk factors, HIV antibody testing, and AIDS knowledge among older Americans. *Journal of Gerontological Social Work, 30*(3/4), 133–146.

Rose, M. A. (1996). Effect of an AIDS education program for older adults. *Journal of Community Health Nursing, 13*(3), 141–148.

Rowe, J. W., & Kahn, R. L. (1998). *Successful aging.* New York: Pantheon Books.

Schmidt, R. (1989). HIV and aging-related disorders. *Generations, 13*, 6–15.

Shilts, R. (1987). *And the band played on: Politics, people, and the AIDS epidemic.* New York: St. Martin's Press.

Solomon, K. (1996). Psychosocial issues. In K. M. Nokes (Ed.), *HIV/AIDS and the older adult* (pp. 33–46). Washington, DC: Taylor & Francis.

Spirduso, W. W. (1995). *Physical dimensions of aging.* Champaign, IL: Human Kinetics.

Stall, R., & Catania, J. (1994). AIDS risk behaviors among late middle-aged and elderly Americans. *Archives of Internal Medicine, 154*, 57–63.

Strombeck, R., & Levy, J. A. (1998). Educational strategies and interventions targeting adults age 50 and older for HIV/AIDS prevention. *Research on Aging, 20*(6), 912–937.

Swenson, N. M., & Siegal, D. L. (1994). Urinary incontinence. In P. B. Doress-Worters & D. L. Siegal (Eds.), *The new growing older: Women aging with knowledge and power* (pp. 300–314). New York: Simon and Schuster.

Timaris, P. S. (1988). *Psychologic bases of geriatrics.* New York: Macmillan.

Tockman, M. S. (1995). The effects of aging on the lungs: Lung cancer. In W. B. Abrams, M. H. Beers, & R. Berkow (Eds.), *The Merck manual of geriatrics* (2nd ed., pp. 569–574). Whitehouse Station, NJ: Merck Research Laboratories.

Umlauf, M. G., & Sherman, S. M. (1996). Symptoms of urinary incontinence among older community-dwelling men. *Journal of Wound, Ostomy and Continence Nurses Society, 23*(6), 314–321.

Wallace, J. E., Paauw, D. S., & Spach, D. W. (1993). HIV infection in older patients: When to suspect the unexpected. *Geriatrics, 48*(6), 61–70.

Wilson, D. L. (1974). The programmed theory of aging. In M. L. Sussman & J. Chesky (Eds.), *Theoretical aspects of aging* (pp. 11–21). New York: Academic Press.

Zelenetz, P. D., & Epstein, M. E. (1998). HIV in the elderly. *AIDS Patient Care and STD's, 12*(4), 255–262.

3

Psychosocial Adjustments to Aging

The last chapter examined the biological changes associated with the aging process. These are the most visible signs the body is growing older. The degree to which these physical changes cause functional impairment is due to a combination of genetic luck, exposure to disease and illness, and lifestyle choices. This chapter explores the psychosocial changes that accompany the biological changes, those adjustments in cognitive functioning, intellectual ability, and social behavior that determine how people think and act as they grow older. Unlike physical changes that follow a relatively predictable path, psychological and social patterns of adjustment are incredibly diverse from elder to elder. Some elders never experience a noticeable loss of memory or lessening of ability to perform complex tasks even well into their 90s and beyond. They are able to maintain active, energetic lives deeply connected to family and friends. Other elders begin to experience serious memory loss as early as 60 years of age or withdraw from social interaction to wait to die. Like physical changes, much of the qualitative experience of the psychosocial changes that accompany the aging process is determined by how elders choose to use their psychological and social resources as they age.

This chapter begins with a look at the psychological changes, including changes in cognitive and intellectual abilities, that are most commonly seen in older adults. This section is followed by an examination of a variety of social theories of aging that speculate about what behavior patterns are commonly observed in elders as they adapt to new and unfamiliar social roles and relationships. Once these adjustments have been identified, it is important to consider what implications those changes have for gerontological social work. The chapter concludes with a look at the findings about psychosocial changes in aging observed in the MacArthur Study, which is the most recent and comprehensive attempt to determine what constitutes successful aging.

Psychological Changes That Accompany Aging

While the biological changes that accompany the aging process are often the most noticeable (and sometimes most bothersome), changes that occur in cognitive and emotional functioning are often those most feared by elders. At the first sign of forgetfulness, middle-aged and older adults may question if they are losing their minds or showing the first signs of Alzheimer's disease. Families worry about an aging relative's ability to follow a complicated regime of multiple prescriptions. A recent widow may wonder if the depression following her husband's death will ever lift or will plague her the rest of her life. This section of the chapter discusses both normal age-related changes in cognitive functioning and personality. The psychological and emotional disorders associated with aging are discussed in Chapter 5.

Cognitive changes are those that occur in the intellectual, memory, learning, and creative processes of elders. Do people actually get smarter as they grow older and accumulate knowledge and experience? Is it inevitable that elders will experience memory problems, forgetting what they had for lunch but remembering details about events from their childhood? Can elders learn new skills? While these are complex questions about very complicated cognitive functions, the answers are both "yes" and "no." Although cognitive changes associated with the aging process have been studied for years, there is often conflicting evidence about exactly what happens in the process. This section will explore general trends in psychological research about these cognitive processes.

Intelligence

Intelligence is the way in which a person gathers information, processes it, develops new ideas, and applies information to new and familiar situations in the activities of daily living. There are two major aspects of intelligence. It follows that as people grow older and accumulate knowledge and experience that they should know more. Planning a garden, reading, cooking, and repair work are all examples of activities that require knowledge acquired from a lifetime of experiences. From the perspective of accumulating information, intelligence does increase or at least is maintained well into old age. Psychologists refer to this type of intelligence as *crystallized intelligence* (Schaie, 1996). How effectively individuals accumulate knowledge is strongly influenced by the amount of information they are exposed to through education and life experience and, to some degree, genetic luck. In terms of accumulated knowledge, elders do become smarter. They do know more than when they were younger. Intelligence testing measures that focus on the recall of accumulated knowledge test crystallized intelligence.

However, determining how to live on a single fixed income or negotiate public transportation after a lifetime of driving—challenges that accompany life changes, such as retirement and widowhood—require a different set of intellectual skills. The ability to secure new information, combine it with accumulated knowledge, and apply it to problem solving is known as *fluid intelligence* (Salthouse, 1992; Schaie, 1996). Elders do not perform as well on intelligence testing measures that measure problem-solving competence or the ability to perform a sequence of tasks. There is no clear evidence that age alone accounts for poor performance in this area of intelligence testing. Most intelligence testing is timed and elders have a slower reaction time due to deterioration in the neurotransmitters, which was discussed in the previous chapter on biological aspects of aging. When time restrictions are lifted from the testing situation, there are only negligible differences between younger and older subjects (Salthouse, 1992).

Factors Contributing to Intelligence.   Intellectual functioning in old age is the product of a variety of factors, a few of which are not related to the aging process at all. Genetic ability may be the most important determinant of all factors (Rabbitt, 1993). Individuals who show high intellectual functioning throughout their lives are most likely to continue to function well in their later years. Higher levels of education and the choice of challenging life work contribute to enhanced intellectual abilities as one ages. In general, innate abilities combined with a lifetime of intellectual exercise are strong predictors of how well intellectual functioning will stand the test of time.

The primary mental abilities associated with intelligence are verbal understanding, spatial relationships, reasoning, and basic fluency in both words and numbers. These activities are those most important to daily functioning for people of all ages. Competence in these areas continues to improve until the late 30s and early 40s. In the absence of disease, primary mental abilities remain stable until the late 60s when a slow, and in some cases almost indiscernible, process of decline begins (Schaie, 1996; Willis, Jay, Diehl, & Marsiske, 1992). By the late 70s, this decline is more noticeable.

Age-related changes in physical health, sensory acuity, and nutrition and the presence of depression have also been associated with a decline in intellectual functioning. Cardiovascular disease, characterized by impaired blood circulation, has been linked to observable changes in an elder's ability to engage in complex problem-solving activities (Gruber-Baldini, 1991). While the efficiency of nerves in carrying messages from the brain is compromised as the body ages, blood circulation also plays a role in general overall healthy functioning of the brain. Sensory input from vision and hearing are an important part of processing information. When these functions are impaired in elders, cognitive functioning is also compromised. Elders may appear to not follow a conversation or a task because they are missing important environmental stimuli. What is especially difficult is that elders may not know they are missing this input and adamantly deny they are having trouble.

Nutrition.   Inadequate nutrition contributes to declining intellectual functioning (Baltes, 1993). Biological changes in the esophagus and stomach result in elders feeling "full" sooner than younger persons, which may result in either insufficient caloric intake or vitamin deficiency. The brain simply does not function as efficiently without adequate nutrients. Along with insufficient nutrition, elders are more prone to dehydration because of diminished sense of thirst or a tendency to restrict fluid intake to avoid frequent urination. The severe dangers of inadequate nutrition and dehydration will be covered in greater detail in Chapter 5, when the organic brain condition, delirium, is discussed. When elders are coping with physical or emotional discomfort, there is less psychic energy available for cognitive tasks. It is not so much that intellectual functioning declines but rather that the amount of psychological energy elders can devote to complicated cognitive functions diminishes (O'Hanlon, 1993).

The Environment.   One of the most important findings about intellectual functioning among elders is the significance of the environment in which elders are required to use cognitive skills. Elders who show poor intellectual functioning in the testing environment of a laboratory are likely to function better in more familiar environments, such as their own homes. Ultimately, the ability to engage in problem solving in the challenges of everyday life is infinitely more important in understanding an elder's cognitive functioning. Research indicates that when elders engage in problem solving that has immediate relevance to their daily functioning, they remain amazingly adept at rallying cognitive resources (Baltes, 1993; Schaie, 1996; Willis, 1996). These same studies have found that retaining one's independence is the strongest motivator for elders to find creative ways to solve problems. If maintaining their independence is contingent on the ability to follow a complicated prescription regime, elders may compensate by writing detailed notes about what medication is to be taken at what time of the day. Posting notes around the kitchen helps to remind them to check to make sure the gas is turned off or doors are locked. This type of behavior is familiar to those who have worked with elders and represents an elder's own efforts to compensate for cognitive losses. The importance of a familiar environment also helps to explain why elders may lose cognitive functioning rapidly in unfamiliar environments, such as specialized elderly housing or a nursing home.

Personality

Personality is an individual's composite of innate and learned behaviors and emotional and cognitive functions that determines how that individual interacts with the environment. From the moment of birth, individuals begin to show their own unique personality. Some individuals are by nature easy going, upbeat, and pleasant while others are intense, have guarded emotionality, and may be less sociable. Although people cannot choose their personality styles, they can control their own behavior. In a sense, personality is both structure and process. It is structure in that an individual's personality remains relatively stable throughout life, and it is process in that it is always changing in response to the environment. In childhood, adolescence, and young adulthood, the personality is relatively flexible and is in constant interaction with the environment in the process of maturation. During adulthood, the mature personality becomes more stable and is less likely to change (Kogan, 1990).

Psychosocial Tasks.   Erik Erikson believed that the personality adapts throughout life in response to a set of psychosocial tasks, or challenges, that accompany the individual's development in the environment (Erikson, 1963). From the first challenge a child faces in developing trust or distrust in those around him or her, Erikson saw the interaction between the genetic endowment of the personality and the context of the environment. If people are to move through each of the life stages successfully, it is necessary to resolve the psychosocial crises germane to that stage. He hypothesized that if early life crises were not resolved, problems in psychosocial functioning would appear later in people's lives. For example, if people have not learned to trust as infants, it is difficult for them to ever develop intimacy with another person later in life. The final life stage in Erikson's work—seen as the work of old age—is resolving the crisis between ego integrity and ego despair. In this stage, individuals must learn to accept all that has happened in their lives and to come to an understanding about what meaning their lives have had. Sometimes that process involves taking care of unfinished business and changing what can be changed, such as repairing damaged relationships. Other times that means letting go of those things that cannot be changed. Either way, if individuals cannot find some peace in their own minds about their lives, the inevitable result is despair—an overwhelming feeling of futility about life.

Coping with Stress.   Personality is an important component of the psychological aspects of aging, primarily because personality affects how people cope with stress. Stressful situations are not unique to elders but old age may bring some of the most difficult stressors in life: physical illness, loss of a life partner, financial stresses from limited resources, threats to independence, and fears about dying and death. While these major issues create significant stress for elders, elders bring a lifetime of knowledge and experience that actually help them handle major stressful events. Elders have usually given some thought to how to handle these events, and while they remain stressful, they are not entirely unexpected.

   Lazarus and Cohen (1977) found that the quality of elders' responses to stress was contingent on four elements. The first was "cognitive appraisal" of a situation—that is, whether elders perceived a situation to be stressful at all. For some elders, a late morning paper will ruin their entire day, while for other elders, it would take a life-threatening event to arouse much anxiety. Some elders are very good at "not sweating the small stuff," while others look for the small stuff to worry about. A second component is how desirable or undesirable the stressful event appears to an elder. One elder might approach a knee replacement as a welcome end to chronic knee pain and accept an uncomfortable recovery process as just part of the process that ultimately will have positive consequences. Another elder might have a hard time seeing beyond the painful recovery period to the benefits of a more comfortable joint. People's personalities give them a different set of lens through which to observe similar events, and thus they have different reactions. A third component in how elders adapt to stress is the availability of a support system. Those elders with partners or extensive family and friend support networks appear to handle stress better because they do not feel they are alone. Being able to rally emotional support from others seems to mitigate the effects of stress. A fourth component is the amount of control people feel they have in responding to stress.

Ruth and Coleman (1996) found that elders face greater stress in association with everyday existence. Maintaining a household, coping with limitations imposed by physical illness, and eating alone are examples of events that are likely to cause ongoing stress that is as difficult as, if not more than, major life transitions. How elders cope with stressful situations is a product of their own personality styles. They identified two distinct patterns in how elders cope with everyday stressors. One group engaged in what Ruth and Coleman described as "planful, active" coping styles in which the elders actively engaged in developing a plan to address the stressful event. These elders tended to be those who had an internal locus of control and felt they still retained some control over their own environments. For example, an elderly widow who dislikes eating alone all the time may invite friends over for meals on a regular basis or make an effort to attend a congregate meal site as a way to counteract the stress of eating alone. The second group engaged in an "avoidance or minimization" approach to stressful events in which they simply ignored or denied the impact of stressors. Those individuals were more likely to possess an external locus of control attributing most of what happened in their lives to forces outside of their control. Elders with this approach to eating alone may simply resign themselves to the situation or turn on the television as a substitute. In essence, they have resigned themselves to a situation and do not see themselves as actors in making a change in this aspect of their lives.

Memory

In the absence of disease, the human brain has almost unlimited capacity for memory. That capacity is not affected by age-related changes in memory. Rather, it is the process by which the human mind remembers that changes as the body ages. There are three components to memory. Sensory memory is what people notice and commit to memory through the senses. A favorite song, the smell of fresh baked bread, and the sight of a beautiful sunset are examples of sensory memory. One does not decide to remember those things but simply does so because the image has made an impression on sensory memory. Sensory memory is the first step in processing information and involves receiving information through one of the five senses. Words and images are first seen through vision. Sounds are heard and often connected to visual images. The smell of fresh bread, for example, stimulates the memory without vision or sound. Touch, the last of the five senses, plays a role in helping elders notice texture or temperature. Sensory memory itself is not affected by age-related changes, although the ability to recognize these sensory images may be impaired when any of the senses are impaired by age-related changes. Elders may not recognize a song because they cannot hear it clearly or not recognize the smell of fresh bread because they cannot smell it. Smells are a very powerful stimulus for memory and will be discussed later in this book in the section describing the use of reminiscence therapy with elders. Perceiving information from the environment through the senses is a precursor to committing information to memory (Craik & Jennings, 1992).

Another component of memory is called primary memory or what is known as a person's working memory. Primary memory requires that an individual "encode" a memory and commit it to storage (Smith, 1996). For example, much of the information you are exposed to as a student starts in primary memory. In order to be able to access that information later, you must be aware of it, be motivated to remember it, and store it along with similar information. This process is not entirely a conscious process. The greater the incentive to remember the information and the more deliberate the effort to remember it, however, the more likely that information will be committed to the third component of memory, secondary memory. Secondary memory is the accumulation of information that is stored until it is retrieved through recall. If the information is reinforced, it becomes part of a person's long-term memory.

For many elders, it is not the capacity to remember that is impaired with aging, but rather the processing of resources that result in remembering. Perceptual speed decreases, making it harder to process information in the same length of time as when the individual was younger (Smith, 1996). For example, when a physician very quickly reviews a number of prescriptions, it may be difficult for an elderly patient to process both the visual and auditory clues and connect them to a specific medication. Is it the blue pill that is taken twice a day but only with food, or is it the white pill? For many elders, too much information given too quickly cannot be processed efficiently enough to be worked through the working memory and committed to secondary memory. This information overload results in elders' inability to remember—not because of reduced memory capacity but because of a difficulty in processing this information into memory.

The Motivation to Remember.   The motivation to remember information also plays an important role in the process of memory for elders (Willis, 1996). Why do elders forget what they had for lunch but remember infinite details about holidays with their families 50 years ago? What one had for lunch lasts in sensory memory only for a limited time. Unless there is some significance to remembering it, it probably will not be remembered (even by much younger persons). However, the memory of holiday celebrations with family members is important. These memories may have been recalled and rehearsed frequently throughout life. This reinforces that memory. When memories are reinforced by strong emotions, they are deeply embedded in secondary memory. The combination of sensory memories combined with strong emotional memories makes this type of memory more significant, therefore more easily remembered. Some elders appear to be forgetful because, on some level, they have decided it is not important to remember.

Recognition of objects and names is easier for elders than strict recall of factual material. Giving people environmental clues to help them remember things, such as a clock or a calendar, facilitates memory. When asked to recall infrequently used information, elders may take longer than a younger person to access that information from secondary memory. It is not that they cannot access the memory but that it simply takes longer. This "tip of the tongue" phenomenon occurs for most people long before they become elderly and is the result of the decreasing efficiency of the process of memory recall (Willis, 1996).

Learning

Adults learn in ways different from the ways children do. Young children are often described as "sponges" soaking up knowledge almost effortlessly, without necessarily questioning why they have to learn it. Adults, on the other hand, learn better when the information or skill they have to learn has some very specific relevance for their lives. Their motivation to learn is based on meeting a specific need for that knowledge rather than simply for the exercise of committing knowledge to memory (Lumsden, 1988). Adults also learn more effectively when they have an opportunity to rehearse new behavior or information. The process of reinforcement is an essential part of adult learning. These two factors—relevance to one's life and the opportunity to rehearse new behavior—are significant factors in an elder's ability to learn. It is not surprising that elders perform poorly on laboratory experiments in learning when asked to memorize long lists of words or numbers (Willis, 1996). Elders appear to be more discriminating learners and need to see the relevance of the knowledge. For example, a recent widow may need to learn to handle the household finances when there is no one else around to do it for her. While she may not be excited about learning how to pay monthly bills or balance a checkbook, she *needs* to learn how to do it and therefore has a very strong motivation. Personal motivation is a strong predictor of whether elders are capable of learning.

Memory is another important factor in an elder's ability to learn. If new information is not processed from sensory reception through working memory and stored in secondary memory, learning has not occurred. If an elder has difficulty hearing the instruction or seeing visual materials, new information becomes more difficult to learn. Elders also learn at a slower rate than young people. Too much information presented too quickly simply cannot be processed by the elderly mind and therefore will not be processed into secondary memory.

Social Theories of Aging

The final section of this chapter addresses social theories of aging, descriptions of various ways social scientists have observed or speculate that elders adapt to the social environment around them. It has been emphasized throughout this chapter that elders are unique in both their biological and psychological response to the aging process and this remains the case in looking at their social response to aging as well. Some elders retain an active, busy life well into advanced old age and stay very involved in the social world around them. Others withdraw into their own limited worlds, dropping out of the social mainstream. For some elders, old age is a positive experience and a time for new friends, new opportunities, and new experiences. For others, the later years are simply a time to be endured as they wait to die.

What has been presented about the biological and psychological changes that accompany the aging process certainly helps us to understand, in part, why the social experience can be so different for elders. The mobility restrictions imposed by severe arthritis, osteoporosis, or cardiovascular disease may make socialization difficult. People, including younger people, do not want to socialize when they do not feel well. Limitations in vision and hearing may make engaging in a conversation taxing for an elder. It is easier sometimes not even to try to communicate with others. If an elder is depressed, he or she may lack the motivation to try to reach out to others in a social exchange. Just trying to maintain some emotional stability takes all the energy an elder may have. However, biological and psychological challenges associated with the aging process alone do not explain the variations in elders' behaviors within the greater social environments.

Our ability to both observe and describe different kinds of social behavior among elders has improved since gerontologists first began observing social behavior. Social science research methods have developed over time, enabling gerontologists to observe larger numbers of elders and to offer more sophisticated analysis of why social adaptation varies so dramatically. Improved observational techniques combined with an evolutionary process in how we think about aging as a social phenomenon has yielded new insight into both the role of the aging population within society and how individual elders react and respond to their position as "elder" in relationship to others in society (Lynott & Lynott, 1996).

Role Theory

One of the earliest attempts to explain how elders adjust to aging as a social role is role theory (Cavan, Burgess, Havighurst, & Goldhammer, 1949; Phillips, 1957). This theory focuses on the behavior and insight of the individual elder rather than viewing the aging process as significantly affected by socioenvironmental factors. Roles are sets of expected behavior patterns defined by an individual's relationship to another person or social institution. For example, the role of parent is defined by the relationship to a child. The role of student is defined by the relationship to an institution of higher learning or a professor. Role theory postulates that life is a series of sequentially defined roles and the quality of an elder's adjustment to the later years is dependent on the ability to move from roles identified with youth and middle age to those associated with aging. Roles associated with middle age may be parent, worker, spouse, and active community member. For an elder, these roles may change to age-related roles, such as grandparent, retiree, and widow. Elders lose some roles from middle age and gain new ones. One's personal self-esteem and social identity are deeply embedded in these social roles. According to role theory, elders demonstrate successful aging when they can move from one set of roles to those appropriate to their age norms. Dissatisfaction with the aging process develops when people are unable to make this shift or cannot identify new roles to replace old ones (Havighurst & Albrecht, 1953). Being able to forge new roles in relationship to other people in society predicts which elders will successfully adapt to old age.

Activity Theory

Another theory that focuses on adaptations in individual behavior to society, rather than societal adaptations to elders, is activity theory. Activity theory predicts that elders who maintain active and reciprocal relationships with their social environment are those most likely to age successfully (Maddox, 1966; Spence, 1975). Elders who travel, work part time, or participate in a wide range of social activities find old age a rewarding and satisfying time in their lives. If elders withdraw from social activities, they are more likely to become depressed and dissatisfied with old age. As with role theory, the responsibility for one's satisfaction or dissatisfaction with aging lies with the individual elder. In theory, few would disagree that purposeful activity for elders contributes to a greater sense of attachment to the social environment and the opportunity for greater personal rewards. Every young person hopes the retirement years will be filled with lots of exciting new adventures. The occasional elder who is still climbing mountains or running a marathon in the 80s is always held up as the optimal adjustment to aging. Everyone can cite an elder who continues to be a vibrant participant in life and looks happy and healthy.

Activity theory, however, fails to account for the physical health problems and socioeconomic limitations that preclude elders' active participation in society (Fry, 1992; Lynott & Lynott, 1996). While this theory is still considered as an ideal in adjustment to aging, it is rightfully accused of being oblivious to the realities that elders of color or elders with disabilities face. For an elderly African American woman who has raised her own children and perhaps her grandchildren, received inadequate preventative health care, and always lived on a subsistence level income, old age may be a time when there is not the time, money, or energy to remain active in the ways this theory implies. A more relaxed, less frenetic life may be a welcome change. Or, the simple lack of finances or transportation may make extensive social activities impossible. For older Native Americans, old age is a time to pass social activities and responsibilities to younger persons. Their own perception of their social roles is not consistent with what activity theory proposes as the path to successful aging.

Disengagement Theory

Disengagement theory was proposed to counteract activity theory and shift the emphasis away from the individual to a focus on the function of aging for society. Aging occurs within a greater social context. Therefore, to understand aging, we must look at it in relationship to younger persons. Disengagement theory proposes that a mutual disengagement by both society and the individual occurs as social and political power transfers from one generation to another (Cumming & Henry, 1961). Adaptive aging occurs when elders disengage from active roles in society to more passive roles to make room for the development of new leadership among younger people. This theory emphasizes the adaptive nature of this mutual disengagement. It does not necessarily imply that elders are happy with this process, but merely that it is adaptive. Ultimately, disengagement serves the best interests of both the individual and society according to this theory.

Disengagement theory has come under extensive criticism both scientifically and anecdotally. The idea that withdrawing from society is adaptive seems to contradict what we know about people staying active physically and intellectually. As social workers, it would leave us wondering what activities would be deemed appropriate for elders. As the sociological and psychological community has learned more about the social process of aging, the validity of disengagement theory as the sole explanation for the function of aging in society has been discounted. This does not mean that the pattern of disengagement is not seen in some elders, but rather that it is an individual adjustment to aging, not a universally accepted pattern of behavior. The theory fails to account for different socio-cultural patterns that dictate diverse roles for elders (Fry, 1992). Rather than disengage, Asian American elders may serve as a vast source of wisdom and support for their family members. This time in an elder's life can be one of actively offering insight and experience to guide a younger generation, not withdraw from it. Elders who serve as caregivers in a large extended Hispanic family are more valuable, rather than less valuable, as they age.

Continuity Theory

The continuity theory states that elders and society fare best when elders continue a consistent level of activity throughout their lives (Atchley, 2000). Contrary to other social theories, elders do not develop a totally new way of approaching their lives as they age. Rather, old age is a continuation of all lifelong activity patterns, and elders are most satisfied when they maintain a mature, integrated personality consistent with previous patterns of activity. If people have led an active, socially engaged life in middle age, they will be happiest when they can continue to do so in old age. If an individual has led a minimally active life as an adult, this pattern will persist into old age. Elders are simply more of what they were when they were younger, according to this theory. Intuitively, this theory makes sense and is consistent with what psychology tells us about the stability of basic personality characteristics over the life span.

The major criticism of this theory, however, is that it fails to account for unanticipated changes in both physical health and social circumstances (Fry, 1992). For example, if a woman has been athletic most of her life and suddenly faces restrictions in physical activity due to the dangers imposed by osteoporosis, does this mean she will not make a satisfactory adjustment to aging and is destined to be unhappy? If an older man has had few friends throughout his life due to family and job responsibilities, does this mean he probably will never be able to develop new social ties as a retired widower? The major criticism of the continuity theory is that it is a very restricted way of thinking about the potential for change among elders as they adapt to new circumstances that will likely accompany the aging process. Social work is a profession that is deeply rooted in the belief that people and society can both change. Gerontological social work is specifically dedicated to helping older people find ways to make old age a constructive and enriching time in their lives despite the physical, psychological, and social changes they may experience.

Social Constructionism

A more recent theory of social aging, social constructionism, moves beyond the restrictive perspectives of role, activity, disengagement, and continuity theories. Social constructionism postulates that people of all ages participate in everyday life on the basis of the social meanings they have created for themselves (Ray, 1996). There is no such thing as a "fixed reality" that exists for all individuals. People create their own realities, and these realities shift over time. A young man may see his world as one in which his responsibility is to his job and his family. His view of the world prioritizes his activities and his attitudes. A young mother may feel her first responsibility is to her children and order her activities to reflect that view. However, when both men and women reach their later years, their social construction of the reality of their world changes. Having raised their children, their priorities may shift away from parenting as a top priority to a renewed focus on being a couple or to participating in activities that focus more on personal rewards than responsibilities for others. The reality people construct for their own lives explains how they behave. If elders see late life as a time for less social, more introspective activities, that is what they will do. If elders see life as a time for doing all the things they did not have time for earlier in life, they are more likely to pursue a more activities-oriented life. This theory does not necessarily see any particular orientation to old age as either functional or dysfunctional, healthy or pathological, but rather a reflection of the individual's perception of this stage in life.

Social constructionists are less focused on adaptation patterns and more interested in how people define these experiences for themselves. Using qualitative methods, such as personal interviews and narratives, social scientists gather information about what social clues elders use to define the reality of old age. While one elderly woman may see widowhood as a new opportunity for self-development, another may see this same event as the beginning of the wait for her own death, with much to be feared and little to be enjoyed. One elderly man may retire to the couch to simply enjoy doing nothing, while another may welcome the lack of job-related activities to take up active leisure pursuits, such as golf or tennis. Social constructionism views aging and its subsequent adjustment as a uniquely individual process dictated by each individual's own social perceptions.

If people construct their own social realities in old age, the gerontological social worker is challenged to try to understand what that reality is for elders. Understanding how people perceive the world in which they function helps the social worker to help elders participate in activities and interventions consistent with their worldviews.

Feminist and Political Economy Theories of Aging

Feminism and the political economy theories of aging are discussed together because both theories describe the role and function of elders in relationship to power structures. Feminism espouses that traditional social theories ignore the experience of women who have historically have been denied access to economic and social power due to gender. Gender is an organizing principle in people's lives, and in order to truly understanding the experience of aging for women, the role of gender must be examined. Feminist theories of aging state that role, activity, and continuity thoeries homogenize the experience of old age as being the same for men and women (Fry, 1992; Hooyman & Kiyak, 1999; Lynott & Lynott, 1996; Ray, 1996). Little sociological research has been done on the unique aspects of the aging experience for women, despite the fact that their longer life expectancies result in the majority of elders being women. Women's experiences in aging are the result of a differential access to power throughout their lives. Therefore, the unique problems women experience as they age are not solely issues in the area of private activities and decisions but rather are political ones.

Political economy proposes that people's social experiences in aging are deeply influenced by access to social rewards and political power, both of which decline in the later years (Hooyman & Kiyak, 1999). As elders retire, they lose their connection to the source of economic reward—work—and the prestige that accompanies a socially productive role in society. For women and persons of color, access to these social rewards has been compromised throughout their entire lives and worsens as they get older. While the political economy theory of aging may appear to be radical from a political perspective, it is actually socially conservative. Such speculations that elders are devalued—because they are in socially unproductive roles—would appear to relegate elders to a second-class citizenship and promote permanent marginality of this population.

The MacArthur Study and "Successful" Psychosocial Aging

In addition to studying the factors that contribute to the maintenance of good physical health in old age discussed in Chapter 2, the dozens of individual research projects that constitute the MacArthur Study examined the psychosocial factors that contribute to successful aging. In general, the study has confirmed what gerontologists have long assumed, that cognitive and intellectual decline among elders is the exception to the rule. It also confirms that a strong social support network is one of the most important predictors of good psychosocial adjustment to aging.

Cognitive and Intellectual Functioning

Much of the functional loss elders fear as they grow older is preventable according to the MacArthur Study. While elders do experience very real changes in short-term memory as they age, severe memory loss is not common or inevitable in old age. For elders who have lost some of their memory function, mental exercises and a concentrated effort to retrain memory can result in almost complete recovery of memory function (Rowe & Kahn, 1998). Those elders studied who retained strong cognitive and intellectual capabilities made an active effort to use their intellectual resources every single day. They continued to do crossword puzzles, play other word games, read the paper, or find other ways to challenge their minds. Exercising the mind is similar to exercising the body—use it or lose it! The study also found that it was important to find a variety of ways to exercise the mind, including activities that required memory recall, energized the artistic and creative abilities of the brain, or involved the assimilation of new knowledge, all of which stimulated different parts of the brain.

Elders who had a positive attitude about their own abilities to handle what life dealt them also showed less likelihood of experiencing a decline in cognitive and intellectual functioning. Those elders who felt a sense of mastery and control over their lives and retained the ability to make choices about their lives showed better mental functioning (Rowe & Kahn, 1998). It is not clear whether good mental functioning produced this personal self-confidence or whether the self-confidence produced good mental functioning, but the two factors appear to be strongly related to one another. It is important that elders still see themselves as masters of their own fates even when faced with physical changes associated with aging or other changes in their social systems.

The Significance of Social Support

The importance of social interaction and support has long been identified as one of the most important predictors of satisfaction and emotional well-being among elders. The MacArthur Study confirmed this assertion (Rowe & Kahn, 1998). Social support plays an important role in buffering the deleterious effects of all kinds of losses that face elders. Having the support of family and friends can help a widowed elder face the array of new challenges that accompany a new life without spouse or partner. Losing a significant, lifelong friend can be devastating to an elder, but may be less painful if his or her remaining friends can offer emotional support during bereavement. Knowing that friends and family are available for emotional and instrumental assistance following surgery can make the experience less frightening.

The study also found that those elders described as successfully aging were often those who survived and thrived because they remained deeply engaged with family, friends, and productive activity (Rowe & Kahn, 1998). These elders were able to identify what was important to them in their lives, who cared about them, and what activities helped them to maintain a positive self-image. They had something to do and someone who cared about them.

Social isolation was found to be a powerful risk factor not only for the development of cognitive and intellectual decline but for physical illness as well. Elders with concerned family or friends are more likely to attend to physical health issues as others encourage them to see a health care provider regularly and help facilitate these medical visits. Knowing that others are concerned about an elder's health and are paying attention may actually encourage elders to be more diligent about maintaining medication schedules or following treatment plans.

Implications of Psychosocial Changes for Social Work Practice with Elders

The findings of the MacArthur Study and other research on the psychosocial changes associated with the aging process are very encouraging in terms of identifying what elders and helping professionals can do to help make this time in life a positive and rewarding experience for elders. Getting older does not inherently mean the loss of memory, cognitive abilities, or intellectual functioning. Nor does getting older mean that elders must face disengaging from the world around them. These findings suggest a number of important implications for gerontological social work practice and ways in which helping professionals can provide opportunities for elders to maximize their psychosocial functioning.

Provide Opportunities but Respect Choice

Elders who continue to challenge their minds and keep their intellectual curiosity alive tend to retain their cognitive abilities longer. Providing opportunities for elders of all income levels to continue to learn through adult education programs, social and cultural experiences, and the acquisition of new skills is an essential part of successful aging. Making sure that obstacles created by lack of financial resources, physical barriers such as lack of transportation or handicapped accessibility, or simple lack of knowledge about the existence of such opportunities do not limit learning opportunities for elders is an important role for social workers. Do elders know about educational programs or learning opportunities? Can they access those resources? Are these opportunities of interest to an elder? If the answer to all these questions is "yes," what can the social worker do to help an elder connect to these services?

One of the most frustrating aspects of working with elders in many settings—especially nursing homes, adult day health centers, or congregate living centers—is developing educational programming and finding elders are not interested in participating. It is hard to hear elders complain about not having anything to do and then discovering they rarely participate in what does exist in these settings. If removing obstacles and providing ongoing support does not result in an elder's participation, it may be necessary to simply respect the elder's decision not to participate. Even though the social worker can be convinced that this is just what the elder needs, the profession's commitment to self-determination requires that the elder's choice be honored.

Everything Takes More Time

In the absence of disease, elders retain the ability to perform complex tasks or remember important information if they are given more time. Under the pressures of large caseloads and the time restrictions of managed care, it is easy for a social worker to rush through the assessment process or become frustrated when it is necessary to take extended periods of time to explain medication regimes and complicated appointment schedules. Slow down! Give the elder time to process what is being said. If need be, explain the same information in a variety of ways to reinforce the information. Adults learn best when they see the relevance of the information for their own lives and are active participants in the process. Rushing elders can make them very resistant.

Psychosocial Health Is Often Contingent on Physical Health

The quality of an elder's psychosocial functioning is highly contingent on the quality of his or her physical health. If an elder is plagued by physical complaints and generally does not feel well, focusing on opportunities to enhance social contact or stimulate his or her intellectual abilities may prove futile. This statement is qualified, however, by the importance of recognizing that elders often somatize emotional problems, making it difficult to tell what is actually an emotional problem and what is a legitimate physical complaint. Therefore, in recognition of the biopsychosocial approach supported by the profession, it is important that elders have access to health care and be carefully monitored by a physician while the social worker is addressing psychosocial issues. The extensive coverage of the biological aspects of the aging process in Chapter 2 was presented explicitly for this reason. The biological changes of aging both enhance and detract from an elder's psychosocial adjustment to this life stage.

Social Isolation Can Be Deadly for Elders

The danger of social isolation for elders and the ways in which it contributes to depression, dementia, substance abuse, and elder abuse is a dominant theme in this book. Elders need to stay connected to someone or something for good psychosocial health. For some elders, this connection is with family and friends. For others, a beloved pet, phone friends, internet chat lines, or even plants can fulfill the need to stay connected. Elders need social interaction of some kind to maintain both intellectual and social functioning. It is not only the sense of social interaction with others that is important to elders but also the sense of being productive and useful, however an elder defines it. For some elders, productivity is as obvious as volunteering in a community agency or school. For others, it may be defined more subtly in the form of gardening, playing cards, taking care of grandchildren, keeping their homes tidy, or surfing the internet. It is most important that elders define the activity as productive for themselves, not as compared to anyone else's judgment.

Change Is Always Possible

While the continuity theory suggests that elders' adaptations to aging are often continuations of lifetime behavior patterns, it is always possible for elders to change their activity patterns. Believing that people can change is a fundamental underpinning of the social work profession. The older woman who never completed high school and spent her entire life concerned with taking care of her family may be an excellent candidate for taking a course at a local community college. Never having had the opportunity earlier in life to participate in some activities is not an accurate indication that an elder would not be interested now. Likewise, an older man who has never even been outside of his hometown may be an enthusiastic convert to bus trips or other travel opportunities. Old age as a time in the life course offers endless opportunities for elders to change and try new things. While continuity theory may provide an important insight into anticipating how any given individual may adjust to old age, it is not a life sentence. The range of new activities an elder may be willing to try may be limited only by the creativity and encouragement of the social worker.

Summary

Contrary to popular belief, a deterioration of cognitive and intellectual functioning is not inevitable in old age. Elders actually have more crystallized intelligence than their younger counterparts, reflecting a lifetime of learning and living. The speed at which an individual is able to perform complex problem solving, known as fluid intelligence, however, does slow down as an individual ages due to changes in the efficiency of the neurotransmitters in the brain. In the absence of any organic brain damage, such as that caused by Alzheimer's disease, depression, or poor nutrition, elders retain the ability to learn new skills and remain active intellectually. Keeping the brain stimulated and engaged is essential to preserving these cognitive abilities.

An elder's adaptation to the social context of aging depends on personal attitudes, the presence of a social support network, and the environmental context in which the elder grows older. Some elders continue to be active and engaged in their immediate social settings, substituting new and exciting activities for those in which they no longer can participate. Others withdraw to a more isolated life by choice or chance. These elders may view their later years as a time to move away from the demands of middle age and take it easy. Still other elders find a way to combine a more modest level of activity with time to relax and enjoy leisure. There is no single "successful" way to adapt socially to aging.

Check Out These Websites!

1. www.journalkeepers.com   This site describes materials available to help elders create memory journals, written and artistic accounts of favorite memories from their lives. Constructing a memory journal can be an important asset in helping elders who are experiencing memory problems to improve memory or retain memories in the face of Alzheimer's disease. The site has links to other sites that address memory loss in aging.

2. www.aarp.org/leisureguide   The American Association of Retired Persons maintains an extensive website with dozens of topics of interest to elders and those who work with elders. This page of the site provides information on chat rooms for elders, online learning resources, and travel opportunities for elders and professionals who have access to the internet.

3. www.med.harvard.edu/programs/necs   The Harvard Medical School and Beth Israel Deaconess Medical Center in Boston are involved in a study of centenarians in an attempt to identify what factors help elders to live long and productive lives. The study has addressed the importance of genetics and lifestyle in promoting a long life. This website describes the research process and provides links to publications that carry the preliminary findings of the study.

References

Atchley, R. C. (2000). *The social forces in later life*. Belmont, CA: Wadsworth.

Baltes, P. B. (1993). The aging mind: Potential and limits. *The Gerontologist, 33*, 580–594.

Cavan, R. S., Burgess, E. W., Havighurst, R. J., & Goldhammer, H. (1949). *Personal adjustment in old age*. Chicago: Science Research Associates.

Craik, F. I. M. (1995). Memory changes in normal aging. *Current directions in psychological sciences, 5*, 155–158.

Craik, F. I. M., & Jennings, J. M. (1992). Human memory. In F. I. M. Craik & T. A. Salthouse (Eds.), *The handbook of aging and cognition* (pp. 51–110). Hillsdale, NJ: Erlbaum.

Cumming, E., & Henry, W. E. (1961). *Growing old: The process of disengagement*. New York: Basic Books.

Erikson, E. (1963). *Childhood and society* (2nd ed.). New York: Norton.

Fry, P. S. (1992). Major social theories of aging and their implications for counseling concepts and practice: A cultural review. *The Counseling Psychologist, 20*(2), 246–329.

Gruber-Baldini, A. L. (1991). *The impact of health and disease on cognitive ability in adulthood and old age in the Seattle Longitudinal Study*. Unpublished doctoral dissertation, Pennsylvania State University, University Park.

Havighurst, R. J., & Albrecht, R. (1953). *Older people*. New York: Longman, Green.

Hooyman, N., & Kiyak, H. A. (1999). *Social gerontology* (5th ed.). Boston: Allyn and Bacon.

Kogan, N. (1990). Personality and aging. In J. E. Birren & K. W. Schaie (Eds.), *Handbook of the psychology of aging* (3rd ed., pp. 330–346). San Diego, CA: Academic Press.

Lazarus, R. S., & Cohen, J. B. (1977). *The hassles scale, stress and coping project.* Berkeley, CA: University of California.

Lumsden, D. B. (1988). How adults learn. *Generations* (Winter 1987–1988), 10–13.

Lynott, R. J., & Lynott, P. P. (1996). Tracing the course of theoretical development in the sociology of aging. *The Gerontologist, 36*(6), 749–760.

Maddox, G. L. (1966). Persistence in life-style among the elderly. *Proceedings on the Seventh International Congress of Gerontology, 6,* 309–311.

O'Hanlon, A. M. (1993). *Inter-individual patterns of intellectual change: The influence of environmental factors.* Unpublished doctoral dissertation, Pennsylvania State University, University Park.

Phillips, B. S. (1957). A role theory approach to adjustment in old age. *American Sociological Review, 22,* 212–217.

Rabbitt, P. (1993). Does it all go together when it goes? *Quarterly Journal of Experimental Psychology: Human Experimental Psychology, 46A,* 385–434.

Ray, R. E. (1996). A postmodern perspective on feminist gerontology. *The Gerontologist, 36,* 674–680.

Rowe, J. W., & Kahn, R. L. (1998). *Successful aging.* New York: Pantheon Books.

Ruth, J. E., & Coleman, P. (1996). Personality and aging: Coping and management of the self in later life. In J. E. Birren & K. W. Schaie (Eds.), *Handbook of the psychology of aging* (4th ed., pp. 308–322). San Diego, CA: Academic Press.

Salthouse, T. A. (1992). Shifting levels of analysis in the investigation of cognitive aging. *Human Development, 35,* 321–342.

Schaie, K. W. (1996). Intellectual development in adulthood. In J. E. Birren & K. W. Schaie (Eds.), *Handbook of the psychology of aging* (4th ed., pp. 266–286). San Diego, CA: Academic Press.

Smith, A. D. (1996). Memory. In J. E. Birren & K. W. Schaie (Eds.), *Handbook of the psychology of aging* (4th ed., pp. 236–250). San Diego, CA: Academic Press.

Spence, D. R. (1975). The meaning of engagement. *International Journal of Aging and Human Development, 6,* 193–198.

Willis, S. L. (1996). Everyday problem solving. In J. E. Birren & K. W. Schaie (Eds.), *Handbook of the psychology of aging* (4th ed., pp. 287–307). San Diego, CA: Academic Press.

Willis, S. L., Jay, G. M., Diehl, M., & Marsiske, M. (1992). Longitudinal change and prediction of everyday task competence in the elderly. *Research on Aging, 14,* 68–91.

4

Conducting a Biopsychosocial Assessment

What Is an Assessment?

In the preceding chapters, the spectrum of changes associated with biological, psychological, and social developments for elders was discussed in detail. This knowledge serves as an important foundation in understanding the physical, psychological, and social changes elders can expect in their lives as well as helping identify those conditions that are not part of the normal course of aging. A gerontological social worker forms preliminary hypotheses about what interventions may be helpful to the elder and determines goals based on how an elder functions within the biopsychosocial context of aging. This chapter will address the process of assessment—the social worker's study of an elder's strengths and challenges as they influence, and are influenced by, socioenvironmental factors. The assessment process gathers a wide variety of information about the quality of an elder's biopsychosocial functioning within the environment in which he or she lives not only from the perspective of the social worker conducting the assessment but from the viewpoint of the elder as well. A productive biopsychosocial assessment of an elder is a dynamic and interactive process. It utilizes the expertise of the social worker as a student of human behavior and the expertise of the elder about his or her own abilities to survive and thrive in the immediate environment. The information gathered in an assessment is used to pinpoint what, if any, services might improve the elder's quality of life.

A gerontological social worker's assessment of an elder is not synonymous with what is often called a geriatric evaluation or diagnostic workup. Geriatric evaluations are usually done by a team of service providers, including physicians, social workers, psychologists, occupational therapists, speech pathologists, and physical therapists. Each professional evaluates an elder within his or her own area of professional expertise, and then the team develops intervention and treatment plans. The term *diagnostic workup* most commonly refers to an in-depth medical or psychiatric evaluation of an elder that is requested after presenting evidence of a medical or psychiatric problem. While both geriatric evaluations and diagnostic workups are important parts of the continuum of care for elders, they are ordinarily preceded by a more basic evaluation referred to in this chapter as a biopsychosocial assessment.

What Is the Purpose of a Biopsychosocial Assessment?

An assessment serves as the basis for identifying how support or rehabilitative services can help aid elders to maintain independent and satisfying lifestyles. An assessment also serves as an educational process to alert both the elder and appropriate support systems to high-risk areas that may threaten the elder's well-being. Assessments are usually conducted following a change in the elder's life, such as a serious illness, fall, loss of a spouse, change in living arrangements, or some evidence of difficulty observed by a family member or caregiver. An honest and thorough assessment should identify areas in which an elder functions adequately as well as those in which an elder faces significant challenges. Once limitations are identified, services can be specified that are aimed at supporting, restoring, or replacing levels of functioning.

Evaluation of Strengths and Obstacles

It is deceptively easy to think of assessment as the process of evaluating what an elder cannot do. Society tends to focus on what the body and the mind *lose* as the aging process occurs rather than focusing on what capabilities are retained (or even improved) as people move into their later years. Assessment is not exclusively about what obstacles elders confront in everyday life. It is also about identifying the strengths elders have retained or developed that help them compensate for other losses. For example, elders who have difficulty managing stairs may turn a downstairs room into a bedroom rather than take the risk of falling on the stairs. This process represents an elder's attempt to "miniaturize" his or her environment, an effort to shrink personal space into a more manageable area (Rubenstein, Kilbride, & Nagy, 1992). While it may appear to the social worker that the elder can no longer live in a lifetime home, this move is actually an indication the elder has considered how to maintain control and mastery over a smaller environment, rather than consider moving out of a familiar living space—a strength, not a weakness. Likewise, an elder may spend most of his or her time in a single, comfortable chair surrounded by the phone, television, and important papers to minimize the number of times he or she has to get up and walk around—a healthy adjustment to mobility and ambulation challenges.

Applying a strengths perspective to both assessment and intervention means that every effort on the part of the social worker is focused on "helping to discover and embellish, explore and exploit clients' strength and resources in the service of assisting them achieve their goals" (Saleebey, 1997, p. 3). Intervention goals that emerge from an assessment are built on the strengths and assets an elder already has, which can be mobilized to overcome obstacles.

Identification of Ways to Support and Maintain Existing Functioning

The assessment process is helpful in identifying those areas in which elders are functioning adequately but may benefit from additional support to maintain self-sufficiency. One of the most important underlying principles in gerontological social work is the merit of maximizing independent functioning and promoting maintenance of personal dignity for elders. With this principle in mind, assessment should be focused, in part, on those areas in which elders are maintaining independent functioning or are capable of doing so with some support. For example, an elderly widower may decide to give up driving because of steadily deteriorating eyesight. While this is a wise decision from the perspective of safety to self and others, that choice has other consequences. It jeopardizes his daily attendance at the local senior center where he gets his noon meal and plays cards with friends. In order to maintain and support his own initiatives to seek socialization outside his home, an assessment can appropriately identify that the elder needs transportation, not necessarily the delivery of home-bound meals. While delivering home meals may address the nutritional concern, it deprives the elder of his initiative in maintaining critical social contacts. Assessment can correctly identify ways in which to encourage and maintain an elder's efforts to maximize independent functioning and meet personal needs.

Identification of Interventions That Restore Lost Functioning

Many of the therapeutic interventions discussed in this text address the importance of working to improve lost functioning. Using music or art therapy to help an elder through a deep depression has the ultimate goal of alleviating the depression, not expecting that the elder will simply learn to live with it. Physical and occupational therapy work specifically toward rehabilitating an elder after an illness or accident to maximize abilities. Assessments can be helpful in identifying what functional capabilities have been compromised and what services might be provided to work toward reestablishing those abilities. For example, a recent widow who relied on her husband to drive her to shopping and medical appointments may need to learn to use public transportation to resume her independence in these areas. An elderly diabetic who has lost a foot to circulatory problems associated with the disease may have to learn to use a prosthetic device to regain mobility or make physical adaptations in his or her house to accommodate a wheelchair.

Identification of Supports to Replace Lost Functioning

Assessments may be used to identify areas in which elders need assistance in replacing lost functioning. For example, an elderly woman who has just suffered a minor stroke may be evaluated to determine if it is realistic for her to return to her own home. An assessment may determine that she can handle the basic activities of daily living, such as getting around her home, using the bathroom independently, and feeding herself but needs assistance in taking a bath several times a week or having meals delivered. An assessment can identify what functioning has been compromised as well as what independent functioning remains. Complementing existing functioning with support services to replace lost functioning helps to reinforce an elder's ability to maintain independence.

Sometimes the assessment process is crucial in helping families and support systems move beyond denial about an elder's abilities to maintain independent living. It is painful to see a loved one become frail and it is easy to hide behind reluctance to seek more skilled assistance for the elder, especially when the elder resists added care. Data gathered from an assessment can provide an important basis for honest, although difficult, discussions between elders and their families.

Special Considerations in Assessing Elders

Assessment is a regular and important part of social work practice with all populations but there are a number of special considerations unique to work with elders.

The Balance between Independence and Dependence

It has been emphasized so far in this chapter that a constructive assessment is a combination of the social worker's impressions and observations and the perspectives of elders themselves about their own levels of functioning. It makes sense that the elder has the most to gain by recognizing his or her own limitations and accepting services that will enhance daily functioning. However, the deep-seated fear of losing independence and being forced to leave home, no matter how unfounded, often keeps elders from either recognizing or admitting functional limitations. These fears and concerns are so powerful that elders may go to great lengths to deny or hide problems they are having. While it would seem easier to have elders move to more accessible living arrangements, the significance of maintaining independence at all costs out of the fear associated with being forced into an institution is a powerful determinant in creating functional denial about abilities. When circumstances dictate an assessment by a social worker or health care professional, elders often fear what the consequences of identifying functional impairments will be. It is important for the person conducting the assessment to be cognizant of the presence and power of this fear. Intervening in the lives of elders may represent a threat to an elder's attempt to maintain the precarious balance between independence and dependence.

Origin of the Request for Assessment

When an individual or family voluntarily requests assistance from a social service agency under normal circumstances, the social worker can assume the clients are at least marginally self-motivated to obtain supportive services to improve the quality of their lives. They alone stand to benefit (or not benefit) from their active participation in the change effort. If an elder has requested assistance in a specific area, such as housekeeping services, a chore service, or homebound meal delivery, the assessment process might be seen as part of a more comprehensive service delivery system that helps the elder to obtain not only the requested service but also others as they are deemed appropriate. In this situation, the request for assessment and intervention is client-centered. The gerontological social worker can expect clients to be more directly involved in being active participants in the assessment process. It is a more straightforward process to work with elders in identifying service needs when they have initiated contact with the service provider and can remain actively involved in the process of self-determination of any service plans. The elder can remain in control of how little or how much intervention occurs.

However, in gerontological social work, a request for assessment and intervention is frequently not initiated by the elder. The situation is much more complicated when an assessment has been requested by members of an elder's family, other caregivers, neighbors, or even public service personnel, such as a police officer. The purpose and goals of an assessment under these circumstances are not as clear. It is important for the social worker to approach the assessment process with a clear understanding of whose goals are being addressed. Has the elder consented to involvement with a social service agency, or is intervention by the social service community being initiated against the elder's will? Is the elder competent to make the decision to refuse intervention? What does the family or caregiver expect to be the result of the assessment process? Are these expectations consistent with the social work profession's commitment to self-determination? These are important questions to consider before the actual assessment process begins so that both the social worker and the elder are clear about the stated purpose of the assessment.

Assessing and evaluating an elder who actively opposes such intervention is similar to working with an involuntary client, and the social worker can anticipate considerable resistance. Children and adolescents may have little choice about receiving treatment due to a more restrictive perspective about their legal rights as minors. However, elders retain full legal rights to self-determine unless determined to be in need of guardianship under a strict legal procedure. The rights and wishes of the elder's family or caregivers do not supersede the rights of the elder.

The Heterogeneity of the Elder Population

As has been reinforced throughout this text, the elder population is very heterogeneous; therefore, the social workers' approach to the assessment process should be unique to each elder. Most elders are able to be very active participants in the assessment process with honest and forthcoming insights as to their own abilities, as well as their needs. Others may show more limited abilities to either participate in the process or recognize their own limitations. Severe hearing and sight losses may preclude using standard assessment tools or make verbal communication extremely difficult. For some elders, the mere idea of being tested for basic competencies may produce such high levels of anxiety that they are unable or unwilling to participate. For yet others, the ravaging effects of dementia or depression preclude the elder from even being emotionally or cognitively available to the assessor.

These circumstances require the social worker to adapt traditional assessment approaches to accommodate physical or cognitive barriers to the process. Make sure any adaptive equipment—such as hearing aids, glasses, dentures, or mobility assistive devices—is available to the elder. Allow the elder to use a magnifying glass or enhanced lighting to access printed or written materials. Use a more conversational tone to minimize the testing atmosphere and reduce performance anxiety. Give elders time to become comfortable with you, and do the assessment at their pace, not yours. Avoid professional jargon that confuses or frightens elders, and be prepared to explain why you are asking any of the assessment questions. Elders have a right to know what you are looking for and why in the assessment process.

Respecting Personal Privacy

One of the most important values of the social work profession is its commitment to respecting the personal dignity of the individual. In most social service settings, clients are asked to disclose some of the most personal aspects of their lives. The profession is often guilty of judging the clients' receptiveness to intervention on the basis of how much of this personal information they are willing to discuss. If clients share this information willingly, they are considered cooperative. If they resist discussing highly personal information with a social worker they have just met, they too often get labeled resistant. Neither of these labels is accurate. The sphere of the deeply personal is one that is aggressively protected by most clients. For elders who may never have come in contact with the social service delivery system, a social worker's attempt to obtain deeply personal information may be interpreted as rude, inappropriate, and intrusive.

Assessments require that the social worker ask very personal questions about health, social relationships, and finances that may be particularly uncomfortable for elders to answer. While the social worker may understand the health risks involved with incontinence and know the condition can often be treated successfully, it is unrealistic to expect that elders will be willing to share the details of their toileting habits. Admitting to a near stranger that one has lost control over urinary output may be intolerably embarrassing for an elder. While the social worker may recognize that occasional memory lapses may be indicative of early dementia that may be treatable, an elder's fears of having Alzheimer's disease may understandably cause an elder to deny such problems. The embarrassment of not knowing exactly what day it is or who is president of the United States may result in an elder becoming resistant or belligerent as a legitimate defense mechanism. Perhaps the most sensitive area for elders may be the area of financial resources. If a person has been socialized over his or her lifetime not to ask others about their finances and not to expect others to ask about personal finances, talking to a social worker about money may be extremely difficult. This holds true for both elders who have no money and those who have considerable resources.

Conditions for Conducting an Assessment

The Physical Environment

The ideal place for an assessment to take place is the elder's home. This places the elder on his or her own turf, reducing the distractions and anxieties inevitable in an unfamiliar setting. The home setting also provides the social worker with invaluable information to corroborate or challenge what the elder says about the ability to function. More details about what to look for in an elder's home will be presented later in this chapter when the actual assessment process is discussed. When the assessment takes place in a hospital or other institutional setting, the social worker may not have much control over the setting. However, keeping the elder in the room or space to which he or she has become accustomed is still more beneficial than moving to an unfamiliar location.

Some basic conditions in the physical setting can be controlled regardless of a home or institutional setting. Make sure the elder has access to any assistive devices, such as hearing aids, glasses, or dentures, or mobility devices, such as a walker or cane. It is also crucial that there be adequate lighting in the setting so that the elder can see any written materials being used and have a clear view of the social worker conducting the assessment. Minimize distractions caused by open doors, background noise, or annoying glare. Radios and televisions should be turned off to ensure that the elder can hear and see the interviewer without interference.

If the assessment involves obtaining specific information on medications, medical record, or financial information, elders should be given ample opportunity to locate the records in question prior to the assessment so as to have them available at the time of the interview. Elders will be more confident during the interview if they have a basic understanding of what the assessment process entails.

Although family members, neighbors, and medical personnel may eventually be helpful in obtaining additional information for an assessment, try to conduct the first assessment session alone with the elder. Having a spouse or family member present may not only influence the content of the answer but also increase the likelihood that others will attempt to answer questions for the elder.

Optimum Functioning

Select a time for the assessment when the elder is not fatigued or feeling poorly. For elders with serious health problems, fatigue may preclude their participation in a lengthy session of questions and answers. If the assessment is lengthy and detailed, schedule it over several shorter periods of time. Elders with some organic brain damage may find mornings and late afternoons disorienting times of the day, making these poor times of the day to get an accurate picture of their functioning.

Be sensitive to cultural and gender issues that influence the quality of the interaction between the social worker and elder. If English is not an elder's first language, arrange for a skilled interpreter who is familiar with the assessment process, not just someone who happens to speak the language. Some Hispanic and Asian women may be extremely uncomfortable sharing deeply personal information with male social workers. Use family members to gauge what special arrangements need to be made.

Explaining the Purpose of the Assessment

It is not uncommon for family members to request an assessment of a elder and then ask the social worker not to divulge that information to the elder. Participating in such deceptive practices is unethical and ill-advised. The elder needs to know very specifically the purpose of the evaluation, who requested the assessment (if he or she did not), and for what end the findings will be used. The elder must be able to consent to the assessment in order to engage him or her in the mutual process of identifying strengths and challenges. This process of securing informed consent is one of the most basic ethical principles of the social work profession.

In cases where elders are not able to give their informed consent or appear unable to competently understand the purpose of the assessment, every effort should be made to protect their rights and dignity. Even if elders do not appear to be able to fully understand the assessment process, social workers should take the time to explain it to them anyway. The explanatory process is a safeguard to the worker that he or she is clear about the purpose and is making a concerted effort to show professional respect for the elder. Family members or designated caregivers need to be completely aware of the dynamics of the assessment process and who will have access to the findings when an elder has limited cognitive abilities.

The Issue of Confidentiality

It is tempting for a social worker to assure a client that everything he or she says will remain absolutely confidential. In assessments of elders, this is simply not true and should not be used as a way to encourage elders to share personal information. Other parties will see the findings of an assessment. Documentation of need is required to determine eligibility for many supportive and rehabilitative services to elders. A visiting nurse will have access to pertinent medical information on the elder. The Social Security Administration will see private financial information if an elder applies for Supplemental Security Income. An art or music therapist will see the documentation of depression or dementia as part of planning intervention services. It is the social worker's responsibility to advise the elder as to what efforts are made to disclose this information only as is absolutely necessary to service providers and/or family members with a vested interest in the elder's well-being. Elders need to be reassured that personal information will be respected and protected within the confines of a specific circle of concerned parties. The obligation to honestly explain the parameters of confidentiality falls on the social worker.

Components of a Comprehensive Assessment

The specific aspect of an elder's functioning that is assessed is determined by the purpose of the assessment. For an elder who has no identified physical or medical problems but has shown evidence of serious depression, the social worker may only be evaluating the elder's mental health. For an elder who has shown no emotional or cognitive problems but struggles with the activities of daily living, a functional assessment of those abilities may be the focus of the assessment. The six major domains included in a comprehensive assessment are physical health, psychological and emotional well-being, social functioning, competence in activities of daily living, financial resources, and environmental safety. The material included in these domains may be used in its entirety, or portions may be excerpted to focus on a specific area of concern. A standard form to be used for an assessment is not presented because most agencies and institutions have a specific format designed for their own purposes. Additional measurement tools social workers might find helpful to provide further validation to their own observations are presented when appropriate. This chapter is intended to give an overview of the general assessment process. The rest of the chapters in the book will go into more detail about specific issues in mental health and social relationships.

The most important activity the social worker can employ is a willingness to observe, to gather as much information as possible from those observations, and to continually engage the elder in the assessment process as an active participant. Open your eyes and look. Open your ears and listen.

Basic Demographic Information

Obtaining basic demographic information first is helpful for several reasons. It is essential that an elder's name, address, date of birth, and marital status are correctly recorded for future use. The process of gathering this information gives the elder an opportunity to become more comfortable with the social worker and to prevent an elder's immediate feeling of being "tested." To acquire a more personal picture of the elder, it is helpful to find out about family members, including siblings and grandchildren, if any, to begin to identify potential support systems. Ask about employment status, military history, and education. Be prepared to listen to more details than you may need for the assessment. Elders may use this opportunity to "test" your willingness to listen to them or to show their pride in their own or family members' accomplishments. It is worth the time it takes to help the elder relax and feel comfortable with you. Discussing hobbies or other interests can also be helpful in getting a more complete picture of the elder as a person. Ask about race and ethnic identification to help you understand what significance these factors play in the elder's life.

Physical Health

Using what you have learned about the normal changes associated with biological aging, carefully observe what physical changes are affecting the elder. What is your first impression about the elder's health? Does the elder have difficulty in walking, in getting up from sitting, or with physical coordination? Do you see evidence of tremors or paralysis? Is there any evidence of a prior stroke, such as slurred speech or weakness on one side of the body? Elders who are having transient ischemic attacks (TIAs) display varying levels of awareness and may appear to be having brief "spells" of distraction or discomfort.

Is the elder aware of any heart trouble? Is there any indication the elder has trouble breathing or appears winded after simple activity? When asking an elder about hypertension—high blood pressure—elders may use the term *high blood* to describe the condition. Likewise, elders may refer to diabetes as *sugar*. If you do not understand the terms an elder uses to describe a health condition, ask for clarification.

Is an elder's hearing impaired? Elders who have a hearing loss may nod and appear to hear you, but fail to answer questions appropriately or ignore your questions. The television may be turned up extremely loud, or the elder may fail to answer the phone or a doorbell when it rings. Hearing loss makes communication tenuous. It is difficult to get accurate answers to assessment questions if you have serious concerns about whether the elder has even heard you. Furthermore, elders may be extremely self-conscious about hearing loss and deny it exists, making communication very frustrating. Figure 4.1 offers some helpful suggestions in how to communicate more effectively with elders who have a hearing loss.

It is equally important in the process of assessment to determine whether an elder has a significant vision impairment. A person with sight loss may squint or tilt his or her head toward the speaker when spoken to—in an attempt to focus on the source of a voice—or may have difficulty locating personal objects in plain sight. When a vision-impaired elder reaches out for objects, he or she may appear tentative, indicating an attempt to feel for an item rather than locate it with the eyes first and then reach for it. Some elders have difficulty identifying color or may dress in inappropriate color combinations. Elders who once found reading enjoyable may give up reading any materials because they cannot read anything

FIGURE 4.1 *Tips on Speaking to Elders with Hearing Loss*

- Face the person and speak clearly.
- Stand where there is good lighting and low background noise.
- Speak slowly and distinctly.
- Do not put your hands over your mouth, eat, or chew gum.
- Use facial expressions or gestures to give useful clues.
- Reword your statement if necessary.
- Be patient; stay positive and relaxed.
- Ask how you may help the listener to better understand you.
- If speaking in public, use a microphone.

Source: Adapted from Administration on Aging, 1995.

that is not magnified significantly. Just watching an elder moving across a room can give the social worker clues as to sight loss. An elder may bump into the walls or objects in plain view or stumble on carpets even though the surface is smooth. While eating, an elder with vision loss may have difficulty getting food on a fork or serving himself or herself from a serving plate. Knocking over cups and glasses or having difficulty determining when a cup or glass is full are common problems for elders with vision impairments (American Foundation for the Blind, 1999).

Do you smell dangerous odors in the home, such as gas or smoke, that the elder does not appear to notice? Note the temperature of the home. Excessive heat or cold may be a warning sign that the elder is at risk for hypo- or hyperthermia. Your own observations are an important adjunct to the questions you ask about physical health.

While only a physician or nurse can professionally evaluate an elder's health, it is important to get basic medical information from the elder as part of the assessment process. What does the elder identify as medical problems, past or present? Is she or he under a physician's regular care? Who is the physician or other health care provider? Is the elder receiving health care from other providers, such as a chiropractor, herbal healer, or acupuncturist? Is the elder relying on the use of herbs or over-the-counter medications to treat a health problem that he or she has not discussed with a health care provider?

Asking about medical insurance is helpful in determining whether the elder has economic, as well as physical, access to medical care. What prescription medication is the elder taking and what is it prescribed for? It is critical to ask about over-the-counter medications, which elders may not even consider to be medications, as well. Ask to see the bottles to confirm the accuracy of the description and to check for outdated medication. What assistive devices are needed, such as glasses, hearing aids, or mobility devices?

Talking to an elder about eating habits can assist in identifying adequate nutrition and the elder's ability to prepare meals. Ask the elder for permission to check the cupboards and refrigerator. This not only indicates whether food is actually available in the house but also gives you an opportunity to check for spoiled food. It is important to ask about alcohol or tobacco in a way that does not threaten an elder or encourage a dishonest response.

Another vital area to explore is to ask the elder about the ability to get to the bathroom on time. Is a bathroom located conveniently to the primary living space in the elder's home? Is there other evidence of incontinence, such as offending odors or soiled clothing? Is the furniture wet or stained, indicating an incontinent episode? This is a sensitive issue, and elders may deny a problem if they are deeply embarrassed. Using other environmental clues may help you to approach the topic in a more direct but less threatening manner. This topic is covered in more detail in Chapter 2.

It is important to ask elders how they rate their own health. Do they consider themselves healthy? What would they identify as any major health concerns? Do health problems prevent them from doing things they would like to do? Have other family members expressed concerns about their health? Elders with lifelong chronic illnesses may have adjusted well to their medical conditions and describe themselves as relatively healthy when you would not describe them as such. Other elders with minor health problems of recent onset may see themselves as unhealthy. Elders are most likely to rate their health as poor or fair when they have a medical condition that restricts normal daily activities.

Does an elder have a health care proxy in which a friend or family member is designated to make health care decisions should the elder become unable to do so? In some states, these are also called durable powers of attorney for health care. These documents will be explained in detail in Chapter 13 in the discussion of issues in dying.

Over a million elders each year are the victims of physical, psychological, or other forms of abuse (Wolf, 1996). Part of the physical assessment process includes looking for signs of elder abuse. Does the elder have suspicious bruises or signs of physical injury that she or he seems uncomfortable talking about? Does the elder change his or her story about how an injury occurred during the course of the assessment? Elders have more fragile skin than younger persons, so that what is a minor injury for a younger person may appear as a more serious bruise for an elder. If the elder has a caregiver, try to ask about suspicious bruises and injuries when the caregiver is out of the room. If you suspect elder abuse, contact the appropriate local office of Elder Protective Services through your local county department of social services immediately. The problem of elder abuse and neglect and how to detect it is discussed in greater detail in Chapter 11.

Finally, after you have explored many of these areas with the elder, is what the elder tells you about his or her health consistent with what you have observed during the assessment? If an elder claims no problems with hearing or sight, does that appear to be the case from your perspective? If an elder denies any mobility limitations, does that coincide with what you observe? Assessment is a dynamic process in which the worker's observations and the elder's insights both contribute to the final designation of problem areas. If your observations differ significantly from the elder's responses, consider why this may be the case. Does the elder appear to be afraid of having to leave his or her home? Are your expectations of adequate functioning unrealistic? If the elder has not been receiving regular medical care, it may be helpful to advise him or her to have a physical exam and even to offer help make the appointment. Obtaining permission to review the results of any recent medical tests is essential to corroborating your and the elder's assessment of physical health but should only be pursued if germane to future planning for services. Visiting nurses and home health care aides traditionally do their own medical evaluations or are more professionally competent to interpret a physician's findings.

Psychological Functioning

Compiling an accurate picture of an elder's psychological functioning begins at the moment you begin interacting with an elder. While talking to an elder about physical health, you will begin to get a preliminary idea of how he or she is able to process and answer questions, recall factual information, and carry on a logical and coherent conversation. Included in psychological functioning for the purpose of an assessment are personality, intelligence, memory, dementia, and delirium.

Personality.   Personality is part of a person's psychological functioning and provides insight into how a person views the world and copes with stress. How would you describe the elder's personality? Ask elders how they feel they have changed since they were younger. What are areas of the elder's life that he or she considers to be great sources of stress? If an elder mentions a particularly stressful event, such as a serious illness or death of a friend or family member, explore how he or she has coped with the stress. The answer will give you insight as to how well the elder is able to mobilize problem-solving skills. Do you get the sense the elder feels control over his or her life or simply reacts as events happen? An elder's sense of mastery over his or her life is one of the strongest predictors of emotional well-being (Rubenstein, Kilbride, & Nagy, 1992).

Intelligence.   What is your basic evaluation of the elder's intelligence? How does the elder keep mentally active—by reading, solving crossword puzzles, or other intellectually stimulating activities? Educational level is not the most accurate indicator of an elder's intellectual abilities, but rather how well he or she uses intellectual resources to problem solve or remain connected to life. Minimally educated elders may be wonderfully creative and resourceful in maintaining a sense of mastery over the environment.

Memory.   An elder's personal assessment of his or her own memory is important to understanding any deterioration in memory functions. Does the elder have more difficulty remembering recent or remote events? Do you notice a deliberate effort on the elder's part to remember information, or does "I do not remember" come as a more automatic response? Does the elder repeat certain pieces of information throughout the assessment without being aware of doing so? Try to determine whether the elder is concerned about memory loss, unaware of it, or just accepts it as part of the aging process.

Dementia.   Dementia is a gradual deterioration in an elder's ability to process and express logical ideas, orient self to time and location, and access recent and remote memory. The most familiar kind of dementia among elders is Alzheimer's disease, which is discussed in detail in Chapter 5. The purpose of a psychological assessment is not for the social work practitioner to diagnose dementia, per se, but rather to document symptoms that suggest further testing for cognitive impairment is advisable. Dementia is caused by actual biological changes in the brain, and its onset is usually gradual rather than sudden. While elders suffering from dementia appear to have normal sleep patterns, appetite, and energy levels, they present with a sense of disorientation or confusion about common activities of daily living. They may exhibit a great deal of difficulty with basic intellectual activities, such as remembering the names of common objects, orienting themselves to the correct day of the month or season of the year, or counting. They may have difficulty concentrating or making simple decisions. The deficits appear in cognitive or intellectual functioning, not in severe alterations in mood or affect. An elder may or may not be aware of these cognitive deficits, yet it is common for an elder with some degree of dementia to confabulate, or make up an answer to a question, rather than respond "I do not know." This is a conscious or unconscious attempt to minimize the loss of cognitive functioning.

A simple and commonly used tool used to identify dementia is the Mini-Mental Status Exam, which appears in Figure 4.2 (Folstein et al., 1975). The exam is intended to help the assessor determine if there are indications of cognitive limitations. An elder is asked about orientation to time and space as well as tested for basic cognitive functions, such as using short-term memory, naming familiar objects, reading and following simple directions, and reproducing a simple line figure. The exam takes about 10 minutes to administer. Results of the exam can give the social worker a baseline idea about the presence or absence of cognitive deficits, which may be indicative of dementia. This exam is not a definitive indicator of dementia but simply gives the assessor some preliminary indications of an elder's cognitive functioning at the time of the assessment. If an elder scores poorly on this test, more in-depth testing for cognitive limitations is advised.

Delirium.   Unlike dementia, delirium is an acute, temporary condition that often mimics dementia. Delirium is characterized by disorientation, confusion, difficulty in making decisions, and decreased alertness, many of which are also symptoms of dementia. The primary difference is that the onset of delirium is rapid and usually connected to an identifiable, precipitating event, such as a toxic reaction to medications, dehydration, poor nutrition, an infection, acute alcohol withdrawal, or hypothermia (American Psychiatric Association, 1994). Elders suffering from delirium may have fluctuating levels of awareness and present with disorganized thinking and severely impaired memory. Both emotional and intellectual stability appear to be impaired with this condition, and the elder may

FIGURE 4.2 *The Folstein Mini-Mental Status Exam (MMSE)*

Cognitive Function	Question/Task	Score
Orientation	1. What is the year? Season? Date? Date? Month?	____ (Maximum 5)
Orientation	2. Where are we? State? County? Town? Hospital? Floor?	____ (Maximum 5)
Registration	3. Name three objects. The words are repeated until the patient learns all three. Examiner should allow 1 second to name each object to the patient, who is then asked to repeat the words immediately. Examiner should record the number of trials the patient needs to learn the three words. One point is given for each correct answer.	____ (Maximum 3)
Attention and calculation	4. Begin with the number 100 and subtract backward by 7s. Stop after five answers.	____ (Maximum 5)
Recall	5. Repeat the three objects memorized above.	____ (Maximum 3)
Language	6. (Show the patient a pencil and a watch.) Name each object.	____ (Maximum 2)
Language	7. Repeat the following: "No ifs ands, or buts."	____ (1)
Language	8. (Ask the patient to follow a three-stage command.) Take this paper in your right hand, fold it in half, and put it on the floor.	____ (Maximum 3)
Language	9. Read and do the following instructions: "Close your eyes."	____ (1)
Language	10. Write a sentence.	____ (1)
Language	11. Copy this design.	____ (1)
		____ Total

Scoring: The lower the score, the greater the degree of impairment. 23 points or less: Suggests cognitive impairment. 30 points: Maximum

Source: M. F. Folstein, S. E. Folstein, & P. R. McHugh, "Mini-Mental State: A Practical Method for Grading the Cognitive State of Patients for the Clinician," *Journal of Psychiatric Research*, 12(3): 189–198, 1975, © 1975, 1998 MiniMental LLC. Reprinted with permission.

experience hallucinations or delusions. Families usually notice the sudden change in functioning following an illness or other event in the elder's life. Delirium is a medical emergency and warrants immediate medical treatment to minimize permanent damage. It is not constructive or medically advised to try to conduct an assessment of an elder who shows symptoms of delirium. Delirium is discussed in greater detail in Chapter 5.

Emotional Well-Being

Depression.   Assessing emotional well-being in the elder requires determining whether the elder's emotional state is stable and appropriate. For example, does the elder appear to be depressed or verbally indicate that he or she feels sad or listless much of the time? While everyone has days when they feel "blue" or sad, a prolonged state of sadness is not a normal part of the aging process. Find out if the elder has suffered a recent loss, such as the death of a spouse, family member, or close friend. In these situations, some level of depression is expected and should not be considered problematic unless the depressed state persists for an extremely long time. The two primary characteristics of a serious depression are a depressed mood and a markedly diminished interest in activities that were a source of pleasure for the elder (American Psychiatric Association, 1994). Secondary characteristics include an extreme feeling of sadness, frequent crying spells, and disruptions in normal sleep patterns, which may include either insomnia or excessive sleeping. Depressed persons usually voice a feeling of chronic fatigue and a loss of normal levels of energy. Elders may focus on what they can no longer do rather than on what strengths and abilities have not been impaired by illness or the general process of aging. Rather than confabulating, as is more apparent in persons with dementia, depressed persons may answer many questions with the response "I do not know," showing little, if any, effort to think about the answer to the question. Depressed elders often have great difficulty making even the simplest decisions, such as what to eat or what to do in a familiar situation. In interviewing a depressed elder, one often gets the sense that the elder simply no longer cares about much in life or cannot rally the energy to participate in any activities (Mosher-Ashley & Barrett, 1997). A common test used to identify preliminary indications of a depression is the Geriatric Depression Scale (GDS).

The GDS is used widely to identify mild to severe depression in elders through a series of 30 simple, yes-no answers. The GDS appears in Figure 4.3. The GDS is simple to administer and seems to work well with elders with a wide range of cognitive abilities. It was designed specifically for elders and has been confirmed to be both reliable and valid as a test instrument (Yesavage, Brink, Rose, Lum, Huang, Adley, & Leirer, 1983). The answers to many of the questions raised in the GDS can be helpful to the social worker in recognizing the need for some supportive counseling and in identifying areas in which an elder may need particular assistance. A single administration of the GDS cannot definitely diagnose depression. It may be necessary to administer the test more than once. Its results are strongly influenced by physical health and may be skewed by recent losses or events that may not be valid indicators of long-term depression.

FIGURE 4.3 *The Geriatric Depression Scale (GDS)*

1. Are you basically satisfied with your life?	Yes	No
2. Have you dropped many of your activities and interests?	Yes	No
3. Do you feel that your life is empty?	Yes	No
4. Do you often get bored?	Yes	No
5. Are you hopeful about the future?	Yes	No
6. Are you bothered by thoughts you can't get out of your head?	Yes	No
7. Are you in good spirits most of the time?	Yes	No
8. Are you afraid something bad is going to happen to you?	Yes	No
9. Do you feel happy most of the time?	Yes	No
10. Do you often feel helpless?	Yes	No
11. Do you often get restless and fidgety?	Yes	No
12. Do you prefer to stay at home, rather than going out and doing new things?	Yes	No
13. Do you frequently worry about the future?	Yes	No
14. Do you feel you have more problems with memory than most?	Yes	No
15. Do you think it is wonderful to be alive now?	Yes	No
16. Do you often feel downhearted and blue?	Yes	No
17. Do you feel pretty worthless the way you are now?	Yes	No
18. Do you worry a lot about the past?	Yes	No
19. Do you find life very exciting?	Yes	No
20. Is it hard for you to get started on new projects?	Yes	No
21. Do you feel full of energy?	Yes	No
22. Do you feel that your situation is hopeless?	Yes	No
23. Do you think that most people are better off than you are?	Yes	No
24. Do you frequently get upset over little things?	Yes	No
25. Do you frequently feel like crying?	Yes	No
26. Do you have trouble concentrating?	Yes	No
27. Do you enjoy getting up in the mornings?	Yes	No
28. Do you prefer to avoid social gatherings?	Yes	No
29. Is it easy for you to make decisions?	Yes	No
30. Is your mind as clear as it used to be?	Yes	No

SCORING: One point for each answer.

1. No	6. Yes	11. Yes	16. Yes	21. No	26. Yes
2. Yes	7. No	12. Yes	17. Yes	22. Yes	27. No
3. Yes	8. Yes	13. Yes	18. Yes	23. Yes	28. Yes
4. Yes	9. No	14. Yes	19. No	24. Yes	29. No
5. No	10. Yes	15. No	20. Yes	25. Yes	30. No

Normal: 0–9.   Mild depressives: 10–19.   Severe depressives: 20–30.

Source: Reprinted from *Journal of Psychiatric Research, 17,* J. Yesavage, T. Brink, T. Rose, O. Lum, O. Huang, V. Adley, and V. Leirer, "Development and Validation of a Geriatric Depression Screening Scale: A Preliminary Report," pp. 215–228. Copyright 1983, with permission from Elsevier Science.

Suicidal Ideation.   A depressed elder may express feelings of personal worth-lessness and have recurring thoughts of death or suicidal ideation. Suicide is the tenth leading cause of death among persons over the age of 65 (Busse, 1992). The risk for suicide among elders is 50 percent greater than among younger popula-tions (Osgood & Thielman, 1990). At particular risk for suicide are elders who ex-perienced a recent change in living situations, such as being widowed or moving from a lifetime home or apartment. White men in poor health who live alone, have a low socioeconomic status, and have few social supports are at particularly high risk.

An elder's risk for suicide must be seriously considered in doing any assess-ment of an elder's emotional well-being. A number of simple questions should be asked during the process of an assessment to clearly determine whether an elder is at increased suicide risk and should be immediately referred for psychiatric evaluation. They include the following:

- Have you ever felt life was not worth living? If yes, when?
- Have you ever considered ending your life? If yes, when?
- Do you feel that way now?
- Have you ever considered how you would do it?
- Do you have a plan?
- What has stopped you from going through with your plan?

These questions should be included in every gerontological assessment even if you do not consider the elder depressed on the basis of your observations of the elder's mood and affect. A more comprehensive look at suicide among elders is included in Chapter 8. The threat to commit suicide should never be discounted or minimized. Take immediate action if an elder appears to be at high risk.

Anxiety and Worry.   While depression is characterized by a long-standing sense of sadness and hopelessness, anxiety is defined as a sense of chronic inter-nal discomfort, dread, a deep foreboding that something bad is going to happen, accompanied by physical symptoms of hyperventilation, nervousness, headache, or trembling (Gurian & Goisman, 1993). Elders may seem to be easily distracted or deeply worried about events that may or may not happen. It may be difficult for them to concentrate on simple tasks; attempts to recall factual information may be impaired by their agitated state. Medical conditions—such as cardiovas-cular problems, Parkinson's disease, Alzheimer's disease, and hormonal imbal-ances—often mimic the symptoms of anxiety and should be considered before describing an elder as suffering from anxiety. Anxiety is also easily confused with worry. Worry is related to specific concerns about identifiable issues, and the el-der is usually able to discuss exactly what he or she is worrying about. Worry it-self is not a pathological response but a legitimate emotional reaction to health and safety concerns. It is important to probe an elder's concerns when conducting an assessment to make this important distinction.

Social Functioning

The purpose of assessing social functioning is both to determine what, if any, social activities an elder participates in or would like to participate in and to determine whether an elder has social supports he or she feels can be mobilized.

Lifestyle.   How does the elder spend a typical day? It is often insightful to ask an elder how he or she decides what to do each day. The answer may help you discern what kind of worldview the elder has constructed for himself or herself. This is the core of the social constructionist understanding of the social process of aging. Activity, disengagement, and continuity theories of social aging posit that elders have unique ways of retaining and discarding activity patterns from earlier in their lives. Does the elder remain engaged in the mainstream of life, or has he or she withdrawn from a more active life? Have any life events forced the elder to unwillingly adopt a less active life? If so, has the elder made an attempt to substitute different activities for those lost?

Social Isolation.   Does the elder feel lonely and want more social interaction with others? How often does an elder leave home to visit friends or family, attend church, or other social activities, such as senior center gatherings, church activities, a card club, shopping, or attending concerts? What transportation is available to the elder? Would the elder like to leave home more often? If the answer is yes, what obstacles prevent the elder from doing so? Not every elder wants to be busy socializing all the time. Respect the elder's wish to spend time alone. There is no specific right or wrong answer to any of these questions, but problem areas can be identified if the elder is not happy with the current situation and sincerely wants to have more social contact. Some elders are extremely content spending lots of time alone and would never describe themselves as lonely. Townsend (1968) distinguished between "isolates" and "desolates" in the following way. The emotional meaning of isolation depends on whether this state is the product of habitual lifestyle choices (isolates) as opposed to isolation imposed on an elder by an emotional or physical loss (desolates). Some elders are loners by choice, and others, as the result of life events. Shanas (1964) found childless elderly widows and many widowers to be at the highest risk for involuntary isolation, especially when the social network prior to being widowed was extremely limited. It is important for the social worker to recognize and acknowledge the significance of losses in an elder's life. Social roles—such as spouse, worker, community member, or friend—may be lost in old age and never replaced. These losses seriously affect the number and quality of social interactions for the elder.

If the elder is homebound, do others visit on a regular basis? Pets, phone conversations, and watching television are often substituted for other social contacts when elders cannot or will not leave home. Is there any social interaction with neighbors? Do other service providers—such as Meals-on-Wheels, visiting nurses, homemaking services, or friendly visitors—come into the elder's home? Are too many service providers already coming into the home? When services are not carefully coordinated, an elder may feel overwhelmed by the number and frequency of services and find the level of intrusion annoying.

In order to help an elder identify those persons who play a significant social role in his or her life, Rubenstein, Kilbride, and Nagy (1992) developed a diagram resembling a bull's-eye surrounded by concentric circles. The elder is represented as the center of the diagram surrounded by three concentric circles, each progressively farther away from the center. In the circle closest to the center, elders were asked to write the names of those persons they felt they were closest to—those who were most important in their lives. In the second and third circles, elders were asked to identify those persons they felt less close to. Elders indicated how often they saw or spoke to each person identified in the diagram. While Rubenstein, Kilbride, and Nagy (1992) used this exercise for social relations research, it can be adapted to be used as an assessment tool with elders. Identifying both the quantity and quality of significant social relationships diagrammatically can supplement an elder's verbal description of his or her level of social contact and identify sources of instrumental and emotional support.

Instrumental and Emotional Support.   Instrumental support refers to any outside assistance the elder may receive, such as financial support, help with household chores, or running errands. Ask the elder who helps him or her in these areas, if anyone. Is this arrangement satisfactory for both the elder and the person providing instrumental support? Are there things the elder cannot do because he or she cannot find someone to help? Answers to these questions will help you understand what support systems exist for the elder and what systems need to be developed. Gaps in instrumental support can often be closed by providing home-based services, such as homemaking or chore services, if family or friends are not available to help.

Emotional support is more personal and involves contact and support from family members or close friends. Who does the elder contact when a problem arises or when he or she feels the need to talk to someone? Does he or she have a confidante with whom troubling or disturbing thoughts can be shared? Women tend to fare better in this area than men, primarily because women are more likely to develop and maintain a network of social relationships. The presence of even a single close emotional friend can help an elder ease the pain of loneliness and continue to feel connected to others.

Competence in the Activities of Daily Living

Activities of Daily Living (ADLs).   Assessing an elder's competence in the activities of daily living (ADLs) determines an elder's ability to complete the basic tasks of self-care, such as eating, toileting, ambulating and transferring, bathing, dressing, and grooming. These functional abilities are influenced by the physical and psychological status of the elder as he or she interfaces with the demands of everyday life. Major limitations in one or more of the ADLs strongly suggest an elder needs supportive services unavailable in independent living without

24-hour care. Can an elder feed himself or herself without assistance, or does he or she require assistance in cutting foods into bite-sized pieces or with buttering bread (eating)? Can an elder get to toilet facilities at the appropriate time and control bodily elimination (toileting)? Is an elder able to get around the living space (ambulation) and get out of bed or a chair without assistance (transfer)? Can an elder bathe independently in a bathtub, in a shower, or by sponge bath? Is an elder able to select clothing, dress independently, and accomplish basic grooming activities, such as combing hair or completing basic dental care?

Instrumental Activities of Daily Living (IADLs). Instrumental activities of daily living are more complicated tasks than ADLs yet remain basic skills necessary to managing an independent household, such as using a telephone or preparing meals. Losses in the ability to perform IADLs may signal the beginning of cognitive decline for elders or the development of disabling health problems. Significant IADLs include the following:

1. Use of the telephone, including the ability to look up and dial a number and receive calls
2. Shopping, including the ability to plan and purchase items if transportation is provided
3. Food preparation, including both planning a complete meal and preparing it without assistance
4. Housekeeping skills, including heavy housework, such as scrubbing floors, or basic chores, such as dusting or making the bed
5. Independent transportation by car, bus, or taxi
6. Administration of medication, including taking the correct dosage at the appropriate time without assistance or reminder from others
7. Money management, including writing checks or securing money orders to pay bills

These activities are usually evaluated on one of three levels: retains the ability to accomplish the activity completely independently, needs assistance in some part of the activity, or is unable to do the task at all. Impairments in any of the IADLs do not necessarily imply an elder is unable to live independently, but rather suggest support services may be needed to help maintain as much independence as possible.

A credible functional assessment requires a combination of both an elder's response to the questions posed and the social worker's own direct observations. What evidence do you have to support or refute the elder's assessment of his or her functioning in each of the areas? This is not to suggest that elders will be dishonest in responding, but rather emphasizes the role that fear of losing independence can play in distorting a realistic evaluation of abilities to do basic activities. It is painful for elders to admit to others they have difficulties performing activities of daily living they successfully accomplished throughout their adult lives.

Financial Resources

If appropriate to the purpose of the assessment, ask an elder about his or her financial resources. While personal finances are a very sensitive topic with elders, the topic can be broached by indirect questions. Does the elder worry about having enough money for regular living expenses? Has he or she delayed getting a prescription filled or buying food because the money was not available? Is money available for emergency expenses? Exploring an elder's financial resources may help identify other sources of financial or material assistance for which the elder is eligible, such as Supplemental Security Income, Medical Assistance, or energy assistance. If an elder believes that your questions are in his or her best interest in helping improve the quality of life, answers to questions about money may be more forthcoming. It is important to respect an elder's personal privacy in this area.

Environmental Issues

Assessing the elder's environment includes observations about the general repair of an elder's home or apartment, the existence of a hazard-free living space, and basic security precautions that ensure an elder's physical safety within the neighborhood environment. A checklist identifying specific questions about possible safety problems in an elder's home appears in Figure 4.4.

General Repair.   Does the elder's home or apartment appear to be properly maintained? Are basic housekeeping tasks attended to, such as keeping floors and windows clean, removing trash, and washing dishes? Does the elder voice any concerns about these household chores? A common behavior pattern among elders is to "miniaturize" their immediate living space as a means of maintaining control over housekeeping tasks (Rubenstein, Kilbride, & Nagy, 1992). For example, elders might completely close off a second floor in a house or a bedroom in an apartment that is not being used. The bed and dining table may be moved into the living room to minimize the need to move about the home. For elders with substantial physical limitations, the activities of living may be compressed into a single room. In this reduced living space, an elder may surround himself or herself with important papers, personal items, the telephone, and television. In essence, the environment has been rearranged and miniaturized to be more manageable. This is a common and creative move by elders to alter a familiar living environment to accommodate age-related limitations.

How has the elder decorated the home? Are there recent pictures of family and friends on display? Are clocks and calendars evident in the home, and are they set to the correct time and date? Most elders take great pride in their homes, no matter how humble, and the home serves as much more than just a place to live. Rather, it is the stage on which they are living out their lives. Some elders are financially and physically able to update home furnishings regularly, while others are more comfortable with old, familiar surroundings.

Hazard-Free Living Space. Elders are at greater risk for falls due to age-related changes in sight, hearing, and coordination. Check the living space for furniture, rugs, or clutter in walkways that could cause an elder to trip and fall. Look for drapery and electrical cords that are difficult to see and easy to stumble over. Do stairs have handrails? Are papers, magazines, or books piled up in a way that could be a fire hazard? Is the home or apartment equipped with smoke and carbon monoxide detectors? Does the elder have an emergency alert device that connects with the local police, fire department, or local hospital if assistance is needed?

Security Precautions. Many elders have lived in the same location for many years while the neighborhood around them has changed significantly. How safe does the neighborhood appear to you? Are other people on the streets, or does the area appear abandoned? Does the elder feel safe in the home? While the socioeconomic class of the neighborhood is not always an issue for elders,

---

FIGURE 4.4 *Older Consumer Home Safety Checklist*

Use this checklist to spot possible safety problems that may be present in the elder's home. Check YES or NO to answer each of these questions. Then go back over the list and take action to correct those items that may need attention.

1. Are lamp, extension, and telephone cords placed out of the flow of traffic? ___YES ___NO
2. Are electrical cords in good condition, not frayed or cracked? ___YES ___NO
3. Do extension cords carry more than their proper load? ___YES ___NO
4. Are all small rugs and runners slip-resistant? ___YES ___NO
5. Are emergency numbers posted on or near the telephone? ___YES ___NO
6. Are smoke detectors properly located? ___YES ___NO
7. Are smoke detectors working? ___YES ___NO
8. Are space heaters placed where they cannot be knocked over? ___YES ___NO
9. Are gas or kerosene heaters properly ventilated? ___YES ___NO
10. Does the elder have an emergency exit plan? An alternative exit in case of fire? ___YES ___NO
11. Are hallways, passageways between rooms, and other heavy traffic areas well lit? ___YES ___NO
12. Are exits and passageways kept clear? ___YES ___NO
13. Are bathtubs and showers equipped with nonskid mats? ___YES ___NO
14. Are medications stored in the containers that they came in and are they clearly marked? ___YES ___NO
15. Are stairs equipped with handrails? ___YES ___NO
16. Is the lighting in the stairwells sufficient to prevent falls? ___YES ___NO

Source: Adapted from the U.S. Consumer Product Safety Commission, 1999.

knowing how the elder feels about leaving the home is an important consideration for future planning of activities. Does the elder have adequate locks on both doors and windows? Too few? Too many? An excessive number of locks may indicate an elder has had difficulty in the past or anticipates trouble with intruders in the future.

Professional Intuition

Finally, what are your general impressions about the elder's ability to participate in the assessment process? How did the assessment "feel" to you? Are there items not included in any of the preceding sections of this chapter that alarmed you? What does your professional intuition tell you about the elder's functioning? Trusting your professional intuition is an essential part of the assessment process and plays an important role in determining what areas you feel are particularly important to study further. If you do not feel you were able to get enough information from an elder, it may be necessary to contact other collaterals to help you draw a solid conclusion about an elder's functioning.

Using Collaterals to Gather Additional Information

If an elder has serious cognitive or communicative difficulties, it may be necessary to involve other collaterals, such as family, friends, or other service providers, in the assessment process. It is important that the elder give permission for you to contact other people and is aware that you will be asking for specific information about his or her abilities in all of the areas of the assessment process. If family members are in regular contact with the elder, they can be helpful in determining what difficulties in functioning have been present for a long time and which are most recent. How has the elder changed in the past six months or in the past year? Was there a precipitating event, such as an illness or personal loss, that exacerbated the problem? What has the family member noticed, if anything, about changes in mood, cognitive abilities, or social involvement? Be aware that families have lifelong, unresolved familial issues and be sensitive to personal agendas that may skew the accuracy of responses. Whatever goals are set for intervention will have an effect on family members as well. Other collaterals, such as lifelong friends, physicians, clergy, or even the postal carrier, may have insights that can help the social worker clarify both the strengths and challenges elders face in their daily lives.

Summary

A comprehensive assessment of an elder's biopsychosocial functioning is the first step in helping the elder obtain services and resources to improve the quality of life and maintain independent living. Strong assessment skills require social workers to open their eyes and look as well as open their ears and listen. Knowledge of the biopsychosocial changes associated with the normal aging process is essential to evaluate how a specific elder is handling these normal changes as well as how he or she is challenged by chronic physical or mental health problems. The assessment process is a dynamic one in which both the social worker and elder contribute to an evaluation of how the elder is functioning physically, psychologically, socially, in activities of daily living, financially, or within his or her home environment. The specific focus of any given assessment is contingent on why the assessment is being conducted and what both the elder's and social worker's goals are for future intervention.

By its nature, an assessment requires gerontological social workers to ask very personal questions. These must be asked with exceptional sensitivity and patience on the part of the worker. Workers should expect resistance to admitting difficulties in highly personal areas, such as bodily functions, sexual activity, family relationships, and personal finances. These areas should be explored only when they have direct bearing on the request for assistance or the eligibility for services. If elders ask why you need to know any particular piece of information, be prepared to tell them. While a social worker may not be uncomfortable with discussing deeply personal information, it is irresponsible to assume an elder is not.

Check Out These Websites!

1. **www.audiologyawareness.com/hhelp**   This site offers an online hearing test and valuable information about identifying and treating hearing loss. It offers both professionals and elders information on what kinds of hearing loss occur in late life.

2. **www.onhealth.com/ch1/interactives**   As part of a larger site devoted to a variety of online information sources about health in general, OnHealth presents several interactive quizzes on personal health assessment issues, including diabetes, heart disease, depression, and high blood pressure. It also includes a set of "calculators" to help elders determine if they are getting enough sleep or have healthy body mass indices.

3. **www.cpsc.gov**   On this site, the Consumer Product Safety Commission offers the full text of the *Safety for Older Consumers, Home Safety Checklist*, which was presented in abbreviated form in Figure 4.4. Detailed suggestions are offered to help elders and their families alleviate safety hazards in the home.

4. **www.igc.org/afb**   Sponsored by the American Federation for the Blind, this site provides further information on recognizing and addressing sight loss in persons of all ages. It offers suggestions for helping persons with vision loss obtain professional help.

*References*_____

Administration on Aging. (1995). *National Institute on Aging Age Page: Hearing and older people.* Washington, DC: Author. Retrieved March 15, 1999 from the World Wide Web: www. aoa.gov.

American Foundation for the Blind. (1999). *How to recognize vision loss in older people.* New York: Author. Retrieved August 3, 1999 from the World Wide Web: www.igc.org/afb/ a_recog.html.

American Psychiatric Association. (1994). *Diagnostic and statistical manual of mental disorders* (4th ed.). Washington, DC: Author.

Busse, E. W. (1992). Quality of life: Affect and mood in late life. In M. Bergener, K. Hasegawa, S. I. Finkel, & T. Nishmura (Eds.), *Aging and mental disorders: International perspectives* (pp. 38–55). New York: Springer.

Folstein, M. F., Folstein, S. E., & McHugh, P. R. (1975). Mini-Mental State: A practical method for grading the cognitive state of patients for the clinician. *Journal of Psychiatric Research, 12,* 189–198.

Gurian, B., & Goisman, R. (1993). Anxiety disorders in the elderly. *Generations, 17,* 39–42.

Mosher-Ashley, P. M., & Barrett, P. W. (1997). *A life worth living: Practical strategies for reducing depression in older adults.* Baltimore, MD: Health Services Press.

Osgood, N. J., & Thielman, S. (1990). Geriatric suicidal behavior: Assessment and treatment. In S. J. Blumental & D. J. Kupfer (Eds.), *Suicide over the life cycle: Risk factors, assessment, and treatment of suicidal patients* (pp. 685–733). Washington, DC: American Psychiatric Press.

Rubenstein, R. L., Kilbride, J. C., & Nagy, S. (1992). *Elders living alone: Frailty and the perception of choice.* New York: Aldine de Gruyter.

Saleebey, D. (1997). Introduction: Power in the people. In D. Saleebey (Ed.), *The strengths perspective in social work practice* (pp. 3–20). New York: Longman.

Shanas, E. (1964). The older person at home—A potential isolate or participant. In *Research utilization in aging: An exploration, proceedings of a conference sponsored by Community Research and Services Branch,* April 10–May 3, 1963. Washington, DC: U.S. Government Printing Office.

Townsend, P. (1968). The emergence of the four-generation family in industrial society. In B. L. Nuegarten (Ed.), *Middle age and aging: A reader in social psychology* (pp. 255–257). Chicago: University of Chicago Press.

U.S. Consumer Product Safety Commission. (1999). *Safety for older consumers, home safety checklist* (CPSC Document #4701). Washington, DC: Author.

Wolf, R. S. (1996). Elder abuse and family violence: Testimony presented before the U.S. Senate Special Committee on Aging. *Journal of Elder Abuse and Neglect, 8*(1), 81–96.

Yesavage, J., Brink, T., Rose, T., Lum, O., Huang, O., Adley, V., & Leirer, V. (1983). Development and validation of a geriatric depression screening scale: A preliminary report. *Journal of Psychiatric Research, 17,* 215–228.

5

Differential Assessment and Diagnosis of Cognitive and Emotional Problems in Elders

Differential Assessment and Diagnosis

This chapter will focus on a more in-depth examination of the cognitive and emotional conditions that are not a normal part of the aging process but rather represent pathological conditions that develop in some elders. The process of distinguishing between different types of cognitive and emotional problems is known as differential assessment and diagnosis. Making distinctions among depression, dementia, delirium, and anxiety is critical to the determination of the appropriate intervention. While these conditions may present very clearly in younger populations, they often mimic each other with elders and are more difficult to differentiate. Elders who show symptoms of dementia often suffer from depression as well. Elders who suffer from delirium may appear to have dementia. Elders who are depressed may also be anxious. While this may seem confusing at first, recognizing the unique symptoms of each condition and comparing their similarities and differences are both essential to sound gerontological social work practice.

Depression, dementia, and delirium will be presented in the first part of this chapter. Presenting symptoms, duration of onset, the essential features of each condition, and risk factors associated with the development of each condition will be discussed and then compared to help identify their distinguishing characteristics—the essence of differential assessment and diagnosis. Anxiety occurs frequently in conjunction with both depression and delirium, but will be discussed separately. While symptoms of anxiety are common among elders regardless of the presence of cognitive or emotional problems, true anxiety disorders are relatively rare.

Depression in Elders

It is estimated that at least 15 percent of community-dwelling elders and one-quarter of all nursing home residents suffer from symptoms of depression (Diagnosis and Treatment of Depression in Late Life, 1991). These statistics are only estimates; depression is one of the most underdiagnosed and undertreated mental health problems of elders. Among elders showing signs of depression, less than 3 percent suffer from what can be appropriately diagnosed as a major clinical depression, a persistent and often recurrent state of depressed affect serious enough to compromise emotional and physical functioning (Mosher-Ashley, 1994). Clinical depression is a debilitating condition in which elders may be reduced to almost total inertia.

Milder and more common forms of depression among elders are known as dysthymic disorders. While dysthymic disorders present with depressed mood, low energy, negative self-talk, and appetite and sleep disturbances—typical characteristics of clinical depression—individuals usually remain functional. Many depressed elders suffer from what is known as an adjustment disorder with depressed mood. An adjustment disorder develops around a specific event, which precipitates a heightened emotional response. For elders, depressive symptoms often develop after major life changes common in later life, such as the loss of a partner or spouse, retirement, or the development of a major physical illness. This type of depression occurs within a complex web of biological, psychological, and social changes in old age. This coexistence with other life-changing events contributes to the tendency of both elders and health care providers to accept feelings of depression as inevitable in aging. Often elders themselves will attribute feeling sad and blue to something that just happens with aging and accept it rather than seek treatment. Health care providers may consider a depressed affect the inevitable response to overwhelming loss or physical illness, failing to identify the condition as a treatable mental illness.

Depression is not part of the normal aging process. Left untreated, elders suffering from depression experience a lower quality of life, greater emotional and physical pain, and greater risk for taking their own lives than elders who are not depressed. In working with elders, it is imperative that the gerontological social worker be able to recognize the factors that place elders at greater risk for depression, pinpoint the symptoms, and help connect elders to the appropriate intervention.

Risk Factors for Depression in Elders

Genetics and Family History.   Depression tends to run in families. Elders who have first-degree relatives, such as parents or siblings, with depression problems are at greater risk to become depressed at some time in life. This form of depression may be caused by a biochemical imbalance that can be corrected with medication. Mental health practitioners are just beginning to understand how depression recurs throughout life. The current cohort of elders may have experienced depression throughout their lives yet it was not specifically diagnosed as depression. Tough times and family tragedies were often seen as events to be endured. It was up to the individual to pull himself or herself out of the blues and get on with life. Current research in mental health has helped us identify depression in young children and teenagers, prompting early and critical intervention. Hopefully, individuals will no longer have to suffer from depression throughout their lives.

Gender. Depression is diagnosed more frequently among women of all races, ethnic groups, and ages than among their male counterparts (Christison & Blazer, 1988; National Institute of Mental Health, 1996). This does not necessarily imply that older women suffer from depression more often than older men. Rather, older women are more likely than men to seek treatment for emotional problems and thus come into the mental health system. Women may seek support from others, including family, friends, and mental health professionals, while men are more likely to use alcohol as a means of coping with depression. A longer life expectancy for women also implies they are more likely to be widowed or lose a partner and face reorganizing their lives around a dwindling social support system. Longer life expectancy also increases the likelihood of developing a serious, chronic illness, which is highly correlated with the development of depressive symptoms. Perhaps most significant is the fact that women often are forced to survive on more limited incomes than men. Chronic financial stress and its effect on adequate health care and living conditions are sources of constant and destructive stress. Low socioeconomic status is one of the most powerful predictors of depression in late life and cuts across both gender and color boundaries. Higher levels of depression appear to be correlated with the hormonal fluctuations women experience during and after their reproductive lives, but this speculation has not been confirmed by scientific research (National Policy and Resource Center on Women and Aging, 1998). So while depression occurs more frequently among older women than younger women, it is more likely the result of an array of biopsychosocial factors rather than gender exclusively.

Living Alone. Living alone does not by itself present a substantial risk for the development of depression (Diagnosis and Treatment of Depression in Late Life, 1991). However, when elders living alone fail to maintain social contacts or when social support systems dwindle as friends and family members die, elders are at higher risk for depression. Social support systems mediate the effects of stressful events for individuals. It is not the number of friends and family members available to an elder for support, but rather the quality and reliability of that emotional support that determines its importance (Mosher-Ashley & Barrett, 1997). Elders can live alone but not feel alone. Even the existence of a single confidante drastically reduces the chances of an elder becoming depressed.

The loss of a significant others—be it a spouse, partner, sibling, or best friend—is strongly associated with the development of depression in elders. Having lived with and cared for another person for a long time creates a bond between individuals that when shattered can cause emotional chaos. The period of grieving the death of a loved one is known as bereavement, which is not the same as depression. Grieving persons often exhibit the same symptoms as depressed persons, such as prolonged sadness, insomnia, and poor appetite, but the symptoms naturally subside throughout the period of bereavement (Gallagher-Thompson & Coon, 1996). An elder who has recently lost a family member or close friend should not be diagnosed as depressed unless the grief reactions last an unusually long time or are accompanied by excessive feelings of guilt and remorse.

Physical Illness.   Physical illness increases the risk of depression for elders. Elders may become depressed when they learn of a serious, life-threatening, or chronic illness (Gallagher-Thompson & Coon, 1996; Mosher-Ashley & Barrett, 1997). A circular connection exists between illness and depression. Immune systems appear to be suppressed, increasing the likelihood of contracting serious illness, when elders are depressed. Likewise, when immune systems are compromised in the presence of illness, depression appears more likely. Regardless of which event occurs first, the connection between illness and depression is both biological and psychological.

Much of the depression that surrounds physical illness is due to the accompanying changes in an elder's ability to carry out the activities of daily living. The loss of ability to feed oneself or to engage in independent toileting, dress, or bath touches the core of an elder's self-esteem. The subsequent dependency generated by loss of these abilities contributes to an elder's feeling of being useless and a burden to others. Burnette and Mui (1994) found that a sense of control over life, the continuing ability to make choices about everyday activities, and self-confidence in one's ability to manage one's life were the strongest deterrents to the development of depression in elders. All of these factors are seriously compromised when an elder faces chronic illness.

Depression may appear as a symptom of diseases seen more frequently in elders—such as brain tumors, Parkinson's disease, congestive heart failure, and lupus (Gallagher-Thompson & Coon, 1996; Mosher-Ashley & Barrett, 1997). Thyroid dysfunctions, gastrointestinal disorders, and endocrine dysfunctions also cause depressive symptoms (Husaini, 1997). In the early stages of Alzheimer's disease as elders become increasingly aware of failing cognitive abilities, they frequently become depressed. Whether depression is itself caused by the Alzheimer's disease or whether the awareness of the progressive debilitation of Alzheimer's disease precipitates the depression is unknown. The comorbidity of Alzheimer's disease and depression is one of the most difficult challenges of mental health services to older adults.

Medications.   Depression is a common side effect of medications prescribed for hypertension, cardiac problems, sleep disorders, and anxiety. A careful check of all of an elder's medications is essential in assessing depression. The toxic interaction of multiple medications can create depression, especially when combined with alcohol. Changing medications or insuring an elder's strict compliance with the time and dosage of all medications may by itself help alleviate depressive symptoms.

The Relationship between Race, Ethnicity, Socioeconomic Class, and Depression

Race and Ethnicity.   Research has shown that racial and ethnic group memberships alone do not contribute to higher levels of depression. Being white is actually a stronger predictor of depression than being a person of color (Burnette & Mui, 1994). While depressive disorders are more common among white elders, depressive symptoms are the most common psychological complaint of African American elders. Lower-socioeconomic class, a greater likelihood of living alone, and the lifelong effects of discrimination contribute more to an increased likelihood of depression than race alone (Turnbull & Mui, 1995).

African American women have lower levels of depression than their white counterparts—when physical illness and income are held constant—due to increased access to the social support systems of family, friends, and organized religion (Dorfman et al., 1995; Husaini, 1997). Seventy-five percent of African American elderly women are church members and 93 percent indicate they pray every day (Levin, Chatters, & Taylor, 1995). Involvement in church activities appears to play a major role in improving black elders' sense of life satisfaction, emotional well-being, and level of social contact.

The relationship between depression and ethnicity among Hispanic elders varies within the subgroups of this population. The incidence of depression among Mexican Americans is similar to that of white elders and is due in some part to the importance and proximity of extended family networks that serve as social supports (Markides & Mandel, 1987). Depression among Mexican American elders may also be less apparent because of extensive use of primary care physicians or indigenous healers instead of mental health professionals. Cuban and Puerto Rican elders showed slightly higher risk for the development of depression than their Hispanic or non-Hispanic counterparts. Mahard (1989) attributed this to chronic problems with loneliness within this population, created by the separation of families in the process of migration. For elders who leave family and friends behind when they migrate to the mainland United States, support systems are less extensive than for Mexican Americans who do not ever leave their place of birth.

Like Hispanics, the incidence of depression differs substantially among Asian Americans depending on what subgroup is being considered. The socioeconomic and cultural experience of Asian Americans is highly dependent on the circumstances in their native country when they immigrated to the United States. The income distribution among Asian Americans in general is bipolar. Lifelong residents of the United States or younger and more highly educated immigrants tend to be represented among the more affluent of Asian Americans, while the most recent immigrants and elders are more destitute. It is difficult even to measure the incidence of depression among Asian American elders because of the paucity of clinical measurement instruments that are sensitive to the cultural differences between Japanese, Chinese, Filipino, Asian Indian, Southeast Asian, and white elders. Koh and others (1986) found that standard, self-administered tests such as the Geriatric Depression Scale (GDS) showed high levels of mental disturbances that did not correspond to the findings from personal interviews with these same elders. This disparity was attributed to the presence of a "pleasure-deficit" view of life among Asian American elders versus what is described as the "Pollyanna outlook" more characteristic of white elders. The Asian self-concept is deeply anchored in group cohesion. Asian elders are less willing to share unacceptable feelings and thoughts with the interviewers—a phenomenon known as the "social desirability" principle (Koh et al., 1986). Using more culturally sensitive testing measures, Hurh and Kim (1988) found higher rates of depression among elderly Koreans, Chinese, and the most recent Southeast Asian immigrants—the Vietnamese, Cambodian, and Hmong.

Unlike African American and Hispanic elderly, the incidence of depression among American Indian elders is much higher than any other ethnic group, including white elders (Manson, 1995). Poor health among American Indian elders appears to be one of the most significant factors in high rates of depression. Almost three-quarters of elders in this ethnic group suffer from mild to severe impairment in the basics of daily living, including preparing meals, independent toileting, physical mobility, and self-care skills, due to chronic illness (National Indian Council on Aging, 1981). Manson (1995) found 32 percent of American Indian elders being treated for physical illness suffered from clinically significant levels of depression, almost 10 times the rate of depression within the general elderly population. Epidemiologists consider this astronomical figure to be an underestimate because of the resistance among American Indian elders to even acknowledge the symptoms of depression and seek treatment (Neligh & Scully, 1990). In American Indian culture, the significance of the person as a whole—not separating illness into physical and mental components—suggests that much of what can be considered mental illness is subsumed into physical illness.

Socioeconomic Class.   Much of the research on depression among elders of color emphasizes that high rates of depression are closely correlated with low-socioeconomic status (Burnette & Mui, 1994; Dorfman et al., 1995; Turnbull & Mui, 1995). Low-socioeconomic class is a more significant risk factor for depression among elders than membership in a racial or ethnic group. Poverty, low education, and poor health caused by a lifetime of inadequate health care (conditions more frequently found in populations of color) are contributing factors to the development of depression (Mosher-Ashley & Barrett, 1997). Low lifetime earnings follow elders into old age and are reflected in low Social Security benefits and small or nonexistent pensions. Serious chronic conditions, such as hypertension or diabetes, left untreated throughout youth have disastrous consequences later in life. Feelings of helplessness and the lack of hope accumulated over a lifetime exacerbate deep feelings of worthlessness and overwhelming sadness among elders. These feelings of a loss of control over life and the stressful events of aging destroy an elder's sense of life satisfaction, choice, and self-confidence (Burnette & Mui, 1994).

The development of depressive symptoms among elders occurs within a complex set of circumstances that make it easy to understand why elders experience depression as well as suggesting that treatment may require instrumental as well as psychological assistance. Husaini (1997) estimated that almost 90 percent of depressive symptoms among elders can be directly related to psychosocial or medical stressors. This means that improving access to health care and addressing problems with low incomes and substandard housing may be among the best treatment options for depressed elders.

Diagnosing Depression in Elders

The first step for a social worker in identifying depression in an elder is the most basic one: What do you see and what do you hear? The two major symptoms of a depression are a depressed affect with overwhelming sadness and a pronounced loss of interest in activities that once gave pleasure (American Psychiatric Association, 1994). For example, if an elderly woman appears to be very sad but cannot quite identify the origin of the sadness and starts to forego a weekly bridge game that once was the highlight of her week, she may be depressed. If an older man who never missed a chance to meet his friends for coffee every morning suddenly finds he just does not care to make the effort, exploring the possibility of depression is critical. Negative self-talk—"No one will miss me if I don't go" or "I am just a nuisance to those guys"—should be obvious warning signs of depression. Elders may describe their worlds as "bland, blank, or boring" (Gallagher-Thompson & Coon, 1996). Other symptoms associated with depression are a lack of energy, a sense of hopelessness or worthlessness, difficulty in concentrating or making decisions, loss of appetite, sleep irregularities, and recurrent thoughts of death or suicide. The length of time an elder has suffered from these symptoms and the degree of debilitation experienced as a result of the symptoms are important considerations in assessing whether an elder is suffering from a major depressive episode or has a depressed mood resulting from a stressful event. A quick checklist of symptoms of depression appears in Figure 5.1.

Self-rating scales, such as the Geriatric Depression Scale (GDS) or the Beck Depression Inventory (BDI), discussed in Chapter 3, may be helpful to the social work practitioner in identifying the basic symptoms of depression. These tools may be helpful in facilitating the elder's awareness of feelings and behaviors that are troublesome but should not be substituted for a more thorough assessment. A thorough assessment includes a physical examination by a health care provider to determine whether depressive symptoms may be caused by illness or medication. This should always be the first step in the treatment process.

Some of the symptoms of depression can easily be confused with age-related changes not connected to depression. Depression is different from sadness. It is

FIGURE 5.1 *Depression Symptom Checklist*

___A persistent sad, anxious, or "empty" mood
___Loss of interest or pleasure in ordinary activities, including sex
___Decreased energy, fatigue, feeling "slowed down"
___Sleep problems (insomnia, oversleeping, early-morning waking)*
___Eating problems (loss of appetite or weight, weight gain)*
___Difficulty concentrating, remembering, or making decisions
___Feelings of hopelessness or pessimism
___Feelings of guilt, worthlessness, or helplessness
___Thoughts of death or suicide; a suicide attempt
___Irritability
___Excessive crying
___Recurring aches and pains that do not respond to treatment

*While indicative of depression in younger populations, these symptoms may be related to causes other than depression.

Source: National Institute of Mental Health, 1996, pp. 4–5.

not unusual for elders to be sad about having to give up a lifelong home, watching friends and family members die, or even losing a treasured pet. Sadness eventually subsides and elders regain a sense of basic happiness about their lives, adjusting to the changes in their lives. Once the gerontological social worker becomes sensitive to depression in elders, noticing the flat affect, blankness, and despair that characterizes depression as opposed to sadness becomes easier. Open your eyes and look. Open your ears and listen.

Depressed elders often complain about difficulties with memory and concentration, which may appear to be the early signs of dementia. The emotional and physical energy required to cope with a serious depression may rob the elderly of the cognitive energy required to perform simple intellectual tasks. In Chapter 3, the role motivation plays in facilitating memory was discussed. If an elder is coping with overwhelming sadness and despair, trying to remember a familiar phone number may not seem worth the effort. Ruling out depression as the reason for compromised intellectual functioning is an important part of correctly identifying dementia, as will be discussed later in this chapter.

While sleep and appetite disturbances are hallmarks of depression in younger populations, they may not always be accurate indicators of depression in elders (Dorfman et al., 1995). Elders may have difficulty sleeping because of physical illness or as a side effect of medications they are taking for the illness. Waking early in the morning and having difficulty returning to sleep may be the result of a very early bedtime rather than depression. Elders experience less efficient sleep. They may compensate by taking frequent naps that disturb their natural circadian rhythm, as described in Chapter 2. Loss of appetite in the elderly may also be indicative of problems with taste, ill-fitting dentures, or the loneliness of eating alone rather than symptoms of depression.

Elders are more likely to express depression as somatic complaints—such as vague feelings of fatigue, pain, and discomfort (Gallagher-Thompson & Coon, 1996; Husaini, 1997)—rather than identifying emotional discomfort. The greater likelihood of physical illness among elders makes discerning depression from physical illness very difficult for health and mental health professionals. This is the primary reason a thorough physical examination by a physician is essential in diagnosing depression. The somatization of depressive symptoms can only be determined when physical illness has been ruled out or at least recognized. Seeking treatment for physical illness rather than mental illness may be more acceptable. Mental illness was and continues to be highly stigmatized for the current generation of elders who may view any emotional problems as indications of personal weakness.

Dementia

While depression is an affective or mood disorder, dementia is a biologically based dysfunction in cognitive or intellectual functioning. Dementia is not a normal part of aging. Some form of dementing illness affects 5 to 10 percent of the population over the age of 65, with the incidence doubling every five years after age 65 (Costa, Williams, & Somerfield, 1996). Dementia is characterized by significant difficulties with short-term memory, orientation to time, space, and person, concentration, and the ability to perform complex tasks. Elders can expect that some cognitive functions will slow as a normal part of aging due to changes in the efficiency of neurotransmitters processing messages to and from the brain. Most older adults, however, can complete very complex tasks if given more time. There is not a loss of these functions, but rather a slowing of them. An elder with dementia may be unable to access cognitive abilities, regardless of time constraints. These abilities are seriously impaired or lost entirely.

Alzheimer's Disease

The most common form of dementia is Alzheimer's disease. It is estimated that 4 million people suffer from Alzheimer's disease (National Institute of Mental Health, 1996). By 2030, this number is expected to climb to 14.5 million as the baby boomer population ages (Hamdy & Turnbull, 1998). This does not mean the actual incidence of the disease is increasing; rather these figures reflect the increase in the sheer number of elders as well as improved diagnostic techniques. One-half of all residents of nursing facilities in the United States suffer from Alzheimer's disease or a related dementing disorder (National Institute of Mental Health, 1996). Direct care costs for patients in both institutional and community settings is estimated at between $24 billion and $48 billion. The indirect emotional and social costs of the disease to people and their families are immeasurable.

Alzheimer's disease is named after Dr. Alois Alzheimer, a German psychiatrist, who first identified the disease in 1906. He was treating a 51-year-old woman who suffered from a rapid decline in cognitive functioning, paranoid delusions, auditory hallucinations, and eventually complete cognitive and physical deterioration. Within four years of the onset of symptoms, the woman was dead. The woman's age, the speed at which her cognitive and physical functioning deteriorated, and her unique brain pathology alerted Dr. Alzheimer to the fact that her condition was not what was known at the time as senile dementia, a slow deterioration of cognitive functioning associated with hardening of the arteries in elders. An autopsy of the woman's brain indicated the presence of neurofibrillary tangles, thick coiled fibers within the cytoplasm of the cerebral cortical neurons. Dr. Alzheimer's findings in this case established the first evidence that neurofibrillary tangles and clusters of degenerative nerve endings—known as neuritic plaques—disclosed brain pathology distinct from other forms of dementia. The impairment caused by the disease is not caused by brain changes associated with aging but rather with cellular-level dysfunction. These cellular changes are accompanied by decreased levels of the brain chemicals dopamine, serotonin, and acetycholine, which are essential to learning and memory. In its early stages, Alzheimer's disease affects primarily cognitive functioning, but eventually it causes physical deterioration.

The main risk factor for developing Alzheimer's disease is advanced age. The incidence of the disease increases from 1 percent of the population between 65 and 74 years of age to over 25 percent of the population over age 85 (National Institute of Mental Health, 1996). This does not mean that, if an elder lives long enough, the development of Alzheimer's disease is inevitable. More likely, the cellular dysfunction that characterizes Alzheimer's disease occurs more frequently as the brain ages. The probability of developing Alzheimer's disease is in some cases affected by heredity. Chromosomal abnormalities have been identified in a limited number of cases in which several generations of a family have one or more members with the disease or with Down syndrome (Hamdy & Turnbull, 1998).

The Medical Diagnosis of Alzheimer's Disease.   An autopsy of the brain remains the only definitive way to diagnose Alzheimer's disease. Unfortunately, waiting to perform an autopsy is not helpful to a physician trying to diagnose the disease or to families who need to make financial and health care plans. Computer-assisted tomography (CAT scans) cannot diagnose Alzheimer's disease at the beginning of the disease, but are able to identify the physical changes that occur in the brain as the disease progresses. In later stages of Alzheimer's disease, the brain shrinks and begins to atrophy, brain tissue indentations widen, and cerebral ventricles enlarge. Magnetic resonance imaging (MRI) can provide structural information about the brain through examining the interaction of the magnetic properties of atoms in the brain and an external magnetic field. Observing this interaction helps physicians delineate healthy portions of the brain from static areas, thus identifying the extent of brain damage caused by the disease. Positive emission tomography (PET) and single photon emission computerized tomography (SPECT) are the most recent tests that can map cerebral blood flow, metabolic activity, and the integrity of the blood-brain barrier (National Institute of Mental Health, 1996). Abnormalities indicated by these tests may provide valuable clues for diagnosing Alzheimer's disease in living patients. Much of the medical diagnosis of Alzheimer's disease occurs by a process of exclusion. Pseudo-dementias and delirium—treatable medical conditions that often mimic Alzheimer's disease—will be discussed later in this chapter.

Fortunately, the mental health community has become quite sophisticated in identifying the biopsychosocial symptoms commonly associated with the disease. The functional assessments discussed in this chapter can contribute to a fairly accurate diagnosis of Alzheimer's disease and other forms of dementia in elders early in the course of the disease.

Diagnosing and Assessing Alzheimer's Disease Using Biopsychosocial Indicators

A Symptoms Checklist. Costa, Williams, and Somerfield (1996) identified a cluster of symptoms to help physical and mental health practitioners recognize the early symptoms of dementia, including Alzheimer's disease. The early warning signs include difficulty in learning or retaining new information, such as recent events or conversations. Frequently used items, such as glasses or keys, may be chronically misplaced. Complex tasks involving a series of steps, such as cooking, cleaning, or balancing a checkbook, may become increasingly difficult. Responding appropriately to simple challenges that require reasoning skills, such as what to do when a sink becomes clogged or an appliance breaks, become overwhelming in the early stages of dementia. Elders may become lost or disoriented even in familiar environments. While the "where is my car in the parking lot?" syndrome happens to everyone, it happens persistently to persons with dementia-related loss. Elders may have accelerating difficulty following and participating in conversations. The inability to find the right word to identify objects, feelings, or ideas is known as *anomia.* Elders in the early stages of Alzheimer's disease may appear more withdrawn and passive or emotionally agitated for no apparent reason. In general, a significant change occurs in both an elder's ability to function in everyday activities and his or her emotional well-being. These symptoms are summarized in Figure 5.2.

Most often in Alzheimer's disease, these symptoms appear in clusters, not as a single event or behavior. Occasionally misplacing the keys does not mean an elder has dementia. Difficulties in memory or social withdrawal are also symptoms of depression or delirium, which must be ruled out before a definitive diagnosis of dementia can be made. Difficulty retrieving familiar words may indicate a stroke rather than dementia. Any positive findings on this list of early symptoms simply suggests additional assessment is warranted.

The onset of Alzheimer's disease and other dementias is gradual. It may take one to three years for noticeable changes in functioning to become apparent. For elders with few, if any, chronic health problems, the disease may progress very slowly. Elders with serious health problems may die of other causes before

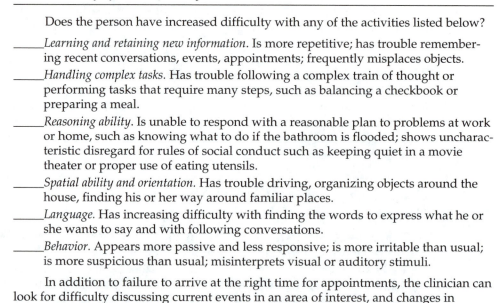

FIGURE 5.2   *Symptoms That May Indicate Dementia*

Does the person have increased difficulty with any of the activities listed below?

_____*Learning and retaining new information.* Is more repetitive; has trouble remembering recent conversations, events, appointments; frequently misplaces objects.

_____*Handling complex tasks.* Has trouble following a complex train of thought or performing tasks that require many steps, such as balancing a checkbook or preparing a meal.

_____*Reasoning ability.* Is unable to respond with a reasonable plan to problems at work or home, such as knowing what to do if the bathroom is flooded; shows uncharacteristic disregard for rules of social conduct such as keeping quiet in a movie theater or proper use of eating utensils.

_____*Spatial ability and orientation.* Has trouble driving, organizing objects around the house, finding his or her way around familiar places.

_____*Language.* Has increasing difficulty with finding the words to express what he or she wants to say and with following conversations.

_____*Behavior.* Appears more passive and less responsive; is more irritable than usual; is more suspicious than usual; misinterprets visual or auditory stimuli.

In addition to failure to arrive at the right time for appointments, the clinician can look for difficulty discussing current events in an area of interest, and changes in behavior or dress.

Source: Costa, Williams, & Somerfield, 1996, p. 2.

the disease progresses to its final stages. When the symptoms of dementia appear abruptly, delirium or other nondementing conditions should be ruled out. (The next section of this chapter discusses delirium specifically.) Elders with any form of dementia may be alert early in the day but become confused by afternoon when they are tired or hungry. While Alzheimer patients may have good or bad days, the deterioration is progressive. Loss of functioning is continuous and intensifies as the disease progresses.

Medical Evaluation.   If elders present with one or more of the early signs of dementia, a more comprehensive assessment is indicated. Health care providers routinely ask about an elder's medical history as a first step in the evaluation process. Information regarding psychiatric history, alcohol and drug use, current or previous infections, and any exposure to environmental toxins is helpful in identifying whether symptoms are due to current medical problems rather than to the development of dementia. Elders' hearing and vision should be checked for acuity. A complete physical examination can reveal the presence of tumors or lesions, vascular obstructions, or infections, all of which can create dementia-like symptoms. A family history of early-onset Alzheimer's disease or other genetic diseases may indicate an elder is at higher risk for development of dementia.

Drug toxicity is the most common cause of reversible dementias among elders. A comprehensive evaluation of medication is a critical part of the medical assessment. This includes over-the-counter preparations, alcohol, and prescription medications. A list of medications that may cause changes in cognitive functioning appears in Figure 5.3. It is important to emphasize that these medications *do not cause dementia.* As the drug interacts with each person's unique body chemistry, some level of impairment in thinking—that may range from vague feelings of being "spacey" to more severe reactions—has been identified in clinical trials as a potential side effect of the medication. Elders should bring all medications with them to a medical appointment rather than relying on either memory or a written list. This allows the physician to double-check the accuracy of an elder's memory as well as determine if medications are expired or inappropriate for the condition being treated.

The physician's interview with the elder is one of the most significant components of the medical evaluation. What does the elder think is going on? What changes in memory or activity does he or she observe? Out of respect for the elder, health care providers need to interview the elder alone regarding the progression and severity of the symptoms. Yet, relying on elders' assessment of their own functioning is not sufficient. In the early stages of Alzheimer's disease, elders tend to minimize the degree of impairment and may deny any difficulty at all. The observations of family and friends are needed to corroborate an elder's assessment. This should be done with the elder's full knowledge. Informants can help health care providers with qualitative assessments regarding the progression and severity of memory loss and decline in cognitive functioning.

Functional Assessment.   Alzheimer's disease is characterized by an elder's progressive inability to perform both the activities of daily living (ADLs) and the instrumental activities of daily living (IADLs). These were discussed in detail in Chapter 4. In the absence of other chronic health conditions, elders with Alzheimer's disease usually do not lose their ability to handle basic self-care functions, such as eating, dressing, or independent toileting (ADLs), until later stages of the disease. The most noticeable losses occur in the IADLs, those activities that require remembering and completing a series of tasks. These include balancing a checkbook, shopping, preparing meals, independent traveling, and remembering appointments. The key to evaluating an elder's functioning is to clarify whether the elder was previously able to do something, such as paying bills, and has progressively lost that ability. Alzheimer's disease and other dementias have a slow onset. Elders do not suddenly lose functional ability with dementia. Gradually, familiar tasks and activities become increasingly more difficult to accomplish.

Mental Status Assessment.   The final component of dementia assessment is the focus on evaluating mental status. An unstructured form of this occurs throughout the evaluation. Physical and mental health providers can get a general sense of an elder's orientation and ability to recall information during the course of the conversation about medical history and functional assessment. The Mini-Mental Status Exam, a brief and simple mental status assessment tool, was presented in Chapter 4. Assessing mental status identifies what, if any, cognitive functions

FIGURE 5.3 *Medications That May Cause Cognitive Impairment*

Antiarrythmic Agents
quinidine (Cardioquin)
tocainide (Tonocard)

Antibiotics
cephalexin (Keflex)
ciprofloxacin (Ciloxan)

Anticholinergic Agents
benztropine (Cogentin)
scopolamine (Isopto)

Antidepressants
desipramine (Norpramin)
impramine (Tofranil)
fluoxetine (Prozac)

Anticonvulsants
carbamazepine (Tegretol)
pheytoin (Dilantin)
valproic (Depakene)

Antiemetics
hydroxyzine (Atarax)
metoclopramide (Reglan)
promethazine (Phenergan)

Antihypertensive Agents
atenolol (Tenormin)
methyldopa (Aldomet)
metoprolol (Lopressor)
propranolol (Inderal)
prozosin (Minipress)
verapamil (Calan)

Antineoplastic Agents
chlorambucil (Leukeran)
cytarabine (Cysar-U)

Antimanic Agents
lithium (Eskalith)

Anti-Parkinsonian Agents
levodopa (Sinemet)
pergolide (Permax)

Antihistamines/Decongestants
chlorpheniramine (Chlor-Trimeton)
diphenhydramine (Benadryl)
phylpropanolamine (Acutrim, Dexatrim)
pseudoephedrine (Sudafed)

Cardiotonic Agents
digoxin (Lanoxin)

Corticosteroids
hydrocortisone (Anusol, Cortaid)
prednisone (Prednisone)

H2 Receptor Antagonist
cimetidine (Tagamet)
ranitidine (Zantac)

Immunosuppressive Agents
cyclosporine (Sandimmune)

Narcotic Analgesics
meperidine (Demerol)
propoxyphene (Darvon)

Muscle Relaxants
baclofen (Lioresal)
cyclobenzaprine (Flexeril)

Nonsteroidal Anti-inflammatory Agents
aspirin
indomethacin (Inocin)
naproxin (Aleve)

Sedatives
alprozolam (Xanax)
diazepam (Valium)
phenobartital

Note: These medications do not cause dementia. Cognitive confusion is listed as a possible adverse side effect of these medications.

Source: Costa, Williams, & Somerfield, 1996.

appear to be impaired and serves as a baseline in tracking the progression of Alzheimer's disease and other dementias. While an elder may have poor recent memory, long-term memory may remain intact until much later in the course of the disease.

The Mini-Mental Status Exam by itself cannot diagnose dementia nor does it always present an accurate picture of an elder's cognitive functioning. Visual, auditory, and linguistic limitations can easily invalidate the diagnostic value of this test. It should only be used as one of several components for evaluating dementia.

Stages of Alzheimer's Disease.   Due to its gradual onset, determining exactly when Alzheimer's disease actually begins is often difficult. However, three distinct stages of the disease in which functioning becomes increasingly impaired can be identified (Andreson, 1992; Sloan, 1998). The first stage lasts between two and four years depending on the individual's physical health and how quickly the disease is diagnosed. The first symptom is loss of recent memory, those events and conversations that have just happened. The elder may or may not be aware that he or she has forgotten something. If elders are aware of this loss, they may attempt to compensate for the loss by making lists or posting reminders throughout the home. Some elders may confabulate answers to questions in an attempt to convince others of their ability to function. They may become confused about following directions or become disoriented in familiar environments. Words or phrases may be repeated or individuals may engage in repetitive motor activities, such as tapping a foot or smacking their lips. In this first stage of Alzheimer's disease, elders may experience mild personality changes, such as loss of spontaneity, social withdrawal, or irritability. Family and friends may first notice these changes because they represent behaviors very uncharacteristic of their loved one. When these changes are drawn to the elder's attention, he or she may deny any difficulty or become quarrelsome.

During the second stage of Alzheimer's disease, which usually lasts between two and twelve years, mental and physical deterioration becomes more pronounced. The elder has more difficulty recognizing family and friends. Memory loss becomes pronounced, characterized by an inability to retain any new information or learn new skills. Elders become restless and tend to wander aimlessly, especially in late afternoon or evening. *Sundown syndrome* is the term used to describe the disorientation and confusion that occurs in elders with Alzheimer's disease. It was first described by Cameron (1941). The restlessness is believed to be caused by the effect that changes in light in late afternoon have on the chemistry of the brain.

An elder's ability to communicate verbally is seriously compromised in the second stage of the disease. While elders may continue to be able to speak, sentences may not make sense or elders may have increasing difficulty finding the right word to express an idea. Elders may lose their ability to dress appropriately or may become incontinent. They may have exaggerated emotional responses, such as excessive irritability, easy crying, or hallucinations.

The final stage of Alzheimer's disease finds elders reduced to total physical dependency. This stage lasts one to three years, ending in death. Elders in the third stage are no longer able to recognize family members or even themselves when seeing their own image in a mirror. Any ability to communicate, walk, or sit may be lost. Total incontinence is common. The lack of physical activity accompanying confinement to bed may lead to the development of pneumonia, urinary tract infection, infected bed sores, or coma, the most common causes of death for elders in the final stage of Alzheimer's disease (Sloan, 1998). The average course of the disease from beginning to end is six to eight years although it may last as few as two years or as long as twenty depending on the elder's physical health and the quality of care received.

Delirium

Delirium is a transient organically based disorder that frequently mimics dementia. An elder suffering from delirium may exhibit symptoms similar to dementia, such as mental confusion, impaired concentration, hallucinations, and erratic moods. The primary differences are that most delirious states develop rapidly and are treatable. That is, the cognitive and emotional symptoms are often due to physical conditions in the body that, once identified, can be corrected. For this reason, delirium is often referred to as reversible dementia.

Symptoms of Delirium

Unlike dementia, delirium has a rapid onset, which is one of the most distinguishing characteristics of the condition. Elders who are normally coherent and oriented may become severely disoriented and emotionally agitated very quickly. They may begin to have visual rather than auditory hallucinations. These symptoms fluctuate so that elders may be intermittently alert rather than experiencing the consistent disorientation normally associated with dementia. Their speech may be coherent during these periods of lucidity but quickly deteriorate without warning. Delirious states are usually accompanied by high levels of emotional anxiety and heightened motor activity. Elders may become combative or verbally abusive with family and friends. It is the acute, almost manic nature of symptoms that serves as the warning that an elder is suffering from delirium rather than dementia.

Delirium is an acute medical emergency. It does not subside without medical evaluation to determine its underlying cause. Left untreated, delirium can result in death. Approximately, 40 percent of elders die from the physical exhaustion or subsequent physical illness that follows the onset of delirium if it is not treated (Butler, Lewis, & Sunderland, 1998). The role of the gerontological social worker is not to treat delirium. Once the condition is recognized, immediate medical treatment must be sought.

Causes of Delirium

There are a variety of underlying causes for delirium in elders, which are generally classified as metabolic, structural, or infectious (Butler, Lewis, & Sunderland, 1998).

Metabolic Causes. Metabolic imbalances in the body may result from the toxic effect of substances introduced into the body or from a dysfunction in endocrine or electrolyte production from within the body. Medication toxicity, recreational drug use, or alcohol are the most common sources of externally introduced substances that precipitate delirium in elders. Elders may take prescription or over-the-counter medications in the wrong dosage or at the incorrect time. Mixing even a small amount of alcohol with narcotic analgesics or anticonvulsants can trigger delirious symptoms in elders.

Metabolic disturbance may also develop when an elder suffers from hyperthyroidism or hypo- or hyperglycemia, a symptom of other underlying medical conditions. Nutritional deficiencies and dehydration are common causes of delirium because of the subsequent effect on electrolyte functioning within the brain. Elders are at high risk for poor eating habits due to low motivation to prepare complete meals, the dread of eating alone, or the inability to purchase nutritious foods. Likewise, elders may restrict fluid intake if they have problems with incontinence or difficulty getting to a bathroom either in their homes or in public places. Delirious behavior may also surface as a result of hyper- or hypothermia. Elders are already at risk for developing these conditions under the best of circumstances due to changes in the cooling and warming functions of the skin and neurological systems. Elders' attempts to keep utility bills under control by lowering the heat in the winter or not using fans or air-conditioning in the summer may threaten their physical well-being.

Brief periods of delirium occur in one-third of all elders recuperating from major surgery (Inouye et al., 1999). The stress placed on the body by the trauma of surgery combined with the presence of multiple drugs in the blood stream may result in periods of delirium.

Structural Causes. The development of structural abnormalities in the body—such as vascular obstructions, brain tumors, or embolisms—can impede blood circulation, depriving the brain of sufficient oxygen and thereby evoking delirium. Parkinson's disease, multiple sclerosis, and other diseases that impair neurological functioning of the body place an elder at increased risk for neurological and chemical imbalances in the body, particularly when the disease has not yet been diagnosed and is not being treated.

Infectious Causes. An infection somewhere in the body is the third general cause of delirium in elders. Pneumonia, postsurgical infections, tuberculosis, encephalitis, syphilis, and HIV/AIDS-related conditions may cause mental confusion and an agitated emotional state. Urinary tract infections, often asymptomatic in elders, may be sufficient to cause these symptoms. Often, these infections cannot be detected without extensive medical testing and a complete physical examination by a health care provider.

Treatment of Delirium

Unlike depression in which a gerontological social worker can use of variety of psychotherapeutic and environmental interventions to help elders improve emotional health, the only treatment for delirium is intervention by a health care professional. The treatment of delirium in elders is contingent on proper identification of the underlying cause. If metabolic imbalances are corrected or substance toxicity reversed, the mental confusion and emotional agitation will subside in most cases. Proper medical treatment of structural causes of delirium and management of chronic illnesses can significantly improve both the physical and emotional health of an elder.

Research has determined that up to 40 percent of dementia observed among elders in the hospital setting could be prevented by a series of simple environmental interventions (Inouye et al., 1999). These include warm milk and back rubs to encourage natural drowsiness, rather than prescription sleeping pills. Hospitalized elders were read to by volunteers, taken on walks to stimulate circulation, and engaged in word games intended to stimulate them intellectually. Focusing on minimizing multiple drug treatments and maximizing cognitive stimulation significantly reduced the development of dementia (Inouye et al., 1999).

Social workers play a critical role, however, in helping family and friends identify delirium in elders. Because the condition mimics dementia, it may go undetected in elders. Family and friends may just assume impairments in memory and mood are warning signs of the onset of dementia. Working with families and friends to help identify the onset of the impairments, any recent illnesses or changes in medications, and nutritional or hydration status will be helpful to a health care provider in determining the underlying causes of delirium. Delirium is a medical emergency. Immediate treatment is imperative, and the gerontological social worker must seek immediate treatment for the elder.

Differentiating between Depression, Dementia, and Delirium

Differentiating between depression, dementia, and delirium is not a simple task. As shown throughout this chapter, the symptoms are often very similar. For example, some degree of mental confusion can occur in all three of these conditions. In the cases of depression and delirium, mental confusion is only temporary. Once an elder's mood is improved (in depression) or the underlying cause of the delirium is discovered, cognitive confusion often disappears. However, cognitive loss is progressive and irreversible in cases of dementia. The presentation and discussion of three case examples will help to clarify the steps in the differential diagnosis process.

CASE 5.1 • *Mr. Charles Curry*

Charles Curry is a 78-year-old widowed male who has lived alone for the past two years, following the death of his wife of 50 years. His suburban home is in good condition, although in need of minor repairs and painting. The place has taken on a cluttered look since his wife's death, with dishes piled in the sink, flower beds overrun with weeds, and papers scattered about the living room. Mr. Curry served as his wife's caretaker prior to her death and did a wonderful job, according to Tom Curry, his eldest son. Mrs. Curry suffered a prolonged illness from cancer but was able to stay at home with hospice support until the time of her death. Hospice maintained contact with Mr. Curry for about a year after her death, but then he requested that they no longer visit him.

Mr. Curry used to be active in the local men's club, the Sons of Hibernia, a social and service organization for those of Irish descent. He went to the club three times a week to play cards and drink beer with other retirees. His friends at the club describe him as having been a jovial, outgoing, friendly guy since his retirement at age 65. He is a retired postal carrier so he knew everyone along his route and seemed to enjoy visiting with lifelong friends and neighbors. He stopped going when his wife became ill and has not indicated any interest in returning to the club since her death. He says the club is too far away and that he is too tired to attend any social activities.

Tom Curry has expressed concern about his father's unwillingness to get out of bed. Mr. Curry says he is always tired after not sleeping very well. As a result, he spends much of the day going back and forth from the couch to the bed, sleeping off and on. At night, he goes to bed at 7:00 P.M. and is up wandering around the house or trying to watch television from midnight on. Tom claims his father appears to be very lethargic and preoccupied. He has trouble remembering whether or not he has eaten but does not express hunger or thirst. He answers "I do not know" to many questions, not seeming to take the time to think about the answer. He frequently expresses a desire to die and join his wife although he has not indicated he has any specific plans to take his life. Tom does not think his father has seen a health care provider for over two years, but Mr. Curry refuses to go because he feels okay. He has lost weight since his wife's death because he does not enjoy cooking and prefers to snack on convenience foods. He has not engaged in any inappropriate behavior and when he concentrates, he appears to be oriented to time, location, and person.

Preliminary Diagnosis

Several clues contained in this case presentation are important to offering a tentative diagnosis for Mr. Curry:

- A significant change in mood or affect
- Loss of interest in activities that were once pleasurable
- Recent loss of his wife, the most significant person in his life
- Minor memory loss and difficulty concentrating
- Suicidal ideation
- Appetite and sleep disturbances

These symptoms fit the classic pattern of depression. Mrs. Curry's death appears to be the precipitating incident in this depression, and Mr. Curry may still be

(continued)

CASE 5.1 • Continued

grieving this loss. However, his mood and demeanor do not seem to be improving, as would be the case in bereavement. He refuses to resume prior social activities, his sleep and eating habits have deteriorated, and he seems to be crippled by his own lethargy. Suicidal ideation is a particularly significant characteristic of depression. Even if a social worker doubts an elder is capable of taking his or her own life, any threat should be taken seriously. If Mr. Curry were suffering from dementia, he would have more difficulty orienting himself to time, space, and person, and a clear, carefully considered wish to die would be unusual. His cognitive functioning would have deteriorated more markedly. There is no indication Mr. Curry cannot perform the activities needed for independent living—he just does not have the interest or energy to do so.

CASE 5.2 • *Mrs. Ellyn Townsend*

Mrs. Ellyn Townsend is an 87-year-old widow who lives alone with her cat in a modest apartment in the center of a large city. She has lived alone for 20 years, following the death of her husband of 40 years from a fatal stroke. She has lived in this neighborhood since she and Mr. Townsend first married. They raised four children in the apartment Mrs. Townsend still occupies. The neighborhood is not as safe as it once was, but many elderly people have stayed in the area because of its convenient proximity to the downtown shopping area. Recently, the neighbors called Mrs. Townsend's daughter, Theresa, to tell her that Mrs. Townsend was wandering around the neighborhood looking for her husband. Mrs. Townsend expressed concern that he was late getting home from work. When reminded that Mr. Townsend died 20 years ago, she became very agitated and argumentative. She accused the neighbors of misunderstanding her and trying to make fun of her. While her concern about the rising crime rate in her neighborhood is warranted, she has become hypervigilant about locking doors and windows.

Mrs. Townsend has various health problems, including heart disease and circulation problems attributed to her late-onset diabetes. She is on almost a dozen different prescription medicines although it is obvious to Theresa that she does not understand when and how to take them. She becomes irritated when Theresa asks her about her medications, insisting she is taking them as required and can prove it. Mrs. Townsend is a retired nurse and until recently was very skilled in monitoring her blood sugar and giving herself insulin. She needs to be reminded how to do this now.

Theresa has noticed recently the house smells of urine and feces and has found soiled clothes stuffed in drawers and under the bed. Her mother denies there is a problem, refusing to even consider she might need an adult hygiene product. The cat runs away frequently, and Theresa suspects that this is because her mother is either not feeding the cat or has become abusive.

Preliminary Diagnosis

Mrs. Townsend exhibits several important symptoms that are significant in reaching a tentative diagnosis:

- Disorientation in a familiar environment
- Loss of ability to perform once familiar tasks (insulin injection)
- Agitation when confronted with losses
- Denial of incontinence even when faced with evidence
- Hypervigilance and almost paranoia about neighborhood

Mrs. Townsend's age combined with a general picture of progressive cognitive confusion would suggest she suffers from the early stages of dementia. However, because of the inconsistency of her medication dosage schedule, the presence of a number of serious health problems, and evidence of disorientation of an unknown period of time, it would be imperative to rule out delirium before proceeding with a diagnosis of dementia. If there are no metabolic imbalances, no structural problems such as tumors or vascular obstruction, and no apparent infection present, a complete evaluation for dementia (most likely Alzheimer's disease) is indicated. The presence of cognitive loss, rather than disturbance in mood or affect, is one of the most important signs of dementia versus depression. Minor disorientation or confusion about a complex prescription regime is not unusual for elders. It is the severity and progressive nature of the loss of intellectual reasoning combined with a loss of care for self or others that distinguishes age-related changes from the organically based changes in dementia, particularly Alzheimer's disease.

CASE 5.3 • *Ms. Rosa Mateo*

Karen Kline works for Elderly Services in a midsize city in the southwest part of the United States. She has been working with Rosa Mateo, age 80, for five years, helping her to obtain light housekeeping assistance and secure a visiting nurse to monitor blood pressure and medications, as well as providing other components of general case management. Karen has not seen Rosa in two weeks but when she comes to her apartment, Rosa refuses to let her in, accusing her of trying to steal her Social Security check. Karen soothes her fears, reminding Rosa that she is her case manager and

(continued)

CASE 5.3 • Continued

not the person who has been victimizing elders in the neighborhood. Rosa appears to settle down and lets her in. For almost an hour, they discuss Rosa's concern about a recent respiratory ailment and the spiraling cost of antibiotics. Karen suspects that Rosa supplements her medication with a healthy dose of vodka on a regular basis and perhaps chooses to purchase alcohol rather than food with her limited income. Today, Karen notices Rosa seems unusually distracted and agitated. She gets up and walks around glancing furtively out of the window every time she passes it. When Karen asks her what she is looking at, Rosa begins to cry and expresses concerns about some man who has been looking in her window. She begs Karen to take her out of the apartment and place her somewhere where the man cannot find her. When Karen goes to comfort Rosa, she becomes verbally and physically abusive.

Preliminary Diagnosis
Without careful consideration of a number of subtle clues, it would be easy for a mental health professional to suggest Rosa is suffering from a mental disorder, such as paranoia, or a psychosis, induced by alcohol. Her behavior patterns are consistent with that diagnosis. However, several symptoms need to be considered more carefully:

- The relatively sudden onset of the conditions which Karen did not observe two weeks ago
- A recent respiratory illness, which may or may not have been treated completely with antibiotics
- Side effects of the antibiotics, some of which are known to cause cognitive confusion
- Agitated erratic mood swings that are not characteristic of Rosa
- Fluctuating levels of awareness, but severe attention deficits

These symptoms suggest Rosa is suffering from delirium and needs immediate medical attention. Karen is in a good position to observe the sudden onset as she sees Rosa on a regular basis and has an ongoing relationship with her. Elders who are suffering from delirious symptoms should undergo immediate medical evaluation with the primary concern of preventing harm to self or others and minimizing the long-term effects of untreated delirium. If there is no underlying cause for delirium, other psychological conditions may need to be considered.

A summary of the distinguishing characteristics that differentiate depression, dementia, and delirium appears in Table 5.1. The social worker needs to consider the presenting symptoms, the duration of onset, cognitive, emotional, and physical factors along with the risk factors present in any particular elder to arrive at a preliminary diagnosis. It is the total picture of all of these factors that will give

TABLE 5.1 *Differentiating Characteristics of Depression, Dementia, and Delirium*

	Depression	Dementia	Delirium
Presenting Symptoms	Depressed mood, negative self-talk, lethargy, appetite and sleep disturbances	Difficulty with memory; disorientation to time, place, and person; disturbances in intellectual reasoning and thinking	Disorientation, mental confusion, emotional liability, manic-like behavior, hallucinations
Onset	Gradual; may be connected to onset of physical illness, loss of family or friends, changes in financial or living situation	Gradual; progressive loss of intellectual functioning; increasing confusion; loss of ability to perform familiar tasks	Sudden; may occur following illness or surgery; deterioration in functioning progresses very quickly
Cognitive Features	Loss of cognitive functioning is rare but elder has difficulty concentrating and making decisions, and may experience minor memory loss	Difficulty remembering recent events, learning new tasks, and communicating. Becomes confused easily about directions and personal location even in familiar area	Mental confusion and disorientation that occurs rapidly. Fluctuating levels of awareness with severe difficulties maintaining attention
Emotional Features	Loss of interest or pleasure in favorite activities; persistent sadness, irritability, guilt, and hopelessness. Seems lethargic and apathetic or intensely worried	Passive and withdrawn as the elder loses touch with the immediate environment. May become agitated when confronted about cognitive losses	Agitated, erratic mood swings, anxious, uncooperative. May become aggressive physically and verbally toward others
Physical Features	Appetite, sleep disturbances, vague somatic complaints that do not respond to medical treatment. Looks very sad	Looks "lost" and confused. May dress inappropriately or show signs of lack of self-care	May have a "wild-eyed" look and appear very disoriented Physical appearance may be disheveled
Risk Factors	Family history of depression, female, social isolation, physical illness, low income, taking medications known for side effect of depression	Family history of Alzheimer's disease or Down syndrome, advanced age	Taking multiple medications, history of drug or alcohol use, poor nutrition and hydration, recent illnesses or surgery, presence of Parkinson's disease or multiple sclerosis or generally poor health

the most accurate and comprehensive differential diagnosis and assessment of these three conditions.

Anxiety Disorders

When faced with physical illness, financial worries, and the pain of loneliness, many elders exhibit anxious behavior. They may worry about how they will live on such a limited income or who will help them get to the doctor or run errands. Everyone experiences this heightened level of emotional discomfort under some circumstances. Anxious behavior is not by itself a form of mental illness but rather the body and mind's way of processing stress. The emotional agitation elders experience often becomes a motivating factor in seeking a solution to the problems precipitating the emotional response. Worry about health may motivate people to seek medical treatment or take better care of themselves. Concern about getting safely to a doctor's appointment might be the impetus for an elder to finally call a senior transportation program to set up reliable, independent transportation rather than obsessing about whether an adult child will be able to provide a ride. Chronic worries about the finances needed to stay in one's own home may lead an elder to finally consider alternative housing, such as assisted living, which may not be as costly and offers assistance with household chores.

However, when a deep sense of dread and fearfulness persists for more than six months and is accompanied by severe physical symptoms—such as headaches, intestinal distress, trembling, fatigue, and insomnia—mental health professionals need to consider the presence of an anxiety disorder. Anxiety disorders are characterized by the intensity and persistence of anxious feelings that may present even when there are no obvious external stimuli. Elders may experience heart palpitations, hyperventilation, dizziness, or excessive sweating. Identifying anxiety disorders may be more difficult in elders because the symptoms often mimic common medical problems, such as cardiovascular disease, dementia, or Parkinson's disease.

Ten percent of elders, most of whom are women, exhibit anxious behavior serious enough to warrant treatment (Markovitz, 1993). While anxious behavior is common in elders, full-blown anxiety disorders affect less than 3 percent of the elderly population (Dickey, 1999). Gurian and Goisman (1993) described anxiety as a "common symptom and an uncommon syndrome" among elders. Elders may experience the development of an anxiety disorder for the first time late in life or may continue to fight a lifelong condition into old age. The emotional and physical resources needed to effectively fight an anxiety disorder take a dangerous toll on an elder's health, making it a legitimate concern for gerontological social workers. These disorders are included in this section of the chapter because physicians often treat elders for anxiety disorders with medication when indeed elders are having anxious reactions to life problems rather than suffering from a mental illness. Anxiety disorders are overdiagnosed and overmedicated. Finding solutions to real problems combined with supportive counseling can eliminate the need for a pharmacological response to the symptoms.

Risk Factors for Anxiety Disorders

Anxiety disorders appear to run in families although there is no clear evidence that the disorder is inherited. Children learn to cope with stress by watching parents and siblings and may begin to mimic the anxiety they observe in their home environment. Gurian and Goisman (1993) observed a greater incidence of anxiety disorders among women of all ages, African Americans, married people, and persons with low incomes and limited education. It is logical to expect that for persons who struggle with inadequate financial resources throughout their lives, in part a by-product of low educational levels, anxiety would be persistent. Illness appears also to be a precipitating factor for the development of anxiety disorders. The neurological damage caused by long-term drug and alcohol use, Alzheimer's disease, asthma, chronic obstructive pulmonary disease, multiple sclerosis, or hypertension places an elder at higher risk for the development of the symptoms associated with anxiety disorders.

Anxiety disorders have a high co-morbidity with depression in elders. Flint (1994) found one-third of depressed elders showed symptoms of anxiety. This may seem contradictory as depression is characterized by a depressed affect and low energy level while anxiety presents with an agitated emotional state. Anxiety develops secondary to depression. Elders may present with a mixture of symptoms. While they show the sad mood, lack of energy, and memory problems typical of mild depression, they may be experiencing excessive worry, insomnia, and agitation—symptoms associated with anxiety. When the depression is treated, the anxiety often disappears.

In one of the few studies of its kind, Bergmann (1978) found that 38 percent of elders with Alzheimer's disease showed symptoms of anxiety as well. The anxious behavior may actually be an indication of the progression of the dementia. The cognitive limitations associated with advanced dementia make the diagnosis of accompanying anxiety extremely difficult. Communicating with patients about what they feel eventually becomes impossible. Mental health professionals must rely on a combination of their own professional observations and those of family, friends, and caregivers about the behavior of the elder. The co-morbidity of these conditions is one of the most important reasons that accurate differential assessment and diagnosis are critical to working with elders.

Types of Anxiety Disorders

Generalized Anxiety Disorder.   Generalized anxiety disorder (GAD) is the blanket term for anxiety disorders that do not have the specific features characteristic of panic disorder, phobia, obsessive-compulsive disorders, or post-traumatic stress disorder. Elders with GAD experience excessive worry and tension that is either unfounded or more severe than is warranted by a situation. They may worry about money, health, work, or family even when no signs of trouble exist. This intense worry is accompanied by physical symptoms, such as muscle tension, restlessness, digestive distress, heart palpitations, and breathing difficulty. An agitated and irritable emotional state becomes a chronic way of life, often interfering with social relationships and daily functioning. Minor events become catastrophic. Elders cannot be talked out these worries when GAD is present.

Panic Disorders.   Panic disorders are characterized by feelings of intense terror and fear that strike suddenly and without warning. They may occur with or without the presence of external stimuli, such as a threat to personal or emotional safety. Elders experiencing a panic attack often complain of their hearts pounding, sweating excessively, and feeling faint, dizzy, or weak. They may feel chest pain or a "smothering feeling" severe enough that they believe they are actually dying. Some elders are flushed while other feel chilled. Hands may feel numb during a panic attack or tingle uncomfortably. Panic attacks can last from a few minutes to almost an hour. When the panic attack subsides, elders usually feel markedly better but become anxious about when they will experience another panic attack. Panic attacks occur without warning and are severely debilitating. As a result, elders may restructure their lives to avoid being in public situations out of fear that a panic attack will strike, leaving them helpless. It is the chronic dread and fear of another attack that creates the anxiety.

Phobias.   The complex constellation of irrational fears are known as phobias. Phobias are intense fears of a particular object or situation—such as a fear of dogs, heights, small spaces, elevators, tunnels, water, or flying, which is the most common phobia. In the presence of the stimuli, people experience all of the classic symptoms of a panic attack, becoming emotionally agitated, fearful, and filled with a sense of impending doom.

Many of the phobias observed in children and adolescents subside as children grow up and are more capable of facing and processing irrational fears. However, some adults never conquer these fears or develop new ones as adults. Middle-aged and elderly people know the fears are irrational, but feel powerless to overcome them. One in ten adults experiences some specific phobia (Dickey, 1999). The disorder tends to run in families, as much fear is learned and is more common in women than men. Agoraphobia, a fear of open spaces and leaving one's home, is the most common phobia among elders (Flint, 1994). Lindesay (1991) found that elders developed agoraphobia as a response to a serious physical illness, falling outside the home, or a mugging or physical attack in the neighborhood.

Fear of flying is an example of a common phobia, but people can get around the fear by taking trains, buses, or automobiles. Unless their professions require regular airplane travel, an adult can function quite well without treating acrophobia. Taking the steps prevents a phobic response to elevators or escalators, but is less functional if an individual has a job in a high-rise building. Elders who are claustrophobic (fear of small spaces) may cope just fine with the condition until they have to give up their own homes or apartments to move into a small room in a nursing home or assisted-living facility. People do not seek treatment for phobias until they cause impossible obstacles to daily functioning.

Social phobia, the intense fear of becoming humiliated in public places, does appear more frequently in elders than other phobias (Dickey, 1999). Self-consciousness about physical changes associated with aging or diseases, such as Parkinson's disease, can seriously restrict an elder's willingness to socialize with others. If an elder has a problem with incontinence, he or she may avoid public events where access to bathroom facilities is uncertain. These are rational fears about being humiliated. Social phobias are irrational fears, and people experiencing such fears know it. While they cannot clearly describe what could happen that would humiliate them, the fear is immobilizing. Despite their own recognition and their desire to attend social functions, the intense fear of being humiliated prevents elders from doing so. This is a good example of a situation in which anxiety can cause or reinforce depression. Social isolation is one of the most common causes of serious depression in elders. If an elder has social phobia and becomes isolated, he or she experiences both the anxiety of the social phobia and the depression caused by social isolation.

Obsessive-Compulsive Disorder.   Persons suffering from obsessive-compulsive disorder (OCD) are plagued by disturbing thoughts or images, called obsessions. In order to prevent or dispel these obsessions, they develop complex rituals, called compulsions. If a person is obsessed with germs and dirt, he or she may resort to hand washing repeatedly during the day. Persons obsessed with the possibility of a burglary may check the locks on doors and windows dozens of times before they retire at night. Some people have developed elaborate rituals around eating, such as eating foods in the exact same order each time, not letting different foods touch on the plate, or avoiding foods that are a certain color. Professional baseball and hockey players may consider it bad luck to shave during a playoff series. Everyone develops rituals and superstitions about certain things. However, when the pattern of obsessive thoughts followed by elaborate rituals to counteract those thoughts consume more than an hour a day and interfere with normal activities of life, this pattern is considered to be symptomatic of an obsessive-compulsive disorder. Obsessive-compulsive disorders rarely begin in late life but are more commonly a continuation of a psychopathology that has been present in an elder since late adolescence or young adulthood.

Post-Traumatic Stress Disorder.   Few emotional conditions have received more attention in recent years than post-traumatic stress disorder (PTSD). Once known as "shell shock," PTSD was identified among veterans returning from war. These men and women were haunted by the thoughts and memories of the original ordeal to the point that they were unable to function normally within society without treatment. While war veterans were the first identified victims of this condition, mental health professionals have since observed similar emotional problems in persons experiencing kidnaping, serious accidents, sexual assault or abuse, natural disasters, or mass destruction, such as a plane or train accident. The disorder is characterized by a person reliving a life-threatening or particularly painful event from earlier in life. For a few minutes up to several days, the person actually re-experiences the original terror and horror. Many persons with PTSD experience flashbacks so real they cannot distinguish that they are not back at the scene of the original trauma. Following a PTSD episode, they may develop serious sleep problems, severe depression, or be easily startled. Sometimes persons who were once affectionate and caring become irritable and emotionally detached as a means of processing the PTSD. The experience may occur shortly after the precipitating event and subside within a few weeks or months. For others, the PTSD appears long after the trauma and lasts the rest of their lives, as is the case for the current generation of elders who survived the Holocaust.

Assessing Anxiety in Elders

Medical Evaluation.   The physical symptoms associated with anxiety in elders often mimic other medical conditions common among elders, such as cardiovascular disease, thyroid dysfunction, and hyperglycemia. It is imperative, therefore, that an elder be examined by a health care professional to rule out any serious medical problem that would explain the physical symptoms. Over-the-counter cold medications and sleeping aids may cause restlessness and agitation as well as any number of prescription medications, indicating a thorough assessment of all medications an elder takes on both an occasional and regular basis. Health care professionals need to know if there is any history of anxiety earlier in an elder's life or in close relatives due to the familial tendency of the condition.

Both physical and mental health professionals need to get a complete picture of the patterns of symptoms and their duration. Is this anxiety related to a recent event in the elder's life? Is the excessive worrying justified or does it seem a catastrophic reaction to a relatively minor event? What is happening in the elder's psychosocial environment that can help both the health care provider and social worker better understand what might be contributing to the elder's agitated emotional state? What does the excessive worrying and agitation mean to the elder? Does the elder show any symptoms of accompanying depression or early signs of cognitive loss? Answers to these questions are critical in determining whether the elder is simply exhibiting anxious behavior or definite symptoms of an anxiety disorder.

Psychological Assessment.   Anxiety, like other mental health conditions, can be rated using existing psychometric measures. One of the most common instruments for measuring anxiety in the general population is the Hamilton Anxiety Rating Scale (HARS) (Beck, Stanley, & Zebb, 1999). The scale consists of 89 indicators of psychic and somatic symptoms of anxiety rated by the observer—usually a social worker, psychologist, or psychiatrist. Although the scale is considered very accurate, its length makes it cumbersome for use with the elderly, who are likely to become fatigued before the test is completed or to overrate the seriousness of somatic symptoms (Sheikh, 1996). The Stait-Trait Anxiety Inventory (STAI) is equally accurate and asks elders themselves to rate their symptoms (Bieling, Antony, & Swindon, 1998). The scale contains only 22 items and is available in a form adapted for elders. Therefore, it may be more appropriate. Psychometric scales combined with a complete physical examination can give the physical and mental health care provider the most accurate assessment of the presence of both anxious behavior and anxiety disorders.

Differential Diagnosis of Anxiety

The symptoms of anxiety disorders, particularly panic disorder, phobias, obsessive-compulsive disorder, and post-traumatic stress disorder, are relatively straightforward. The differentiation of anxiety and its co-morbidity with other disorders is a more complicated process. The following case example will help identify the features of anxiety and other emotional or cognitive conditions when they appear together.

CASE 5.4 • *Mrs. Grace Ardine*

Grace Ardine is an 83-year-old African American woman who lives with her husband in a senior housing complex in the central city. Her husband requires extensive care following a stroke that has paralyzed him totally on the right side. He is able to communicate quite well although, at times, he cannot remember the names of common objects and becomes very frustrated. He tends to take this frustration out on his wife in the form of verbal abuse. He requires assistance with toileting, feeding, and transferring from his wheelchair to the bed. Mrs. Ardine is very healthy and has remained strong; therefore, helping her husband has not been a problem for her. She does heavy physical work around the house and remains extremely active for a woman of her age. Two afternoons a week, she also cares for three of her grandchildren. She enjoys the company of the children, and they help to keep Mr. Ardine entertained. Both Mr. and Mrs. Ardine are retired teachers with excellent pensions. Combined with insurance coverage, they have more than sufficient income to provide for both necessities and some luxuries in their lives.

Mrs. Ardine has begun to worry constantly about what will happen to her husband if she dies, despite the fact his health is much more precarious than hers. She does not explore skilled nursing facilities or assisted-living arrangements and resists when her adult children offer to do so. She simply broods about how he will never cooperate with anyone but her and probably die from neglect. The couple have long-term care insurance to cover the possibility that one or both of them would someday need such care, but this does not appear to be much of a consolation to her. She has developed headaches for the first time in her life that do not respond to over-the-counter remedies. Although Mr. Ardine's health has not deteriorated further since the stroke, Mrs. Ardine pesters his doctor a couple of days a week with concerns about minor changes in his physical condition. She feels he is not eating enough, is irritable more than usual, and seems weaker on the side of his body not

(continued)

affected by the stroke. Mr. Ardine has been examined by his physician who is unable to find any new medical problems, but cannot convince Mrs. Ardine of that fact.

Despite constant attention from her grandchildren, Mrs. Ardine says she feels lonely. Caring for her husband has isolated her from friends and extended family members and restricts how often she can leave the apartment to visit with others in the neighborhood. She always feels tired. She tries to nap when her husband is sleeping during the day, but she has difficulty falling asleep and staying asleep.

Preliminary Diagnosis
Mrs. Ardine has several clear symptoms of anxiety:

- Excessive worry about her husband's health and well-being despite no apparent problems in addition to the stroke; yet, an unwillingness to find a solution to the problem as she perceives it
- Chronic concern about finances even with a good income
- Sleep disturbances
- Somatic complaints of fatigue and headaches

The distinguishing feature of these symptoms is that there are adequate safeguards in place for Mrs. Ardine's worries about her husband's health and their finances. His health is not deteriorating according to the physician, and both income and insurance are adequate should this situation change. She is not asking that anything change, but appears fixated on situations that are essentially not problematic. Looking more closely, a number of other symptoms indicate that anxiety is not the only issue for Mrs. Ardine:

- Fatigue despite good health
- Sleep difficulties
- Sense of isolation and loneliness
- Brooding mood

These symptoms would indicate Mrs. Ardine is probably struggling with depression as well as anxiety. Her husband's occasional verbal abuse, the stresses of caregiving for both her husband and grandchildren, and a lack of social contacts with old friends and neighbors are all factors that would contribute to depression. Further evaluation is needed to determine whether the depression is the primary condition with secondary anxiety or vice versa.

Summary

Depression, dementia, delirium, and anxiety are four of the most common cognitive and emotional problems observed in elders. Depression is distinguished by its primary effect on an elder's mood and affect, while dementia affects cognitive and intellectual functioning. Delirium mimics dementia, but is distinguished by its sudden onset and relationship to a biological cause that can frequently be reversed. Anxiety is typified by an excessive worrying, irrational fears, and somatic complaints, but may be anxious behavior and not an anxiety disorder. Distinguishing between the major presenting symptoms, essential features of each condition, and the risk factors associated with the development of each is the essence of differential assessment and diagnosis, which are the focus of this chapter. Assessment and diagnosis are complicated because the conditions frequently mimic each other or occur together. An inaccurate assessment of any of these conditions can have disastrous consequences. Untreated depression can lead to an elder's attempt to commit suicide just to escape the pain of chronic sadness and feelings of worthlessness. Elders who show signs of increasing inability to manage in familiar home environments may suffer accelerated decline in physical health or be dangerous to themselves or others. Left untreated, delirium can result in death for an elder who succumbs to physical exhaustion or physical illness. Chronic anxiety can leave elders prisoners in their own homes, suffering increasing social and emotional isolation. It is imperative that the gerontological social worker be able to make the preliminary distinctions between these four conditions and encourage elders and their families to secure treatment, the topic of the next chapter.

Check Out These Websites!

1. www.alz.org The Alzheimer's Association has 220 local chapters and 2000 support groups throughout the country. This website is aimed at both families who need more information about the disease and professionals who work with elders. It includes exceptional educational materials that describe Alzheimer's disease in detail, discuss current treatment options, and identify resources in different areas of the country.

2. www.ahcpr.gov/guide Sponsored by the Agency for Health Care Policy and Research, this site offers extensive materials on Alzheimer's disease, including clinical practice guidelines, aimed at health and mental health practitioners. It offers helpful suggestions for working with families and community resources.

3. www.nimh.nih.gov/publica/over65.htm An educational booklet describing depression can be downloaded from this site and shared with elders and their families. The material is presented in simple language and offers suggestions for finding resources in local communities. The website also describes current treatments for depression in a hopeful and encouraging tone. Links to other information on dementia and anxiety from the National Institute of Mental Health are provided.

4. www.healthindex.org This site identifies links to a wide variety of information about depression, dementia, and anxiety as well as other mental health problems found in elders. It includes links to the American Medical Association and the Centers for Disease Control. These organizations provide information on current research being conducted in the general field of elder mental and physical health and aimed primarily at health and mental health professionals.

References

American Psychiatric Association. (1994). *Diagnostic and statistical manual of mental disorders* (4th ed.). Washington, DC: Author.

Andreson, G. (1992). How to assess the older mind. *RN* (July), 34–40.

Beck, J. G., Stanley, M. A., & Zebb, B. J. (1999). Effectiveness of the Hamilton Anxiety Scale with older Generalized Anxiety Disorder patients. *Journal of Clinical Geropsychology, 5*(4), 281–290.

Bieling, P. J., Antony, M. M., & Swindon, R. P. (1998). The Stait-Trait Anxiety Inventory, Trait version: Structure and content re-rexamined. *Behaviour Research and Therapy, 36*(7/8), 777–778.

Bergmann, K. (1978). Neurosis and personality disorder in old age. In A. D. Isaacs & F. Post (Eds.), *Studies in geriatric psychiatry* (pp. 176–194). Chichester, England: John Wiley & Sons.

Burnette, D., & Mui, A. C. (1994). Determination of self-reported depressive symptoms by frail elders living alone. *Journal of Gerontological Social Work, 22*(1/2), 3–19.

Butler, R. N., Lewis, M. I., & Sunderland, T. (1998). *Aging and mental health: Positive psychosocial and biomedical approaches.* Boston: Allyn and Bacon.

Cameron, D. E. (1941). Studies in senile nocturnal delirium. *Psychiatric Quarterly, 15*, 47–53.

Christison, C., & Blazer, D. (1988). Clinical assessment of psychiatric symptoms. In M. S. Albert & M. B. Moss (Eds.), *Geriatric neuropsychology* (pp. 82–99). New York: Guilford Press.

Costa, P. T., Jr., Williams, T. F., & Somerfield, M. (1996). *Early identification of Alzheimer's Disease and related dementias. Clinical practice guideline, Quick reference guide for clinicians, No. 19* (AHCPR Publication No. 97-0703). Rockville, MD: U.S. Department of Health and Human Services, Public Health Service, Agency for Health Care Policy and Research.

Diagnosis and treatment of depression in late life. (1991). *National Institute of Health Consensus Statement Online.* November 4–6 (cited 2/3/99), *9*(3), 1–17.

Dickey, M. (1999). *Anxiety disorders* (NIH Publication #99-3879). Rockville, MD: National Institute of Health.

Dorfman, R. A., Lubben, J. E., Mayer-Oakes, A., Atchinson, K., Schweitzer, S. O., DeJong, F. J., & Matthias, R. E. (1995). Screening for depression among a well-elderly population. *Social Work, 40*(30), 295–304.

Flint, A. J. (1994). Epidemiology and co-morbidity of anxiety disorders in the elders. *American Journal of Psychiatry, 151*(5), 640–649.

Gallagher-Thompson, D., & Coon, D. W. (1996). Depression. In J. I. Sheikh & I. D. Yalom (Eds.), *Treating the elderly* (pp. 1–44). San Francisco: Jossey-Bass.

Gurian, B., & Goisman, R. (1993). Anxiety disorders and the elderly. *Generations* (Winter/Spring), 39–42.

Hamdy, R. C., & Turnbull, J. M. (1998). Alzheimer's disease: An overview. In R. C. Hamdy, J. M. Turnbull, J. Edwards, & M. M. Lancaster (Eds.), *Alzheimer's disease: A handbook for caregivers* (3rd ed., pp. 1–7). St. Louis, MO: Mosby.

Hurh, W. M., & Kim, K. C. (1988). *Uprooting and adjustment: A sociological study of Korean immigrants' mental health.* Final Report to National Institute of Mental Health (Grant No. 1 RO1 MH40312-01/5 RO1 MH 40312-02). Macomb, IL: Department of Sociology and Anthropology, Western Illinois University.

Husaini, B. A. (1997). Predictors of depression among the elderly: Racial differences over time. *American Journal of Orthopsychiatry, 67*(1), 48–58.

Inouye, S. K., Bogardus, S. T., Charpentier, P. A., Leo-Summers, L., Acampora, D., Holford, T. R.,

& Cooney, L. M. (1999). A multicomponent intervention to prevent delirium in hospital-ized older patients. *New England Journal of Medicine, 340*(9), 669–676.

Koh, S. D., Ceca, K. M., Koh, T. H., & Liu, W. T. (1986). *Mental health and stress in Asian American elderly.* Chicago: Pacific/Asian American Mental Health Research Center.

Levin, J. S., Chatters, L. M., & Taylor, R. J. (1995). Religious effects on health status and life satis-faction among Black Americans. *Journal of Gerontology, 50B,* S154-163.

Lindesay, J. (1991). Phobic disorders in the elderly. *British Journal of Psychiatry, 159,* 531–541.

Mahard, R. (1989). Elderly Puerto Rican women in the continental United States. In C. Garcia & L. Mattei (Eds.), *The psychosocial development of Puerto Rican women* (pp. 75–91). New York: Praeger.

Manson, S. M. (1995). Mental health status and needs of the American Indian and Alaska Native elderly. In D. K. Padgett (Ed.), *Handbook on ethnicity, aging, and mental health* (pp. 132–141). Westport, CT: Greenwood Press.

Markides, K., & Mandel, C. H. (1987). *Aging and ethnicity.* Newbury Park, CA: Sage.

Markovitz, P. J. (1993). Treatment of anxiety in the elderly. *Journal of Clinical Psychiatry, 54*(5-supp.), 64–68.

Mosher-Ashley, P. M., & Barrett, P. W. (1997). *A life worth living: Practical strategies for reducing depression in older adults.* Baltimore, MD: Health Sciences Press.

National Indian Council on Aging. (1981). *American Indian elderly: A national profile.* Albuquer-que, NM: Author.

National Institute of Mental Health. (1996). *If you're over 65 and feeling depressed: Treatment brings new hope* (NIH Publication No. 96-4033). Rockville, MD: Author.

National Policy and Resource Center on Women and Aging. (1998). Identifying and coping with depression. *Women and Aging Letter, 2*(5), 1–9.

Neligh, G., & Scully, J. (1990). Differential diagnosis of major mental disorders among American Indian elderly. In U.S. Department of Health and Human Services, *Minority Aging* (DHHS Publication No. HRS-P-DV 904). Washington, DC: U.S. Government Printing Office.

Sheikh, J. I. (1996). Anxiety disorders. In J. I. Sheikh & I. D. Yalom (Eds.), *Treating the elderly* (pp. 75–103). San Francisco: Jossey-Bass.

Sloan, P. (1998). Neuropsychological assessment of dementia. In R. C. Hamdy, J. M. Turnbull, J. Edwards, & M. M. Lancaster (Eds.), *Alzheimer's disease: A handbook for caregivers* (3rd ed., pp. 27–40). St. Louis, MO: Mosby.

Turnbull, J. E., & Mui, A. C. (1995). Mental health status and needs of black and white elderly: Differences in depression. In D. K. Padgett (Ed.), *Handbook on ethnicity, aging, and mental health* (pp. 73–98). Westport, CT: Greenwood Press.

6

Social Work Interventions in the Socioemotional and Cognitive Problems of Elders

Introduction

This chapter describes interventions used to treat elders who struggle with depression, early stages of dementia, and anxiety. They include cognitive-behavioral work, reminiscence, and life review, interventions designed to help elders gain insight into their own behavior and feelings. These interventions are generally geared toward elders who are verbal and capable of the intellectual and emotional rigor exacted by "talk" approaches to resolving emotional difficulties. The next chapter will explore alternatives to talk therapies—such as art, music, exercise, and pet therapy—which may be appropriate for both high-functioning elders and elders who have severe cognitive or communicative limitations. The use of drug and electroconvulsive therapies is discussed briefly to familiarize gerontological social workers with medical interventions that may be prescribed to accompany verbal approaches to treating depression and anxiety.

In reality, every contact with elders whether through a formal clinical setting or sharing a cup of coffee during a home visit is potentially therapeutic. Every connection a social worker makes through developing a relationship with an elder can improve the elder's psychosocial functioning. Intervening in the socioemotional and cognitive problems of elders combines knowledge of the process of aging with a systematic, carefully considered approach to identifying the problem, exploring alternative solutions, applying solutions, and evaluating the intervention.

What Happens in the Process of an Intervention?

What do gerontological social workers do when they implement an intervention? Despite a social worker's magical thinking about "saving people" or "changing the world," social workers do one of two things in working with clients. In some cases, social workers help clients *change* a situation that is painful, dangerous, or unbearable. Interventions aimed at helping depressed elders may focus on ways to address the origin of the depression—such as inappropriate medication, physical illness, or prolonged bereavement—and help elders to modify something in an effort to alleviate the depression. Finding new social contacts, getting more physical exercise, or addressing grief through traditional "talk therapy" are all aimed at changing the situation causing emotional distress. In other situations, social workers are working with elders to help them *adjust* to a situation that cannot be changed. The medical community does not know how to reverse the debilitating effects of Alzheimer's disease or totally rehabilitate an elder left paralyzed by a stroke. Spouses and lifelong friends cannot be replaced when they are lost to death. In these cases, situations facing elders may not be able to be changed, but elders can change their responses to the situations. While there is no cure for Alzheimer's disease today, good physical and emotional care for elders can slow the devastating effects of the disease and improve the quality of life for both elders and caregivers. The physical damage caused by a stroke may not respond to efforts at physical rehabilitation, but assistive devices, such as an electric wheelchair, can help elders regain some sense of control over their environment, thereby improving their emotional well-being. A lonely widow may learn to reconnect to a world without her husband by directing her affection and concern to children in an intergenerational day care center or a children's hospital. The cause of the problem cannot be changed, but the elder's response can be. It is important for both the elder and the social worker to be clear about the exact focus of any intervention effort.

Empowerment as a Goal of Intervention

A sense of control over life and the ability to continue to make decisions about both long- and short-term plans are the best predictors of emotional well-being among elders. Elders need to feel that despite health problems or loss of friends and family members, they are still in charge of their lives, continuing to function as independent and competent adults. Family members may be well intentioned when they assume responsibility for all financial and logistical decisions for frail elders, but taking all decision making away from elders is ill-advised. Rather than looking for ways to take power away from elders, sound gerontological practice looks for ways to empower elders, to enhance the areas over which they have control in their lives. For elders living in the community, it means the choice of where to live and what to do with their time. For elders living in institutional settings, choice and power may be limited to deciding what to wear or what personal belongings to bring to a new living setting. Often it is not the size of the decision, but the ability to make it that empowers elders.

    The empowerment perspective in social work practice refers to a collection of theoretical approaches that emphasizes the process and product of helping clients gain or reclaim power over their lives (Cox & Parsons, 1994; Gutierrez, 1990).

The approach has been applied to a wide variety of client populations, but has become particularly appealing in social work interventions with women, elders, and persons of color as a response to their sociohistorical oppression. The actual process of gaining or reclaiming power is therapeutic. Empowerment is also a philosophical attitude about working with elders that intentionally avoids the hierarchical distinction between social worker as expert and elder as client. The relationship between social worker and client is one of mutual power with both worker and client engaged in collective action to bring change. The worker and client focus on strengths and assets rather than weaknesses and liabilities.

Cox and Parsons (1994) developed an empowerment model for work with elders that employs change on four dimensions. Dimension One focuses on individual work through the identification of individual needs and raising the individual's awareness of the powerlessness from which the problem originates or through which it is maintained. Coping with the tasks of the aging process through small-group or educational activities is the primary focus of Dimension Two of the empowerment approach. The small self-help group process sensitizes elders to their shared interests and lays the groundwork for the collective action targeted in the next two dimensions. Dimension Three addresses change in clients' immediate environment, such as access to local health care, social services, income maintenance, or transportation. Dimension Four moves beyond the immediate world of the client to focus on the political problems of groups of elders, such as age discrimination, health care, or other social policy dimensions. While it may be unusual for a gerontological social worker to have the opportunity to apply all four dimensions of the empowerment model in work with elders, the philosophical tenet of approaching elders' problems from the perspective of loss of power can be done on any level of intervention (McInnis-Dittrich, 1997). It is important to find ways to maximize an elder's sense of empowerment over his or her life regardless of the elder's emotional or cognitive condition.

Whose Goals?

Working toward empowerment of elders also implies that the social worker respect and honor what elders want for themselves. It is easy to acknowledge the importance of self-determination in facilitating clients' choice about the direction and focus of any proposed change effort. However, it is more difficult to see this principle in action in working with elders. How does the worker balance the wishes of the elder with the requests of the family? Whose goals take priority? For example, Mrs. Elway is a 88-year-old widow who wants desperately to stay in her home of 60 years. This is possible if she has homemaker services, Meals-on-Wheels, and a visiting nurse. Her family, however, is afraid as she becomes increasingly frail that she will fall and would like to see her moved to an assisted-living facility. Whose goals should guide the final decision?

Does the answer change if the family informs the worker that they will help pay for assisted-living but not in-home services? Does it make a difference if the worker agrees that she could fall even if she has not fallen yet? Does it matter if

Mrs. Elway shows the early signs of dementia although she seems to manage fine in her home with the identified support systems? Working with elders who face difficult decisions about maintaining their independence, relinquishing power over their finances, and making end-of-life decisions is an ethical minefield. Elders are adults who retain legal rights to decide about their own well-being unless otherwise determined by a court of law. Never lose sight of *whose goals* are the focus of any intervention effort.

Obstacles to Intervention and Treatment with Elders

Attitudes about Interventions

One of the most difficult obstacles to securing interventions for elders, especially conventional mental health treatment, is a prevailing attitude that the intervention of a gerontological social worker is for crazy people or people who have been dysfunctional their entire lives. The current cohort of elders may not be familiar with or interested in psychological theories about human behavior and emotions. Some elders harbor the continuing belief that people bring their troubles on themselves. They may believe that depression and anxiety are due to character flaws rather than to emotional reactions to a complex array of difficult biopsychosocial events that occur in the lives of many older adults. For elders who have functioned well throughout their lives, the idea of talking to a complete stranger who is most often younger than they are about deeply personal problems is simply not acceptable. They cannot believe anyone outside of the immediate circle of family and friends could possibly understand, nor is it any of their business. Elders who have these attitudes about involving a helping professional in problem solving and mental health practices may offer formidable resistance to any efforts to engage them in the intervention process.

Somatization of Emotional Conflicts

Elders may be unfamiliar with the language of professional helping and find it difficult to identify feelings at all. Either they feel okay or they do not feel okay, and those feelings are more likely to be associated with physical health than emotional well-being. The tendency of elders to somatize feelings—convert unpleasant emotions into physical complaints—has been emphasized throughout this book. It is the reason they are more likely to seek treatment from physical health care providers than from mental health professionals. Helping elders develop an awareness of a variety of feeling states may be an essential part of the intervention process. Part of this phenomenon is the resistance to engage in self-reflection, which may be seen as self-centeredness, a socially unacceptable character trait. They may feel that people who obsess about themselves are selfish or bring on undesirable feelings by fixating on what they are feeling. Thinking about depression or talking about it with others may be seen as a road to creating, rather than curing, depression.

Physical Barriers

There are also very real physical barriers to implementing services for elders including a lack of specially designed services for elders in both rural and urban areas. Social workers who have great expertise in working with children and adolescents may be poorly trained to understand the unique needs of elders. Inappropriate services may be more detrimental than no service at all. If services do exist, elders may not be able to access those services due to lack of transportation or an inability to get into a building that is not equipped to handle wheelchairs or walkers. Negotiating the obstacles of phone trees and voice mail needed to make an appointment may be discouraging for elders who prefer to talk to a real person. Faced with too many choices of what service to call or no choices at all may force elders to abandon any efforts to get help.

Cultural Barriers

Cultural barriers present another obstacle for elders seeking help for both mental health and socioenvironmental problems. They may feel uncomfortable talking to a social worker of a different racial or ethnic background, who is not intimately familiar with "the ways things are" in their own cultural group. English may not be their native language. It is difficult enough to talk about personal problems in one's own language, but straddling the language barrier while trying to convey feelings and thoughts may be overwhelming. Even if it is possible for elders to find a mental health professional who speaks their own language, the age difference between them presents an obstacle for both the elder and the worker. In many cultures, elders hold a deeply respected position, and younger persons are expected to defer to their elders and honor them. Probing for deep feelings or confronting the elder is not acceptable. Asking an elder to change a behavior or challenging long-held beliefs—a necessary part of many interventions—is considered offensive.

For the vast majority of elders who have neither the personal resources nor excellent private medical insurance, the inability to pay for services remains a formidable obstacle. If an elder has supplementary insurance to Medicare or relies on Medical Assistance alone, both the mental health care provider authorized to provide treatment and the number of treatment sessions are usually strictly regulated. While a worker may consider ten sessions the minimum needed to treat a serious depression or anxiety disorder, insurance companies are more likely to authorize far fewer sessions. Medicare pays for only part of the cost of mental health treatment considered medically necessary and requires elders to cover the rest. The cost of treatment may simply be prohibitive for elders to even consider.

Developing a Relationship with an Elder

Helping Elders Understand the Purpose and Process of an Intervention

Elders may be particularly suspicious about engaging in a professional helping relationship. In part, this is due to prevailing attitudes among elders about who needs to see a social worker or equating any intervention with mental illness. Seeking help is a sign of strength, not a sign of weakness. In their later years, elders may experience a host of changes they cannot control, such as physical aging and the loss of family or friends. Applauding their efforts to exert control over their emotional well-being and to be active participants in solving their problems rather than resigning themselves to live with uncomfortable emotional states helps elders to build confidence in their abilities to do something that will make them feel better. This is a situation in which the social worker can play the role of coach as well as counselor.

Emphasize the mutuality of the goal-setting process. Too often clients of all ages assume the social worker knows best and is most qualified to decide the goals of the intervention effort for them. This can spell disaster. Taking the time to find out what elders want to be different and what they expect to accomplish in their time with the social worker is absolutely essential. Reiterating the fact that any intervention is about what they want, not what the worker wants, is extremely important. It is often during this initial discussion that the social worker finds out who really thinks there is problem—the elder or family members. Sending an elder to a social worker "to get fixed" will not work. Elders need to be actively involved in establishing goals that they are willing to commit to, not those goals that reflect what others expect of them.

Elders may be particularly uncomfortable about disclosing personal information out of concern about who will have access to the information shared. Elders who are dependent on caregiving from family members may hesitate to ever reveal feelings or concerns that might imperil the caregiving relationship. Be totally honest about who has access to the content of case records. If you can assure elders of absolute confidentiality, do so. If, in fact, your findings will be shared with family members or other health care providers, you owe the elder complete honesty. Elders have an ethical and legal right to know who will have access to the social worker's records and how much of what transpires during the intervention process will be shared with others.

Recognize that elders may have great difficulty identifying and expressing feelings. Social workers may be hypersensitive about the significance of feelings. Another's inability to identify feelings may be misinterpreted as resistance rather than a genuine difficulty in figuring out how they feel. Reassuring elders that identifying and processing feelings is not an easy process and that it becomes easier with more experience should help the elders feel more comfortable.

Explain what the helping process entails. What will happen in a typical session? What is the social worker doing while the elder is talking about his or her life? How long do sessions last? Who pays for the sessions? Even if adjustments need to be made in these areas, elders need to have a preliminary idea of what they can expect before they invest in the helping process. Social workers need to be prepared to answer questions about their qualifications and what makes them knowledgeable about working with elders. Elders may identify a social worker as synonymous with a caseworker with the public assistance office and be very confused about his or her competence in the range of activities involved in gerontological social work.

Developing Rapport

Slow down! Most novice social workers jump into the intervention process too quickly, leaving elders overwhelmed and frightened. Elders need time to warm up and feel comfortable sharing personal information with a social worker. Taking several minutes to visit with the elder before broaching deep psychological issues gives the elder some space and time to make the transition into the session. Showing concern about the elder as a total person also conveys the message that the social worker sees the elder as a person, not as a psychological or social problem.

It is essential in every helping relationship to communicate respect for the client. For elders, this means valuing and utilizing their life experiences. Talking about how it was so different years ago is important in helping elders to identify previous coping strategies and consider how these coping strategies can be applied to current situations. Acknowledging the "way it used to be" may be important to processing the reality of life today. The social worker needs to be able to help the elder make the psychological connection between earlier life experiences and current life challenges. The point here is not to encourage elders to dwell on the past but to use the value of perspective for insight. Elders may repeat the same story over and over during the intervention process. It is important that the social worker acknowledge that he or she is familiar with the story the elder is telling and probe for the meaning of its being repeated. Knight (1996) suggested that elders repeat themselves because they are so used to not being listened to in the first place. The social worker should use active listening skills to convey the message that he or she is listening and is interested in what these stories mean to the elder.

Acknowledge cultural differences when they exist. Expressing an interest in learning about how an elder's experience is different because of membership in ethnic and cultural groups is a wonderful way to build rapport with an elder. Drawing on the strengths of an elder's cultural group is essential to the success of the intervention process. Ignoring cultural differences is its own kind of prejudice and devalues the importance of the cultural and ethnic context in which elders have lived.

The importance of recognizing and accommodating physical limitations has been emphasized throughout this book and is especially significant in individual work with elders. If an elder has hearing limitations, speak slowly and clearly. An elder with impaired vision may need more visual clues to utilize written materials. If an elder has physical disabilities that make sitting for long periods of time uncomfortable, take more frequent breaks or schedule shorter meetings.

Cognitive-Behavioral Therapy

Cognitive-behavioral therapy (CBT) is a common intervention approach used in all age groups for a variety of emotional problems, including depression and anxiety. This type of therapy explores the relationship between thoughts (the cognitive sphere) and subsequent feelings and behavior (Adler, 1963; Beck, 1995; Ellis, 1962; Lantz, 1996). Events that occur in people's lives generate automatic, unpremeditated thoughts about what those events mean. An individual's interpretation of the meaning of those events in turn precipitates a feeling state that determines people's behavior. As a student, you are very familiar with the sequence of events that follow the announcement of a paper deadline. Your immediate thought may be, "I am not good at writing papers, and this will be very difficult for me." The feeling state that follows may be one of panic and terror or, for others, mild anxiety. The behavioral response for those who panic may be to delay the paper writing activity for as long as possible to avoid the panic and anxiety. For others, the anxiety may be a good incentive to get started on the paper early or to get additional help from the instructor in an effort to control the anxious response. The same event (announcement of a paper deadline) elicits different emotional responses or feeling states (panic, confusion, or anxiety) and consequently different behavioral responses (avoid the paper, start the paper, or drop the course). See Table 6.1.

Cognitive-behavioral therapy is based on the assumption that both cognitive and behavioral responses to events are learned. Therefore, through a process of relearning, people can change both their emotional responses to events and situations and the behavior that follows. This process involves helping people to identify emotional and behavioral responses to events and substitute more adaptive, effective responses. The ultimate goal of CBT is change in both an individual's emotional state and behavior patterns. This type of therapy is considered a

TABLE 6.1 *The Cognitive-Behavioral Connection*

A	B	C	
Situation or Event	*Thought Following the Situation/Event*	*Mood/Feeling State*	*Behavior*
Announcement of a paper deadline	"I am not good at writing papers. This will be difficult for me."	Anxiety, panic, withdrawal, or denial	Procrastinate, start the paper immediately, get help, or withdraw from the course

Source: Adapted from Mosher-Ashley & Barrett, 1997, and Yost et al., 1986.

psychoeducational approach to treating both depression and anxiety in elders. It is not enough for elders to begin to connect situations, thoughts, and feelings with behavior. They also need to learn about common errors in thinking and what to do about them to eliminate troubling thoughts and feelings. In this context, CBT will be applied to working with individuals, although some mental health professionals believe that this approach is most effective with elders when applied in the group setting (Yost, Beutler, Corbishley, & Allender, 1986) or when used in conjunction with medication.

Elders Who Respond Best to Cognitive-Behavioral Therapy

Cognitive-behavioral therapy is not appropriate for use with all elders who experience depression or anxiety. It is most effective with elders who are verbal and have few, if any, cognitive impairments because the cognitive-behavioral process requires that elders be able to identify thoughts and discuss feelings. This ability to engage in abstract thinking and analyze behavior is the cornerstone of the cognitive-behavioral approach. Elders must also be able to self-disclose and be willing to do so with the social worker. The approach has shown limited usefulness in work with elders who are highly autonomous or have extreme difficulty asking for or receiving help (Mosher-Ashley & Barrett, 1997). In other words, elders have to want to participate in the process of making connections between thoughts and feelings. No matter how much the social worker can see how cognitive distortions are causing an elder to remain depressed or become anxious, it is the elder's insight, not the worker's, that changes how the elder feels.

Elders with severe memory problems or a limited attention span may not be appropriate for CBT. Elders have to first learn which situations trigger painful thoughts and emotions and recognize those triggers in future situations. This requires not only the ability to concentrate intensely but also the willingness to do so. Severely anxious elders may not be able to concentrate during sessions and internalize the process. In cases of severe depression or later stages of dementia, memory is often impaired, making it difficult for elders to retain information about the process from one week to another. This approach is also not appropriate for elders who have exhibited suicidal ideations (Yost et al., 1986).

Cognitive-behavioral therapy may not be appropriate for elders who are actively abusing alcohol or drugs. These substances interfere with normal cognitive functioning. However, once elders are free of mind-altering substances, CBT may prove helpful not only in treating depression and anxiety but also in addressing some of the underlying dynamics of the addictive process.

The Process of Cognitive-Behavioral Therapy

The process of CBT involves four distinct phases, which have been adapted for use with elders by Yost and others (1986). These phases will be described briefly, using examples of how the process begins with identifying a simple connection between events and feelings and then expands into an analytical approach to recognizing the intricate connection between events, thoughts, feelings, and behavior.

Preparation.   Before actually helping elders identify the connection between thoughts and feelings, it is important for the worker to spend time developing the relationship with the elder. Elders need to have clear ideas about what they expect to change as a result of participating in the process. During the preparation phase, the social worker discusses the symptoms of depression or anxiety (whichever is appropriate to the intervention) including common causes of the condition, how it can affect an elder's functioning, and reassurances that the condition can be treated. This phase gives the social worker an opportunity to explain what CBT entails and why it is important to identify how situations, thoughts, feelings, and behavior are connected.

These activities serve two purposes. They allow elders to carefully consider their own role in the process and to clarify their expectations. What do they want to be different in their lives? Are they willing to be critical observers of their own behavior? Do they believe they can change? These questions form the basis for what is known as the pre-affiliation process in therapy. Second, it gives the social worker the opportunity to consider whether CBT is the right approach for the elder and to lay the initial groundwork for developing the helping relationship with the elder. Does the elder have realistic expectations about the process? Does the elder have the ability and interest in committing to a process of intense introspection? Can the social worker and elder develop a trusting, open relationship?

Collaboration-Identification.   Once the social worker and elder have decided to continue with CBT, it is important that both commit to collaborating with each other. In work with elders, it may be necessary for the worker to self-disclose more than is usually typical in other kinds of intervention. The elder may need more personal information about the worker to feel comfortable and develop trust.

In this phase of CBT, the elder is introduced to the process of identifying the relationship between situations and feelings. The worker verbally explores situations in which an elder is acutely aware of being depressed or anxious, helping the elder see how certain situations and events are followed by particular feelings. These situations may be recorded on a chart similar to the one that appears in Table 6.2. It may take some time for elders to feel comfortable making the connections. The worker plays an important role in helping the elder clarify situations and subsequent feelings. Completion of the chart is often assigned as homework between sessions to give the elder an opportunity to consider the connections outside sessions.

Once the elder is able to make these connections independently, another step is added to the process. The elder is asked to identify what thought preceded the emotional response to the situation. What did the event mean to him or her?

TABLE 6.2   *Sample of Two-Column Record Used in the Identification/Collaboration Phase of Cognitive-Behavioral Therapy*

A *Situation or Event*	B *Mood/Feeling State*
Elderly woman does not hear from one of her children on her birthday	Sad, alone, unloved
Elderly man needs to use walker after hip surgery	Foolish, handicapped, useless, dependent, embarrassed
Elderly woman can no longer cook for extended family members on Sundays	Useless, failed in family responsibilities, no longer a productive family member

Source: Adapted from Mosher-Ashley & Barrett, 1997.

This additional step is shown in Table 6.3. Through this activity, the elder becomes aware of the threefold connection of situations or events, the cognitive response or thought, and the subsequent feelings. The worker uses the charts as educational tools to help elders identify triggers for troublesome feelings.

Yost and his associates (1986) suggested that, during this phase of CBT, behavioral components be introduced to the helping process. It is not enough for a depressed or anxious elder simply to identify the triggers for bothersome feelings. An awareness of dysfunctional thoughts does not by itself alleviate elders'

TABLE 6.3   *Sample of Three-Column Record Used to Introduce the Thought Process in Cognitive-Behavioral Therapy*

A *Situation or Event*	B *Thought Generated by Situation or Event*	C *Mood/Feeling State*
Elderly woman does not hear from one of her children on her birthday	"I am not important enough to remember on my birthday. He must not care about me."	Sad, alone, unloved
Elderly man needs to use walker after hip surgery	"I cannot even walk without help. I cannot let my friends see me like this. What kind of man am I?"	Foolish, handicapped, useless, dependent, embarrassed
Elderly woman can no longer cook for extended family members on Sundays	"It is my job to take care of this family and keep it together. Now I cannot do that."	Useless, failed in family responsibilities, no longer a productive family member

depression or anxiety. They must begin to look at active ways to facilitate more positive feelings as well as a means of regaining mastery over their lives. For example, when elders are depressed, they often lose interest in activities they once considered pleasurable, such a gardening, socializing, or reading. Loss of these pleasurable activities exacerbates the depression. The more depressed an elder becomes, the less interest he or she has in returning to favorite activities, and the downward spiral continues. A behavioral component often introduced in this phase of CBT is helping elders identify those once pleasurable activities and committing time to resuming them. The social worker may ask an elder to construct a chart of his or her daily schedule and mutually identify a time when the elder will make a concerted effort to engage in those activities. Other times, it may be more helpful to break down resumption of such activities into small steps that can be accomplished every day. If an elder once enjoyed reading, it may be necessary to start with the identification of a book to read. Getting the book is the second step. Reading one chapter is the next step. The process continues until the elder is once again engaged in the reading process. This process is intended to empower the elder to regain control over life as a part of treating a depression. For elders suffering from anxiety, this behavioral component may include systematic desensitization, thought stopping, or relaxation techniques to be employed when an elder feels anxious. Giving elders specific tools to apply when they are feeling either depressed or anxious is part of the behavioral component of CBT.

Change Phase.   Once elders recognize the connection between events, thoughts, and feelings, they can begin to identify and correct their own cognitive distortions. What is dysfunctional about the way I am thinking? Am I reacting in a rational manner or perhaps reading more into a situation than is warranted? Examples of cognitive distortions include globalizing, "awfulizing," mind reading, self-blaming, unrealistic demands on others, unrealistic expectations of self, and exaggerated self-importance. It is easy to see how errors in thinking can lead an elder to have a very painful emotional reaction. If an elder believes that not receiving a phone call on Sunday from an adult child means the child does not love him or her anymore, it is not surprising that the elder would get depressed. If an elder thinks that every wrong number is actually an harassing phone call, it is not surprising that several wrong numbers in a row could create some level of anxiety. Cognitive-behavioral therapy is aimed at helping elders recognize these cognitive distortions and examine their own thought processes.

The three-column connection between thoughts and feelings created in the identification phase of treatment can then be expanded to include a fourth column that helps the elder identify corrective techniques, as shown in Table 6.4.

Not only can the elder catch the distorted thinking before it creates emotional havoc, but also he or she can employ corrective behavioral actions to gain control over the situation. For example, if an adult child does not call on Sunday afternoon as is expected by an elder, the elder can call the adult child. In many respects, the process should give elders the power to decide, "What can I do to make myself feel better?" Taking positive steps empowers the elder to regain

TABLE 6.4   *Sample of Introducing Corrective Techniques to the Cognitive-Behavioral Connection*

A Situation or Event	B Thought	C Mood/Feeling State	D Corrective Action
Elderly woman does not hear from one of her children on her birthday	"I am not important enough to remember on my brithday. He must not care about me."	Sad, alone, unloved	This is an example of *awfulizing,* taking one situation and deriving global disaster from it. Substitute thinking: "He must be very busy these days. I should call him to let him know how much I love him."
Elderly man needs to use walker after hip surgery	"I cannot even walk without help. I cannot let my friends see me like this. What kind of man am I?"	Foolish, handicapped, useless, dependent, embarrassed	This is an example of having *unrealistic expectations of oneself.* Substitute thinking: "I am happy I can get around with a walker. My friends will be happy to have me back even if it takes me a little longer."
Elderly woman can no longer cook for extended family members on Sundays	"It is my job to take care of this family and keep it together. Now I cannot do that."	Useless, failed in family responsibilities, no longer a productive family member	Another example of *unrealistic expectations of oneself.* Substitute thinking: "I did a good job of cooking all these years. Now it is time for me to pass on the responsibilities to my daughters. People will under-stand."

mastery over the environment. Regaining control helps individuals move from re-acting to things over which they feel they have no control to becoming proactive.

Behavioral techniques employed in this phase of intervention include stimu-lus control and behavioral rehearsal. *Stimulus control* refers to rearranging, elimi-nating, or minimizing the effect of troublesome stimuli. For example, if Sunday afternoons are a particularly difficult time for a recently widowed elder who asso-ciates that time with special time with his or her spouse, it may help to redefine that day with new activities. Instead of staying home getting depressed thinking about what Sundays used to be like, the elder may make a concentrated effort to visit with friends out of the house. Going to a movie or having dinner with a friend or family members on a regular basis may redefine what Sundays mean to the elder. Sundays become less of a stimulus for depression and are directed to more pleasurable activities. *Behavioral rehearsal* involves learning and rehearsing new behavior patterns for old or recurrent situations that are problematic. The social worker can be very helpful in suggesting new ways to handle old situations. Elders may have a lifetime of behavioral patterns that they simply do not know how to change.

Consolidation and Termination.   The final phase in CBT is the consolidation and termination stage. This stage is an integral part of the entire intervention process and means more than simply graciously ending a helping relationship. During the final phase of treatment, the social worker's job is to consolidate the changes observed during the treatment process. Reviewing with elders how far they have come, discussing what strengths they have developed in identifying emotions and thoughts, and reinforcing the belief that they can handle future challenges is part of this process. Elders need to leave the intervention process confident that they have learned the skills to continue to fight depression or anxiety. It may be helpful to outline specific strategies elders can employ in the future if troublesome emotions return. This can help relieve some of the fears elders may have about managing on their own.

The final task in this stage is for the social worker and elder to separate from each other. This may be accomplished in stages by scheduling appointments less frequently or moving from personal contacts to phone conversations. Talking about what the relationship has meant for both worker and elder is helpful in easing into the end of a professional relationship or at least redefining it. Worker and elder need to have a clear understanding about the ground rules for any future contact.

Cognitive-behavioral intervention offers elders opportunities to examine the connections between what they think and how those thoughts affect subsequent feelings and behaviors. The sense of self-awareness that develops as elders participate in CBT is intended to be carried over beyond the therapeutic relationship so that if troubling thoughts develop in future situations, elders have learned how to identify the source of those thoughts and feelings and to develop corrective actions on their own.

Validation Therapy

While a cognitive-behavioral approach may be appropriate for high-functioning elders, it is not effective in working with elders who experience cognitive dysfunction, such as that observed in dementia including Alzheimer's disease. In the 1960s, Naomi Feil, a gerontological social worker, developed an approach to communicating with elders with dementia, known as *validation therapy.* This approach is based on the assumption that all behaviors of persons with dementia are need driven. That is, even if what an elder says does not seem to make sense to anyone, every statement is an attempt to communicate with caregivers and others (Feil, 1967, 1984, 1993). Rather than attempt to orient elders with dementia to time and space, validation therapy respects the reality of the confused elder and uses the elder's reality, not the caregiver's, to understand what the elder is trying to communicate (Keady, 1999).

The Principles of Validation Therapy

Caregivers and professionals using a validation approach never argue with an elder with dementia regarding what constitutes reality or attempt to orient the elder to time or space if he or she does not explicitly want to be oriented. This approach recognizes that retreating to another time in life may be an attempt to reestablish a sense of safety and security (Day, 1997; Keady, 1999; Touzinsky, 1998). Elders with dementia may retain distant memories long after they have lost the ability to accurately determine where they are in the present. Other adult memories may represent a time when the elder felt a sense of mastery and control over his or her environment, therefore may be a "safe" place to retreat when the demands of living with dementia become overwhelming. For example, if an elderly widow with dementia keeps asking "Where is my husband?" even though her husband has been dead for many years, validation therapy would contend that this statement reflects the older woman's needs. Rather than correct the woman by reminding her that she is widowed and that her husband has been gone for many years, a validation approach would respond with a statement such as "You must miss your husband very much" or "I know it must be frightening to be alone right now." Rather than interpret the elder's statement as a reflection of her confusion, a validation approach interprets the statement as her expression of loneliness or grief that her husband is not with her.

A validation approach does not attempt to reinforce or extinguish behavior that is troublesome or annoying but accepts such behavior as an attempt on the part of the elder to communicate some need, thought, or feeling. For example, an elder with dementia who always gets agitated during bath time in a nursing home may be expressing a strong personal reaction to being bathed by a relative stranger or to the loss of privacy elders in an institutional setting often experience. The cognitive damage caused by the progressive nature of the dementia prevents the elder from saying explicitly, "I am uncomfortable with a woman I do not know bathing my naked body." Rather, the sentiment is expressed through uncooperative or hostile behavior. Rather then attempting to restrain the agitated elder or trying to reason with him or her, a validation approach would acknowledge to the elder that this must be embarrassing and reassure the elder that every attempt has been made to protect his or her privacy. Accepting the feelings of elders with dementia and respecting their attempts to communicate sheds a different light on caring for elders with dementia. Rather than just accepting difficult behavior as inevitable, a validation therapy approach takes a step back and tries to understand what the difficult behavior means.

The major focus of a validation approach is maintaining communication with an elder with dementia rather than actively resisting the cognitive decline that accompanies Alzheimer's disease and other dementias (Touzinsky, 1998). Family members and other caregivers who constantly try to correct the confusion inherent in elders with dementia soon become angry, resentful, and exhausted. It becomes so difficult for some family members to interact with an elder with dementia that after a while they do not even try to have any meaningful interaction. It is easier to make an obligatory visit to the elder and just accept that fact that he or she is not aware of visitors or can no longer interact with the visitor in any meaningful way. The validation approach suggests that caregivers and family members accept elders with dementia *where they are*. If an elder is lost in the reality of another time, respond to, rather than refute, that reality. For example, if an older woman is concerned about making sure someone is taking care of her young children (who are now all adults), reassuring her that someone she knew and trusted from that time in her life is caring for the children is more likely to calm her agitated state than trying to get her to understand that her children are all grown up and do not need to be looked after. Her concern is real and needs to be acknowledged rather than dismissed. Understanding the meaning of her behavior, rather than creating an awareness of reality, is the goal of this application of the validation approach (Day, 1997).

The Pros and Cons of the Validation Approach

Although the scientific validity of the validation approach has not been consistently demonstrated in controlled studies, small qualitative studies and anecdotal evidence support the effectiveness of this approach (Day, 1997). Feil (1993) observed improved speech, less regression, less crying, less wandering behavior, and improvements in gait, interaction, and eye contact among elders who were treated using the validation approach rather than a reorientation approach. She also found less need for physical or chemical restraints because of the reduction in aggressive or violent behavior. Other observers found that elders and their family members were able to communicate more successfully during visits, resulting in less frustration on the part of both the elder and caregivers (Babins, Dillion, & Merovitz, 1988; Fine & Rouse-Bane, 1995).

Other controlled studies found no statistically significant connection between the use of a validation approach and improvements in behavior among elders with dementia (Robb, Stegman, & Wolanin, 1986; Scanland & Emershaw, 1993). In the studies that both supported and refuted the effectiveness of validation therapy, very small, non-randomized samples were used without matched control groups without the establishment of credible pre-intervention behavior baselines. These limitations make it impossible to discount the value of the validation approach as well as fail to support it as an effective alternative to traditional reality orientation. Regardless, it offers an alternative to traditional approaches worthy of future research.

Reminiscence and Life Review

Reminiscence—the processing of remembering prior life events—serves a specific function for elders even when not applied in a strictly therapeutic sense. Erickson (1963) identified the final life stage task as resolving ego integrity versus ego despair. In order to do that, elders need to look back on their lives and derive a sense of accomplishment and meaning. "Did my life make a difference? Did it mean anything?" Elders may find their memories a source of great joy at a time when their social support networks are dwindling or their health is failing. Recalling positive accomplishments and identifying ways in which their lives were purposeful may contribute to their ability to achieve ego integrity. Other elders find their memories and reminiscing about their lives very painful. It is difficult for them to identify what good they have accomplished throughout their lives. They may come to the conclusion that their lives were a waste. Rather then achieve ego integrity, they experience ego despair.

Butler (1963; Butler et al., 1998) built on the work of Erik Erikson's developmental stage theory to suggest life review as a universal event in the lives of aging persons. He contends that life review is prompted by the awareness of the proximity of death—the reason the life review process is more likely to occur in elders than in younger populations. The process of returning to past events in one's life can bring a heightened awareness of unresolved conflicts. When unresolved conflicts are recognized and confronted, the elder may experience banishment of guilt, resolution of intrapsychic conflict, and reconciliation of family relationships. Resolving these conflicts through guided life review gives elders an opportunity to mend fences and take care of unfinished business as part of the process of achieving ego integrity versus ego despair. It is the process of remembering with the intent of identifying negative as well as positive emotional memories. When problematic experiences and memories are uncovered, professional counseling skills are used to help an elder reframe and accept past events or take steps to resolve them. Life review assumes negative emotions and events will be uncovered.

Life review and reminiscence are discussed separately in this chapter and are not considered to be the same thing. Reminiscence is designed to help elders retrieve *positive* events and feelings through the process of reminiscing. It does not focus on helping elders resolve lifelong conflicts or attend to unfinished business although certainly those events may come up in the process of remembering the past. Reminiscence therapy is specifically geared to guiding elders to remember events that reinforce the belief that they are worthwhile, valued human beings. It is intended to improve an elder's mood but does not attempt to achieve insight, as is the goal of life review.

Goals of Reminiscence

One goal of reminiscence work with elders is to access pleasant, happy memories to help improve elders' current mood. It is more than just remembering "the good old days," but rather a facilitated effort to recreate a more adaptive mood state. Talking about childhood memories surrounding a family vacation or holiday tradition may make an elder relive the positive emotions associated with the past event. The feeling state can be transported to the present, helping to relieve depression or calm anxiety. This type of reminiscence is narrative reminiscence, retelling factual events that invoke happy feelings (Watt & Wong, 1991).

Another purpose of reminiscence is to improve an elder's self-esteem and coping ability by examining how elders successfully faced difficulties in the past. Mosher-Ashley and Barrett (1997) described this process as remembering "victories over life challenges." When elders are faced with stressful life events—such as learning to manage finances, chronic health problems, or painful isolation—they tend to focus on the present, according to Puentes (1998). This orientation to the present may prevent the elder from drawing on a lifetime of coping and adaptation skills that could be successfully applied to a current life situation. For example, reminiscence was used with an 85-year-old woman who expressed trepidation about handling her own finances after the death of her husband. Through guided reminiscence, the woman thought back to the time when her husband was in the armed services during World War II and she was in charge of both earning and budgeting their money. She managed to pay off their house and had accumulated a tidy nest egg by the time her husband returned from the service. She reasoned that she did not need to earn more money, just learn how to manage it. If she had done that successfully before, she could do it again. Retrieving that memory helped her realize she had money management skills. She just had to regain her confidence about financial manners. Helping an elder to identify concrete situations from the past and draw on those same coping skills can empower him or her to regain control over what appears in the present to be an overwhelming situation. Watt and Wong (1991) referred to this as instrumental reminiscence—drawing on past experiences to solve current problems. Instrumental reminiscence can also be topic specific, such as remembering how the individual made friends in a new situation or tackled big projects. The purpose is to rekindle personal initiative and restore self-confidence in elders, who may not have used those skills in many years.

A third goal of reminiscence is to improve social skills. It is easy for elders to lose social skills when they become alienated or isolated. They may forget how to talk about anything other than their own aches and pains. Whether reminiscence is employed in an individual setting, which involves conversation with at least one other individual, or in a group setting, reminiscing about social events, dating and courtships, or raising children can help elders learn to reconnect with others in a more positive, reciprocal way.

How Effective Is Reminiscence?

Therapeutic reminiscence has been found to have a positive influence on depression, self-esteem, and socialization among elders (Blankenship, Molinari, & Kunik, 1996; McDougall, Blixen, & Suen, 1997; Orten, Allen, & Cook, 1989;

Youssef, 1990). It remains unclear whether reminiscence is therapeutic specifically because of the power of memories in changing behavior or evoking feelings or due to the socialization that occurs when the process is applied in an individual or group setting (Comana, Brown, & Thomas, 1998). Reminiscence may be less effective in working with elders who suffer from severe cognitive limitations, such as dementia, or have other severe mental illnesses that produce disruptive behavior. Elders who are unable to tolerate even brief periods of sustained attention and concentration due to physical or mental illness are not good candidates for reminiscence. Elders with mild forms of dementia may show surprising benefits from reminiscence because it relies on long-term rather than short-term memories, many of which are in tact for these elders (Jaccoma, 1990; Ott, 1993).

The cultural assumption that some ethnic groups, such as Asian American or Hispanic elders, may be unwilling to share deep personal memories outside their own ethnic groups or be uncomfortable discussing individual achievements has not been supported by research (Atkinson, Kim, Ruelas, & Lin, 1999). Hispanic elders may be even more inclined than non-Hispanic elders to share life experiences and resolve problems through reminiscence. Zuniga (1989) and Atkinson and associates (1999) found reminiscence gave Hispanic elders an opportunity to reinforce the traditional roles of elders in Hispanic culture and transmit important cultural values and ethics to younger Hispanics.

The Process of Therapeutic Reminiscence

Group Size and Session Length.   Reminiscence groups are traditionally composed of seven to nine members and a group facilitator. The exact number depends on the level of functioning of the elders, both cognitively and physically. If group members have communicative limitations, such as hearing loss or speech problems, additional facilitators may be necessary to help with verbal interaction. The group may accommodate more than nine members if all members are able to function independently. It is advisable to have more, rather than fewer, members to ensure an adequate number of participants for any given session. Health problems for elders may contribute to a tendency for elders to miss frequently.

Reminiscence groups usually meet for six to twelve sessions depending on the location of the group meetings. A longer course of group meetings is more realistic in congregate housing, adult day health centers, and nursing homes than it might be in senior centers where a twelve-session commitment may be too difficult for community-dwelling elders. Sessions are usually planned for 30 to 60 minutes in length. As group members become more comfortable with each other, the sessions may go longer.

Group or Individual Formats.   Reminiscence therapy can be offered in both group and individual formats. The primary advantage of presenting reminiscence in a group format is the ability to reach more elders. It is easily adapted for use in institutions, such as assisted-living centers, congregate living, adult day health centers, and nursing homes. If the goal of the reminiscence is to improve socialization, the group has the obvious advantage of increasing the individual's inter-action with other elders who may live in proximity. The socialization that occurs within the group setting may carry over beyond the reminiscence group, improv-ing social interaction for more elders than is possible when working with individuals. The group format also may be better for elders who are too uncom-fortable in a one-on-one setting and prefer the more passive participation afforded by the group approach.

The individual approach also has specific advantages. Mosher-Ashley and Barrett (1997) pointed out that conducting reminiscence with an individual allows the worker to tailor the intervention to the specific needs of the individual and adjust the pace to reflect the needs and abilities of the individual elder. For elders with sensory losses, such as hearing or communication difficulties, or for an elder who is homebound, this may be preferable. The worker can devote his or her indi-vidual attention to the elder in a way not possible in the group setting. This may be particularly important if the worker suspects that reminiscing will trigger pain-ful or difficult memories in an elder.

Selecting Topics for Sessions.   One approach to reminiscence is chronological in which the social worker meets with the elder for ten sessions. Two weeks are devoted to each of the major developmental stages, childhood, adolescence, early adulthood, middle age, and old age. If the goal is to improve self-esteem, the worker might help the elder identify the major accomplishments of each of those life stages. If the goal is to identify coping strengths, elders may recall how they handled difficult times during specific times in their lives. If the goal is to generate positive, happy family memories, the worker may guide the elders to recount their happiest memories from these times in their lives. The topics selected for each of the chronological periods is determined by the goals of the reminiscence intervention for the specific elder. The chronological approach is also used in life review but with a very different purpose, and workers should have clear goals in mind as to why the chronological reminiscence approach has been chosen over a more structured life review approach.

A less structured approach can also be used in which elders explore certain topics not necessarily connected to developmental periods in their lives. If the goal is to focus on positive feelings, the worker can focus reminiscing on favorite foods from the past, holiday celebrations, vacations, or social events. These "safe" topics can help the elder relax and become comfortable with the process (Mosher-Ashley & Barrett, 1997). Once the elder is comfortable, it may be easier for the worker to progress to more personal topics. For example, if the goal of the inter-vention is to review life accomplishments, elders may focus on work or family-related events during one session, relationships during another, and service to others in another.

Burnside (1993) cautioned workers about failing to involve elders in the se-lection of topics or pursuing topics that are of more interest to the worker than elders. She found the litany of "firsts"—such as first kiss, first date, first playmate, or first memory—were not good choices in reminiscence groups of elders. Many

found those topics traumatic rather than happy or felt pressure to distinguish between what they really remember and what had been recounted to them as a
"first." More general topics—such as holiday memories, early work experiences,
or favorite childhood pets—evoked fewer traumatic memories and elicited more
conversation when applied in a group format. Burnside (1993) recommended topics take into account the gender of group members, the cohort experiences of elders, geographical location, and culture.

The Use of Structured Activities and Props.   It may be necessary to provide
props to stimulate elders' memories. One way to involve group members is to ask
them to bring something to the group that brings back memories of another time.
It may be an article of clothing, a piece of music, an old newspaper, collectibles
associated with a time in history, such as depression glass, or photos of common
events. Anything that stimulates one of the senses can be even more powerful
than words in stimulating memories. Ott (1993) recommended familiar scents,
texture boards, music, or poetry. Depending on the abilities and interests of group
members, more structured activities can include writing autobiographies for family members, organizing photos to give to family members, constructing family
genealogies, or putting together a cookbook of family recipes (Mosher-Ashley &
Barrett, 1997).

The most important thing that gerontological social workers need to remember in conducting reminiscence groups is that the group is supposed to improve
an elder's mood and that all activities need to be directed toward that goal. The
purpose of reminiscence is to make elders feel good through accessing life memories and sharing those with other group members and the social worker. It is not
intended to be deep psychotherapy nor is it intended to access painful emotions.
If the social worker finds elders in a reminiscence group focusing on unresolved
issues or problematic emotions, it may be appropriate to refer the elder to more
structured therapy or life review work.

Life Review

Based on his assumption that reminiscence is a natural part of the aging process,
Butler (1963) advocated that guided life review could be used to help elders work
through unresolved developmental issues from earlier stages in their lives to resolve lifelong intrapsychic conflicts. Resolution of those conflicts could help
elders attain a sense of satisfaction and acceptance about their lives and help them
make the most constructive use of the time remaining. His work is based on Erik
Erikson's eight developmental stages. At each major developmental period in life,
individuals are faced with resolving specific conflicts. If the life stage conflict is
not resolved during the appropriate stage, it may reappear throughout an
individual's life, impairing that person's ability to achieve psychological and social maturity.

Bengston and Allen (1993) proposed a different metaphor for the concept of life review based on their perception of the life course, which emphasizes the contexts of one's cohort and family members as indicators of changing social roles. Bengston and Allen (1993) offer the image of the life course as a series of clocks. The biological clock refers to the maturation process of the human body from infancy through old age. Certain physical changes in the body mark the passing of time, such as adolescence, reproduction, and physical aging. The cohort clock refers to the social forces that shape an individual's identity within an historical and sociological context. Age cohorts share a common frame of reference that defines their lives in a unique way. The family clock indicates one's sense of relationship to the family of origin and a family of procreation. Certain ages suggest a time for establishing one's own family and then eventually being relieved of family responsibilities as children grow up and leave home. The final clock in this image is the age-linked clock, which defines people's expectations about where they should be at what age in their lives. While a 25-year-old may be at the beginning of his or her career, a 65-year-old is more likely to be winding down in the workplace and anticipating retirement.

Goals of Life Review

Unlike reminiscence, life review focuses on both positive and negative events in an elder's life history. It is intended to recreate a sense of the elder's developmental stages and life history. Through confronting negative emotions and events, it is possible to identify unresolved issues from earlier life stages. In guided life review, the social worker is able to help an elder identify those issues and determine what can be changed and what cannot. Sometimes fences can be mended with family members who elders perceive as having hurt them or been hurt by them earlier in life. Sometimes unfinished business can be finished while an elder still has time. When issues involving parents who are dead are uncovered, it may be the social worker's job to help an elder reframe past hurts and let go of the pain.

Life review may also be used to help an elder review life accomplishments and identify coping skills that can be applied to current life challenges—a goal similar to that used in reminiscence. While elders may find the challenges of their later years particularly painful, they have coped with very serious crises throughout their lives successfully and unsuccessfully. Focusing on what has worked (and not worked) in the past not only contributes to improving an elder's problem-solving skills but also helps to improve self-confidence and self-esteem.

When Can Life Review Be Beneficial?

Knight (1996) recommended life review for elders who are struggling with constructing a "new view of themselves" after a life crisis, such as widowhood. An elder may need help visualizing a future without a life partner—one that focuses on a "me" rather than a "we." After many years of being part of a couple, an elder may be unable even to envision how he or she will carry on alone. Regaining a sense of individuality through reviewing personal strengths and assets may help an elder to regain the self-confidence needed to start a new phase in life. Lewis and Butler (1974) included widowhood as one of many role transitions elders face as social and familial constellations change in later life.

Life review can be useful in helping elders face a crisis, such as a chronic illness or disability. Assisting elders to place current health problems within a life course perspective encourages them to isolate poor health as dominating a very small part of their lives. As Puentes (1998) emphasized, it is easy to focus only on the present and globalize current problems to encompass one's entire life, past and present. Rather than become immersed in self-pity, an elder can learn to accept the illness as a small part of a much larger lifetime experience.

This approach may be most helpful for elders who are struggling with finding meaning and purpose in their lives. It may be difficult for elders to see how their lives have had value when they feel alone and isolated. Will it have mattered that they lived at all? For many elders, identifying their positive influence on life may be easy—through raising a child or making a meaningful contribution through their life's work. It is also possible that elders will come to the sad conclusion that their lives were a waste. The negative issues raised by life review can actually contribute to the occurrence of late life disorders, especially depression (Merriam, 1993). Butler, Lewis, and Sunderland (1998) warned of this possibility and encouraged helping professionals to make careful consideration of this chance prior to engaging a client in the life review process. Life review may not be the best intervention for some elders.

The Process of Life Review

Group vs. Individual Formats.   Life review can be conducted in both an individual or group format. The group format has the advantage of reaching a greater number of elders, who may be facing similar life challenges. Elders may find their own memories kindled by the memories of cohorts—similarly to what happens in group reminiscence therapy. Elders may also feel less self-conscious as part of a group.

Because life review often involves very personal and at times painful memories, however, it may be more beneficial to some elders when offered on an individual basis. The group format makes it difficult to make sure that each elder has an adequate chance to work on individual goals and gets an equal opportunity to participate verbally in the group. When painful memories or events are uncovered, the social worker may need to devote undivided attention to helping the elder process and understand intense emotions.

Establishing Pre-Intervention Baselines.   One of the key elements of life review is that it is evaluative as well as therapeutic. Prior to engaging in the chronological process, a social worker should establish a baseline for an elder's emotional well-being. This can be done using the Geriatric Depression Scale (GDS) discussed in Chapter 4 or the Life Satisfaction Index (LSIA) (Neugarten, Havinghurst, & Tobin, 1961), depending on the overall goal of the intervention. Life review is focused on helping elders not only to better understand their own life histories but also to apply the insight gained in this process to present and future behavior. Life review does not aim to fixate elders in the past, but to use the insight gained to move them away from past conflicts to more productive and satisfying lives now. Building a pretest and posttest into an intervention helps both the social worker and the elder assess how successful the effort has been in accomplishing the basic goals of the intervention.

The Structure of Life Review.   Guided life review generally takes place in six to twelve sessions contingent on the elder's goals for participating in life review, the elder's health, and the personal preferences of both social worker and elder. Approximately two sessions are spent on each of the major developmental periods. Burnside and Haight (1994) offered a structured format, the Life Review and Experience Form (LREF). This protocol covers areas such as death, grief, fear, religion, school, hardships, sex, work, and relationships over the life span. Obviously, some topics receive greater attention at different developmental stages. It is not necessary to ask all of the questions in each of the developmental stages. These questions have been validated in previous research (Burnside & Haight 1994; Haight, 1992). Social workers may develop their own style after applying life review techniques for some period of time and add or delete content areas as they find useful. There is no one "right" way to conduct a therapeutic life review.

It is important to explore the influence of membership in a cultural or ethnic group with elders during the process of life review. What did belonging to a cultural or ethnic group mean to them? What were their first experiences of being "different" from others, and what did this mean to them? What changes have they seen between the generations in experiencing and valuing the ethnic experience? This does not apply only to members of distinct racial and ethnic groups, such as African Americans, Hispanics, American Indians, or Asian Americans. For example, belonging to a white ethnic group, such as Irish, German, Jewish, Scandinavian, or French, among others, may have a very significant meaning for elders and define much of their life experience.

Knight (1996) cautioned helping professionals conducting a life review to pay special attention to what the elders do not include as they chronologically review their lives. Are there gaps of several years that an elder cannot remember or systematically deletes from the review? Psychological editing, the conscious or unconscious deletion of life events, may be the key to unresolved conflicts. The elder may not mention events as significant as failed marriages, deceased or estranged children, or problematic social relationships (Knight, 1996). A social worker's intuition is the most valuable tool in assessing what may be missing in an elder's recounting of his or her life history.

The Role of the Social Worker.   During the process of therapeutic life review, the social worker often takes on the role of editor (Knight, 1996). It is the social worker's job to probe for additional content, a common activity in much of the counseling process. Helping the elder to slow down and make a concentrated effort to remember important events is necessary for a comprehensive review.

While elders may have difficulty remembering more recent events, often their long-term memories are extremely sharp (Butler, Lewis, & Sunderland, 1998). The social worker plays an important role in facilitating the process of remembering and recounting earlier events in elders' lives.

The social worker can help elders to reframe events from their past. For example, if an elder has a great deal of hostility and resentment toward his or her parent, the social worker may be able to assist the elder in seeing the offending parent in a different light. Maybe an elder feels his or her father was not there for him or her while growing up because of job responsibilities. This event reframed as "he was doing the best he knew how to take care of his family" may help the elder to let go of negative feelings and move to accept the absent parent's motives as worthy, even if the behavior was not. This technique is especially powerful in helping elders understand family members who may have struggled with alcohol or drug abuse at the expense of the well-being of their families. The purpose of this technique is to help elders accept life events and let go of negative and dysfunctional feelings or at least find a way to live with them when they cannot be changed.

This may be especially difficult when dealing with issues surrounding sexual abuse and incest, which may emerge as a result of life review. Sexual abuse cannot be justified or reframed to make it acceptable, no matter how impaired the perpetrator may have been nor should this be the aim of life review. In earlier work done by this author, life review was used with older female survivors of childhood sexual abuse to help these women move ahead in challenges they were facing in their current life situations (McInnis-Dittrich, 1996). For example, an 85-year-old woman refused to go into the hospital for medical care because of her fears about who would care for her severely disabled daughter. Professional, high-quality respite care arrangements were available, but she was convinced her daughter would not be safe. The process of life review revealed that she had been sexually abused as a child by a close relative when her own mother had been hospitalized nearly 80 years before. Using props such as a favorite doll and family pictures, she was able to recall the event and make the connection to her present reluctance to leave her daughter with anyone. After working through some of these painful memories, she eventually consented to her daughter's respite placement but on her terms. No men were allowed to care for her daughter, she would talk to her daughter several times a day on the phone, and none of her other children or relatives were to be made aware of her own childhood abuse. Insight became a way for her to understand her current behavior and empower her to set boundaries to assure her that this would not happen to her daughter.

The role of the social worker in life review also includes helping elders to identify themes in their life histories and to acknowledge how life themes have influenced past and current behavior. McDougall, Blixen, and Suen (1997) identified themes in life review as disempowering or empowering. Disempowering themes include anxiety, denial, despair, helplessness, isolation, loneliness, and loss. Throughout the process of life review as intrapsychic conflict is resolved, empowering themes such as connection, coping, efficacy, hope, and trust should become more prevalent. Helping elders to move toward the identification of empowering themes becomes part of the purpose of the life review intervention.

Constructing a Product of the Life Review Process. As in reminiscence work, it may be helpful for the life review process to result in a distinct product, such as a photo album, a video, or life history journal. The product of life review need not be limited to these traditional formats. Quilts, sculptures, paintings, and other art forms can also be used. One elder involved in life review used her childhood dollhouse and transformed each room in the house to represent a different developmental stage in her life. She furnished the rooms with mementos, furniture, or photos that reminded her of this particular time in her life. The completed dollhouse was a concrete reminder of her many happy memories in life and a tribute to her creative skills. Constructing a product of the life review process is not necessary, and the discretion of the social worker should dictate whether this will be considered.

The Evaluative and Summary Component. The most important part of the life review process is the evaluative and summary component. This gives an elder a chance to integrate all of the events of the developmental life stages into a life course perspective. It is important for elders to come to some determination about what kind of life they have had. What would they change? What would they leave the same? What are their satisfactions and disappointments? What are they most proud of? How have significant life events affected an elder's life? How can negative events be balanced against more positive events in the elder's life? Achieving this balance has been described as a "freeing" process that allows the elder to move ahead to the rest of life (Burnside & Haight, 1994).

Once past events have been integrated, the social worker can help the elder move to a discussion of what he or she hopes to accomplish in the time left in life. Life review is intended to move the elder beyond the past to more functional and satisfying life choices in the present and future. What else would he or she like to accomplish in the future? What business needs to be "finished" to resolve old hurts and painful events? During this final stage of the life review process, the posttest is usually given to determine if there has been an improvement in an elder's emotional well-being during the life review process. Repeating the same evaluative measure given during the preliminary session is essential to evaluating the success of the intervention.

Medical Interventions for Depression and Anxiety

Drug Therapy

While many gerontological social workers are convinced that elders receive medication *instead* of treatment, medication is often a valuable adjunct to traditional mental health treatment. It is important for the social worker to work closely with the health care provider prescribing the medication both to monitor its effectiveness in conjunction with talk therapy and to identify any problematic side effects.

The most common medications prescribed to treat depression in elders are tricyclic antidepressants and heterocyclic antidepressants (Gallagher-Thompson & Coon, 1996). The brand names for these medications include Elavil, Pamelor, Norpramine, Tofranil, and Sinequan. While very effective in alleviating depression among elders, the side effects of these medications may deter elders from maintaining the proper dosage schedule. Minor side effects can include drowsiness, dry mouth, and constipation. Some elders experience much more severe symptoms, such as memory problems, confusion, blurred vision, and labored breathing (Gallagher-Thompson & Coon, 1996). Serotonin selective reuptake inhibitors (SSRIs), which include Prozac, Zoloft, and Paxil, represent a new class of antidepressants. These drugs have shown great promise in alleviating depression, especially when depression presents with anxiety without severe physical complaints. However, they remain prohibitively expensive for elders on limited incomes. Once an elder begins taking any prescription antidepressant, it is imperative that he or she be carefully monitored to guard against drug toxicity.

Some physicians and psychologists (Markovitz, 1993; Sheikh, 1996) recommend elders begin drug therapy for anxiety before they try any of the talk therapies. Relieving the physical symptoms of anxiety—which include extreme fearfulness, heart palpitations, and cold sweats—may help elders to regain the concentration necessary to focus on the intervention process. The adage for treating anxiety in elders with medication is to "start low and go slow" (Sheikh, 1996). The metabolic changes associated with the normal aging process often make an elder particularly sensitive to the effects of antianxiety compounds, known as anxiolytics. Aging bodies may have an impaired ability to process these drugs, leading to the rapid formation of toxic levels of the drug in the bloodstream. Benzodiazepines, such as Valium, Traxene, and Centrax, are the most frequently prescribed medications for anxiety in elders (Butler, Lewis, & Sunderland, 1998). SSRIs, other antidepressants, betablockers, neuroleptics, and even antihistamines have been found to offer elders significant relief from the symptoms of anxiety (Markovitz, 1993; Sheikh, 1996). Like antidepressants, these medications must be carefully monitored and adjusted as needed throughout the course of treatment.

Among the most significant obstacles to drug therapy for anxiety and depression in elders are the side effects produced by the medications and the time it takes for these medications to offer symptom relief. It may take weeks for the medication to reach therapeutic levels in the bloodstream, which often leads elders and their families to decide the medication is not working and discontinue its use. An elder may have difficulty remembering whether the medication has been taken and either double dose or skip it completely. Strict compliance to dosage schedules is imperative for these medications to be effective. Another obstacle to drug therapy is the high cost of these medications. All of an elder's prescriptions may cost hundreds of dollars a month, forcing an elder to chose between food and medicine. Drug therapy is neither a quick nor inexpensive fix for depression and anxiety in elders.

Electroconvulsive Therapy

Electroconvulsive therapy (ECT) is considered to be a highly effective intervention for severely depressed elders for whom all else has failed. Butler, Lewis and Sunderland (1998) recommended ECT in cases of depression that are antidepressant resistant and psychotherapy resistant or have created life-threatening suicidal behavior. Other times, it is indicated in cases where an elder's cardiological or neurological problems are so severe that antidepressant medications are contraindicated. Gallagher-Thompson and Coon (1996) also recommended ECT in cases where an elder's depression is accompanied by acute psychotic features, such as hallucinations or delusions. It is considered a treatment of last resort by the mental health community, but should not be discounted as a treatment choice in cases of severe depression.

Despite its inhumane reputation as "shock therapy," ECT is actually a very safe process. A normal course of treatment consists of six to ten sessions, which are administered in a hospital. Elders are sedated and anesthetized to prevent the uncontrolled flailing once associated with the therapy. It appears to be effective because the electrical current apparently resets the receptor sites that receive the neurochemical substances responsible for mood—an electrical version of what antidepressants achieve chemically (Blazer, 1990; Jenike, 1988). Improvements in mood may occur within as short a time as a week.

The treatment approach is not without side effects, the most common of which are impairments in short-term memory and difficulty in concentration. These side effects, however, disappear within six months of treatment. The side effects of ECT may not be as severe as the memory and concentration impairments that a severe depression can cause for elders. The decision to pursue ECT treatment is not made by a social worker but must be prescribed by a psychiatrist or primary care physician. It is important that elders be offered this intervention as a choice in the treatment of severe depression.

Summary

A wide variety of treatment options are available to elders who suffer from depression and anxiety. Elders respond well to treatment when changing attitudes and behaviors are their goals, not simply those of a social worker or family members. The development of a trusting and respectful relationship with an elder is the most important part of the treatment process. Elders may be highly suspicious of what mental health treatment entails and need to be fully informed about the process. Consistent with the principle of empowerment, elders need to be intimately involved in identifying their own goals for any intervention effort.

Cognitive-behavioral approaches are beneficial for elders who are depressed or anxious. These approaches help identify faulty thinking patterns that lead to uncomfortable emotions and problematic behavior. Reminiscence is aimed at improving an elder's mood by accessing happy memories from earlier in life. By sharing within a group or in an individual setting, elders can recreate positive and productive memories that help them feel better and cope better with the challenges of the present. Similar to reminiscence, life review explores an elder's past to better understand the present. Unlike reminiscence, life review is aimed at facing unresolved conflicts in an elder's past that may be presenting emotional obstacles to achieving a sense of ego integrity rather than despair. Both life review and reminiscence are aimed at validating an elder's life experience and recognizing the influence of those experiences on an elder's life satisfaction.

Drug therapy and electroconvulsive therapy are medical interventions aimed at relieving the symptoms of anxiety and depression. These approaches are most effective when used as adjuncts to traditional verbal approaches or as a last resort for elders who do not respond to talk therapies. The interventions described in this chapter are aimed primarily at those elders who can be active participants in talk therapy—those who retain the cognitive and emotional resilience needed to use insight effectively to change emotions or behavior.

Check Out These Websites!

1. **www.pharminfo.com/drugfaq**   If you are interested in more information about what medications are used to treat depression and anxiety in elders, this website offers extensive information about these medications by both their trade and generic names. Information on these drugs includes treatment regimes, side effects, and contraindications.

2. **www.psych.org/public_info**   The American Psychiatric Association offers fact sheets on a wide variety of psychological and emotional problems common among elders, with especially informative materials on anxiety and electroconvulsive therapy. The website also describes current research under way to determine the therapeutic benefits of popular herbal treatments, such as St. John's wort, on depression.

3. **www.medinfo.ufl.edu**   Sponsored by the medical school at the University of Florida, this website describes current research under way using life review, specifically in the hospice setting. It recounts ways in which life review is being used to help elders and others with terminal illnesses put their lives in order in preparation for death.

4. **www.nacbt.org**   The National Association of Cognitive Behavioral Therapists offers this website as a support for professionals and those persons interested in pursuing CBT. Online CBT discussion groups are available to both novice and experienced therapists as well as links to other sites that offer more information on this therapeutic approach.

References

Adler, A. (1963). *The practice and theory of individual psychology.* New York: Premier Books.

Atkinson, D. R., Kim, A. U., Ruelas, S. R., & Lin, A. T. (1999). Ethnicity and attitudes toward facilitated reminiscence. *Journal of Mental Health Counseling, 21*(1), 66–81.

Babins, L., Dillion, J., & Merovitz, S. (1988). The effects of validation therapy on disoriented elderly. *Activities, Adaptation, & Aging, 12*(1/2), 5–11.

Beck, J. (1995). *Cognitive therapy: Basics and beyond.* New York: Guilford Press.

Bengston, V. L., & Allen, K. R. (1993). The life course perspective applied to families over time. In P. G. Boss, W. J. Doherty, R. LaRossa, W. R. Schumm, & S. K. Steinmetz (Eds.), *Sourcebook of family theories and methods: A contextual approach* (pp. 469–498). New York: Plenum.

Blankenship, L. M., Molinari, V., & Kunik, M. (1996). The effect of a life review group on the reminiscence functions of geropsychiatric inpatients. *Clinical Gerontologist, 16*(4), 3–18.

Blazer, D. (1990). Depression in late life: An update. In M. P. Lawton (Ed.), *Annual review of gerontology and geriatrics, Vol. 9* (pp. 197–215). New York: Springer Publishing.

Burnside, I. (1993). Themes in reminiscence groups with older women. *International Journal of Aging and Human Development, 37*(3), 177–189.

Burnside, I., & Haight, B. (1994). Reminiscence and life review: Therapeutic interventions for older people. *Nurse Practitioner, 19*(4), 55–61.

Butler, R. N. (1963). The life review: An interpretation of reminiscence in the aged. *Psychiatry, 119*, 721–728.

Butler, R. N., Lewis, M. I., & Sunderland, T. (1998). *Aging and mental health: Positive psychosocial and biomedical approaches.* Boston: Allyn and Bacon.

Comana, M. T., Brown, V. M., & Thomas, J. D. (1998). The effect of reminiscence therapy on family coping. *Journal of Family Nursing, 4*(2), 182–197.

Cox, E. O., & Parsons, R. J. (1994). *Empowerment-oriented social work practice with the elderly.* Pacific Grove, CA: Brooks/Cole.

Day, C. R. (1997). Validation therapy: A review of the literature. *Journal of Gerontological Nursing, 23*(4), 29–34.

Ellis, A. (1962). *Reason and emotion in psychotherapy.* New York: Stuart.

Erikson, E. (1963). *Childhood and society* (2nd ed.). New York: Norton.

Feil, N. (1967). Group therapy in a home for the aged. *The Gerontologist, 7*, 192–195.

Feil, N. (1984). Communicating with the confused elderly patient. *Geriatrics, 39*(3), 131–132.

Feil, N. (1993). *The validation breakthrough.* Baltimore: Health Professions Press.

Fine, J. I., & Rouse-Bane, S. (1995). Using validation techniques to improve communication with cognitively impaired older adults. *Journal of Gerontological Nursing, 21*(6), 39–45.

Gallagher-Thompson, D., & Coon, D. W. (1996). Depression. In J. Sheikh (Ed.), *Treating the elderly* (pp. 1–44). San Francisco: Jossey-Bass.

Guiterrez, L. (1990). Working with women of color: An empowerment perspective. *Social Work, 35*(2), 149–154.

Haight, B. K. (1992). Long term effects of a structured life review process. *Journal of Gerontology, 47*(5), P312–P315.

Jaccoma, R. (1990). Reaching the present through the past. *Milestones, 3*(5), 6–7.

Jenike, M. (1988). Depression and other psychiatric disorder. In M. S. Albert & M. B. Moss (Eds.), *Geriatric neuropsychology* (pp. 115–144). New York: Guilford Press.

Keady, J. (1999). Dementia. *Elderly Care, 11*(1), 21–26.

Knight, B. G. (1996). *Psychotherapy with older adults* (2nd ed.). Thousand Oaks, CA: Sage.

Lantz, J. (1996). Cognitive theory and social work treatment. In F. J. Turner (Ed.), *Social work treatment: Interlocking theoretical approaches* (pp. 94–115). New York: Free Press.

Lewis, M. I., & Butler, R. N. (1974). Life review therapy: Putting memories to work in individual and group psychotherapy. *Geriatrics, 29*, 165–172.

Markovitz, P. J. (1993). Treatment of anxiety in the elderly. *Journal of Clinical Psychiatry, 54*(5 suppl), 64–68.

McDougall, G. J., Blixen, C. E., & Suen, L. J. (1997). The process and outcome of life review psychotherapy with depressed homebound adults. *Nursing Research, 46*(5), 277–283.

McInnis-Dittrich, K. (1996). Adapting life-review therapy for elderly female survivors of childhood sexual abuse. *Families in Society: The Journal of Contemporary Human Services, 77,* 166–173.

McInnis-Dittrich, K. (1997). An empowerment-oriented mental health intervention with elderly Appalachian women: The women's club. *Journal of Women and Aging, 9*(1/2), 91–105.

Merriam, S. B. (1993). Butler's life review: How universal is it? *International Journal of Aging and Human Development, 37*(3), 163–175.

Mosher-Ashley, P. M., & Barrett, P. W. (1997). *A life worth living: Practical strategies for reducing depression in older adult.* Baltimore: Health Professions Press.

Neugarten, B., Havinghurst, R., & Tobin, S. (1961). The measurement of life satisfaction. *Journal of Gerontology, 14,* 134–143.

Orten, J. D., Allen, M., & Cook, J. (1989). Reminiscence groups with confused nursing center residents: An experimental study. *Social Work in Health Care, 14*(1), 73–86.

Ott, R. L. (1993). Enhancing validation through milestoning with sensory reminiscence. *Journal of Gerontological Social Work, 20*(1/2), 147–159.

Puentes, W. J. (1998). Incorporating simple reminiscence techniques into acute care nursing practices. *Journal of Gerontological Nursing, 24*(2), 15–20.

Robb, S. S., Stegman, C. E., & Wolanin, M. O. (1986). No research versus research with compromised results: A study of validation therapy. *Nursing Research, 35*(2), 113–118.

Scanland, S. G., & Emershaw, L. E. (1993). Reality orientation and validation therapy: Dementia, depression, and functional status. *Journal of Gerontological Nursing, 19*(6), 7–11.

Sheikh, J. I. (1996). Anxiety disorders. In J. I. Sheikh (Ed.), *Treating the elderly* (pp. 75–104). San Francisco: Jossey-Bass.

Touzinsky, L. (1998). Validation therapy: Restoring communication between persons with Alzheimer's disease and their families. *American Journal of Alzheimer's Disease, 13*(2), 96–101.

Watt, L. M., & Wong, P. T. (1991). A taxomony of reminiscence and therapeutic implications. *Journal of Gerontological Social Work, 16*(1/2), 37–57.

Yost, E. B., Beutler, L. E., Corbishley, M. A., & Allender, J. R. (1986). *Group cognitive therapy: A treatment approach for depressed older adults.* New York: Pergamon.

Youssef, F. A. (1990). The impact of group reminiscence counseling on a depressed elderly population. *Nurse Practitioner, 15*(4), 32–38.

Zuniga, M. E. (1989). Mexican-American elderly and reminiscence: Interventions. *Journal of Gerontological Social Work, 14*(3/4), 61–73.

7

Alternative Interventions in the Socioemotional Problems of Elders

Traditional and Alternative Interventions

In the last chapter, traditional social work interventions with elders with depression and anxiety were presented. These interventions are considered "traditional" only in the sense that they are the most common approaches used and reflect a social work focus on talk therapy. These approaches offer social workers and elders choices in determining which intervention is best suited for the intellectual and cognitive abilities of any given elder. However, there is a rich repertoire of "alternative" approaches that incorporate music, art, drama, and animals into the therapeutic process. These modalities are referred to as "alternative" in this chapter in the sense that they offer an alternative to traditional social work intervention. While widely used in hospitals, nursing homes, residential treatment centers, adult day health centers, and rehabilitation centers, they are only recently being seriously considered by social workers as an adjunct to social work intervention.

Music, art, and drama therapy all require specialized training and education. Therapists in these areas usually are required to have a graduate degree and extensive experience in the field before they can be certified. Social workers should not be conducting therapy using these modalities without supervision and training. However, all of these creative forms of therapy and animal-assisted therapy can be adapted as part of a total intervention plan for elders with socioemotional problems. Music, art, drama, and animals can play an important role in improving the quality of life for elders. Music can soothe a troubled soul. Art can bring beauty into the lives of elders who face emotional and physical challenges every day of their lives. Drama can offer a creative outlet to elders, both as actors in the dramatic process or as observers of another's performance. A friendly dog can offer love and affection to an isolated elder. All of these therapeutic modalities offer elders an alternative to living with the crippling effects of untreated emotional turmoil.

The Therapeutic Use of Music

Music can be used formally and informally as part of an interdisciplinary approach to treating the emotional and psychological problems facing elders. While social workers may choose to include music as part of a therapeutic intervention plan with elders, it must be emphasized that music therapy is a distinct profession with a well-developed knowledge and skill base. This section of the chapter is intended to familiarize the social worker with the basic principles of music therapy as a means to access emotions and thoughts among elders. It is not intended to replace professional training in music therapy. Social workers who conclude that music therapy is appropriate for use with their older clients should consult a trained music therapist on staff at most hospitals, nursing homes, or adult day health centers for specific treatment options.

Some form of music has existed in every known culture throughout history, leading scientists to believe that making and enjoying music is an essential part of human neurological development (Gfeffer, 1990). It serves as a medium for expressing the entire range of human emotions from profound sadness to overwhelming joy. Music accompanies many of life's most important rituals, such as weddings and funerals. It has served as a means to preserve history, celebrate the present, and anticipate the future.

While its therapeutic value for health and healing have long been known, music therapy as a distinct therapeutic approach only emerged in the latter half of the twentieth century. *Music therapy* is defined as the use of rhythm and melody to enhance the psychological, emotional, and physical well-being of people (Bright, 1997). Music's therapeutic value is not attained solely by having elders listen to music and be entertained although that is one appropriate use of music. Music can also help individuals and mental health professionals access emotions and thoughts as they influence behavior. Music stimulates the central nervous system in a way that actually evokes a range of emotional responses that can be used to modify affect and behavior in nonmusical situations (Thaut, 1990). The structural properties of music (tempo, beat, rhythm) together with the associative properties of music (memories, events) elicit strong emotional responses either by how it makes people feel or what it makes people remember. For example, there is probably no more effective way to conjure up all the turbulent feelings of adolescence than to listen to the music that was popular at the time. Relationships and events become strongly associated with certain music in both positive and painful ways.

While cognitive-behavioral approaches to resolving emotional problems focus first on identifying thought patterns and connecting those thoughts to subsequent emotional states, music therapy does the opposite. Thaut (1990) explained this process as a series of facilitative steps. First, music facilitates the experience of emotions, which is essential to the second step of identifying what those emotions are. Once emotions have been identified, they can be expressed either verbally or through behavioral manifestations. Once an individual becomes aware of the connection between the experience of emotions and the expression of those emotions in behavior, music therapy can facilitate the synthesis, control, and modification of those behaviors to be more functional for the individual. This phenomenon makes this approach particularly attractive in work with elders who may be resistant to sharing troublesome thoughts with a therapist or who are unable to do so due to communicative and cognitive limitations.

Music as Psychotherapy

When music is used as a component of psychotherapy with elders, it should be considered as part of a comprehensive interdisciplinary approach. Coordinating medical care, support services, and mental health services is imperative to avoid both duplication of and gaps in service. Elders are usually referred to music therapists by a physician whose knowledge of the individual patient suggests that a less verbal, more experiential approach to resolving emotional problems is warranted. Appropriate referrals are contingent on the physician being aware of the benefits of music therapy, having enough personal knowledge about the elder to surmise that music might be therapeutic to him or her, and knowing what music therapy resources exist in the institution or community. While the social worker may not be in the formal role to refer an elder for music therapy, he or she may be a valuable resource for providing physicians with options for referral that include the therapeutic use of music.

The first step in music therapy is to identify the goals of the therapeutic intervention. Goals for music therapy may be similar to other psychosocial interventions such as increasing socialization, relieving depression or anxiety, stimulating cognitive abilities, facilitating personal insight, or improving self-esteem. Music therapy has specific goals that, like other forms of psychotherapy, need to be attainable and measurable. What do elders want to be different in their lives? What do they hope to accomplish in participating in the therapeutic effort? Elders participating in music therapy often are given the Geriatric Depression Scale (Chapter 4), the Life Satisfaction Index, or other baseline assessment tools before and after the intervention to measure empirically the effectiveness of the intervention (Mosher-Ashley & Barrett, 1997).

The second step in the therapeutic process is to select the appropriate music. The music needs to reflect the goals identified for the helping process as well as the elder's personal preference. For elders who are unable to participate actively in this process, families can serve as an important resource. Once music therapists have access to a variety of musical selections, they can select specific pieces that coincide with therapeutic goals. For example, if the goal of intervention is to help relieve depression, livelier pieces may be more appropriate than the soft, slow selections chosen to relax an anxious elder. Elders and their families should be encouraged to select favorite pieces from childhood, adolescence, or young adulthood, particularly if these have been happy times in an elder's life.

Establishing a trusting therapeutic relationship is as crucial to the success of music therapy as it is to any other approach. The elder has to trust the therapist and learn to feel safe sharing deeply personal information. Elders may be emotionally more vulnerable during music therapy than with other psychotherapeutic approaches because the focus is on eliciting emotions first and making sense of the related thought patterns later. Direct access to the emotions makes it difficult for anyone to filter out material they find threatening. As with a good social work relationship, a music therapist takes the time and steps necessary for an elder to understand and fully participate in the intervention.

Individual sessions in music therapy usually take between 30 minutes to an hour depending on the cognitive and emotional capabilities of the elder. For high-functioning, healthy elders, weekly sessions with a music therapist combined with daily homework can result in very rapid improvements in mood or affect. For less high-functioning, frail elders, more than 30 minutes once a week may simply be too exhausting. Music therapists traditionally begin the session with a focusing exercise to relax the elders and help them concentrate on the session. Goals for the overall intervention effort, as well as for the individual session, are articulated, as is done in traditional counseling work. The selected piece or pieces of music are presented and then processed with the music therapist. For some elders, this may involve accessing remote memories and the accompanying feelings—a process similar to reminiscence and life review therapy. The role of the therapist is to move elders from the meaning of the events in the past to their relevance for the present and future. Music helps the elder and the therapist access those emotions. More traditional therapeutic techniques, such as support, identifying dysfunctional defense mechanisms, and promoting insight, help the elder process the feelings generated by the music and apply the insight to desired thought and behavioral changes in the present.

For other elders, the therapeutic process may involve the music therapist leading guided imagery. The music helps the elder and therapist to access troublesome emotions. In guided imagery, troublesome or stressful thoughts are replaced with more positive, happy thoughts through the process of mental imaging facilitated by the therapist. For example, an elder who is troubled with sadness about deceased loved ones can learn to replace sad images with the happy images of all of the good shared times with the loved one or the mental image that the loved one is still with him or her in spirit. This complex interaction between accessing emotions and applying therapeutic techniques to resolve emotional conflicts is the part of music therapy that requires a high level of professional competence in both music and counseling.

The music therapy process can also be applied within a group setting with elders, particularly when improving communication skills or increasing opportunities for socialization are among the goals for a music therapy intervention. Group sessions tend to be composed of six to ten members depending on the abilities of group members. Sessions run between thirty minutes and two hours depending on the setting and group composition. Music therapy group sessions have basically the same format as more traditional social work groups, with specific activities to mark the beginning, middle, and end of the session. As in social work groups, the relationships that develop between members of the group and the therapeutic effect of the group process are as important as the relationship between group members and the group leader. When deep emotions surface in the context of a shared musical experience, it is important that group members respect each others' vulnerabilities and offer mutual support.

Therapeutic Music with Elders with Alzheimer's Disease

The cognitive damage caused by Alzheimer's disease and other organic brain disorders limits the usefulness of more traditional talk therapies. Music therapy may prove among the most beneficial in allowing the social worker to reach into the emotional world of the elder. When other psychotherapeutic efforts fail, music has an amazing ability to help connect health and mental health professionals to the inner life of a person with Alzheimer's disease. Beatty and associates (1988) and Aldridge (1996) found that both the participatory and reactive musical abilities of persons with Alzheimer's disease remain intact, even when many of their cognitive abilities have been lost. People who are no longer able to orient themselves to time, space, or person may continue to play a musical instrument, sing, or react appropriately to music. Clair and Bernstein (1990) found the ability to sing remained in some elders with Alzheimer's disease long after these elders had lost their ability to speak, suggesting that singing and speaking are distinct human abilities rather than variations of the same. These researchers also found that even when elders with Alzheimer's disease were no longer able to communicate verbally in any form, they retained the ability to rhythmically respond to music using drums or other percussion instruments. Music may remain one of the most resilient forms of maintaining some kind of communication with elders with dementia.

Hanser and Clair (1995) and Towse (1995) maintained that music focuses on elders' strengths and abilities rather than their disabilities. The receptive experience of hearing music only requires them to hear and appreciate the music on their own terms. For high-functioning elders, music can be an intellectually invigorating experience as they seek to identify musical themes or understand the emotional essence the music is intended to convey. For this group of elders, it is often helpful to incorporate an educational component into the experience of attending a musical performance. Discussing the specific music before and after a concert gives elders an opportunity to exercise their minds and learn something new. Elders with cognitive limitations can enjoy the same piece of music on a much more basic level, experiencing the music as simply a blend of pleasing sounds that creates a positive emotional experience.

For elders in the last stages of Alzheimer's disease who have lost all communicative abilities, the ability to keep rhythm to a variety of musical pieces may represent the only way in which professional helpers can know a relationship with the outside world still exists.

Music can also be used effectively to calm an agitated elder with Alzheimer's disease as an alternative to the use of restraints or medication. Agitation and restlessness are common with this disease and present a formidable challenge to caregivers in both home and institutional settings. Familiar music from earlier in their lives or selected classical pieces can calm agitated elders as well as increase their attention span and reduce the incidence of disruptive behaviors (Casby & Holm, 1994; Clark, Lipe, & Bilbrey, 1998; Norberg, Melin, & Asplund, 1986). Music appears to tap into a part of the brain that is not damaged by Alzheimer's disease and serves to soothe agitated emotions.

Hanser and Clair (1995) used a music therapy group approach with moderate- to high-functioning elders with Alzheimer's disease and their caretakers as a way to improve the relationship between elder and caregiver and to provide stress reduction for both parties. Activities included using self-massage, guided imagery, sleep induction techniques, or a combination of music and movement to reduce stress. Elders and their caregivers identified ways in which these activities could be incorporated into the daily schedule of both parties as the homework part of the intervention effort. Other activities included group singing, improvisational techniques, and listening to music for pure enjoyment. Elders and their caregivers were given the opportunity to process the emotions accessed by the sessions in a way that led them to a general discussion of the stresses of having Alzheimer's disease as well as those of caring for persons who have it.

Receptive or Passive Use of Music

Music can be used as part of the intervention effort with elders in ways that do not require the knowledge base required for professional music therapy. The most obvious therapeutic use of music with elders simply involves listening to music for both enjoyment and relaxation, either on an individual basis or as part of a social event. Going out with others to attend a concert, based on a shared interest in enjoying the spectacle and the sound of the music, promotes socialization (Standley, 1995). Many of the emotional problems facing elders are exacerbated by social isolation—too much time alone. The anticipation of attending a musical event, joining others for a performance, and sharing an enjoyment of music can be powerful tools in combating loneliness and encouraging the development of new friendships among elders.

Active Participation in Making Music

More free time in later life may afford elders the opportunity to renew musical skills attained earlier in life or to learn to play an instrument for the first time. Playing an instrument requires the coordination of the cognitive skills needed to read the music with the physical coordination used to play an instrument. This is an excellent way to stimulate intellectual activity in elders. An individual can play alone for his or her own personal enjoyment or join with others for a more social experience.

The current cohort of elders may find group singing an important component of making music with others. Singing requires elders to remember both the words and melody of songs from earlier in their lives. Recalling old songs often stimulates the sharing of memories among elders as they recount where they used to sing these older songs and what events are associated with them. Singing also requires the physical exercise of vocal cords, which may not be used often among elders who live alone. Invariably a good rousing song can provoke laughter (or tears), exercising emotional muscles as well. Even if elders are unable or unwilling to sing, making music can consist of using rhythmic instruments, such as drums, maracas, or other percussion instruments, to follow the beat of music.

Music Combined with Other Art Forms

Art therapists have learned that music can stimulate other creative activities, such as drawing, painting, or writing poetry (Rosling & Kitchen, 1992). Elders may be asked to listen to a piece of music and express the mood created by it artistically or through creative writing. A lively piece can motivate and stimulate an elder struggling with depression. A more subdued piece may calm an agitated or anxious elder. Using music to set the mood and then capture the emotion through an artistic medium can help elders to deal with troublesome emotions.

Music can be used to accompany exercise programs for elders, both as a source of entertainment and as a means of setting the pace for the exercise (Standley, 1995). Elders who have had a stroke or other debilitating illness may find music a pleasurable experience during somewhat unpleasant physical therapy needed to restore physical functioning. If the physical exercise experience can be made more pleasurable for elders, they are more likely to follow through with an exercise regime. Elders may also enjoy dancing, even with severe physical limitations. The effort required to move one's body (or mobility device) to the beat of the music, the emotional stimulation of the central nervous system generated by the sound of music, and the social aspects of dancing can be invigorating (Hanser, 1990).

Art as a Therapeutic Activity

Art has long been viewed as a way to convey ideas and to capture deep emotions in a more poignant manner than verbal expression alone. Using a variety of media, including painting, drawing, sculpture, fabric, photography, and multimedia installations, artists are able to transform thoughts and feelings into a visual product. Malchiodi (1990) proposed that art may have developed in civilizations throughout history as a means to achieve or restore psychological equilibrium.

From primitive cave drawings to today's highly abstract creations, art may be used to alleviate or contain feelings of trauma, fear, and anxiety as well as psychological threats to self and community. Even for those people for whom art is recreation not vocation, art provides an opportunity to be both an active and passive participant in the creative process. Using art as a therapeutic approach in working with elders can be as complex as a professionally designed art therapy program or as simple as arranging for elders to attend a museum exhibit or gallery opening.

Art Therapy

Like music therapy, art therapy practice is a recognized professional intervention that requires an extensive knowledge and skill base. Art-as-therapy and art-as-psychotherapy are based on the principle that art reflects both an individual's perception of his or her inner world and an attempt to order or express one's view of the outer world (Johnson, 1995). The mind and the body operate as one so that when feelings and experiences are expressed through art, the body is affected as well (Kaplan, 1998). Visually representing fears, joys, or dreams through various art media is accompanied by a biological response, such as lowered blood pressure or a rise in pleasure-inducing hormones. The profession requires extensive knowledge of the same psychological theories that guide social work practice, including psychodynamic, cognitive, and behavioral theories, as they affect the understanding of how people develop social skills, manage behavior, and engage in problem solving. In addition, art therapists are trained in the use of assorted artistic media available to meet the therapeutic goals identified for each client. Entrance into the profession requires a master's degree and certification by the Art Therapy Credentials Board (ATCB) (American Art Therapy Association, 1998).

Art therapists, like social workers, work with clients to help identify the underlying conflicts that impair social functioning. Adults and children who may not be able to talk about what is bothering them may be more successful in identifying problems through drawing or sculpture. For example, a drawing of a troubled family may tell the therapist much more than hours of talk therapy. A self-portrait presented in modeling clay may be infinitely more revealing in helping to identify problems with self-esteem in a depressed elder. Art therapy is not just "doing art." It is a complex process of facilitating and interpreting the expression of emotions and ideas in a supportive therapeutic environment (Brooke, 1996).

Art therapy relies on projective methods, the unconscious processes of the inner experience as it is expressed through an artistic medium, such as painting or drawing (Brooke, 1996). People may not be aware of processes in their unconscious or may be unable to verbally express thoughts, fears, and wishes. Expressing those subconscious processes may be facilitated by using nonverbal and nonthreatening artistic means (Coleman & Farris-Dufrene, 1996). Art brings those processes to a conscious level where the client and therapist can express them. Professional art therapy requires a high level of skill in being able to interpret what the client has expressed through the artwork. However, even art therapists agree that interpreting the meaning of symbols expressed through art is a subjective process. There is no ultimate truth about what artistic symbols mean, and these representations should be interpreted with great caution (Kaplan, 1998).

Art therapists are frequently on the professional staffs of hospitals, nursing homes, residential treatment centers, and psychiatric facilities. Psychiatrists and social workers are increasingly using art therapy as part of a broader intervention approach with elders with a deep depression or communicative impairments who seem resistant to more traditional talk therapies. Many elders welcome the opportunity to be creative and to work with a therapeutic modality that is completely novel for them. Elders need to be actively involved with the social worker and art therapist in determining if this approach should be tried. Not all elders will be interested in art therapy or able to work with artistic materials, but art therapy should be seriously considered as one of the many alternatives to traditional counseling. While intense art therapy remains in the purview of a professional art therapist, the gerontological social worker can incorporate art into intervention plans for elders in a variety of other ways.

Art as a Therapeutic Group Activity

Art groups can be developed in nursing homes, assisted-living centers, congregate living centers, adult day health centers, and senior centers as creative outlets that also serve therapeutic purposes. For most elders, the therapeutic use of art is less about introspection into the unconscious and more about the power of group dynamics, task completion, stimulation by the use of colors or shapes, and reminiscence trigger (Fausek, 1997). Incorporating artistic activities into the recreational programs in these facilities can be both enjoyable and helpful in promoting socialization.

Special Considerations in Selecting Activities.   Several issues must be considered before instituting an art activity group with elders. It is important that the activity chosen not resemble an arts and crafts project. While there is merit in giving elders an opportunity to make bird houses or jewelry, art as a therapeutic activity needs to have specific goals that meet the needs of the participating elders and should not be considered solely as an activity to pass time or relieve boredom. Any materials, such as crayons or finger paint, that are associated with children's art activities should be avoided (Harlan, 1991). Even elders with cognitive limitations sense the infantilizing nature of doing activities associated with children and will resist. Activities selected should respect the dignity and abilities of elders as adults. Finally, Fausek (1997) suggested that elders not be placed in the position of competing with each other. Competition for whose work is the best inhibits creative expression and rekindles lifelong concerns about one's creative talents. One of the most common responses of elders when asked to consider art as a therapeutic modality is "I cannot draw." Creative ability is equated with the ability to draw rather than being valued as the production of a visual product that is uniquely one's own. Celebrating the diversity of interests and talents among elders is an essential part of the therapeutic effect of incorporating artistic outlets into their lives.

Themes and Art Projects.   When applied in a group setting, art projects should have a theme related to the established goals for the group. For example, if a group of elders is facing challenges unique to aging, such as widowhood, living with a chronic illness, or adjusting to a new living situation, the project selected might revolve around the general theme of meeting challenges. Fausek (1997) suggested elders be asked to express their feelings about those challenges in a painting using color to depict emotions or obstacles. Depicting the meeting of challenges—crossing a bridge or climbing a fence—can remind elders of other times in their lives when they successfully handled challenges.

Using textured fabrics as part of a wall hanging can spur a discussion about the importance of touch. The textured fabrics provide tactile and visual stimulation, particularly for elders with cognitive limitations. Assorted fabrics can also be used to help elders think about their own unique personal characteristics and how fabric can be viewed as a symbolic representation of those differences. When combined into a decorative wall hanging, the richness of the diversity of the fabric reflects the richness of the diversity of people.

Art as a Means of Orientation or Self-Esteem.   Group art activities may serve as a means to orient elders with cognitive or memory limitations (Fausek, 1997; Mosher-Ashley & Barrett, 1997). For example, certain colors and symbols are associated with seasons. Painting, dying fabrics, or making paper flowers associated with the season may reinforce an elder's seasonal orientation. If elders are unable to participate in these activities, pictures in magazines can be made into a collage to depict the seasons. Elders may be asked to identify shapes and colors and arrange precut pieces into a mosaic. These activities ask elders to interact with the group leader and each other in a creative way that stimulates orientation as a therapeutic end. Working together in a group encourages group interaction and promotes socialization for elders who may be painfully isolated from others.

High-functioning elders may be dealing with more complex issues of self-identify or self-esteem, which can be incorporated as themes in an art project (Sterret & Pokorny, 1994). Asking elders to paint self-portraits using only colors but no identifiable form can help elders and the group leader identify feelings (Fausek, 1997). Using color as a metaphor for feelings may tap into deep emotions in a way that cannot be accomplished verbally. If elders are asked to share their self-portraits with others in the group, the activity can be further used to promote social interaction. Fausek (1997) also recommended the use of what she called "The Echo" in helping elders improve self-esteem. Elders are asked to identify an object or animal that symbolizes themselves, such as a bird, flower, or rock. They are asked to draw ripples around the item such as those that appear when a stone is thrown in the water. The ripples symbolize the many ways that people affect others that they do not know or cannot see but know are there. Elders who feel they have had little influence on others throughout life can gain a better appreciation of the ripple effect of their own lives.

Art as Recreation

Artistic endeavors can have therapeutic value simply as recreation. Elders who enjoyed painting, weaving, or sculpting as a hobby earlier in life may have put those activities aside as they were busy with careers or raising a family. Other elders have always been interested in doing art but may have lacked the encouragement or financial means to pursue their interests. With more time and access to organized activities, such as those offered by senior centers, elders may have the luxury of returning to those interests. In many states, elders can audit classes at local public colleges or universities at no charge or for reduced tuition. Art classes are also available through community recreation programs or local senior centers. The physical act of creating art and the personal enjoyment derived from the process can improve both the physical and emotional health of an elder.

Art appreciation can also be therapeutic. Similar to attending a musical performance, attending an art exhibit or gallery show is a social activity that can help elders develop new social relationships and stimulate their minds. Incorporating an educational element into the experience with a preshow lecture and postshow discussion may be particularly appealing to high-functioning elders. The visual stimulation provided by art offers an improvement in the quality of life for many elders.

The Therapeutic Use of Drama

Another alternative approach to working on the socioemotional problems of elders is the therapeutic use of drama. Drama as it is used in this section of the chapter includes all forms of performance that allow actors to tell a story, reenact a real or imaginary event, or use props, such as puppets or familiar items, to convey an idea or feeling. While the use of drama as a therapeutic technique may not be considered in the mainstream of social work approaches to working with elders, it offers great promise as a means to encourage elders of all levels of ability to explore their own creativity and stimulate their imaginations. Dramatic approaches work with elders specifically because the drama forms are unusual. Like music and art, drama appeals to a creative sphere in elders that is often overlooked in the traditional focus on an elder's physical and cognitive abilities. Elders have a rich repertoire of lifetime experiences and memories to bring to the various "stages" on which therapeutic drama takes place.

Three distinct forms of therapeutic drama have particular relevance in work with elders. The most traditional use of drama to address socioemotional problems is psychodrama, a prescribed sequence of activities designed to help elders identify and resolve emotional conflicts. This approach is very psychoanalytic in its approach and requires therapists to be trained in the use of the technique.

Drama as therapy and attendance at dramatic performances are two other ways of incorporating drama as a therapeutic element as part of an intervention that require more creativity than technique. Drama therapy, like music and art therapies, is a distinct mental health profession. Formal drama therapy requires extensive training in both counseling techniques and drama. Registered drama therapists (RDT) are certified by the National Association of Drama Therapy (National Association of Drama Therapy, 1995).

Psychodrama

Psychodrama as a specific therapeutic technique was originally developed by Jacob Levy Moreno in the 1930s (Blatner, 1995; Kipper, 1992). Moreno proposed this method as an approach to group treatment offered in contrast to the growing popularity of psychoanalysis as developed by Sigmund Freud. His focus was on promoting health and creativity rather than the more Freudian emphasis on psychopathology. He saw psychodrama as helping a client move away from the deep solitary introspection of psychoanalysis to the group arena where clients could work out their neurotic conflicts in the context of real people. Rather than focusing on a verbal exchange with a therapist, Moreno saw the therapeutic value of people reenacting conflicts and role-playing solutions to their problems in the context of both peers and the therapist (Kipper, 1992). This dramatic presentation of clients' problems in front of others helped to access not only the therapist's insights about the cause of problems and possible solutions but also those of group members.

Moreno felt the way to encourage people to take a more creative approach to life rather than justifying existing behavior patterns was to encourage spontaneity, improvisation, and willingness to experiment with new behavior patterns (Blatner, 1995). When presented in the context of role-playing rather than the real world, participants could stretch their own creative behaviors in a safe context. In other words, psychodrama is a kind of interpersonal and social laboratory (Blatner, 1995).

Membership in a psychodrama group requires group members to be willing both to participate as an actor and to offer feedback as an observer. In psychodrama, the therapist serves as director and group members as auxiliaries, or actors, in the therapeutic process. The client whose problems are being addressed is known as the protagonist and selects other group members to serve as actors in his or her dramatic presentation. Group members who are not taking the parts of significant others in the process serve as the audience. The "stage" is wherever the action is taking place. Typical psychodrama sessions last between 60 and 90 minutes and have three distinct phases.

Warm-Up Phase.   The warm-up phase resembles the beginning phases of traditional group therapy. Members of the group are asked by the therapist (director) to focus on specific recollections of holidays or events with special significance to the group, such as the death of a loved one, the diagnosis of a chronic illness, or a lifetime milestone. As the group identifies feelings connected with the event, a client (protagonist) volunteers or is selected by the group to act out the event for others in the group. Throughout the lifetime of the group, all members who are willing should have an opportunity to take the part of the protagonist. This part does not require dramatic talent in the conventional sense of the word but rather a willingness to tap one's own creativity to best convey feelings and reenact events for others in the group.

Action Phase.   Once a protagonist has been selected, he or she selects other group members, known as auxiliaries, to take significant roles in playing out the event. For example, an elderly woman who is trying to work out conflicts she is currently having with her adult children might select one group member to play her overbearing, meddlesome daughter and another to play her neglectful son. From her descriptions of the actions of her adult children, group members take on those roles to help the woman visually recreate these problematic relationships. Props may be used to set the scene within the woman's home or elsewhere where interaction between the primary players occurs. The protagonist then plays out the complaint (Kipper, 1992). Auxiliaries and other group members become an active part of the process through asking about thoughts and feelings or clarifying what actions and statements mean. The protagonist is free to reenact actual events or rehearse new behaviors in an attempt to work through conflicts.

In the action phase, the therapeutic process becomes interactive. This interaction between the protagonist and members of the group is known as the *tele*, the two-way flow of both positive and negative feelings that binds the group together (Mosher-Ashley & Barrett, 1997). The director may ask actors to reverse roles or engage in "doubling." Doubling is a technique during which one person acts or reacts to others and a "double" verbalizes what the actor is feeling in contrast to what they are doing (Kipper, 1992). The elderly woman used as an example previously may be outwardly friendly and cooperative with her daughter but in her mind she is voicing strong negative feelings about how her daughter is treating her like a helpless child. The public self engages in one kind of behavior while the private self carries on quite another nonverbal dialogue. This can also be accomplished by the use of "asides" in which the actor turns his or her head to the audience and speaks what is going on in his or her mind. Both techniques help the actor to clarify feelings and thoughts that contradict or coincide with public actions.

Acting out events is meant to offer the actor, and perhaps the auxiliaries, an opportunity for an emotional catharsis. Strong emotions are expressed through a situation the actor can control. Presenting the script of an important event or situation gives the actor the chance to give his or her side of the story to both a therapist and other group members who can assist the actor in resolving conflict.

Kipper (1992) suggested that actors can take one of three roles during this process of presenting a conflict in psychodrama. A client may play himself or herself and simply recreate an event as it did or might happen. This simulation may be most effective for elders who are self-conscious about playacting. Another technique is mimetic replication in which the person imitates a well-known response of a familiar person, such the elderly woman imitating her daughter's doting behavior or her son's neglectfulness rather than reenacting her own behavior. The third role that can be assumed by an actor is mimetic pretense in which an individual plays the part of an imaginary or fantasy person. This role is often therapeutic for a person trying to develop new and nontraditional behavior patterns. Rather than play herself or her daughter, the elderly woman may create the part of an imaginary friend who confronts the daughter about her oppressive treatment of her mother—a part in which she may verbalize her feelings about being overprotected in a way not possible through other roles. Or she may play the part of her late husband admonishing his son for neglecting his mother.

Closure: The Sharing/Processing Phase.   After an actor has presented a situation or event, group members are asked to react to the events they have viewed. Group members may share their insights about the situation suggesting ways in which the protagonist might handle the situation in the future. Seeing the similarity between the protagonist and their situation and discussing it can lead group members to their own catharsis. The most valuable part of this phase may be the opportunity for elders to gain new perspectives on familiar problems. For example, a daughter may seem overbearing and meddlesome because she is deeply concerned about her mother's well-being. While her elderly mother may resent all the intrusiveness of a overprotective daughter, the daughter might see her constant attention as a source of comfort and support for her mother. Her son may seem neglectful because he finds it too painful to admit that his mother is older and needs his help, rather than vice versa. His inattentiveness comes from fear and denial, rather than from lack of affection for his mother. It may be difficult for an elder to see these alternative explanations for others' behavior without the input from group members.

In addition to new perspectives on old problems, elders can benefit from the social interaction that takes place during group problem solving. Discussing personal problems may be difficult, if not impossible, for elders to do with family members, especially if the family member is part of the problem. Other elders who can relate to common problems elders experience as part of the aging process may be more credible confidants and advice givers than younger friends.

The Benefits of Psychodrama

Practicing New Behaviors.   Psychodrama offers elders an opportunity to learn and practice new behavior patterns (Mosher-Ashley & Barrett, 1997). It is human nature to resort to tried and true methods of solving problems. Elders may seem rigid and set in their ways because they have found a repertoire of behavior patterns that continues to work and they do not need to learn new ways of doing things. The suggestions of both a therapist and other group members in the psychodrama process can give elders new approaches that they might not even have considered. Developing new behavior patterns in the context of the group can offer elders a source of support not available to them in their immediate environment.

Relieving Social Isolation.   Social isolation is one of the most common themes among elders who have developed socioemotional problems. The opportunity to interact with others afforded by psychodrama can help to draw elders out of an isolated world and encourage them to interact with others (Carman & Nordin, 1984). Despite the seriousness of problems presented in psychodrama, elders often find humor in the interaction with other elders around problem solving. The opportunity to imitate others or reenact events in their lives can actually be fun. Moving troublesome feelings from within one's mind to the public arena of a small stage may help elders to put these feelings into better perspective.

Resolving Grief.   Grief is also a common theme. Elders may get stuck in the bereavement process and be unable to move into resolving the loss of a loved one. Acknowledging the grief and expressing the depth of the personal pain in a supportive environment of other elders can be a cathartic experience. Presented within the supportive environment of other elders who truly do know how devastating loss can be may help an elder to move on. The grief needs to be acknowledged before people can move forward.

Reenacting Previous Roles.   Psychodrama may also give elders an opportunity to recall and reexperience past roles. Carman and Nordin (1984) relayed a powerful story of an elderly woman in a nursing home who reenacted her family's Thanksgiving traditions as part of a psychodrama therapy group. She selected other group members as family members and seated them at a large table. Very carefully and precisely, she played out all of the roles she played as hostess for the festivities, including greeting family members, preparing food, making sure everyone got enough to eat, and shooing people away from the table so that she could clean up. In the nursing home, she had limited opportunities to be a nurturer and caregiver, which were cherished roles from earlier in her life. Reenacting a family holiday gave her the opportunity to replay these roles and vicariously derive the same satisfaction she experienced earlier in her life.

"My Clients Would Never Do That!"   Some gerontological social workers react with disbelief when psychodrama is suggested as a therapeutic intervention in treating the socioemotional problems of elders. They find it hard to believe that an elderly man in a wheelchair or an older woman who will barely speak to staff members in a nursing home or congregate living situation would ever agree to participate in a psychodrama group. Psychodrama has been criticized for its psychoanalytic focus and may at a cursory glance seem inappropriate for elders. However, it was Jacob Moreno's earliest contention in developing this approach that it moved away from the intense focus on the internal thought processes and subconscious material emphasized in the psychoanalytical approach to helping the client solve real problems in the context of real people in the real world

(Blatner, 1995). That is precisely what social work with elders entails—giving elders important insights to help change behavior to derive greater satisfaction from their lives as older adults. Psychodrama can work because it goes beyond traditional talk therapies and offers elders a refreshing alternative to explore feelings. It may be particularly attractive to elders because it is so different and intriguing. If the belief that elders can change is an important part of gerontological social work, it is imperative the social worker become familiar with and explore a variety of therapeutic interventions.

Other Forms of Drama as Therapy

Psychodrama may be the most highly developed form of the therapeutic use of drama, but drama can be used in other, less structured formats for the purpose of promoting personal and emotional growth. Elders can use puppets to act out difficult situations or simply to enjoy as an art form. For example, Hansel and Gretel puppets have been used by elders with mild to moderate forms of dementia to explore the fear associated with getting lost in familiar places. As Hansel and Gretel left a trail of crumbs to help find their way home, elders can explore ways in which to regain their orientation when they find themselves lost. The puppets become a medium for acting out those fears and also for exploring options for problem resolution.

In improvisation, elders are assigned a role or situation and asked to create a character and spontaneous dialogue (Kavanaugh, 1993). Improvisation is therapeutic because participants often incorporate aspects of their own personality into this role, consciously or unconsciously. It is safe to act out these personality traits or emotional issues because the actions, thoughts, and feelings can be attributed to the character, not the elder. When used over time as a means of self-expression, both the elder and social worker will recognize recurring themes. These themes may be indicative of unresolved emotional conflicts, which can be addressed in individual or group therapy.

Pantomime, similar in many ways to improvisation, can be used to help elders convey feelings about familiar situations shared by many elders, such as going to the doctor or completing difficult household chores. This activity requires elders to think about how to convey feelings and ideas nonverbally, a task that can stimulate an elder's creativity in a variety of ways. Charades and other games requiring pantomiming can also lead to great laughter, one of the best therapeutic interventions for elders. The laughter combined with the social interaction that occurs in any group activity has both direct and indirect therapeutic benefits.

Elders may be interested in organizing their own theatrical production, brushing up on dramatic talents long left behind or trying an art form that has always interested them. Presenting a play or musical for others' enjoyment is not so much the therapeutic activity as the organizational, social, and personal skills that are mobilized in the process of putting together a dramatic presentation. Elders can make new friends, develop new interests, and feel they are participating in something creative as members of a dramatic troupe.

For elders who are not interested in participating in a dramatic presentation, attending a play or dramatic presentation can be therapeutic by itself. Like concerts and art shows, theater presentations are a good way to offer a stimulating break from everyday life and facilitate social interaction with other elders.

Animal-Assisted Therapy

If you are an animal lover, you do not need to be convinced that the presence of a dog, cat, bird, or any other domesticated pet can be a source of both pleasure and comfort. Pets receive and give love unconditionally and touch a part of the human psyche that even other human beings cannot reach. For this reason, animals are being used in a variety of ways to help elders overcome depression, reduce anxiety, and improve social skills. Animal-assisted therapy refers to a wide range of opportunities for elders and animals to interact in a therapeutic way. Animal-assisted therapy does not require the level of knowledge and skill required for interventions such as music, art, or drama therapy, but it does require a solid understanding of the significance of the animal-human connection and the practical considerations in using animals for therapeutic purposes.

The Human-Animal Bond

People of all ages need to form attachments to other humans in order to grow and thrive in the process of human development. Babies attach to caregivers, children to parents and siblings, older children to friends, partners to one another, and so on throughout the life course. For elders, often these bonds have been severed by death of significant others or social isolation from family and friends. While bonding with animals should never substitute for interaction with humans, animals are often good substitutes for affectional ties when other outlets are not available. The ability to unconditionally unite with another living being, in this case an animal, requires people to move outside themselves and care for something else (Dossey, 1997). Animals do not care about physical disabilities or communication difficulties nor do they pass judgment about cognitive abilities. If given attention and basic care, animals can reciprocate with affection and devotion.

Interaction with animals has been shown to reduce blood pressure and slow both heartbeat and respiratory rates (Carmack & Fila, 1989; Proulx, 1998; Raina et al., 1999). Pets may provide an acceptable outlet for rubbing, petting, stroking, and scratching, meeting the needs of elders to touch and be touched (Dossey, 1997). Interacting with animals both verbally and nonverbally has been shown to approximate contact with humans, meeting a person's need to make a connection to another living being. This is particularly important for elders who are either socially or cognitively isolated (Barba, 1995). Animals can provide valuable companionship for elders who live alone. Ownership of a pet has been found to buffer the effects of stress caused by poor health or the loss of significant others in an elder's life. A pet's ability to comfort and console can help an elder face other life challenges as well as provide a buffer against social isolation (Raina et al., 1999).

Animals' Roles as Social Connections

Animals can also serve as a social catalyst in facilitating better communication between people. Walking one's pet is a good way to meet neighbors and start conversations that might not otherwise happen. Animals are a nonthreatening topic of conversation that can open a connection between people. Even in more institutional settings, such as adult day health, congregate living, and nursing homes, an animal can give people an excuse to start talking to each other even when they believe they have little in common. A shared affection for animals may be the start of new relationships for elders.

Interaction with animals can also facilitate reminiscence. Elders may fondly recall family pets from earlier in their lives, thereby retrieving happy memories. Accessing happy memories as a way to improve current mood states is one of the purposes of reminiscence therapy, as discussed in the previous chapter. Animals can serve as a good catalyst for this reminiscence process. As elders share with one another memories of a family pet, they are socially interacting and developing reciprocal relationships—an essential part of helping elders build and maintain social support systems.

Types of Animal-Assisted Therapy

Pets as Companion Animals.   For elders who retain a moderately high level of independent functioning and are willing to take on the responsibilities, owning a pet may be a source of comfort and social support. Pet ownership has been found to foster feelings of happiness, love, security, and a sense of responsibility similar to the benefits of interaction with humans (Raina et al., 1999). Pet owners make fewer visits to a physician, have better physical health, and stay more physically active than persons who do not own pets (Seigel, 1990; Willis, 1997). The caregiving involved with dogs and cats may actually provide people with a purpose in their lives encouraging them to stay healthier and more active precisely because their pet depends on them for care (Francis, 1991). Pets need to be fed and exercised, giving elders a way to keep busy through an established routine every day. Raina and associates (1999) found that elders who had pets retained their ability to perform the activities of daily living (ADLs) longer than elders without pets even after controlling for factors in health and mental health. Pets actually helped these elders stay healthy.

Of course, these positive benefits are contingent on an elder's interest in the responsibilities of full-time pet ownership. While some elders would love to have a pet, they may not be able to do so in their living situation or simply do not have the time or energy to take on pet ownership. Veterinary care, food, and other supplies can be expensive and present a formidable obstacle to elders with limited incomes. After a lifetime of responsibilities to family, friends, and jobs, some elders simply do not want to make the commitment required to care for a pet full time. Some communities have developed pet loaning programs in which an elder may have the companionship of a pet for a limited amount of time such as a few hours a week. While they may cherish the time the pet visits, they do not have the full-time responsibility or expense of pet ownership. These arrangements can be informally arranged with family, friends, or neighbors or may involve more formal arrangements through programs, such as Pet Partners.

Visiting Pet Programs.   Pet Partners is one of many such programs in which elders are visited by animals either in their own homes or in institutions, such as adult day health centers and nursing homes. Pet Partners is a nationwide program sponsored by the Delta Society, a voluntary organization established in 1977 to promote the mutual benefits of relationships between people and animals and to help people improve their health, independence, and quality of life (Delta Society, 1999). Pet Partners trains volunteers and screens pets to become visiting animals in nursing homes, hospitals, schools, rehabilitation centers, and private homes. The purpose of Pet Partners and other such programs is to provide opportunities for people to connect with animals in an environment that respects the needs of both people and the animals. The screening and training programs ensure that there will be the best match between the animal and the people benefitting from the program. Although dogs are the best known "pet partners," this program also uses cats, guinea pigs, rabbits, horses, goats, llamas, donkeys, pot-bellied pigs, and birds.

Pet Partners and other visiting pet programs accomplish their therapeutic purpose by putting people and pets together and letting them enjoy one another. The goal of the program is primarily recreational and may not be tied to any specific mental health goals, although it is assumed that the interchange will benefit both animal and person. Whether the animals are presenting a structured performance or simply mingling with elders, the purpose is to get elders to connect with the animal. Visiting pet programs have a particular appeal in working with elders. The programs involve minimal expense as most are run by volunteers in the community. It does not involve a specific commitment on the part of elders to the regime of caring for a pet, but allows short exposure to the benefits of a pet.

Structured Animal-Assisted Therapy.   Animal-assisted therapy can also take a more structured approach than the interaction afforded by a visiting pet program. Nurses, social workers, occupational and physical therapists, and psychologists may decide to include animal-assisted therapy as part of a psychosocial intervention with elders. When offered as true "therapy," health and mental health professionals establish specific goals for the use of animals and continually evaluate the effectiveness of animal-assisted therapy in reaching those goals. An elder is assessed for both an interest in working with a pet and the ability to actively interact with a pet.

Once an elder has been consulted and evaluated, it is necessary to decide what kind of animal would be most appropriate. Dogs have been found to be somewhat more appropriate for pet therapy than cats, due to their temperament. While there are cats that enjoy being handled and are affectionate, many prefer not to be touched and will not offer the reciprocal affection that dogs do. Mature dogs are often better than puppies because they tend to be less exuberant and easier to handle. Some elders will respond better to small animals that they can hold in their laps, while those in wheelchairs or confined to their beds might do better with big dogs that they can pet without reaching down. These decisions are usually made between the mental health professional, the facility in which the therapeutic encounter will take place, and the elder.

Animal-assisted therapy sessions with groups usually consist of a 30-minute presentation or show given by the animals followed by an hour or longer visit with residents or patients. The presentation is often given for pure entertainment and gives elders an opportunity to focus on the animals and for the animals to become comfortable with them. An hour-long visit allows the animal to wander among the elders, giving them the opportunity to pet, talk to, or touch the animal. Elders are given the option to be as involved as they feel comfortable being, without feeling required to touch the pet. Individual sessions in pet therapy usually last about 30 minutes during which time an elder can touch, talk to, or just hold the pet. In both group and individual settings, elders are encouraged to talk to staff and each other about the experience. Animal-assisted therapy can also provide benefits to the staff of institutions where a program in initiated. The presence of an animal can present an opportunity for both elders and staff to have fun together. The positive effects animals have on elders can also be translated into positive physical and psychological benefits to caregivers (Willis, 1997).

As in other therapeutic interventions, once goals are established and an action plan is developed and initiated, the intervention must be constantly monitored to assess how it is reaching the identified goals in a measurable fashion. If the goal is to improve socialization, how is this going to be measured? What observable differences in behavior indicate that animal-assisted therapy has improved an elder's mental health or social skills? How can the benefits of interaction with an animal be translated into general mental health benefits for the elders and others in their environment? Animal-assisted therapy becomes most beneficial when mood and behavior changes persist beyond the specific encounter with an animal.

Service Animals.   Another kind of animal-assisted therapy to be discussed in this chapter is the use of animals as providers of personal service. For persons with disabilities or elders with restricted mobility, pets can provide concrete assistance that may help an elder to maintain independent living. Most service animals are dogs although some monkeys have also been trained to provide assistance. Service dogs may serve as hearing dogs for elders with impaired hearing, alerting an elder to the phone or door bell, or intruders. Seeing-eye dogs have long provided assistance to persons with visual impairments, both in assisting with mobility and providing protection. The National Service Dog Center, also sponsored by the Delta Society, provides a link to learning more about service dogs and advocating for persons of all ages who have service dogs (Delta Society, 1999).

Animal-Assisted Therapy and Elders with Alzheimer's Disease

Animal-assisted therapy, similar to music therapy, appears to have an amazing ability to reach elders in all stages of Alzheimer's disease (Batson, McCabe, Baun, & Wilson, 1998; Fritz, Farver, Kass, & Hart, 1995). When traditional talk therapies fail to make a connection with an elder, nonverbal methods appear to be much more successful. Churchill, Safaoul, McCabe, and Baun (1999) found that allowing elders with Alzheimer's disease to talk to and pet an animal significantly reduced the agitation commonly associated with the disease. They observed increased verbalizations in patients who did not verbalize with humans, greater attentiveness, more facial expressions, and more touching behavior in the presence of a pet than was observed when the pet was not present. The animals appeared to be able to reach elders with Alzheimer's disease in a way that nurses, social workers, and other therapists could not. These researchers found the calming effects to be very effective in counteracting the Sundown Syndrome, discussed in Chapter 5. This disorientation and agitation that frequently occurs in elders with Alzheimer's disease in the late afternoon has been attributed to the effect of changing light on the senses. When animals were presented to elders at this time of day, the elders appeared to be more relaxed. Their blood pressure and skin temperature were lowered. The presence of the animal also appeared to stimulate reminiscence and memories among persons with Alzheimer's disease. Other benefits to persons with Alzheimer's disease included the opportunity to both receive and give more personal affection. The elders benefit from the unconditional acceptance of the animal despite the significant changes in both physical appearance and cognitive abilities that accompany Alzheimer's disease.

Precautions in Establishing Animal-Assisted Programs

Despite all the benefits of connecting animals and elders, there are a number of issues to consider seriously before establishing a program on either an organizational or individual basis. The Delta Society offers phone consultation and on-site assessment to groups considering programs and can offer invaluable advice in planning the best match between animals and elders (Delta Society, 1999).

The primary consideration is to make sure elders want interaction with animals. People can enjoy animals but have no interest in playing with them—no matter how adorable the dog or cat seems to be. This issue reinforces the point that social workers need to constantly remind themselves about whose goals are the focus of the intervention. Some elders are afraid of animals as a result of earlier life experiences of being bitten or scratched. Frail elders may fear that an energetic dog or cat may be too frisky for them and could hurt them. Other elders with sensory limitations may find the quick moves of a pet confusing and annoying, making them more anxious rather than calming them. Good communication with the elders being considered for animal-assisted therapy is essential to the development of a successful program.

Matching animals with the appropriate temperament with elders is a second consideration in establishing an animal-assisted program. Not every animal is gentle or patient enough to come into a room full of strangers without getting upset. Animals need to be carefully assessed for an even temperament and a willingness to be vigorously petted and touched. Pets that are good-natured with children are usually also good with frail elders. Animals should also be in good health, free of infectious diseases, and fully immunized before they are considered for a program (Mosher-Ashley & Barrett, 1997).

Careful consideration of the appropriate time in an elder's day for animal-assisted therapy is a third precaution in establishing a program. Pet therapy should be used as an adjunct to a broader plan for improving an elder's psychosocial functioning and should not interfere with established mealtimes or therapy sessions (Bruck, 1996). Visitation with a pet should not be attempted when an elder is tired or feeling poorly. The exception to this may be the institution of pet therapy for elders with Alzheimer's disease during the period of restlessness and agitation associated with Sundown Syndrome, which was discussed earlier in this chapter.

In an institutional setting, it is important to consider carefully whom to include in animal-assisted therapy programs. Limited cognitive abilities or sensory deficits are not necessarily reasons to exclude elders when, in fact, they may benefit the most. However, elders who are prone to becoming aggressive or violent when overstimulated may not be appropriate.

Finally, it is crucial that adequate staff be assigned to supervise any animal-assisted therapy. An animal in an institutional setting may create a temporary chaos that requires enough staff presence to insure that every elder has access to the animal without risking personal injury. Usually getting staff to volunteer for this responsibility is not a problem as it provides a welcome change from the institutional regime.

Summary

The alternative therapies presented in this chapter offer social workers another set of tools in working with elders experiencing socioemotional problems. These therapies can serve as adjuncts to more traditional social work approaches. Music can help elders retrieve happy memories from earlier in their lives, uncover unresolved conflicts, or offer the simple enjoyment of listening to a beautiful sound. It offers great promise in helping a social worker establish a connection with elders with cognitive limitations because the ability to receive and process music appears to remain long after other cognitive abilities have faded.

Doing art can be both fun and therapeutic for elders. The therapeutic use of art, whether in the form of art therapy or art as an activity, can stimulate rarely used creative abilities. Elders who return to painting or take it up for the first time later in life may find the artistic process deeply rewarding. For elders with cognitive limitations, art can serve as a medium to reconnect the elder both to his or her deepest feelings and to other elders in the environment. The beauty of both art and music for elders is that there is no one universal way for these to work therapeutically. Each individual elder can participate and therefore appreciate art and music in their own unique way.

Drama and psychodrama are less commonly used with elders but offer other creative ways to access emotions and develop social skills. Psychodrama is the most structured drama-related approach and requires extensive training. However, other conventions, such as puppets, improvisation, and pantomime, can be included as part of a comprehensive approach. The use of drama is limited only by the social worker's creativity. Animal-assisted therapy is less focused on a formal therapeutic intervention and more attuned to providing simple enjoyment and companionship for elders. Receiving the unconditional love and affection of a pet full time or for a few hours a week can help isolated and lonely elders feel loved and needed.

Perhaps the most important part of including alternative therapies in an intervention effort with elders is that all of these approaches can be therapeutic—simply because they are fun and promote social interaction. Finding an occasion to laugh and interact with others may be the most therapeutic aspect of all.

Check Out These Websites!

1. **/www.petsforum.deltasociety/default/html** The site offers detailed information about the therapeutic use of pets as well as a full description of the various activities of the Delta Society. It also provides useful links to other kinds of animal-assisted therapy programs throughout the United States and Canada.

2. **www.ncata.com** The National Coalition of Arts Therapies Association site offers specific information about a number of the alternative therapeutic methods discussed in this chapter, including drama therapy, creative arts therapies, and music and dance therapies. It identifies the educational requirements for therapists practicing within each of these disciplines and provides links to undergraduate and graduate programs in the United States and Canada.

3. **www.arttherapy.org** This site is the organizational web page for the American Art Therapy Association. It provides viewers with an in-depth description of art as a therapeutic modality, state legislative updates, conferences, and educational programs.

4. **www.namt.com** The American Music Therapy Association website provides links to several sites of interest to individuals who would like to learn more about music therapy. It provides information about finding a music therapist in a geographical area, resources for finding out more about music therapy as a career

and as a therapeutic intervention, and the educational requirements to gain certification in music therapy.

References

Aldridge, D. (1996). *Music therapy research and practice in medicine: From out of the silence.* London: Jessica Kingsley Publishers.

American Art Therapy Association. (1998). Frequently asked questions about art therapy. Retrieved from the World Wide Web, September 15, 1999. Available at http://www.arttherapy.org/fact.html.

Barba, B. E. (1995). The positive influence of animals: Animal-assisted therapy in acute care. *Clinical Nursing Specialist, 9,* 199–202.

Batson, K., McCabe, B., Baun, M., & Wilson, C. (1998). The effect of a therapy dog on socialization and physiological indicators of stress in persons diagnosed with Alzheimer's disease. In C. C. Wilson & D. C. Turner (Eds.), *Companion animals in human health* (pp. 203–215). Thousand Oaks, CA: Sage.

Beatty, W. W., Zavadil, K. D., Bailly, R. C., Rixen, G. J., Zavadil, L. W., Farnham, N., & Fisher, L. (1988). Preserved musical skill in a severely demented patient. *International Journal of Clinical Neuropsychology, 10*(4), 158–164.

Blatner, A. (1995). Psychodramatic methods in psychotherapy. *Psychiatric Times, 12*(5). Retrieved from the World Wide Web, September 15, 1999. Available at http://www.mhsource.com/edu/psytimes/p950520.html.

Bright, R. (1997). *Wholeness in later life.* London: Jessica Kingsley Publishers.

Brooke, S. L. (1996). *A therapist's guide to art therapy assessment: Tools of the trade.* Springfield, IL: Charles C. Thomas Publishing.

Bruck, L. B. (1996). Today's ancillaries, part 2: Art, music, and pet therapy. *Nursing Homes* (July/August), 36–45.

Carmack, B. J., & Fila, D. (1989). Animal-assisted therapy: A nursing intervention. *Nursing Management, 20*(5), 96–101.

Carman, M. B., & Nordin, S. R. (1984). Psychodrama: A therapeutic modality for elderly in nursing homes. *Clinical Gerontologist, 3*(1), 15–24.

Casby, J. A., & Holm, M. B. (1994). The effect of music on repetitive disruptive vocalizations of persons with dementia. *The American Journal of Occupational Therapy, 48*(10), 883–889.

Churchill, M., Safaoul, J., McCabe, B., & Baun, M. M. (1999). Using a therapy dog to alleviate agitation and desocialization of people with Alzheimer's disease. *Journal of Psychosocial Nursing, 37*(4), 16–22.

Clair, A. A., & Bernstein, B. (1990). A preliminary study of music therapy programming for severely regressed with Alzheimer's type dementia. *Journal of Applied Gerontology, 9,* 299–311.

Clark, M. E., Lipe, A. W., & Bilbrey, M. (1998). Use of music to decrease aggressive behaviors in people with dementia. *Journal of Gerontological Nursing, 24*(7), 10–17.

Coleman, V. D., & Farris-Dufrene, P. M. (1996). *Art therapy and psychotherapy: Blending two therapeutic approaches.* Washington, DC: Accelerated Development.

Delta Society. (1999). *Delta Society overview.* Renton, WA: The Delta Society. Retrieved from the World Wide Web, September 5, 1999. Available at http://www.petsforum.deltasociety/default/html.

Dossey, L. (1997). The healing power of pets: A look at animal-assisted therapy. *Alternative Therapies, 3*(4), 8–16.

Fausek, D. (1997). *A practical guide to art therapy groups.* Binghamton, NY: Haworth Press.

Francis, G. M. (1991). Here come the puppies: The power of the human-animal bond. *Holistic Nursing Practice, 5*(2), 38–41.

Fritz, C. L., Farver, T. B., Kass, P. H., & Hart, L. A. (1995). Association with companion animals and the expression of noncognitive symptoms in Alzheimer's patients. *The Journal of Nervous and Mental Disease, 183,* 459–463.

Gfeffer, K. E. (1990). Cultural context as it relates to music therapy. In R. F. Unkefer (Ed.), *Treatment of adults with mental disorders: Theoretical bases and clinical interventions* (pp. 63–69). New York: Schirmer Books.

Hanser, S. B. (1990). A music therapy strategy for depressed older adults in the community. *Journal of Applied Gerontology, 9,* 283–297.

Hanser, S. B., & Clair, A. A. (1995). Retrieving the losses of Alzheimer's disease for patients and care-givers with the aid of music. In T. Wigram, B. Saperston, & R. West (Eds.), *The art and science of music therapy: A handbook* (pp. 342–360). Chur, Switzerland: Harwood Academic.

Harlan, J. E. (1991). The use of art therapy for older adults with developmental disabilities. *Activities, Adaptation & Aging, 15,* 67–79.

Johnson, G. (1995). *Fire in the mind: Science, faith, and the search for order.* New York: Vintage Books.

Kaplan, F. F. (1998). Scientific art therapy: An integrative and research-based approach. *Art Therapy: Journal of the American Association of Art Therapy, 15*(2), 93–98.

Kavanaugh, K. M. (1993). Drama therapy enlivens the creative spirit. *The Council Close-Up, 33,* 1–4.

Kipper, D. A. (1992). Psychodrama: Group psychotherapy through role-playing. *International Journal of Psychotherapy 42*(4), 495–521.

Malchiodi, C. A. (1990). *Breaking the silence: Art therapy with children from violent homes.* New York: Brunner/Mazel.

Mosher-Ashley, P. M., & Barrett, P. W. (1997). *A life worth living: Practical strategies for reducing depression in older adults.* Baltimore, MD: Health Professions Press.

National Association of Drama Therapy. (1995). *Drama therapy.* Retrieved from the World Wide Web, September 5, 1999. Available at http://www.nadt.org.

Norberg, A., Melin, E., & Asplund, K. (1986). Reactions to music, touch, and object presentation in the final stages of dementia: An exploratory study. *International Journal of Nursing, 23*(4), 315–323.

Proulx, D. (1998). Animal-assisted therapy. *Critical Care Nurse, 18*(2), 80–84.

Raina, P., Walter-Toews, D., Bonnett, B., Woodward, C., & Abernathy, T. (1999). Influence of companion animals on the physical and psychological health of older people: An analysis of a one-year longitudinal study. *Journal of the American Geriatrics Society, 47,* 323–329.

Rosling, L. K., & Kitchen, J. (1992). Music and drawing with institutionalized elderly. *Activities, Adaptation & Aging, 14*(4), 59–64.

Seigel, J. (1990). Stressful life events and the use of physician services among the elderly: The moderating role of pet ownership. *Journal of Perspectives in Social Psychology, 58,* 1081–1086.

Standley, J. (1995). Music as a therapeutic intervention in medical and dental treatment. In T. Wigram, B. Saperston, & R. West (Eds.), *The art and science of music therapy: A handbook* (pp. 3–22). Chur, Switzerland: Harwood Academic.

Sterret, P., & Pokorny, M. (1994). Art activities for patients with Alzheimer's and related disorders. *Geriatric Nursing, 15,* 155–159.

Thaut, M. H. (1990). Neuropsychological processes in music perception and their relevance in music therapy. In R. F. Unkefer (Ed.), *Treatment of adults with mental disorders: Theoretical bases and clinical interventions* (pp. 3–31). New York: Schirmer Books.

Towse, E. (1995). Listening and accepting. In T. Wigram, B. Saperston, & R. West (Eds.), *The art and science of music therapy: A handbook* (pp. 324–341.). Chur, Switzerland: Harwood Academic.

Willis, D. A. (1997). Animal therapy. *Rehabilitation Nursing, 22*(2), 78–81.

8

Addictive Disorders and Suicide Prevention in Elders

Substance Abuse and Elders

It is not difficult for anyone who works with elders to see how depression and anxiety can be major problems for this population in view of the myriad of life challenges and changes they must face in this period of their lives. Our notion of an elder with an alcohol or drug problem, however, may be difficult to separate from media images of the skid-row bum, a disheveled, incoherent old man lying in an alley. Health and mental health providers' ageist stereotypes about the typical substance abuser actually prevent professionals from both identifying potential abusers and providing treatment. Too often an elder's tendency to use alcohol frequently and heavily is dismissed as "the only vice she has left" or "something to help him sleep." While use of illicit drugs may be rare among elders, self-medication with prescription tranquilizers and sedatives is often overlooked as constituting an unhealthy drug dependency. Professionals and family members may inadvertently enable an elder to develop and continue substance abuse.

This chapter examines the problem of alcohol and drug abuse within the elderly population. It explores what is considered problem alcohol and drug use, who is at greatest risk for abuse, how to assess substance abuse problems, and what interventions are available to elders and their families. The chapter concludes with a frank discussion about suicide—too often the consequence of untreated alcohol and drug problems among elders.

Alcohol Use and Abuse by Elders

Alcohol use and abuse by elders remains one of the most invisible problems of elders, even though the frequency of drinking and the amount consumed declines with age (Adams & Cox, 1997; Dufour & Fuller, 1995; Helzer, Bucholz, & Robins,

1995). It is estimated that 49.4 percent of persons over the age of 65 years of age drink alcohol at least on a semiregular basis, compared to 73.1 percent of persons between the ages of 18 and 29 (National Institute on Alcohol Abuse and Alcoholism, 1998). Approximately 10 percent of elders are defined as problem drinkers (Adams & Cox, 1997). This figure is hotly debated with other estimates ranging from as low as 1 percent of the elder population to much higher than 10 percent. The National Institute on Alcohol Abuse and Alcoholism (1998) has observed that 6 to 11 percent of elders admitted to hospitals show signs of alcoholism, while 20 percent to 40 percent of elders in institutions, such as psychiatric facilities and nursing homes, show clinical signs of alcohol dependence. With such high abuse rates documented in health care facilities, the 10 percent figure may even be a modest estimate of this problem.

These statistics refer strictly to the current cohort of elders that spans the ages of 65 to over 100. Many of today's elders grew up in an environment with strict social and religious mores about the use of alcohol, which may account for the dramatic differences in the sheer numbers of elders who drink even casually compared to younger cohorts. Current attitudes about the social acceptability of alcohol consumption suggest that the numbers of elders who drink and consequently those who will develop problem-drinking habits will increase in coming decades (Adams & Cox, 1997). The casual attitudes about drug and alcohol use among baby boomers as well as high school students and college-aged young adults will no doubt follow these cohorts throughout life. This is another example of the importance of assessing the influence of birth cohort and the influence of a life course perspective when discussing the biopsychosocial problems of elders. The seeds of any substance abuse problem can often be traced to a lifetime of both behavior and attitudes. Contemporary research on the use of alcohol among elders is traditionally based on cross-sectional research in which current elders are compared to current cohorts of younger drinkers. Longitudinal research that traces long-term patterns in alcohol use over time indicates that alcohol consumption patterns remain relatively stable (Gomberg & Zucker, 1998; Levenson, Aldwin, & Spiro, 1998; Smith, 1997).

Problems in Assessing Alcohol Abuse among Elders

Defining Problem Drinking. Defining what constitutes problem drinking or alcoholism for elders is one of the most controversial aspects of determining its prevalence. The traditional criteria for alcoholism include alcohol consumption equivalent to one fifth of distilled spirits during a drinking episode, alcoholic blackouts, withdrawal symptoms once consumption of alcohol is stopped, high blood alcohol levels without appearing intoxicated, and the continuation of drinking even in the face of serious financial, legal, or social problems (Butler, Lewis, & Sunderland, 1998). While these criteria may be appropriate for younger persons, they may miss the more subtle indicators that an elder has an alcohol problem. Elders who abuse alcohol may not have the legal, social, occupational, or financial problems that often bring younger problem drinkers into treatment (National

Institute on Alcohol Abuse and Alcoholism, 1998). Younger persons who drink heavily are more likely to be arrested for drunk driving or to face job-related problems caused by alcohol use, both of which eventually force the person into treatment. Elders are more likely to drink at home, less likely to be convicted of drunk driving, and likely to begin heavy drinking after retirement. It is much easier to keep drinking behavior private without the public consequences other age groups experience.

Age-Related Changes.   Alcohol-related impairments are also easily confused with physical changes associated with aging. Loss of memory, difficulty in concentrating, insomnia, erratic mood swings, depression, and falling accidents (all signs of alcohol problems) may be attributed to biological and psychological changes associated with the early onset of dementia or declining physical health (Gomberg & Zucker, 1998; Smith, 1997). Health and mental health providers may not even consider these symptoms to be caused by alcohol use. Elders are more likely to receive medical attention for the consequences of alcohol use rather than for problem drinking as the presenting problem.

Determining Blood Alcohol Content.   Estimates of blood alcohol content are also inaccurate indicators of alcohol problems among elders. Normal age-related changes affect the way in which an older body absorbs and reacts to alcohol in the bloodstream (Gomberg & Zucker, 1998). Elders have a higher blood alcohol content than younger persons after consuming the same amount of alcohol due to a decrease in the amount of water in the body and a decrease in the amount of lean muscle mass (Holland, 1999; Smith, 1997). Each drink consumed results in greater intoxication. A person may have been able to have two or three beers when he or she was 30 and show no signs of intoxication. Those three beers will have a very different effect on a 70-year-old body.

The Problem of Self-Reporting.   Estimates of alcohol use and abuse are computed using a combination of self-reports and medical records. Self-reports of drinking behavior tend to underestimate an individual's drinking behavior especially when drinking is heavy. Elders who are heavy drinkers may purposely underreport their drinking when asked by a health care provider or may have a poor memory about how much alcohol they have actually consumed. Medical records that rely on health care providers to obtain and record drinking behavior assume health care providers have actually asked elders about their drinking. This rarely occurs unless there is a medical problem or accident which necessitates asking that question. Nurses and physicians may feel uncomfortable asking elders about such personal matters or erroneously assume it is not a problem.

Using More Qualitative Measures.   Gomberg (1990) suggested that the criteria for identifying alcoholism in elders should include less quantitative measures about alcohol consumption and more qualitative criteria that capture the ways in which alcohol has compromised an elder's biopsychosocial well-being. Included in these criteria are the incidence of falls and other accidents caused directly or indirectly by the use of alcohol, the presence of nutritional deficiencies when alcohol interferes with healthy eating, social isolation, family problems, and medical problems associated with the use of alcohol. These are the criteria to be used in this discussion to identify alcohol abuse among elders rather than more structured measures, such as the amount of alcohol consumed or incidence of blackouts cited by Butler, Lewis, and Sunderland (1998).

Early- versus Late-Onset Alcoholism

There are important differences between elders who have lifelong heavy drinking habits versus those who begin heavy drinking late in life. Early-onset alcoholism refers to problem drinking that begins prior to age 40 and is usually the maintenance of self-destructive behavior patterns that precede the stresses of aging. This population is more likely to be male and represents two-thirds of all older adults manifesting alcohol dependence (Butler, Lewis, & Sunderland, 1998; Holland, 1999). These problem drinkers are more likely to have severe alcohol-related medical problems that result from a long history of excessive alcohol consumption. Before current medical advances, early-onset alcoholics rarely lived into old age but with improved nutritional care, antibiotics, and better hospital care, many are living much longer lives. Years of heavy drinking can cause chronic liver disease, cardiomyopathy, and alcohol-induced dementia—medical problems that can be severe and irreversible. These alcoholics are more likely to have intense emotional and psychological problems, which either caused the original addiction to alcohol or have been exacerbated by its use (Liberto & Oslin, 1997). The legal, social, and financial problems that plague younger alcoholics affect these older drinkers as well. Alcohol has left its indelible mark on the life histories of these elders, who are more likely to be divorced, separated, or never married and have limited incomes due to erratic employment histories.

Family and social support systems may long have disappeared due to the frustration and anger that chronic alcoholism creates for those who love or live with a problem drinker. The population most in need of psychosocial support may be least likely to have it. Lifelong alcoholics are more likely to have spent time in treatment programs at some point in their lives due to the problems created by drinking at the time they had job and family responsibilities. While they may be more familiar with various treatment approaches, they are also less confident that treatment will work for them due to previous failures (Liberto & Oslin, 1997).

Late-onset alcoholism among elders, which represents the other one-third of alcohol-dependent elders, is characterized by problem drinking that starts during middle age or early old age (Holland, 1999). Often referred to as "reactive" drinking, elders may begin heavy drinking in reaction to retirement, bereavement, or the onset of a chronic medical problem (Chenitz, Stone, & Salisbury, 1999). These drinkers are more likely to report that they feel intense depression or loneliness prior to starting a drinking episode. Drinking becomes the way to alter negative emotions or cope with the boredom created by long stretches of unstructured time. Brennan, Moos, and Mertens (1994) stressed that late-onset problem drinking is not so much a reaction to life stressors as it is a maladaptive coping strategy used to deal with those stressors. When these maladaptive patterns are replaced by more constructive activities, late-onset drinking responds very well to treatment.

In late-onset alcoholism, problem drinking starts well after the time in life when employment and family responsibilities are major life activities. It is rare that these drinkers have the history of legal, medical, and social problems that face early-onset alcoholics. They are less likely to have lifelong emotional or psychological problems, and as a result, they are more likely to have intact support systems, which form the basis for any intervention effort in addressing the problem drinking (Schonfeld & Dupree, 1997). Members of these support systems are often those persons who seek treatment for and offer their support to elders who have developed problems with alcohol.

Unfortunately, late-onset alcoholics are also less likely to see their alcohol use as a problem. This denial presents obstacles to both the identification of alcohol problems and an elder's willingness to seek treatment (Liberto & Oslin, 1997). They have not lost a job or a life partner due to alcohol use. They may not have ever been arrested for driving under the influence of alcohol or hurt themselves or others while drinking. Without these outward manifestations of what is considered problem drinking, it is easy to deny that alcohol consumption is a problem. In fact, many elders who have been moderate social drinkers their entire lives develop the symptoms of alcoholism as they get older. The casual cocktail hour may progress from one drink to several or begin earlier in the day due to the more leisure-oriented pace of a retiree's life. Combining even a slight increase in the amount of alcohol consumed with the body's declining ability to metabolize alcohol can create both intoxication and alcohol dependence in a once moderate social drinker. It is more common that these problem drinkers come to the attention of health care providers because of falls, accidents, or injuries associated with acute intoxication.

Risk Factors Associated with Alcoholism

Why do some elders become alcoholics while others do not? The exact reasons are not known, but medical and social science have been able to identify a number of factors that place some elders at greater risk than others.

Familial and Social Factors.   Alcoholism tends to run in families, especially among early-onset alcoholics, suggesting that there may be social, ethnic, and genetic proclivities among some members of the elderly population for developing an alcohol problem (Holland, 1999). It is probably not a single factor but the complex interaction of early family experiences surrounding alcohol use, its acceptability, its availability, and role-modeling that influences how an individual will use alcohol throughout the life course. Other psychosocial factors, including peer influence in young adulthood and the social context in which alcohol is consumed, contribute to lifelong use patterns. While binge drinking in colleges and universities may seem an innocent part of the campus experience for young persons, health care professionals are concerned about the number of young adults who will continue heavy alcohol use into adulthood, moving from innocuous partying to entrenched patterns of alcohol dependency.

Social Isolation and Depression. Older problem drinkers show higher levels of loneliness and lower levels of social support than their counterparts who do not have a drinking problem (Schonfeld & DuPree, 1997; Hanson, 1994). Social isolation is one of many contributing factors to the development of depression in elders and is more highly correlated with the development of problem drinking than age, gender, education, or health status (Graham & Schmidt, 1999). Divorced, separated, or never-married men and women are more likely to develop alcohol-related problems than persons who are married or widowed (Brennan & Moos, 1990)—another manifestation of the dangers of social isolation in encouraging alcohol abuse.

Elders who have recently experienced major changes in social roles are at greater risk for problem drinking (Ebersole & Hess, 1998). While retirement may be a welcome relief from employment responsibilities, it creates a major role change from productive worker to retiree. For elders whose self-worth is determined to a great extent by their professional identification and a sense of being productive, retirement may be extremely difficult. For recently widowed elders, the transition from being part of a couple with the concomitant responsibilities of caring for another person to being alone may create an unbearable emptiness. The same role transition problem may present itself when an elder goes from being relatively healthy to being chronically ill. Any major role transition in late life may precipitate heavy alcohol consumption to counter the stresses of the transition.

Leisure Lifestyles. Elders of higher socioeconomic class, particularly white men, are more likely to develop alcoholism than their lower income counterparts (Gomberg & Zucker, 1998). Clearly, one of the reasons for this is that alcohol consumption is an expensive habit. Higher incomes are associated with higher socioeconomic class. Higher income elders are also more likely to participate in social activities in retirement that encourage alcohol use, particularly in retirement communities. A leisure-oriented lifestyle may feel very much like a constant vacation. With few, if any, responsibilities, there is less need to curtail alcohol consumption. In this environment, casual use of alcohol can easily turn to alcohol dependency.

Race and Ethnicity. Moore, Hays, Greendale, Damesyn, and Reuben (1999) found no relationship between race and alcohol consumption. The support for this finding is ambiguous in other studies in which race did account for differences when gender was taken into consideration. Alcohol problems appeared more frequently among white elders than elders of color with the exception of low-income African American men. Gomberg and Zucker (1998) found upper-income white men and low-income African American men had the highest levels of alcohol use. However, African American men drank larger quantities of alcohol, preferred high alcohol-content beverages, and reported a larger number of alcohol-related health problems due to alcohol use. These problem drinkers were more likely to have combined alcohol with illicit drugs and to have begun the pattern of self-destructive behavior earlier in their lives.

African American and Hispanic women consume smaller amounts of alcohol than their white counterparts, however, and little is known about alcohol use among Asian and Native American women (Eliason, 1998). These lower levels of alcohol consumption may be due, in part, to the fact that elders of color have stronger social support systems, lower incomes, and are more likely to be members of religious organizations that discourage alcohol use.

Alcohol and Older Women

Among the most invisible segments of elder problem drinkers are women. While men are two to four times as likely to develop drinking problems at some point in their lives, women are more likely than men to become late-onset problem drinkers (Cowart & Sunderland, 1998; Eliason, 1998; Hooyman & Kiyak, 1999). Health and mental health providers are particularly reticent to ask older women about their alcohol consumption, assuming the church-going grandmother-type is highly unlikely to be a problem drinker. Yet, it is these erroneous assumptions about older women and alcohol that prevent women from receiving treatment.

This higher incidence of late-life drinking is associated with the longer life expectancy of women, making them more vulnerable to the stresses that precipitate drinking reactive to loneliness, depression, and loss of family and friends (Cowart & Sunderland, 1998). Women who are divorced, separated, or never-married are disproportionately represented among problem drinkers as compared to widowed and married older women, reinforcing the point that social isolation places elders at high risk for excessive alcohol consumption. Among elderly women who are married to heavy drinkers, drinking patterns are similar to those of single women.

Alcohol consumption is higher among older women who currently work outside the home or have worked outside the home, especially in professional or managerial positions (Eliason, 1998). While older women appear to drink because of the pressures associated with employment, older men drink more heavily when they become unemployed or retired.

Women's aging bodies are also more susceptible to becoming physically addicted to alcohol as they age. Women weigh less; therefore, each ounce of alcohol they consume has a more intoxicating effect within the body. Women's bodies have a greater ratio of fat to muscle, which results in their bodies excreting alcohol more slowly than men. This higher level of alcohol concentration accelerates the speed at which liver damage occurs.

Alcohol Problems in Nursing Homes

Estimates of problem alcohol use in nursing homes range from 2.8 percent to 49 percent depending on the setting and how alcohol abuse levels are assessed, although 15 percent probably is the most accurate figure for this population (Joseph, 1997). Lower rates are found in facilities that are predominately female, while the numbers soar when assessing alcohol abuse rates in male-dominated facilities, such as Veterans Administration nursing homes. After dementia, problem alcohol use is the second most common diagnosis upon admission to a nursing home (Stockford, Kelly, & Seitz, 1995). Persons with alcohol problems in a nursing home are more likely to be male, younger, currently without a spouse, and with lower incomes than nonalcoholic residents (Joseph, 1997). They are also more likely to show symptoms of depression and be tobacco dependent as well.

It is incorrect to assume that alcohol-dependent elders stop consuming alcohol once they are admitted to a nursing home. While many are forced to stop, due to lack of access to alcohol and the controlled environment of most skilled nursing facilities, others continue to drink surreptitiously. Family and friends may bring the elder alcohol during visits despite strict alcohol-free policies of the home. Other elders who leave the facility on a regular basis to visit family may bring alcohol back with them. Elders who are not able to get alcohol from the outside may turn to drinking mouthwash or shaving lotion, two common substances with high alcohol content.

If addicted elders cannot get alcohol, they may exhibit serious withdrawal symptoms, such as tachycardia, hypertension, tremors, or confusion. If the medical staff is unaware of alcohol dependency, these physical symptoms may be treated as medical problems instead of signs of alcohol withdrawal. Surreptitious use of alcohol can have fatal consequences when combined with other medications used to treat chronic health problems.

Psychological and Medical Consequences of Alcohol Abuse

Medical problems caused by heavy alcohol use are the primary reason elders with alcohol problems come to the attention of health care providers. As has already been mentioned, the aging body metabolizes alcohol at a different rate, creating a greater blood alcohol concentration in elders than in younger people for the same amount of alcohol consumed. This higher level of alcohol in the blood affects every psychological and physical system.

Psychological and Cognitive Consequences.   Tarter (1995) hypothesized that heavy alcohol consumption actually causes premature aging, accelerating short-term memory loss, impairing abstract-reasoning abilities, and hampering an elder's ability to process information. Elders who are abusing alcohol tend to exhibit more erratic mood swings and become argumentative with little provocation. These behavior changes may be due to biochemical changes in the frontal lobe of the brain, the part of the brain most responsible for intellectual and emotional functioning. Alcohol has been shown to contribute to the shrinkage of the frontal lobes, resulting in loss of functional brain tissue (Pfefferbaum, Sullivan, Mathalon, & Lim, 1997). Once they begin to abstain from alcohol use, older alcoholics are less likely to regain these intellectual functions than are younger alcoholics.

Depression often precedes the development of an alcohol problem but it is also a consequence of heavy drinking. Persons over the age of 65 with an alcohol problem are three times more likely to exhibit a major depressive disorder than elders who do not abuse alcohol (Grant & Hartford, 1995). Moderate and heavy drinkers are 16 times more likely than nondrinkers to die of suicide, which is commonly associated with depressive disorders (Grabbe, Demi, Camann, & Potter, 1997).

Malnutrition.   Problem drinkers of all ages often lose interest in food or the ability to eat properly, resulting in serious malnutrition. For elders who are at greater risk for malnutrition already due to the loss of smell, difficulty preparing meals, and a dislike for eating alone, inadequate nutritional intake places them at greater risk for acute and chronic illness (Tyson, 1999). Vitamin deficiencies combined with toxic levels of alcohol in the bloodstream can lead to disorders of the central nervous systems, such as seizure disorders and gait impairments. The older problem drinker often walks with a hesitant, wide-based gait with rigid arms and a forward-leaning stance, which results in frequent falls (Chenitz, Stone, & Salisbury, 1999). Alcohol intoxication already impairs physical coordination and movement and, when combined with age-related changes in the central nervous system, causes falls to present as great a danger to an elderly problem drinker as any other illness. The incidence of hip fractures increases with alcohol consumption (Bilke, Stesin, Halloran, Steinbach, & Recker, 1993) not only because of a greater tendency to fall while drinking but also because of the effect of prolonged use of alcohol on bone density in elders.

Damage to Body Systems.   The liver and kidneys often show the first effects of prolonged alcohol use. The liver may become enlarged, develop fatty deposits, or fail, as is the case in cirrhosis of the liver—an irreversible deterioration of liver functioning. High blood levels of alcohol may overburden kidneys already stressed by normal age-related changes, resulting in an inability of the kidneys to regulate bodily fluid levels and filter toxic substances from the blood. Renal failure results in a process similar to the body poisoning itself.

Long-term alcohol use can damage heart muscles and result in the development of high blood pressure. For elders who already suffer from a cardiovascular condition, heavy alcohol use places the elder at increased risk for heart attack or stroke. The emphasis here is on heavy alcohol use. Medical researchers have found a U-shaped relationship between heart disease and alcohol use, which gives support to the theory that moderate alcohol intake may actually improve cardiovascular functioning. Heart disease is most prevalent among elders with very heavy alcohol use and those who abstain completely (Ashley & Ferrence, 1994; Smith, 1997). Moderate use may actually decrease the probability of developing heart disease.

Recognizing Alcohol Problems in Elders

Physical Presentation.   There are a number of distinct physical indicators that an elder is acutely intoxicated. The smell of alcohol (or attempts to disguise the smell of alcohol by use of breath mints or mouthwash), a flushed face, swollen or reddened eyes, hand tremors, and poor concentration or attention span are among the most obvious (Molony, Waszynski, & Lyder, 1999). Elders may slur their speech or seem particularly unsteady on their feet. Unexplained bruises and injuries are often indicators that they have had several falls, which may be attributable to excessive alcohol consumption. Elders may begin to show disheveled or improper dress or fail to practice good personal hygiene. Family and friends get the very strong sense that something is wrong, although it may be difficult to identify alcohol use per se as the problem. Health care providers may notice increased complaints about insomnia, which leads to excessive daytime sleepiness. Uncontrollable hypertension, attacks of gout, impotence among men, and a bloated appearance may be further indicators of heavy drinking. Medical examinations may reveal old injuries and bruises that the elder cannot (or will not) explain that have occurred while drinking.

Behavioral Indicators.   Some family members observe distinct personality changes when alcohol consumption becomes problematic. Outgoing and friendly elders become withdrawn and moody, while more withdrawn elders become socially aggressive or hostile, creating social discord with family and friends. Excessive alcohol use may contribute to elders' missing regular medical or social appointments. These changes indicate that the elder has lost control over the use of alcohol and may be rearranging his or her life to facilitate a drinking habit.

Visiting an elder in the home may provide further clues about alcohol use. The smell of alcohol, especially in the morning or early afternoon, and physical evidence of alcohol use, such as lots of glasses, empty bottles, or beer cans lying around an elder's living area, offer evidence of drinking. Sometimes elders who are drinking heavily become incontinent during periods of intoxication, and their living spaces may smell of urine or feces. Living spaces may appear unusually cluttered or messy during periods of active drinking. Opening closets or the refrigerator may reveal stockpiles of alcohol. Open your eyes and look. Open your ears and listen.

Getting an elder to admit to heavy alcohol use may not be easy. Denial about the amount of alcohol used and defensiveness when confronted with questions about alcohol use are common among problem drinkers of all ages. An elder may need time and help learning to recognize the signs of their own problem drinking. The Administration on Aging (1999) offers elders a simple problem checklist to help them identify the signs of alcohol abuse. These appear in Figure 8.1.

FIGURE 8.1   *How to Recognize a Drinking Problem*

Not everyone who drinks regularly has a drinking problem. You might want to get help if you:

- Drink to calm your nerves, forget your worries, or reduce depression
- Lose interest in food
- Gulp your drinks down fast
- Lie or try to hide your drinking habits
- Drink alone more often
- Hurt yourself, or someone else, while drinking
- Were drunk more than three or four times last year
- Need more alcohol to get "high"
- Feel irritable, resentful, or unreasonable when you are not drinking
- Have medical, social, or financial problems caused by drinking

Source: Administration on Aging, 1999.

Screening and Diagnostic Tools.   One of the major problems in identifying alcohol abuse in elders is the paucity of age-sensitive alcohol screening instruments. Many instruments used to screen for alcoholism among younger populations, such as the Michigan Alcohol Screening Test (MAST), determine the problematic aspects of alcohol use by questions that refer to the social and legal problems that alcohol use may have created for the user (Selzer, 1971). While this test is highly effective in identifying alcohol problems in younger populations, it misses several important indicators that may be more sensitive in identifying alcohol abuse in elders, such as frequent falls, driving mishaps, and other dysfunctions more likely to bother elders. The MAST has been adapted for use as the MAST-G. This 24-item screening tool is specifically geared to behavior patterns of elders.

A shorter and less complicated instrument used to identify alcohol use is the CAGE screening questionnaire, which consists of four simple questions shown in Figure 8.2. Any positive response to these questions suggests the person needs further evaluation regarding alcohol use. The limitations of both the MAST-G and the CAGE screening questionnaire are that they rely on self-reports to identify alcohol use. They assume an elder will be truthful about reporting alcohol problems. If an elder is not truthful, both have limited use. A medical examination may be more reliable in identifying the physical consequences of excessive alcohol consumption and should be used in conjunction with self-reporting instruments.

Treatment of Alcohol Problems in Elders

The prognosis for treatment of alcohol problems in elders is excellent, particularly among late-onset drinkers (National Institute on Alcohol Abuse and Alcoholism,

FIGURE 8.2   *CAGE Screening Questionnaire*

1. Have you ever felt you should *cut down* on your drinking?
2. Have people *annoyed* you by criticizing your drinking?
3. Have you ever felt bad or *guilty* about your drinking?
4. Have you ever had a drink first thing in the morning to steady your nerves or get rid of a hangover (*eye-opener*)?

Source: American Journal of Psychiatry, 131, pp. 1121–1123, 1974. Copyright 1974, the American Psychiatric Association. Reprinted by permission.

1998). Much of late-onset drinking occurs in reaction to the stresses of aging; therefore, identifying those stressors and helping elders develop more functional coping skills often addresses and eliminates problem drinking behavior successfully.

Barriers to Treatment

Family Attitudes.   Despite an excellent prognosis for successful treatment, a number of barriers prevent elders from seeking treatment. Elders are less likely to reach out for help with their drinking problems because problem alcohol use rarely has the social or legal consequences it has for younger drinkers (Pruzinsky, 1987). Friends and family members may have unknowingly become "enablers" of the drinking problem in elders because they are entrenched in the belief that their loved one's drinking is relatively harmless. They may also resist a health or mental health provider's recommendation for treatment. It may take a serious illness or accident before family members can get beyond their own denial to support active intervention.

Attitudes of Professionals.   The ageist attitudes of health and mental health providers also serve as obstacles to treatment. Like well-meaning family and friends, physicians, nurses, and social workers may deny an elder has a problem or overlook its seriousness. If an elder is alone, seriously ill, and depressed, who would blame him or her for wanting to escape the pain with alcohol? Does it matter if he or she no longer drives, is retired, and has no family responsibilities? Yes, it matters. Excessive alcohol consumption is a life-threatening condition for many elders. As this chapter has emphasized, alcohol can endanger psychological, social, and physical functioning in older adults. It compromises the quality of life for elders who abuse it and should not be considered an innocuous little vice.

Fear and Resistance.   Elders may show resistance to pursuing treatment that requires them to leave their homes. Going to a hospital or nursing home, even for a short period, is a frightening experience for elders because of its association with impending death. Elders need to be reassured they are not being "put away" and have a complete understanding of any course of treatment. The decision to pursue treatment must be their own decision, not the goal of the family or the social worker. Recovery from any substance abuse is extremely difficult for anyone, but is doomed to failure if it is not the goal of the person who has to do the work.

The Detoxification Process

Alcohol treatment for persons of any age involves a number of stages. The first stage is the process of detoxification, which involves a medically supervised withdrawal from alcohol that usually takes place in a hospital or treatment setting. It takes five to seven days for younger persons to cleanse alcohol from their bodies, but it may take up to 30 days for older persons (Molony, Waszynski, & Lyder, 1999; Tyson, 1999). Depending on the severity of the physical addiction to alcohol and an elder's general health, detoxification is often accompanied by severe physical symptoms, such as delirium tremens (DTs), anxiety, hallucinations, an accelerated heartbeat, and a precipitous rise in blood pressure. Elders must be carefully monitored during detoxification, which can be fatal if an elder is already suffering from cardiovascular disease or hypertension. Benzodiazepines, anti-anxiety medications, are frequently administered to elders to ease both the physical and psychological discomfort experienced during alcohol withdrawal (Chenitz, Stone, & Salisbury, 1999). While detoxification might sound like it is as dangerous as chronic alcohol abuse to an elder's body, the short-term risks far outweigh the long-term dangers associated with prolonged alcohol use. The medical risks unique to elders make it essential that elders be encouraged to go through detoxification in a medical setting rather than simply "going on the wagon" at home without professional help.

Follow-Up Treatment for Recovery

Medications.   Antabuse, a medication that causes nausea and vomiting when combined with alcohol, is frequently prescribed for persons in the early stage of recovery from alcohol abuse. The fear of such a violent physical response to alcohol can be an effective deterrent to resuming alcohol use when tempted by social situations or physical craving. While it can be highly effective for younger people, it is not advised for use with elders (Butler, Lewis, & Sunderland, 1998; Gomberg & Zucker, 1998). The violent physical response induced by Antabuse may be life threatening to elders. It can lead to dehydration, uncontrolled abdominal bleeding, and high blood pressure in elders who may already have serious medical problems. The use of Antabuse without supportive counseling fails to teach elders new coping skills and the behavioral changes necessary to continue an alcohol-free lifestyle. Rather than prescribe Antabuse, antidepressants have been found to be helpful to support elders in the recovery process (Zimberg, 1995). Bouts of depression often precede a drinking episode for elderly alcoholics. If the depression is treated, elders may be less likely to succumb to the temptation to resume drinking.

Alcoholics Anonymous (AA).   Alcoholics Anonymous is a 12-step program that has been used worldwide among all age groups with excellent success rates. The program requires that participants acknowledge that they are powerless over alcohol and that they surrender themselves to a "greater power" to help themselves maintain sobriety. Alcoholics Anonymous uses the power of a therapeutic community of other recovering alcoholics to provide support at various stages of recovery. Alcoholics Anonymous offers the benefits of a built-in support system and ongoing socialization, essential components for elders recovering from alcohol abuse (Schonfeld & Dupree, 1997). The supportive element of AA is very helpful to elders whose isolation is often one of the precipitating factors of heavy drinking. However, the confrontational nature of AA, which holds people accountable for their own behavior and attacks the defenses that people use to rationalize alcohol use, appears to be less effective with elders than with younger populations (Schiff, 1988). Kashner, Rodell, Ogden, Guggenheim, and Karson (1992) found that elders were almost three times more likely to complete group treatment successfully if confrontation was used less than it is used in traditional AA treatment.

Schonfeld and Dupree (1997) recommended that traditional AA groups be modified for elders in a number of ways. The groups should be more slowly paced to reflect age-related changes in cognitive processing. Elders may find the intense, hard-hitting pace of the traditional AA meeting upsetting and overwhelming. They suggest specific AA groups be designated for "elders only" to reflect the unique challenges that face a recovering elderly alcoholic. Loss is a dominant theme for elders who develop drinking problems, and elders need to learn self-management and cognitive-behavioral skills to overcome their losses. They must relearn the interpersonal skills needed to make new friends and reconstruct social support systems. Elders also need to be connected to other resources in the community to help with financial, medical, or social problems that frequently develop later in life. Alcoholics Anonymous groups need to combine the benefits of a supportive therapeutic community with the development of practical skills to counteract the stressors that precipitated heavy drinking.

Individual Counseling.   For elders who find the group approach too frightening or painful, individual counseling following detoxification is recommended. If elders can learn to identify and correct faulty thinking patterns, as is done in a cognitive-behavioral approach to treatment for depression and anxiety, they are better prepared to intervene in counterproductive behavior. Identifying what social situations and thought patterns are high risk for a return to alcohol use can help an elder avoid them. The benefits of individual therapy include the ability to tailor any intervention efforts to an elder's specific problems and personal coping styles. The one-on-one approach allows for teaching and rehearsing new social skills that can be applied to difficult situations the elder will face in sobriety. The most beneficial aspect of the individual approach may be its ability to allow the elder to maintain personal dignity and share deeply personal issues in a private relationship.

Drug Misuse and Dependency

Elders are the largest consumers of both prescription and over-the-counter medication. Although they constitute only 13 percent of the population, elders consume one-third of all prescription medications (Sloan, 1992). This translates into elders using between two and six prescription medications and one to three over-the-counter medications per person (Stewart & Cooper, 1994). Drug dependency develops more rapidly among elders due to the same metabolic factors that contribute to alcoholism in this population. Like alcohol, medications are metabolized more slowly, contributing to the presence of higher levels of drugs in the bloodstream than occurs among younger persons. The kidneys and liver are less efficient at removing these substances from the body. Combining the decreased efficiency of the body in processing drugs with the sheer numbers of elders taking multiple medications compounds the risk for developing problems in drug misuse and dependency.

Drug misuse and dependency as used in this discussion refer to the use of multiple medications that places an elder at high risk for the development of serious adverse drug reactions or physical dependency. Drug misuse and dependency among elders falls into two categories, the use of illegal drugs and the misuse of prescription medication.

The Use of Illegal Drugs

Among the current cohort of elders, less than one percent are lifelong users of illegal drugs, although by its nature, illicit drug use is difficult to identify with any statistical accuracy (Caracci & Miller, 1991). This small number is most likely due to two major factors. First, individuals who use illegal drugs beginning in youth often burn out on drugs early in life and never live to become elders. Hustling for drug money, escaping the health risks involved sharing needles and other drug paraphernalia, and the uncertain quality of drugs purchased on the street often result in premature death for serious addicts. Other lifelong drug users adjust their habits to reflect the realities of aging. With reduced incomes, less accessibility to suppliers, and more frequent health problems, aging drug addicts may substantially reduce drug use (Rosenberg, 1997). Primarily, these drug users have been lucky to have managed recreational drug habits without serious legal or medical consequences.

Another reason for the small numbers of elders addicted to illegal drugs may be what Winick (1962) called "maturing out" of the drug culture. Some of the psychosocial stresses that precipitate drug use in adolescence and young adulthood moderate with maturity. People's lives settle down as they assume the responsibilities of raising a family or managing a career. They have fewer opportunities to secure drugs or are more worried about the ramifications of legal trouble if they get caught. This phenomenon is an excellent example of the cohort effect. The current cohort of elders grew up during a time when illegal drug use was associated with the lifestyles of artists, musicians, or criminals, not respectable middle-America. Or at least respectable people did not discuss drug use publically. However, with longer life expectancy, increasing numbers of elders as the baby boom ages, and widespread acceptance among more recent generations of casual recreational drug use, the incidence of illegal drug use is expected to rise dramatically (Barnea & Teichman, 1994; Finlayson, 1997).

Drug Dependency and Prescription Medications

Risk Factors.   Women are at highest risk for becoming dependent on prescription and over-the-counter medications—specifically, white women with lower incomes and education levels (Kail, 1989; Gomberg & Zucker, 1998). Women use the health care system more often than men and physicians are more likely to prescribe psychoactive drugs for women than men because of women's tendency to describe troublesome feelings as part of other somatic complaints (Finlayson, 1997). Three-quarters of all elder visits to physicians result in a new or refilled prescription (Montamat & Cusack, 1992).

Elders who suffer from chronic pain, have previously used a psychoactive drug, suffer from chronic insomnia or depression, or currently use alcohol appear to have increased risk of developing a drug dependency (McLouglin & Farrell, 1997). The risk of becoming addicted also increases among elders with existing mental disorders or hypochondriasis regardless of gender (Finlayson & Davis, 1994).

Drug dependency on prescription medicines is relatively rare among elders of color although noncompliance with medication regimes is very common (Kail, 1989). Elders of color can rarely afford to get all of the medications prescribed for them by physicians and therefore are more likely to use less rather than more medication. Rather than overmedicate on prescription drugs, they are more likely to use prescriptions minimally and resort to less expensive and more accessible folk medicines.

Psychoactive Medications.   The most common drug misuse among elders occurs in the course of treatment for depression, anxiety, pain associated with chronic illness, and insomnia. Antidepressants, tranquilizers, analgesics, and sleeping pills (prescribed respectively for those conditions) are psychoactive medications, meaning they have direct chemical effects on the central nervous system, creating modifications in mood or feeling states. While some of these psychoactive medications create actual physical dependency, others create psychological dependency. Sustained use or misuse can result in an unhealthy relationship between an elder and the medication.

Benzodiazepines and other sedative hypnotics have the most addictive potential in the aging body. The use of benzodiazepines has increased significantly in the past 20 years as health care providers have become increasingly aware of the dangers of long-term use of barbiturates (Finlayson, 1997). While indicated for the treatment of anxiety in elders, benzodiazepines tend to be overprescribed by primary care physicians because of the difficulty in accurately distinguishing between anxiety and depression in elders (Adams, 1991). Depressed elders may present with anxiety. If the depression is not treated, the anxiety will persist regardless of prescription drug treatment.

Developing a dependency on prescription medications is an insidious process. Elders may lack knowledge about the correct dosage of potentially addicting medications and use the drug inappropriately from the beginning. If the medication fails to work as expected, elders may reason that more is better and escalate the amount they are taking. For example, if one tranquilizer helps calm one's nerves, several logically should help one sleep better; similarly, if the analgesic works so well for arthritis, it must work just as well for a headache.

"Nerves" as a Medical Condition.   There is a tendency among the current cohort of elders to use the term *nerves*—defined as "feelings of nervousness and aggravation, anger, impatience, or fearfulness"—to describe what is actually anxiety or depression (Van Schaek, 1988, p. 90). Medication may be prescribed to treat anxiety and depression caused by marital or family problems, retirement, loneliness, work stress, or the chronic stresses of poverty, reinforcing the belief that "the nervous system, not the social system is to blame" for mental health problems in elders (Van Schaek, 1988, p. 98). Despite its apparent connection to psychological and social stressors, "nerves" is actually a medical problem to be treated with medication. If an elder is feeling particularly anxious about an event or situation, it would make sense to take more medication in the same way the elder might take pain relievers for physical discomfort. Medications that are not addictive in proper dosages may become addictive when elders engage in self-medication or fail to follow proper dosage schedules.

Multiple Sources of Medication.   Elders may be receiving treatment from several physicians and having prescriptions filled by multiple pharmacists, thereby decreasing the probability that duplicate, interactive, or lethal dosages will be identified (Raffoul & Haney, 1989). Rarely do elders ask for details about why the medication is being prescribed or offer the health care provider complete information about what other medications are being taken. It is not because elders do not care. More likely, they feel uncomfortable questioning the physician, may feel rushed while in the doctor's office, or cannot remember what the physician said. In most cases, the practice of using multiple health care providers is coincidental or unintentional. For a small number of cases, however, elders intentionally seek the same prescriptions from different sources to protect their drug supplies.

The Interaction of Alcohol and Prescription Medications

Excessive use of either alcohol or prescription medication is extremely dangerous for elders as has been demonstrated in this chapter. One-quarter of all admissions of elders to emergency rooms in the United States are due to the interaction of alcohol and prescription drugs, a life-threatening combination (National Institute on Alcohol Abuse and Alcoholism, 1998). Occasional alcohol consumption inhibits the metabolism of prescription drugs in an elder's body allowing the drug to remain in the body for longer periods of time at more toxic levels. In other words, the alcohol increases the potency of the prescription medication. Even at the prescribed dose, elders are more likely to experience the symptoms of a drug overdose when drugs are combined with alcohol on a short-term basis.

With the exception of narcotics and sedatives, chronic alcohol ingestion creates the opposite effect on the effectiveness of medication. The alcohol activates drug metabolizing enzymes causing the drug to be processed out of the body more quickly, thus decreasing the potency of a drug. An elder may need more of a particular drug to achieve the same effect from it. Alcohol can also reduce the therapeutic effect of antibiotics, benzodiazepines, and many cardiovascular medicines. However, alcohol magnifies the effect of sedatives and narcotic substances. Therapeutic doses of sleeping pills and tranquilizers become lethal when combined with alcohol.

Treatment for Drug Dependency

Drug Detoxification.   As with alcoholism, elders with drug dependencies must undergo a detoxification process in which the offending drug is cleansed from the body. Unlike alcoholism, it may not be possible for an elder to abstain totally from an addicting prescription medication for medical rather than psychological reasons. The original intent of the medication—whether to treat pain, depression, anxiety, or other medical conditions—must be considered in the detoxification process. Detoxification from drug dependency involves a medically supervised reduction in the amount of medication an elder takes until the drug level in the bloodstream has reached therapeutic levels (Finlayson, 1997; Kostyk, Lindblom, Fuchs, Tabisz, & Jacyk, 1994). This process is best accomplished within a hospital or rehabilitation setting so that vital signs and an elder's general health can be carefully monitored. Detoxification from the drug is essential prior to undertaking the cognitive and emotional task of long-term treatment.

Identifying Underlying Issues.   Following detoxification, the most important issue in treating drug dependency among elders is to address the underlying cause of the initial addiction. This process is primarily in the domain of the health care provider but a social worker can be helpful in facilitating communication between the elder and physician. If an elder is misusing analgesics, it is necessary to identify the cause of the chronic pain. Is there an underlying medical condition that is undiagnosed? Can less addictive pain medications be used? What other pain management techniques can be taught to the elder?

It is important to identify underlying socioenvironmental stressors that are contributing to an elder's feelings of anxiety or depression. Using the assessment techniques for diagnosing depression and anxiety discussed in Chapter 5, a social worker can isolate issues that are causing the emotional reactions elders treat with medication rather than intervention. While the detoxification process and future decisions about prescription medication are medical decisions, the social worker plays a critical role in helping both the elder and the physician understand the social context of current drug dependency. Does the elder take prescribed psychoactive drugs intentionally to control troublesome emotions or is misuse the result of simply not understanding how the drug is to be properly used? Does the elder even understand what medications are prescribed for what conditions?

Group Approaches to Treatment.   Age-specific group treatment approaches have been shown to be highly successful in treating drug dependency as well as alcohol dependency among elders (Barnea & Teichman, 1994; Finlayson, 1997). This group approach is not just about developing a better understanding among elders regarding the dynamics of drug dependency but also about addressing the underlying stresses of aging that contribute to drug dependency. Connecting elders with medical, social, and economic resources in the community may be helpful in moving the elder beyond the depression or anxiety that helped sustain the drug use. Treatment groups can help isolated elders recreate a supportive social network.

The group approach can also be used to work with families of drug dependent elders. Families may unintentionally "enable" elders to continue drug dependencies. No family member wants to see a loved one suffer and even with the best intentions, family members may directly contribute to the maintenance of a drug problem (Goldmeier, 1994). Increasing the family's awareness of the signs of drug dependency and the ultimate dangers of psychoactive substance addiction may shock the family into supporting an elder's treatment. Families are the main line of communication to elders and need to be intimately involved in the treatment process.

Drug Regime Alterations.   Changing the elder's drug regime is an important part of the treatment process (Ascione, 1994). Social workers can work with physicians to identify ways in which to consolidate dosage schedules so that the likelihood of confusion about or misuse of any medication is reduced. Can medication schedules be reduced to two times a day rather than four? Can medications that need to be taken with food be taken only in the morning and those that require an empty stomach be taken only in the afternoon?

Encouraging elders to consolidate all prescriptions at one pharmacy is important. Pharmacists are trained specifically to identify potential drug interactions. The system of identifying adverse drug reactions has become so sophisticated that pharmacy record software automatically flags dangerous or duplicate drug combinations. However, this can only prevent problems if all prescriptions are dispensed through a single pharmacy.

Patient Education.   The current cohort of elders grew up placing complete trust in their primary physicians and rarely ask for more information about the drugs they are taking. If a physician prescribed the medication, it must be okay. Elders need to have specific instructions regarding proper dosage and identification of troublesome side effects. If an elder does not feel medication is working, he or she needs to discuss it with the health care provider, not self-medicate until it feels like it is working. Many elders who became addicted to prescription drugs never knew the medication was addictive.

Elders also need to monitor their own drug usage to guard against abuse. Are they aware of what situations prompt the taking of "nerve" pills? What other ways can be developed to help an elder cope with anxiety or depression? Teaching elders cognitive-behavioral techniques for managing stress and developing coping skills gives them alternatives to using medication to improve moods or change feelings.

Suicide among Elders

Suicide is most frequently associated with younger adults who struggle with turbulent personal relationships, difficult career choices, and alcohol and other drug problems. While this is a legitimate concern, the highest suicide rate within the population occurs in persons over the age of 65. Elders constitute only 13 percent of the population but account for 20 percent of all completed suicides in the United States (National Institute of Mental Health, 1999). This disproportionate incidence indicates that there are factors unique to the aging process and the psychosocial experience of elders that places them at high risk for taking their own lives. Yet, elders are rarely targeted for special intervention efforts to prevent suicide. Elders being treated for medical and emotional problems may never be asked about suicidal ideation. An elder who bemoans the uselessness of his or her life may be dismissed as attention seeking or demented. The tendency to see suicide as primarily a threat to younger persons may blind both health and mental health providers to identifying high-risk elders.

Accurately determining the exact number of suicides among elders is a very difficult task. Ruling a death a suicide is actually a legal judgment. If wounds are obviously self-inflicted, a suicide note is left, or the death is witnessed, it may be determined to be a suicide. However, this obscures deaths ruled accidental or due to natural causes that may be covert suicides. An overdose of medication, an automobile accident, or more passive methods, such as refusing to eat or to comply with medical treatment, may actually be suicides though not identified as such on the death certificate.

Suicide among elders may be considered as a rational, preemptive choice to avoid prolonged suffering from a chronic illness. While professionals and family members may be devastated by an elder's suicide, they often accept it as the last element of control an elder may have had over life. Knowing the elder is no longer in pain or lonely may serve as a source of consolation for those close to the elder. This is a dangerous rationalization that allows health and mental health professionals to continue to ignore the emotional turmoil that precedes and follows the act of suicide among elders. One of the primary values of the social work profession is the premium it places on human life. We consider the safety and well-being of children so important that we have given units of government the power to intervene over the rights of parents when a child's life is in danger. We struggle to help adolescents recognize their importance in a confusing and often hostile world with hotlines and residences for runaway teens. We offer shelters for families who are caught in the web of family violence. Yet, few active efforts are made to identify and offer support for elders who are considering taking their own lives.

Risk Factors for Suicide among Elders

Gender. Suicide occurs more frequently among men than women at all ages. This difference is accentuated among elders, particularly among men who are not married. Men account for 84 percent of all suicides committed over the age of 65, making them 4.5 times as likely as women to take their own lives (National Institute of Mental Health, 1999; Segal, Coolidge, & Hersen, 1998). The increased incidence of suicide among men may be due to the dramatic role changes men experience once they retire or to the greater difficulties they may experience in adapting to serious illness or living alone. Alcoholism, which occurs more frequently in men than women, also contributes to these higher rates. Women are more likely to show indirect life-threatening behavior, such as self-starvation or refusal to follow medical regimes, a more passive form of suicide (Osgood, Brant, & Lipman, 1991). Childhood abuse, lifelong difficulties in personal relationships, substance abuse, and chronic depression are highly correlated with suicide among elderly women (Osgood & Malkin, 1997).

Depression and Social Isolation. After gender, depression is the most serious risk factor for suicide in the elderly. A sense of personal worthlessness and feeling sad and helpless, compounded with lack of a social support system, place the elder at high risk to conclude that life is not worth living and to commit suicide. Depression is often caused by social isolation, most common among elders who live alone. Elders who do not feel connected to family or friends may surmise that no one would miss them anyway if they died.

Alcoholism and Drug Abuse. The connection between depression and substance abuse is well documented throughout this chapter. The comorbidity of substance abuse and depression increases the likelihood an elder will commit suicide regardless of gender. Alcohol is a depressant that not only escalates any existing depression but also impairs an elder's judgment. The inhibitions that might prevent an elder from committing suicide while sober are lowered when the elder is intoxicated.

Physical Illness. Elders who are suffering from painful and debilitating chronic illness commit suicide more frequently than elders with only minor health problems (Lindesay, 1997). Higher rates of suicide have been observed in elders with cancer, musculoskeletal disorders, such as osteoporosis, multiple sclerosis, or Lou Gehrig's disease, and AIDS (Blumenthal, 1990). Faced with a lengthy period of chronic illness before natural death, suicide may be seen as the only way to allevi-ate the pain. Elders may see suicide as a preferable alternative to burdening a spouse or family member with the financial and emotional costs of a long illness. Physical illness also compounds the risk of suicide because it is frequently accom-panied by depression, which has already been cited as a high-risk factor. Elders become depressed because they are ill. When they are ill, they may lose social and community roles or become isolated, exacerbating the depression and creating a cyclical relationship between illness, depression, and social isolation.

Race and Ethnicity.   White elders commit suicide at three times the rate of elders of color, although little is known about suicide patterns among the non-white elder population (Surgeon General, 1999, Osgood, 1985). While Native American youth have one of the highest rates of suicide in the United States, Native American elders have among the lowest (Surgeon General, 1999). Native Americans who live to be elders may have exceptionally good coping skills that have helped them overcome the medical and social challenges that they face. Asian American women have the highest suicide rate among women of all races (Surgeon General, 1999). It is tempting to conclude that this happens because of different attitudes about suicide in Asian culture, but it is more likely due to the fact that Asian American women also have higher levels of depression than other women.

Lower suicide rates among elders of color may also be due to the crossover effect discussed in Chapter 1. The current cohort of elders of color have survived a lifetime of discrimination, substandard medical care, and social ostracism. The very skills that have helped them meet with these challenges earlier in life may help them to cope with changing health and social status in old age. Only the strongest elders of color have survived to old age. Therefore, they represent an unusually hardy group of elders. Elders of color have lower rates of alcohol abuse and greater social support networks. They may also have stronger connections to religious organizations, which are likely to have strong prohibitions against suicide.

Recent Loss and Bereavement.   The risk of suicide is greatest for elders in the year immediately following the death of a partner or loved one and subsides each year after. Yet, the vast majority of elderly who are grieving do not commit sui-cide. Those most likely to take their own lives as a reaction to mourning are those who are suffering from "complicated grief" according to Szantos and associates (1997). Complicated grief reactions include unrelenting intrusive thoughts about the deceased, lingering feelings of bitterness and shock over the death, survivor guilt, and a prolonged inability to accept the death. Many elders who suffer from complicated grief have a history of previous psychopathology. It appears as though the recent loss precipitates a more serious depression in these elders, thus increasing suicidal risk. Complicated grief is discussed in more detail in Chap-ter 13.

Other Risk Factors.   Suicide is more likely among elders who come from families with histories of attempted or successful suicide or serious mental illness. The tendency of depression to run in families explains this tendency to some degree as well as the fact suicide has been introduced as an option to ending psychological pain. Elders who have attempted suicide at some earlier time in their lives may be more likely to attempt it again when they are older. Haight and Hendrix (1998) identified several themes that ran through the life stories of older women who have suicidal ideation. These included dysfunctional families of origin; poor role models for being wives, mothers, or friends; a lifelong feeling of isolation; and a generally pessimistic outlook about life.

Assessing Suicidal Tendencies in Elders

It may be more difficult to assess suicidal tendencies in elders than in younger persons because elders are less likely to verbalize their suicidal intent, but are much more likely to complete a suicide attempt successfully (Mosher-Ashley & Barret, 1997). However, most elders do offer some important clues that they are considering taking their own lives. Seventy percent of elders who commit suicide have seen their primary health care provider within the month preceding the suicide with somatic complaints that may be manifestations of a deep depression (National Institute of Mental Health, 1999). It is rare that health care providers directly ask about suicidal ideation. An elder may interpret this failure to ask as rejection, reasoning that even the physician does not seem to be interested in his or her emotional well-being (Osgood, 1985). While there is certainly no way to know for sure if asking about suicidal ideation would have prevented a suicide, this last visit to a health care provider may be the last effort to ask for help. An elder's presentation with a seriously depressed affect cannot be ignored! Health and mental health care providers need to be aware of the risk factors associated with elder suicide and assess those within the context of direct, indirect, and behavioral clues.

Direct Clues.   Direct statements, such as "I am going to kill myself" or "Sometimes I just want to end it all," are not the ramblings of an attention-seeking elder. They are direct clues that the person is considering ending his of her life. If elders express such direct statements, they need to be asked the screening questions for suicide presented in Chapter 4. Those questions are:

- Have you ever felt life was not worth living? If yes, when?
- Have you ever considered ending your life? If yes, when?
- Do you feel that way now?
- Have you ever considered how you would do it?
- Do you have a plan?
- What has stopped you from going through with your plan?

If an elder has a specific plan and has access to the means for carrying out the plan, take immediate action. An elder who is threatening to shoot himself and owns a gun with ammunition is serious about suicide. An elder who would use an overdose of medication and has stockpiled the pills already is determined to end her life. The more lethal the means being considered and the greater the opportunity the elder has to carry out the plan, the more at risk the elder is for completing a suicide attempt (Knight, 1996).

Indirect Clues.   Less direct statements indicating intent to commit suicide may include, "I won't be around here much longer" or "I'm tired of it all." Sometimes elders fish for responses from loved ones with statements such as "You would be better off without me" or "I am too much trouble these days" (Osgood, 1985). These statement are direct requests for reassurance that their lives are valuable and that they are important to someone. Although family members and professionals may find such statements irritating, they are desperate cries for help and cannot be ignored.

Behavioral Clues.   Some elders offer no verbal clues at all. They have decided to end their lives and are beyond being willing to be talked out of it. These elders often show behavioral indicators that should serve as warning signs. Osgood (1985) offered the following behaviors as clues for suicidal tendencies in elders:

- Actually attempts suicide or has in the past
- Buys a gun or other weapon
- Stockpiles medications
- Makes or changes a will unexpectedly
- Begins making funeral plans suddenly
- Gives away valuable possessions suddenly
- Shows a sudden disinterest in religion or worship
- Uncharacteristically neglects self-care or household tasks
- Suddenly becomes calm and peaceful after a long period of agitation or depression

Any of these behaviors by themselves are not necessarily indicators of suicidal tendencies. However, when risk factors are present along with direct or indirect clues, an elder may be at high risk for completing suicide successfully. Health and mental health professionals need to consult with family members if they consider an elder at high risk to get a more complete picture of an elder's behavior in the recent past.

The Role of the Social Worker with High-Risk Elders

Gerontological social workers need to take a proactive role with elders when suicidal tendencies become apparent. Focus on the current crisis that has precipitated an elder's decision to end his or her life. Often it is a relatively minor event that pushes the elder into this decision. Setting a very short-term goal that can be attained may help relieve the pressure an elder is feeling. For example, if an elder has just received a cut-off notice from a utility company, get on the phone and make immediate arrangements with the utility company. If the elder has no money to pay for medication and simply cannot face chronic pain, talk to the physician or pharmacist about a short-term solution.

Remove any immediate danger, such as a gun or stockpiled medication. Ask the elder about getting someone to stay with him or her during this difficult time or contact the health care provider about hospitalizing the elder for further evaluation. Contracting for safety with the elder involves his or her promise not to commit suicide before your next visit. Reaffirming this promise during every contact can ease the elder over the crisis period until the long-term problem can be addressed. It may be necessary to do a shortened version of reminiscence therapy in which you actively work with the elder to identify strengths and coping skills used in the past. What difficult times has the elder had in the past? What did he or she do to get beyond that pain? How can those coping skills be used again? The purpose is to rally emotional strengths to help the elder get grounded emotionally.

It is also important to rally resources from the elder's external environment, such as family members and friends. Who would the elder most like to see right now? What friend or family member has always been a source of comfort? Who would make him or her feel better right now? Would the elder feel comfortable talking to a clergy member? If an elder is overwhelmed with household chores or discouraged by things that need to be done around the house, find someone to do those tasks. The purpose of such activity is to show the elder immediately that you are taking the threats to end life seriously and want to come up with an action plan to avoid that end. Elders often consider suicide as an alternative when they cannot see that anything else will help. Developing an action plan that offers solutions to seemingly overwhelming problems may give the elder hope.

Long-Term Treatment for Suicidal Elders

The most important component in long-term treatment for suicidal elders is to correctly identify and treat the underlying cause for the desire to end life. For those elders who suffer from chronic pain, it is necessary to address pain management with a health care provider. Changing medication, the dosage, or training the elder in other pain management techniques is crucial. If the pain problem is not addressed, an elder will consider or attempt suicide until he or she is successful. Hospitalization that includes a complete physical exam may uncover other medical problems that account for the intense pain, which can be treated once identified.

Elders suffering from depression or anxiety may benefit from any of the treatment approaches discussed in Chapters 6 and 7. Support groups that address the problem of social isolation and reestablish social networks may relieve the intense loneliness that often precedes a suicide attempt. Individual therapy using the cognitive-behavioral approach may help elders to identify those triggers that intensify their depression or anxiety and help them learn corrective behavioral techniques. Reminiscence and life review approaches may help elders address unresolved issues from earlier in their lives and give them an opportunity to make reconciliatory efforts. Elders who are stuck in the bereavement process may need help with guided mourning to help process their grief and move ahead of it. Family members and friends can be valuable resources in helping a suicidal elder. They need to be encouraged to reaffirm the importance of the elder not just by words but by actions as well (Osgood, 1985). Family and friends can introduce the elder to new activities and facilitate those new interests by offering transportation and encouragement. Maintaining regular contact with elders and including them in family activities can help them to reconnect to others and ease their social isolation. The most essential component is finding the cause of an elder's decision to commit suicide and addressing that problem.

Preventing Suicide among Elders

There is no certain way to prevent suicide among elders. Those elders who are determined to take their own lives may not even talk about it. They choose methods and circumstances that maximize the chances they will be successful. However, for those elders who are less sure of this course of action and can be prevented from taking the final step, there are a number of preventative measures social workers can initiate before it reaches the crisis intervention stage.

Depression screening should be a routine part of every social work assessment of elders in every setting. The simple tools presented in this book can help identify high-risk elders before suicide even becomes a consideration. Elders may not even know they are depressed and attribute sad feelings and lethargy to the normal process of aging. Identifying depression and connecting elders to treatment is perhaps the most important step the social work profession can take in preventing suicide. In this effort, social workers need to maintain contact with health care providers, such as physicians and nurses, who are most likely to see a depressed elder within the health care setting.

Alcoholism and drug abuse are strongly correlated with suicidal tendencies in elders, and therefore it is imperative to improve efforts to identify elders with alcohol and drug abuse problems as part of any preventative efforts. The regular practice of having a few cocktails to dull the pain of a chronic illness or help an elder to sleep are not innocent little vices. The physical and psychological consequences of these substances can be fatal. Educating elders and their families about the dangers of excessive alcohol use or abuse of prescription and over-the-counter medications is needed to increase sensitivity to this problem.

Part of any suicide prevention effort needs to center on encouraging leisure education before elders retire. While many companies focus extensively on the financial aspects of a retirement lifestyle, few pay attention to the psychosocial aspects of long-term leisure. Elders may have grand ideas about travel and volunteer activities, good choices if financial and personal resources are available. Healthy elders can usually occupy several years pursuing all the activities they never had time for before retirement. This however, does not address what happens when health problems develop or when incomes are limited. What will people do for the 20 or 30 years past work? Helping elders to plan and develop leisure activities is essential in preventing the development of depression or social isolation in the first place.

Churches and community organizations need to engage in aggressive outreach programs to identify troubled and isolated elders. It is hard to counter an elder's claim that no one cares about him or her when no one ever calls or visits. The painful loneliness of social isolation can create a personal prison for a homebound elder. Every day is the same. There is never anything to look forward to. Elders may feel they are just waiting to die. It is not hard to see why such a life would lead an elder to consider ending life prematurely.

The last preventative effort focuses on professional education, not only of social workers but also of health care providers and attorneys. Few professionals ever think seriously of suicide among elders as a significant problem and fail to look for the direct and indirect indicators that an elder is considering suicide. Physicians and nurses may discount the seriousness of an elder's depression or hesitate to ask about suicidal ideation because they do not want to offend the elder. Attorneys who work with elders in drafting a will may not connect an elder's sudden interest in settling affairs as a warning sign for suicide. It is unfortunate that often postal carriers and liquor store clerks have a better read on an elder's emotional health than the professionals who can offer the most assistance.

Summary

The problem of substance abuse among elders has been seriously overlooked, thus underestimated by mental and physical health care providers. This seems to occur because elders with alcohol problems do not fit the stereotype of lifelong alcoholics or because use of alcohol is seen as the sole remaining vice for elders who are facing chronic illness, loneliness, or depression. With alcohol abuse rates speculated to be as high as 10 percent of the population over 65 years of age, problem drinking among elders is a serious threat to the physical and emotional well-being in this population. Alcohol affects elders differently from the way it affects younger populations because of age-related physical changes, such as decreased amounts of water in the body and a slower rate of metabolizing alcohol. Elders are more likely than younger persons to be taking prescription drugs, which pose serious interaction problems with alcohol. Late-onset alcohol abuse appears to be a problem particularly for older women, who are more likely to live longer than their male counterparts and therefore are susceptible to the stresses of late life including living alone, depression, and social isolation. The encouraging news is that elders with alcohol problems respond well to treatment once problem drinking has been identified. The special needs of elders require that the social work profession routinely screen for alcohol problems, determine the causal factors contributing to the chronic use of alcohol, and adapt traditional treatment modalities, such as Alcoholics Anonymous and residential treatment, to the specific needs of adults in this stage of life.

While illicit drug use is very rare among elders, misuse of prescription medications continues to be a threat to elders' health. Complicated drug regimes for elders taking multiple medications and a tendency to overprescribe psychoactive drugs has created a confusing and dangerous situation in which elders self-medicate with alarming frequency. The social worker has an important role in including medication monitoring as a regular part of the assessment process, working with health care providers, and serving as a patient educator in preventing the deadly consequences of improper medication compliance.

The disproportionately high rate of suicide among elders should alert the social work profession to the need to routinely include suicide screening as part of a total assessment of elders. The population at highest risk for committing suicide is white men who live alone and have alcohol problems—highlighting the comorbidity of depression, social isolation, and substance abuse with a likelihood of suicide. Treating the depression and chronic pain that often precede a suicide attempt and identifying those elders at high risk for taking their own lives can help prevent this tragedy.

Check Out These Websites!

1. **www.health.org/pubs/resguide/olderams.htm** This site is a collaborative effort between the Center for Substance Abuse and Prevention and the Alcohol, Tobacco, and Other Drugs Council. It is a rich source of materials—available online or through the mail—for identifying and preventing alcohol and drug abuse among elders. The site provides information about studies, articles, and reports on this subject as well as a listing of groups and organizations that can help professionals and elders access treatment options.

2. **www.ncoa.org/subabuse/intro.htm** The National Council on Aging in conjunction with the Substance Abuse and Mental Health Service Administration of the U.S. Public Health Service offers this website as a resource for professionals who want to know more about the problem of alcohol abuse among elders. A series of brief papers offers an overview of the problem, guidelines for detecting problem alcohol abuse, and suggestions for treatment resources.

3. **www.members.tripod.com/lifegard/elder.html** This site offers an excellent primer in the problem of suicide among elders. It gives an overview of the problem, identifies warning signs for high-risk behavior, and offers numerous suggestions to both professionals and family members for preventing suicide. Links to dozens of other sites are offered as well.

4. **www.merckusa.com/pubs/mm_geriatrics** This site offers actual material from the *Merck Manual of Geriatrics,* a professional resource for mental and physical health care providers. Topics include problem alcohol use among elders, the connection between drug and alcohol abuse and suicide, and clinical indicators of substance abuse problems.

References

Adams, R. (1991). Anxiety and personality disorders. In J. Sadavoy, L. W. Lazurus, & L. F. Jarvik (Eds.), *Comprehensive review of geriatric psychiatry* (pp. 369–386). Washington, DC: American Psychiatric Press.

Adams, W. L., & Cox, N. S. (1997). Epidemiology of problem drinking among elderly people. In A. M. Gurnack (Ed.), *Older adults' misuse of alcohol, medicine, and other drugs* (pp. 1–23). New York: Springer.

Administration on Aging. (1999). National Institute on Aging, National Institute on Alcohol Abuse and Alcoholism Age Page. Washington, DC: Author. Retrieved August 1, 1999 from the World Wide Web, August 1, 1999. Available at http://aoa.dhhs.gov/aoa/pages/agepages/alcohol.html.

Ascione, F. (1994). Medication compliance in the elderly. *Generations* (Summer), 28–33.

Ashley, M. J., & Ferrence, R. (1994). Moderate drinking and health: The scientific evidence. *Contemporary Drug Problems, 21*, 1–3.

Barnea, Z., & Teichman, M. (1994). Substance misuse and abuse among the elderly: Implications for social work interventions. *Journal of Gerontological Social Work, 21*(3/4), 133–148.

Bilke, D. D., Stesin, A., Halloran, B., Steinbach, L., & Recker, R. (1993). Alcohol-induced bone disease: Relationship to age and parathyroid hormone levels. *Alcohol: Clinical and Experimental Research, 17*(3), 690–695.

Blumenthal, S. J. (1990). An overview and synopsis of risk factors, assessment, and treatment of suicidal patients over the life cycle. In S. J. Blumenthal & D. J. Kupfer (Eds.), *Suicide over the life cycle: Risk factors, assessment and treatment of suicidal patients* (pp. 685–733). Washington, DC: American Psychiatric Press.

Brennan, P. L., & Moos, R. H. (1990). Life stressors, social resources, and late-life problem drinking. *Psychology of Aging, 5*, 491–501.

Brennan, P. L., Moos, R. H., & Mertens, J. R. (1994). Personal and environmental risk factors as predictors of alcohol use, depression, and treatment-seeking: A longitudinal analysis of late-life problem drinking. *Journal of Substance Abuse, 6*, 191–208.

Butler, R. N., Lewis, M. I., & Sunderland, T. (1998). *Aging and mental health: Positive psychosocial and biomedical approaches* (5th ed.). Boston: Allyn and Bacon.

Caracci, G., & Miller, N. S. (1991). Alcohol and drug addiction in the elderly. In N. S. Miller (Ed.), *Comprehensive handbook of drug and alcohol addiction* (pp. 179–191). New York: Marcel Dekker.

Chenitz, W. C., Stone, J. T., & Salisbury, S. A. (1999). *Clinical gerontological nursing: A guide to advanced practice* (rev. ed.). Philadelphia: W. B. Saunders.

Cowart, M. E., & Sunderland, M. (1998). Late-life drinking among women. *Geriatric Nursing, 19*(4), 214–219.

Dufour, M., & Fuller, R. K. (1995). Alcohol in the elderly. *Annual Review of Medicine, 46*, 123–132.

Ebersole, P., & Hess, P. (1998). *Toward healthy aging: Human needs and nursing response* (5th ed.). St. Louis, MO: Mosby.

Eliason, M. J. (1998). Identification of alcohol-related problems in older women. *Journal of Gerontological Nursing, 24*(10), 8–15.

Finlayson, R. (1997). Misuse of prescription drugs. In A. M. Gurnack (Ed.), *Older adults' misuse of alcohol, medicine, and other drugs* (pp. 158–184). New York: Springer.

Finlayson, R., & Davis, L. J. (1994). Prescription drug dependence in the elderly population: Demographic and clinical features of 100 inpatients. *Mayo Clinic Proceedings, 69*, 1137–1145.

Goldmeier, J. (1994). Intervention with elderly substance abusers in the workplace. *Families in Society, 75*(10), 624–629.

Gomberg, E. (1990). Drugs, alcohol, and aging. In T. Kozlowski, H. Annis, H. Cappell, F. Glaser, M. Goodstadt, Y. Israel, H. Kalant, E. Sellers, & E. Vingilis (Eds.), *Research advances in alcohol and drug problems* (pp. 171–213). New York: Plenum.

Gomberg, E. S. L., & Zucker, R. A. (1998). Substance use and abuse in old age. In I. H. Nordhus, G. R. VandenBox, R. S. Bera, & P. Fromholt (Eds.), *Clinical geropsychology* (pp. 189–204). Washington, DC: American Psychological Association.

Grabbe, L., Demi, A., Camann, M. N., & Potter, L. (1997). The health status of elderly persons in the last year of life: A comparison of deaths by suicide, injury, and natural causes. *American Journal of Public Health, 87*(3), 424–431.

Graham, K., & Schmidt, G. (1999). Alcohol use and psychosocial well-being among older adults. *Journal of Studies on Alcohol, 60*(3), 345–351.

Grant, B. F., & Hartford, T. C. (1995). Comorbidity between DSM-IV alcohol use disorders and major depression: Results of a national survey. *Drug and Alcohol Dependency, 39,* 197–206.

Haight, B. K., & Hendrix, S. A. (1998). Suicidal intent/life satisfaction: Comparing the life stories of older women. *Suicide and Life Threatening Behavior, 28*(3), 272–284.

Hanson, B. S. (1994). Social network, social support and heavy drinking in elderly men: A population study of men born in 1914, Malmo, Sweden. *Addiction, 89,* 725–732.

Helzer, J. E., Bucholz, K., & Robins, L. N. (1995). Five communities in the United States: Results of an epidemiologic catchment area survey. In J. E. Helzer & G. J. Canino (Eds.), *Alcoholism in North America, Europe, and Asia* (pp. 71–95). New York: Oxford University Press.

Holland, B. E. (1999). Alcohol problems in older adults. In M. Stanley & P. G. Beare (Eds.), *Gerontological nursing* (pp. 301–311). Philadelphia: F. A. Davis.

Hooyman, N., & Kiyak, H. A. (1999). *Social gerontology: A multidisciplinary perspective* (5th ed.). Boston: Allyn and Bacon.

Jenike, J. (1988). Depression and other psychiatric disorders. In M. S. Albert & M. B. Moss (Eds.), *Geriatric neuropsychology* (pp. 115–144). New York: Guilford Press.

Joseph, C. L. (1997). Misuse of alcohol and drugs in the nursing home. In A. M. Gurnack (Ed.), *Older adults' misuse of alcohol, medicine, and other drugs* (pp. 228–254). New York: Springer.

Joseph, C. L., Ganzini, L., & Atkinson, R. M. (1995). Screening for alcohol use disorders in nursing homes. *Journal of the American Geriatrics Society, 43,* 368–373.

Kail, B. L. (1989). Drugs, gender, and ethnicity: Is the older minority woman at risk? *Journal of Drug Issues, 19*(2), 171–189.

Kashner, T. M., Rodell, D. E., Ogden, S. R., Guggenheim, F. G., & Karson, C. N. (1992). Outcomes and costs of two VA inpatient programs for older alcoholics. *Hospital and Community Psychiatry, 43,* 985–989.

Knight, B. G. (1996). *Psychotherapy with older adults* (2nd ed.). Thousand Oaks, CA: Sage.

Kostyk, D., Lindblom, L., Fuchs, D., Tabisz, E., & Jacyk, W. R. (1994). Chemical dependency in the elderly: Treatment phase. *Journal of Gerontological Social Work, 22*(1/2), 175–191.

Levenson, M. R., Aldwin, C. M., & Spiro, A. (1998). Age, cohort, and period effects on alcohol consumption and problem drinking: Findings from the Normative Aging Study. *Journal of Studies on Alcohol, 59*(6), 712–722.

Liberto, J. G., & Oslin, D. W. (1997). Early versus late onset of alcoholism in the elderly. In A. M. Gurnack (Ed.), *Older adults' misuse of alcohol, medicine, and other drugs* (pp. 94–112). New York: Springer.

Lindesay, J. (1997). Suicide in later life. In I. J. Norman & S. J. Redfern (Eds.), *Health care for elderly people* (pp. 163–174). New York: Churchill Livingstone.

Mayfield, D., McLeod, G., & Hall, P. (1974). The CAGE questionnaire: Validation of a new alcoholism screening instrument. *American Journal of Psychiatry, 131,* 1121–1123.

McLoughlin, D. M., & Farrell, M. (1997). Substance misuse in the elderly. In I. J. Norman & S. J. Redfern (Eds.), *Mental health care for elderly people* (pp. 205–221). New York: Churchill Livingstone.

Molony, S. L., Waszynski, C. M., & Lyder, C. M. (1999). *Gerontological nursing: An advanced practice approach.* Stamford, CT: Appleton and Lange.

Montamat, S. C., & Cusack, B. (1992). Overcoming problems with polypharmacy and drug misuse in the elderly. *Clinics in Geriatric Medicine, 8,* 143–158.

Moore, A. A., Hays, R. D., Greendale, G. A., Damesyn, M., & Rueben, D. B. (1999). Drinking habits among older persons: Findings from the NHANES I Epidemiologic Follow-up Study (1982–1984). *Journal of the American Geriatrics Society, 47,* 412–416.

Mosher-Ashley, P. M., & Barret, P. W. (1997). *A life worth living: Practical strategies for reducing depression in older adults.* Baltimore, MD: Health Sciences Press.

National Institute on Alcohol Abuse and Alcoholism. (1998). *Aging and Alcohol: Alcohol Alert, 40.* Rockville, MD: Author. Retrieved from the World Wide Web, August 1, 1999. Available at http://www.silk.nih.gov/silk/niaa1/publicationaa40.html.

National Institute of Mental Health. (1999). Older adults: Depression and suicide facts. Bethesda, MD: Author. Retrieved from the World Wide Web, August 15, 1999. Available at http://www.nimh.nih.gov/publicat/elderlydepsuicide.cfm.html.

Osgood, N. J. (1985). *Suicide in the elderly: A practitioner's guide to diagnosis and mental health intervention.* Rockville, MD: Aspen Systems.

Osgood, N. J., Brant, B. A., & Lipman, A. (1991). *Suicide among the elderly in long-term care facilities.* Westport, CT: Greenwood Press.

Osgood, N. J., & Malkin, M. J. (1997). Suicidal behavior in middle-aged and older women. In J. M. Coyle (Ed.), *Handbook on women and aging* (pp. 191–209). Westport, CT: Greenwood Press.

Pfefferbaum, A., Sullivan, E. V., Mathalon, D. H., & Lim, K. O. (1997). Frontal lobe volume loss observed with magnetic resonance imaging in older chronic alcoholics. *Alcohol: Clinical and Experimental Research, 21*(3), 521–529.

Pruzinsky, E. W. (1987). Alcohol and the elderly: An overview of problems in the elderly and implications for social work practice. *Journal of Gerontological Social Work, 11*(1/2), 81–93.

Raffoul, P. R., & Haney, C. A. (1989). Interdisciplinary treatment of drug misuse among older people of color: Ethnic considerations for social work practice. *The Journal of Drug Issues, 19*(2), 297–313.

Rosenberg, H. (1997). Use and abuse of illicit drugs among older people. In A. M. Gurnack (Ed.), *Older adults' misuse of alcohol, medicine, and other drugs* (pp. 206–227). New York: Springer.

Schiff, S. M. (1988). Treatment approaches for older alcoholics. *Generations, 12,* 41–45.

Schonfeld, L., & Dupree, L. W. (1997). Treatment alternatives for older alcohol abusers. In A. M. Gurnack (Ed.), *Older adults' misuse of alcohol, medicine, and other drugs* (pp. 113–131). New York: Springer.

Segal, D. L., Coolidge, F. L., & Hersen, M. (1998). Psychological testing of older people. In I. H. Nordhus, G. R. VandenBos, S. Berg, & P. Fromholt (Eds.), *Clinical geropsychiatry* (pp. 231–257). Washington, DC: American Psychological Association.

Selzer, M. L. (1971). The Michigan Alcoholism Screening Test: The quest for a new diagnostic instrument. *American Journal of Psychiatry, 127,* 1653–1658.

Sloan, R. W. (1992). Principles of drug therapy in geriatric patients. *American Family Physician, 45,* 2709–2718.

Smith, J. W. (1997). Medical manifestations of alcoholism in the elderly. In A. M. Gurnack (Ed.), *Older adults' misuse of alcohol, medicine, and other drugs* (pp. 54–93). New York: Springer.

Stewart, R. B., & Cooper, J. W. (1994). Polypharmacy in the aged: Practical solutions. *Drugs & Aging, 4,* 449–461.

Stockford, D., Kelly, J., & Seitz, K. (1995). *Report on the 1990 and 1994 Surveys of VA nursing homes.* Washington, DC: Department of Veteran Affairs.

Surgeon General of the United States. (1999). *The Surgeon General's call to action to prevent suicide, 1999.* Washington, DC: Office of the Surgeon General. Retrieved from the World Wide Web, August 10, 1999. Available at http://www.surgeongeneral.gov/osg/calltoaction/fact2.html.

Szantos, K., Prigerson, H., Houck, P., Ehrenpreis, L., & Reynolds, C. F. (1997). Suicidal ideation in elderly bereaved: The role of complicated grief. *Suicide and Life Threatening Behavior, 27*(2), 194–207.

Tarter, R. E. (1995). Cognition, aging, and alcohol. In T. E. Beresford & E. S. L. Gomberg (Eds.), *Alcohol and aging* (pp. 82–98). New York: Oxford University Press.

Tyson, S. R. (1999). *Gerontological nursing care.* Philadelphia: W. B. Saunders.

Van Schaek, E. (1988). The social context of "nerves" in eastern Kentucky. In S. E. Keefe (Ed.), *Appalachian mental health* (pp. 81–100). Lexington, KY: University of Kentucky Press.

Winick, C. (1962). Maturing out of narcotic addiction. *Bulletin on Narcotics, 14,* 1–7.

Zimberg, S. (1995). The elderly. In A. M. Washton (Ed.), *Psychotherapy and substance abuse* (pp. 413–427). New York: Guilford Press.

9

Group Work with Elders

Using the Group Work Approach with Elders

The social work profession has used the group format to address the socio-emotional challenges facing populations of all ages since the early days of the profession. Developing knowledge of and skills in working with elders in groups is an essential part of the repertoire of practice approaches needed by a gerontological social worker. This chapter will discuss the advantages of using a group approach in meeting the psychosocial needs of elders and highlight what is unique about group work with this population. The process of planning and running a group will be reviewed and then applied to a variety of groups currently being used with elders. The chapter concludes with a discussion of the special considerations of group work with cultures different from that of the group leader and situations that may raise ethical conflicts for the social worker as group leader.

Advantages of the Group Work Approach

The Therapeutic Effects of Group Dynamics. Working with elders in groups is markedly different from one-on-one interventions. Group work utilizes both the therapeutic skills of the social worker and the power of group dynamics—the psychosocial forces that occur when three or more individuals interact with each other around a common goal or purpose. While the group leader plays an important role in facilitating the interaction between group members and in providing the structure within which the work of the group occurs, it is the power of a congregate sense of "we-ness" within the group that is the therapeutic aspect of this approach. Group members develop a web of relationships within the group, learning to use each other as a source of support and feedback. The group solidarity that develops can create a sense of belonging and purpose for group members. Something "magic" can happen in a group context that cannot be accomplished in working with elders individually. This sense of purpose and social connectedness can be particularly powerful for elders who may be socially isolated and need to relearn the social skills required to develop and maintain relationships (Toseland, 1995). The power of group dynamics places the elder in the middle of an interactive environment that can encourage even the most reluctant elder to mingle with fellow group members.

Efficiency. Group work offers the opportunity to reach a larger number of elders with supportive and therapeutic services than is possible in a one-on-one approach (Thomas & Martin, 1992; Toseland, 1995). In nursing homes, senior centers, congregate living centers, and adult day health settings where there may be only one or two social workers to meet the needs of hundreds of elders, devising intervention strategies that meet the needs of a large number of elders is essential. Rather than conduct reminiscence therapy with a single elder, the group approach can be used to deliver the same service to six or eight elders. The therapeutic benefits of painting or pottery can be offered to five or six elders rather than one when the group approach is used. Expanding the therapeutic focus to include a number of elders may be the only way "resource challenged" physical and mental health settings can provide services to some elders at all.

Effectiveness. Group work with elders can be an efficient way not only to provide services to elders, but also to effectively meet their psychosocial needs. Although there are hundreds of examples of the use of group work with elders in both the social work and nursing literature, it is important to note that few of these studies have used a rigorous research approach to documenting the effectiveness of the group approach (see Burnside & Schmidt, 1994; Rose, 1991; Toseland, 1995). Anecdotal evidence about improved mental health and social functioning and the practice wisdom of experienced group workers constitute much of what is considered evidence of "effectiveness" in using this practice intervention. It has not been demonstrated that group work with elders is more effective than individual intervention, but there is considerable support for the notion that group treatment is better than no treatment (Burnside & Schmidt, 1994; Toseland, 1995).

Socialization. A recurring theme in this book is the danger of social isolation for elders. Social isolation contributes to higher levels of depression, a greater likelihood of alcohol or drug dependency, and higher suicide rates (Dufour & Fuller, 1995; Gomberg & Zucker, 1998; Lindesay, 1997; Mosher-Ashley & Barrett, 1997). Group work with elders directly addresses the problem of diminishing social relationships and opportunities by creating a small social system that eases the pain of isolation and helps elders develop the social skills needed to reconstruct a social network outside the group (Toseland, 1995). New behaviors can be learned and rehearsed within the safety of the group context.

   Elders with significant health problems or those who are deep in grief about losses in their lives may develop an intense preoccupation with self. They may become so concerned about their own problems that they lose sight of the value of connecting with others as a way to manage their personal problems and think about something other than their own aches and pains. In the group context, elders may reconnect with others and find opportunities for enjoyment in their lives even in the midst of debilitating physical or social losses.

Consensual Validation.   Part of the benefit of the social interaction derived from the group experience is what Toseland (1995) called "consensual validation and affirmation" (p. 17). Groups can offer elders the sense that what they are feeling and experiencing at this time in life is shared by others. It is difficult for a recently widowed elder to imagine that anyone else can relate to his or her pain and offer meaningful suggestions as to how to cope with the grief. A group can convey to an elder that it is normal to be sad, angry, or frightened following this traumatic event. Knowing that other elders are working through the adjustment and finding ways to alleviate the intense loneliness can be a source of hope and support.

Reestablishing Meaningful Life Roles.   Group participation may give elders an occasion to share their own experiences and insights—a rare opportunity for an elder living alone or in an institutional setting. Elders can share with others their own expertise in a particular area—such as gardening, music, sports, or politics— or other areas presented in the group setting. Toseland (1995) identified this as an important way for elders to focus on their past and present capabilities rather than their disabilities. Reaffirming lifelong competencies helps elders improve personal self-esteem and renew their confidence about acquiring new roles and learning new activities at this time in their lives (Weisman & Schwartz, 1989).

Flexibility and Diversity.   Two of the major advantages of group work are its flexibility and diversity. Groups can be formed and executed in almost any setting of elders. Groups do not require extensive equipment or special arrangements other than a space in which the group can meet without outside interruptions. Nursing homes, congregate living centers, and adult day health settings all have large common spaces suitable for group meetings. There are also a variety of group formats that can be used with elders of all interests and abilities. For example, reminiscence groups can be used with elders with moderate cognitive impairments as well as with high-functioning groups. Social and recreational groups can use activities as simple as listening to music or as demanding as discussing opera or politics. Task groups can focus on the basic activities of daily living, such as learning to move about in a wheelchair, to more complex activities, such as drafting legislation or running a Senior Advisory Council for a unit of government. The basic principles of the group approach can be applied in flexible ways in diverse settings.

The Unique Characteristics of Group Work with Elders

Despite the advantages of using the group approach with elders, a number of unique characteristics in using this modality with elders deserve mention. The more extensive the social worker's knowledge about the aging process in general and the psychosocial characteristics of elders in particular, the easier it will be to make the adjustments necessary to make group work with elders successful.

Physical and Sensory Limitations.   Unlike groups of healthy children, adolescents, or young adults, elders face a variety of physical and sensory limitations that need to be accommodated within a group setting. For example, elders may be in wheelchairs or rely on walkers or canes, requiring that any room designated for the group meeting have enough space for the elders to maneuver these mobility devices. Some chronic health conditions, such as arthritis or osteoporosis, preclude elders from sitting for long periods of time without great discomfort. Elders need to have ready access to bathroom facilities. If the group consists of elders with some level of confusion, accommodations need to be made for wanderers or those whose confusion results in high levels of anxiety. Vision and hearing impairments require the group leader to adapt visual materials or amplify verbal communication to allow these elders to participate actively in the group.

The Role of the Leader.   Traditional approaches to group work assume that the group leader will take an active role at the beginning of the group but, as it develops, will gradually relinquish the direction of the group to its members. The leader's role becomes systematically less directive. In group work with elders, the group leader may need to take a more active role throughout the life of the group (Burnside, 1994a; Capuzzi, Gross, & Friel, 1990). The current cohort of elders may be more passive than groups of younger people for a number of reasons. Elders with cognitive limitations or those suffering from depression may need more encouragement by the group leader to participate in member-to-member interactions instead of focusing on member-to-leader exchanges. Elders may also be hesitant to interact with other members out of deference to the professional social worker, whom they see as expert and leader. They may see themselves as polite attendees rather than active group participants until the leader implicitly and explicitly gives group members permission to focus on each other rather than the group leader.

The group leader may also need to devote extra time to developing individual relationships with group members—more than is normally expected in the group process. Elders may need to be "courted" to attend initial and future group meetings. The group format may be uncomfortable and unfamiliar for an elder who has functioned independently for years and feels some trepidation about speaking within a group.

The Pace of the Group.   How dynamic and interactive the group becomes is a function of the purpose of the group and the physical and mental health of its members. A tendency to be more passive in the group setting, a preoccupation with one's own problems, and some level of discomfort about sharing in the group setting may result in the pace of group work with elders being much slower than in groups of younger persons (Burnside, 1994a; Toseland, 1995; Weisman & Schwartz, 1989). Inexperienced workers may become discouraged quickly when groups tend to move very slowly through the stages of group process and wonder if any progress is being made toward accomplishing group goals. It becomes important for the group leader to be able to see small accomplishments, such as a disengaged member beginning to pay attention or even brief interactions between group members, as indicators that the group process is working. As is true in different areas of social work with elders, important change is possible but may simply take longer than it does in work with younger populations.

When Group Work Is Not Appropriate

Practical Barriers. Group work may not be appropriate if elders are too frail, cannot access the location of the group due to mobility restrictions, or have insufficient command of the language in which the group will be conducted. If appropriate accommodations cannot be made, it may also be necessary to exclude elders with severe hearing loss. Amplifying sound sufficiently to include elders in the conversation may be logistically impossible. These practical barriers may preclude some elders from becoming part of the group.

Disruptive Behavior. Although group interventions can be designed for elders of all levels of cognitive and physical abilities, there are circumstances when it is not advisable that an elder be considered for group work. Elders in the late stages of Alzheimer's disease or other organic disorders who are extremely confused or unable to focus on social interaction do not do well in the group setting. The group leader may not be able to manage physically keeping the elder within the group setting or not be able to insure the elder's safety if he or she wanders away from the group. Elders who are extremely withdrawn in a severe depression or are actively engaging in psychotic thinking or behavior patterns are also not appropriate for inclusion in a group of other elders. Their behavior may prove too disruptive or frightening to others.

Personality Types. One of the challenges facing social workers who are planning an elder group in the institutional setting is exercising control over who is included in the group. Nurses and other staff members may recommend (or insist) that a particularly difficult elder be included in a group in hopes of changing problematic behavior. While these elders may represent those most in need of social interaction with others, it should remain the prerogative of the social worker to determine the composition of the group. Elders with severe behavior problems or hypochondriacal tendencies can undermine the entire group process. There are elders who are simply not able or interested in interacting with others due to their personality attributes. Some elders have become obsessed with their own problems and show limited promise in being able even to listen to others in a group setting. Individual interventions may be more appropriate for these personality types.

Elders in Acute Crises.   Elders who are in the middle of an acute crisis—such as the diagnosis of a fatal illness or the very recent loss of a loved one—or a personal trauma—such a rape or accident—are inappropriate for a group work intervention. They are often too emotionally vulnerable even to participate on a meaningful level. The emotional chaos created by a traumatic event needs to subside before an elder can move beyond the immediate pain and process these events in a group setting (Toseland, 1995). These elders would benefit from individual attention immediately and perhaps can be considered for group membership later.

Cultural Issues in Group Work

The importance of sensitivity to differences between elders of dominant cultural groups and elders of color has been emphasized throughout this book. It is critical that a group leader develop a solid sense of cultural awareness before developing group interventions with elders of color. The group leader must be sensitive to the dynamics of cultural difference on the functioning of the group.

Developing Cultural Sensitivity

Developing cultural awareness goes beyond just learning about another racial or ethnic group. It entails a willingness on the part of the social worker to explore personal attitudes about his or her own ethnic group membership and past experiences in dealing with different cultures. Green (1999) suggested individuals engage in the brutally honest process of exploring how their own racial and ethnic backgrounds have subtly influenced their feelings about different cultures. What messages were sent about the values and cultural practices of other cultures? What significant others in the social workers' life promulgated negative stereotypes or judgmental attitudes? How have adult experiences helped or hindered the individual in reevaluating these stereotypes? Becoming culturally sensitive is not a process of becoming "color blind" but rather becoming acutely aware of the importance racial and ethnic group membership play in determining how an elder sees himself or herself as being different.

Social workers who have little exposure to racial and ethnic groups different from their own need firsthand exposure to other cultures that goes beyond reading about differences. Visiting senior centers or congregate housing sites that cater to specific ethnic or racial groups, talking with other social workers who work with these populations, and meeting with community leaders are important activities to begin the process of developing cultural awareness. Attending ethnic festivals can expose a social worker to the diversity within any given racial group and acquaint them with the food, music, and art of the culture. Open your eyes and look! Open your ears and listen!

Toseland (1995) suggested that if a group leader does not have the time or opportunity to develop at least a moderate degree of cultural awareness before running a group of culturally diverse elders, the group itself can be a good learning experience. Elders of color are often eager to talk about their own cultural beliefs and values. It is an excellent way to appeal to the competencies of elders as well as to work on the specific problems that bring elders into the group context. Conveying a group leader's interest in learning about elders' cultural practices places elders in the role of expert, a source of pride and accomplishment.

This type of discussion in a group context also helps the group leader to identify important differences within a group of elders of colors. The term *Hispanic* includes Mexicans, Puerto Ricans, Central and South Americans, Cubans, and a variety of other nationalities, all of which consider themselves culturally distinct from each other. African Americans who live in the southern part of the United States have had a much different experience from that of those living in northern, urban areas of the country. The hundreds of tribes within the general classification of Native Americans have distinct languages, lifestyles, and traditions. Asian Americans range from very recent immigrants from Southeast Asia to Chinese families who have lived in this country for generations. Sharing the differences between, as well as within, racial and ethnic groups can be a broad educational experience for both the group leader and the members of the group.

Cultural Diversity and Group Dynamics

Members of diverse racial and ethnic groups bring a psychological framework that can have profound effects on the dynamics within a group (Axelson, 1993; Toseland, 1995). It may be difficult to achieve a sense of cohesion among group members if the group members perceive themselves as very different from each other. For example, Asian elders may be horrified by another elder's description of a confrontation with a caregiver daughter. In Asian culture, conflict within families is often discouraged in deference to the importance of maintaining family harmony. An African American elder who has struggled her entire life to provide a modest living for a large family may have little sympathy for a more affluent widow who complains that she can no longer afford domestic help. The animosities created by cultural differences can threaten the integrity of group functioning. The attitudes of elders are the culmination of a lifetime of experiences, and while elders may be reluctant to admit their own prejudices, they will affect the group process in subtle ways. Discriminatory and prejudicial remarks by group members cannot be tolerated. The group leader plays an important role in promoting tolerance among group members who may be judgmental about cultural practices they do not understand (Toseland, 1995). Within the current cohort of elders, many have had little or no exposure to other cultures except through the media. Their prejudicial attitudes may be more the product of ignorance than of true negative feelings toward another ethnic group.

While group diversity can create problems within a group, it can also be an important asset to the group. Exploring the range of ways in which elders solve problems using the unique adaptation techniques of different cultures exposes elders to new ideas and thoughts. For example, a Native American elder may use meditation and traditional tribal spirituality to counteract feelings of depression—a technique that can easily be adapted to other cultural traditions. African American and Hispanic Americans have strong religious traditions that may be more commonly expressed in a group setting but do not preclude private prayer and meditation. The issue becomes how to incorporate the strengths of diverse cultures into problem-solving techniques that can transcend cultural differences.

The Group Process

Before discussing the specific kinds of group interventions that can be used with elders, it is helpful to review the stages of the group process—those distinct aspects in the life of any group in which the congregate "we-ness" of the group is developing along with the components of group dynamics.

Stages in the Group Process

Engagement.   Groups begin as a composite of individuals who bring a variety of expectations and concerns to the group setting. During the pre-engagement stage, group members have not yet identified themselves as members of the group but see themselves as onlookers. What am I doing here? Who are these people and what can they do for me? What is this group thing all about? These are the kinds of questions new group members ask themselves. One of the most important parts of the group process is for the group leader to demonstrate that the benefits of participating in the group are greater than those of not participating. Group members need to understand clearly the purpose and activities of the group and to identify potential benefits of their participation. It is important in working with groups of elders to be very clear about the purpose of and planned activities for the group. Members need to know why the group has been formed, where and when the group will meet, and the number of sessions planned.

Once group members have determined, on either a conscious or subconscious level, that participation in the group has benefits and they begin to identify as members of a given group, they have engaged in the group process. During this time, the group leader can help members identify expectations and concerns about the group, establish group rules about participating in the verbal interaction of the group, and clarify the importance of confidentiality about what goes on in the group.

The Middle or Working Phase.   The actual "work" of the group depends on the purpose of the group but does not actually begin until group members have engaged in the group, both as an idea and as a process. During the middle phase, the group establishes group norms, such as where people traditionally sit during group meetings or what kinds of verbal exchanges are acceptable in the group. As group members develop relationships with other group members, interactions within the group become less member-to-leader and more member-to-member.

This phase of group development is characterized by a growing sense of cohesion among group members and a sense of loyalty to the group (Toseland, 1995).

In the beginning of the middle phase, groups often experience conflict for the first time as members juggle for power or status within the group. Conflict serves a purpose in groups and should not be consciously avoided if the group is to move on in the therapeutic nature of the group process. However, the current cohort of elders may not be comfortable with the expression of negative feelings among peers, many of whom may be strangers, and avoid it just to help maintain an emotional equilibrium in the group. If elders join the group with the anticipation that the group will be an enjoyable experience, it is not surprising that conflict will be avoided at all costs. The group leader may find elders very resistant to the open expression of conflict, even though it is operating within the group. Conflict may come out in more subtle ways, such as private asides to the group leader, interrupting each other, or even dropping out of the group. The group leader should encourage members to deal with conflict openly when possible but respect elders' hesitations. If conflict stalls the group, members need to be encouraged to tolerate alternative viewpoints and explore ways to resolve disagreements and tensions within the group.

During this phase, the leader's role is to encourage participation by all members of the group, drawing in those who appear on the fringes and toning down members who dominate the interaction to the exclusion of others. Encouraging elders to address one another, not just the leader, will help facilitate the interaction process. The group leader plays an important role in clarifying communication between group members, especially for those with sensory or cognitive limitations.

Termination. When the group has accomplished its goals or completed its planned activities, the group is usually terminated. Time-limited groups are planned with the intent of operating only for a specified number of sessions. Open-ended groups last for months or even years with a complete turnover in group membership and even in the group leadership. Open-ended groups may never terminate.

The group leader has a number of specific tasks to accomplish during a group's termination phase. Group members need to be prepared for a group's termination through periodic reminders of the termination date. Often groups will plan special events for the final meeting to create a festive atmosphere to ease bad feelings about the termination. Group members should be given the opportunity to process their feelings about the termination because the ending of the group may trigger strong emotional reactions by elders who experience so much other loss at this time in their lives. The group leader also has the responsibility to help group members identify any personal or social changes that have occurred as a result of involvement in the group and offer group members ways to apply new social skills learned in the group to social interactions outside the group. Personal enjoyment is a noteworthy accomplishment for any group but helping its members acquire skills that improve their lives outside the group is the ultimate goal.

Specialized Groups for Elders

A variety of specialized groups can be used in work with elders. Reality orienta-tion, reminiscence, or remotivation groups can be used with elders with signifi-cant cognitive limitations. Higher-functioning groups may benefit more from formal group therapy, social or recreational groups, or task groups that focus on achieving a single activity, such as getting a piece of legislation passed. The selec-tion of the appropriate group requires the social worker to have very clear goals in mind and choose a format tailored to meet the psychosocial functioning of the target group of elders.

Reminiscence groups are among the most common and important in group work with elders. The purpose and process of reminiscence was covered in detail in Chapter 6 and will not be repeated here.

Reality Orientation Groups

The Process of Reality Orientation.   Reality orientation is a process in which mild to moderately confused elders are given environmental clues to help them determine orientation to time, location, or person. Reality orientation groups are commonly conducted in nursing homes, hospitals, or adult day health settings. Elders are usually receiving supervision and support services in recognition of their mild to moderate levels of confusion. The assumption underlying reality ori-entation is that providing elders with consistent stimulation and appropriate en-vironmental clues to help them reorient themselves to the current setting may help stop memory loss (Williams, 1994). Ideally, reality orientation groups are part of a continuous process in these settings. Caregivers reinforce environmental clues to orient elders throughout the day, not just during group meetings. The group modality is therefore only part of an institution's overall commitment to keeping confused elders connected to the present environment.

Reality orientation groups are usually held once or twice daily for 30 min-utes (Taulbee, 1986; Toseland, 1995; Williams, 1994). The primary benefits of participation are not only support in learning how to reorient oneself in the insti-tutional environment but also social interaction with both peers and staff mem-bers. The opportunity to make a warm, compassionate connection with other human beings on a regular basis may be the greatest benefit to elders (McMahon, 1988; Toseland, 1995).

Group Membership Issues.   Elders who exhibit mild to moderate confusion or memory loss are most appropriate for inclusion in a reality orientation group. El-ders need the motivation to want to orient themselves and possess the cognitive ability to use orientation techniques. However, high-functioning elders will find the simple techniques used in the orientation process simplistic and may be of-fended by the implication that they need reorientation at all. Conversely, elders who are chronically disoriented or confused may become agitated by the constant efforts of the staff to reorient them (Taulbee, 1986). The most appropriate elders for reality orientation groups are those who are aware of their diminishing abilities to orient themselves to time, space, or person but still retain the ability to mobilize enough cognitive skills to use environmental clues to reorient themselves. Group members should have similar levels of ability. Ideal group membership is five to seven members and one leader. Two leaders may be needed for groups of lower-functioning elders.

Group Activities. Reality orientation groups usually combine a variety of activities intended to stimulate elders with the actual process of orienting elders to time, space, or person. The center focus of a reality orientation group is the reorientation board, a flip chart, bulletin board, or chalkboard, which displays the current date, season, weather conditions, upcoming holidays and activities, location of the meeting, or other environmental clues to help the elders orient themselves. At the beginning of the meeting, the group as a whole is asked what day, season, and so forth it is. Elders who do not know are referred to the reorientation board (Williams, 1994). Encouraging elders to seek out environmental clues for themselves helps elders develop the skills to engage in reorientation on a regular basis as a matter of habit.

The actual process of reality orientation is followed by group activities intended to stimulate the senses, teach the elders something new, or involve them in planning future activities around holidays or events (Williams, 1994). These activities may include listening to music, creating art, or doing simple physical or mental exercises, as well as any activity that stimulates cognitive awareness and improves physical functioning. Reality orientation groups are geared to helping elders reconnect with reality by becoming more aware of their immediate surroundings by becoming part of it. Stimulating an elder's sense of sight, smell, touch, taste, or hearing are intended to regenerate cognitive abilities or at least minimize further memory loss. The process of interacting with other elders in the group encourages the elder to pay attention to and focus on the immediate surroundings. Suggestions for reality orientation group activities appear in Figure 9.1.

The Role of the Leader. In reality orientation groups, the leader takes both supportive and directive roles. Elders who experience mild to moderate memory loss know they are missing something. This realization can be a source of tremendous anxiety and embarrassment and requires the group leader to be encouraging and supportive as elders struggle with this issue. Being aggressive with or infantilizing toward an elder who is trying to regain enough mastery over the environment to know where he or she is and what time of the day or month it is will only succeed in agitating an already anxious elder. The group leader needs to be directive in planning activities for the group that will promote interaction between group members rather than allowing confused elders to drift off into their own world. Given the nature of the limitations reality orientation groups address, it is less likely the group will develop an independent sense of "we-ness" without continued reinforcement and guidance from the group leader.

FIGURE 9.1 *Reality Orientation Group Activities*

1. Cook dishes that use seasonal fruits and vegetables.
2. Discuss current events, such as upcoming elections, important local news stories, and the anniversaries of important historical events.
3. Play simple interactive games, such as dominoes, checkers, or tic-tac-toe, that require an elder to work with another person.
4. Listen to current music and familiar music from the past.
5. Take photographs using Polaroid film, video, or digital cameras to produce instant results.
6. Give theme parties specific to holidays.
7. Walk through gardens or nature trails during different seasons of the year.
8. Show current and old favorite movies.
9. Watch fireworks displays for Independence Day or New Year's Day.
10. Take car or bus trips through local neighborhoods to see holiday decorations.
11. Provide educational presentations by health care providers, local historians, or political figures.
12. Invite local school music groups to perform seasonally appropriate music.

Limitations of the Reality Orientation Approach. The reality orientation approach has some serious limitations that should be considered before it is implemented with elders who have cognitive limitations. The approach appears to be most beneficial for elders in the early stages of dementia who *want* to maintain their orientation to time, space, or person, but has shown minimal effectiveness for elders in the later stages of dementia who may find regression to an earlier time in life or a different location a less frightening experience (Woodrow, 1998). The approach also assumes there is a single reality—that of the person conducting the reality orientation sessions. If an elder with dementia does not share that reality, he or she may become frustrated and respond aggressively to the orientation process. For elders in later stages of dementia, Woodrow (1998) suggested that validation therapy (discussed in Chapter 6) may be a more appropriate approach to maintaining communication and much less frustrating to professionals and caregivers who are constantly attempting to orient elders. Validation therapy respects the elder's reality as he or she believes it to be and is less concerned about the accuracy of an elder's perception of time and space. It seeks to understand the meaning of confusing and disorienting statements made by an elder with dementia.

Remotivation Groups

The Purpose of Remotivating Elders. One of the most difficult tasks facing gerontological social workers is getting elders to participate in both individual and group activities. It is important to emphasize that elders retain the right to choose what they want or do not want to do despite how good the social worker thinks a particular choice will be for them. It is a constant struggle in this field to balance a respect for self-determination with the professional knowledge that personal and social isolation reinforces depression and a sense of being detached from the environment, especially for elders with no or very mild limitations. While elders may complain of loneliness, the lethargy that develops over time from lack of social contact can become crippling, reinforcing a tendency to remain withdrawn. Remotivation groups are aimed at "stimulating and revitalizing individuals who are no longer interested or involved in either the present or the future" (Dennis, 1994, p. 153). Group activities are designed to help elders reconnect with others and move beyond a constant preoccupation with themselves and their own troubles (Capuzzi, Gross, & Friel, 1990).

Remotivating elders both individually and within the group context is intended to help elders improve self-esteem, regain a sense of competence in their lives, and learn new roles and skills that will invite them back into the mainstream of life. One of the major complaints of elders is that they no longer feel a purpose in their lives. They define their life roles in terms of what they no longer have—such as identifying as widow or retiree—rather than in terms of active and meaningful functions (Scharlach, 1989). Remotivation group work is intended to respect the self-determination of elders but provide opportunities for them to reaffirm lifelong competencies and skills or develop new interests. It involves a careful process of combining past memories and experiences with activities that draw elders into the present and promote interest in the future.

Membership. The elders who need the group experience the most may be minimally motivated to join it. Selecting group members who know each other or have common interests may alleviate some of the hesitancy about joining a group. The social worker needs to know each individual elder well enough to develop a slate of group activities that will appeal to potential group members and then use that knowledge to pique an elder's interests. Often social workers can parlay the warmth of a personal relationship with an elder into an agreement with the elder to join a group for at least one session with the hope that he or she will have a good time and continue to attend. Remotivation groups traditionally consist of 10 to 15 elders who are able to hear and speak well enough to be active participants and who do not suffer from dementia or debilitating depression (Dennis, 1994). Sessions are held once a week for 6 to 12 sessions.

Remotivation Activities. Dennis (1994) emphasized that remotivation groups should focus on pleasurable activities and avoid focusing on troubled relationships, health problems, or personal despair. It is an obsession with all these problems that distracts elders from staying connected to life in the first place. Elders should find the group a source of enjoyment and fun, giving them an opportunity to develop new friendships, be stimulated by new and familiar areas of interest, and renew their interest in a world outside their own problems. Dennis (1994) recommended such topics as holiday traditions, vacation memories, pets and animals, gardening, the arts, and hobbies. Unlike reminiscence groups that focus primarily on past memories, remotivation groups attempt to connect past pleasurable memories to present and future aspirations. For example, a widow who has fond memories of having a big Christmas tree in the family home but has discontinued the tradition because it is too much work might substitute a smaller, artificial tree decorated with some of her favorite ornaments to recreate past plea- sures in the current environment. The same widow may miss traditional holiday baking, which she has given up because her children and grandchildren live too far away to enjoy the treats. Joining forces with other widows who have similar interests can result in returning to the holiday baking but sending the goodies to distant family members or giving the product to a local children's home. Past pleasures are rekindled with the adaptations necessary to reflect the elder's cur- rent reality. The focus on activities that rekindle an elder's feelings of competence brings elders feelings of both pleasure and purpose. Dennis (1994) found that ac- tivities that stimulate the senses are those that appear to be of the greatest interest to remotivation groups. For example, cooking an actual meal rather than talking about cooking stimulates an elder's sense of smell and taste—a more effective way to engage an elder in the remotivation process. Planting a small herb garden, giving elders a chance to feel the dirt and plants, rather than just recalling memo- ries of past gardens, pulls an elder into the present and the future and out of a fixation on the past. One of the most exciting technologies available to elders is computers. While elders may resist learning about computers (which can baffle even those who need to use them all the time), once they learn about e-mail or the informational and educational resources available on the internet, their attitudes may change quickly. Other suggestions for remotivation activities are listed in Figure 9.2.

The Role of the Group Leader.   In remotivation groups, the leader takes the ini- tial responsibility for identifying and developing group activities and continuous monitoring of how responsive group members are to each of the topics. Elders will often express interest in certain topics for future activities once the group is under way. The group leader should also steer elders away from unpleasant or anxiety-provoking topics that elicit negative memories or feelings. The purpose of

FIGURE 9.2 *Remotivation Group Activities*

1. Gardening
2. Holiday preparation
3. Meal preparation tips for cooking for one or two people
4. Arts and crafts
5. Demonstrations of current computer technology
6. Makeup and fashion shows (for women)
7. Simple, inexpensive home decorating ideas
8. Visits from pets
9. Reading a novel out loud by chapters
10. Educational television programs
11. Opportunities for volunteering

the group is to help elders enjoy the activities and find them a source of motivation and pleasure. The group interaction should appeal to those areas in which an elder has competence or could develop competence and should not emphasize lost abilities. The leader needs to be supportive of an elder's hesitance to try something new but encouraging as well, akin to the role of motivational coach.

Social and Recreational Groups

The Purpose of Social and Recreational Groups.   While remotivation groups focus on rekindling elders' interest in reconnecting with others and finding enjoyment in group activities, social and recreational groups are designed to serve those elders who want to remain socially stimulated. These groups appeal to elders who are actively involved in their environments already but are looking for companionship, the opportunity to learn something new, or share their interests with other elders. The focus of these groups is primarily enjoyment.

Group Membership.   Social and recreational groups are most successful when the members bring diverse talents and interests to the group but have similar ability levels. For example, travel groups for elders vary from those designed for "physically active elders" who are capable of lots of walking, have no health limitations, and are looking for adventure to those for moderate- or low-energy level elders who would enjoy a less demanding, more structured approach to travel. The composition of the group should reflect a similarity in basic abilities to minimize competitiveness and maximize each group member's ability to participate in the group.

A balance of very verbal and less verbal members is important. Too many assertive elders in a group can wreak havoc with power struggles, while too many quiet, reserved members can reinforce each other's passivity. This balance of temperaments benefits all members but may not be easy to achieve when the group leader has limited input as to the composition of the group.

Group Activities.   The scope of social and recreational groups is unlimited. It is entirely contingent on the interests of the target group of elders. A recreational group can be as simple as a weekly bingo game in an assisted-living or congregate-living setting or as rigorous as a group of elders interested in learning how to sky dive. The most important thing is to identify activities that elders, not just the leader, are interested in pursuing. For example, the author designed a group for socially isolated, rural elderly women who were frequently restricted to their homes due to transportation problems or inclement weather. The focus of the group was supposed to be the common interests of women in rural areas, such as gardening, food preservation, cooking of regional dishes, and local ethnic traditions. When the group got together, they were thrilled to have the company of others but were not interested in talking about these topics at all! They wanted to go to fast food restaurants, see movies, shop at a local discount store, and talk about their soap operas. They proved to be a much more "with it" group than originally presumed. The group goals of socialization were accomplished, but the group was a better judge of what activities would achieve those goals.

Role of the Leader.   In social and recreational groups, the role of the group leader is less directive and more facilitative. The leader may plan and arrange for the basic activities of the group and facilitate the beginning phases of engagement in the group. However, group solidarity may develop quickly in these groups. Natural leaders may emerge from within the group, or the group as a whole may assume responsibility for the momentum of the group. The leader, however, maintains responsibility for clarifying communication between members when needed, monitoring the development and resolution of conflict, and keeping the group focused on the social or recreational activities. Observing how each individual group member is faring within the group setting remains an ongoing activity of the group leader. Some members need additional encouragement to move from bystander status to that of active participant. Sometimes damaging subgroups develop within social and recreational groups that exclude other group members or threaten the role of the leader. The distinct advantage of working with this kind of group is that the leader really gets to see the group process in action, both a delight and a challenge.

Support Groups

The Therapeutic Benefit of Support Groups.   While all group formats are intended to provide some measure of social support for elders, support groups are specifically intended to help elders cope with the difficult life transitions associated with aging, such as widowhood, chronic illness, housing transitions, or stressful family relationships (Toseland, 1995). Support groups require a high level of personal disclosure and rely on the therapeutic effects of the group, offering members both support and concrete suggestions for coping with the focus problem. Ultimately, support groups are intended to move an elder beyond the current emotional trauma associated with an adverse life event to find ways not only to adjust to the situation but also to grow beyond it. A credibility is attributed to others who are experiencing or have experienced a similar life crisis that the group leader often does not have.

To facilitate growth in its members, support groups often contain an educational component (Burnside, 1994b). For example, elders coping with recent widowhood often need concrete information about settling estates, disposing of property, or learning how to manage their finances. Similarly, caregivers of elders with Alzheimer's disease and elders themselves need to learn more about the disease and what can be expected in the months and years ahead as the disease progresses.

Group Membership.   The common bond in support groups is formed by members who are experiencing the same life event. It is often beneficial to include elders who have successfully met a life challenge along with elders who are new to the crisis. This balance is helpful in moving the elder from fixating on the loss or crisis to identifying better adaptive techniques. It is also important that members be emotionally stable enough to be able to listen to others and participate in a group context. Elders who are still in emotional chaos may be too vulnerable to participate in the group or be so obsessed with their own pain that they cannot hear others. Group members must also be willing and able to share intense personal feelings with others. Elders who are unwilling to discuss feelings or process personal crises outside a circle of intimates may not be appropriate for inclusion in a support group.

Support Group Activities.   The success of any support group depends on the development of an atmosphere of warmth and respect that encourages members to share their own "story" with the group. Sharing their feelings about a life transition can help elders move along in the process. For example, resolution of grief requires that elders acknowledge deep feelings of pain, anger, or loss while identifying ways to cope with these feelings. The leader needs to be familiar with the normal progression of the grieving process as well as be able to identify when an elder is "stuck" in the process (Toseland, 1995). Other group members serve as a reality check when elders are having trouble moving along in the process and can offer invaluable feedback to both the grieving elder and the group leader.

The work of the support group is not just to allow elders to vent troublesome feelings but also to help group members identify ways in which they can move beyond these feelings to adjust to life as it has changed. For example, a recent widow who feels very lonely but resists every effort by family and friends to attend social events may need to be challenged about the apparent contradiction in her behavior. Other widowed women who understand the self-consciousness accompanying rejoining social activities are in a better position to offer the woman the encouragement she needs to take the first step than family and friends may be. Fellow support group members may be able to offer concrete suggestions and motivate a recent widow because of their own experiences with a similar situation.

In preparation for termination of the group, the mutual support shared within the group is gradually transferred to formal and informal helping networks outside the group (Toseland, 1995). The support networks developed in the group may continue beyond the life of the group if members have developed strong personal relationships with each other. However, it should not be assumed that a promise to call each other is evidence that ongoing support is in place for group members. Connecting group members with ongoing social and recreational activities that promote social interaction, referring group members for additional individual counseling when indicated, and alerting members to other support services in the community are more reliable ways to assure that members who continue to need other forms of support will receive them.

Role of the Leader.   The primary role of the group leader is to provide support and facilitate mutual aid to group members by encouraging the development of bonds between group members. Exercises that help members become acquainted and comfortable with each other are important in the beginning of the group. Using go-round exercises or ice-breaker activities starts the process of members interacting with each other, not just with the leader.

When a support group is working, the level of group interaction is high and laden with emotional content. The leader helps group members identify the manifest and latent content of group communications, striking a balance between offering an opportunity to ventilate emotions and preventing a total emotional meltdown. At the conclusion of intense sessions, the leader is responsible for putting a sense of closure on the session so that group members do not leave group sessions in an emotionally agitated state.

Homework assignments may be devised by the group leader to foster the application of coping techniques discussed in group to members' lives outside the group. Group members tend to be more invested in the group process when they feel they are getting concrete ideas about how to cope with the life crisis. Reporting back to the group after doing this homework holds group members more accountable to actually practice these skills outside the group.

Support groups can be successfully led by peers rather than professionally trained group leaders as is evidenced by the success of Alcoholics Anonymous and other peer support models (Thomas & Martin, 1992). Peers who have experienced similar life crises have a degree of credibility that group leaders do not. Utilizing a professional group leader and a peer coleader is a compromise that recognizes the need for credibility along with the necessity of professional training (Kostyk, Fuchs, Tabisz, & Jacyk, 1993). Professional group leaders can benefit from the insight and wisdom of peer leaders' experiences while peer coleaders profit from training in general group work techniques, conflict resolution, and communication skills.

Therapy Groups

The Focus of Group Therapy.   While all group work with elders is intended to be therapeutic, therapy group work with elders focuses on the power of group problem solving to help elders change maladaptive or dysfunctional behavior patterns (Toseland, 1995). Rather than intentionally avoiding painful or unpleasant emotions as is often done in remotivation, social and recreational, or reminiscence groups, therapy groups are designed to address problems directly and elicit the input of group members in identifying solutions. The group approach is used to enhance or restore an elder's functioning during the process of coping with or recovering from a variety of mental health problems. For example, elders coping with recurrent depression may join a group aimed at helping them identify the triggers for depressive episodes and ways in which they can help themselves alleviate the intense feelings of sadness. In another instance, elders may benefit from a group approach to overcoming antisocial behavior that has contributed to their isolation and loneliness by helping them become aware of their own behavior and by learning appropriate social skills.

Ageist attitudes on the part of mental health professionals and elders themselves can be formidable obstacles to even considering the formation of therapeutic groups for elders. The stereotypes that elders' behavior patterns are too entrenched to be changed or that elders have limited interest in and ability to engage in personal introspection often result in a group therapy approach being dismissed even before it is seriously considered. If the prospective group leader harbors either of these ageist attitudes, the group approach will not work. One of the most serious mistakes made in both health and mental health settings is allowing elders to give up too easily. Professional helpers may reinforce elders' perceptions that they are too tired, too sick, or too old to continue to take an active role in managing their lives and behavior. While mental health professionals may be well-intentioned, allowing elders to relinquish personal responsibility to others robs elders of the psychological value of continuing to seek some control over their environments. When professionals expect little from elders, that is exactly what they get. Assuming elders with emotional or psychological problems have limited ability to benefit from personal insight or the insights of others in changing dysfunctional behaviors relegates elders to a chronically unhappy existence. The expectations placed on elders become self-fulfilling prophecies (Toseland, 1995). It is important for the social worker to examine his or her own personal attitudes about elders' abilities to be active participants in a group change effort before considering group therapy as an intervention choice.

Group Membership. Members of therapeutic groups are usually selected because they share a similar mental health problem although their life circumstances may present very unique challenges to each member. Unlike support groups that help elders through a transition with the hope that life can return to some semblance of normalcy when the elders adjust to the changes in their lives, true therapy groups do not assume people will "get over" a mental health problem. For example, depression can be successfully treated but elders will need to learn that "success" is dependent on taking medication on a regular basis or avoiding situations that exacerbate the condition. Alzheimer's disease will not magically disappear, but its deleterious process can be slowed by good medical care, nutrition, and continued stimulation of cognitive abilities. Those who benefit from group membership are those elders who are willing to accept that group therapy is not a cure but a treatment for mental health problems.

Group members should be voluntary participants in the group process and not have been forced to join by family members or physical or mental health professionals. Participating in group therapy requires members to be motivated to examine their own behavior and willing to listen to the feedback of both group members and the group leader.

Group Activities in Therapy Groups. Developing individual and group goals is the primary activity in the early stages of a therapy group. While the leader may have general goals in mind for each participant, members are more likely to commit to the group process if they have identified their own goals. Members may need input from both group members and the leader in identifying goals; however, the purpose of being in the group needs to be clearly articulated early in the group process.

The activities in any therapy group are chosen contingent on both the presenting problems of group members and the theoretical orientation of the group leader (Toseland, 1995). Group therapeutic approaches can include reminiscence, life review, or reality orientation, which have been discussed elsewhere in this book. These approaches have a prescribed protocol for group activities and offer a structured intervention in the group process. A cognitive-behavioral approach helps elders to identify faulty thinking patterns that result in maladaptive behavior. Using the expertise of the leader combined with the feedback of the group, elders can learn to identify their own cognitive distortions. Once an elder is able to identify what thinking patterns are followed by dysfunctional behavior, he or she can learn new behavior patterns. A psychodynamic approach to group therapy with elders focuses on the emotionally distressing behavioral effects of unresolved conflicts from both an elder's past and present, emphasizing how defense mechanisms can create maladaptive behavior (Tross & Blum, 1988). The specific approach employed by a group leader is the function of his or her expertise and the challenges facing group members.

Weekly check-in is a technique frequently used in all types of groups. Having each group member speak briefly about experiences since the last group meeting or bring current concerns to the attention of the group helps to develop continuity between sessions and focus the group on the activities of the day (Toseland, 1995). This technique also gives less verbal elders an opportunity to contribute to the group process.

Frequently, group therapy involves assigning homework to each member as a way to provide opportunities for group members to apply what has been learned in the group setting to life outside the group consistent with individual goals. Trying out new behaviors and approaches to familiar situations provides immediate feedback and gives the elder an opportunity to process new behaviors with group members in the next meeting. The power of the collective sense of "we-ness" holds the elder accountable for actually making a concentrated effort to change unwanted behaviors. Homework assignments encourage members to engage in the group process because they feel they are actually doing something that will help them. An awareness of the need for behavior change is immediately followed with concrete suggestions about implementing those changes.

Role of the Group Leader.   In therapy groups, the leader assumes the roles of expert and change agent—more directive and interventive roles than are taken in support or social groups of elders (Toseland, 1995). The leader is engaged in a constant process of assessing the functioning and coping skills of individual members, providing insight and concrete suggestions to members as needed. It may become apparent as the group progresses that some members are in need of more intense therapeutic work than is possible in the group setting and should be referred to other support services outside the group. Other group members may simply need more support from the group leader than others to avoid dangerous scapegoating by group members. In therapy groups, the group leadership process is a dynamic one requiring constant reassessment of the group's functioning.

Emphasizing group members' abilities and drawing on group members' experiences can create an atmosphere that encourages elders to build on their own competencies in the process of behavioral change. A skilled group leader guides the group to develop its own solutions to problems, a process that helps group members develop insight and confidence as part of the therapeutic process. The willingness to let the group struggle and find its own solutions requires the group leader to be firmly committed to the conviction that group members are capable of finding appropriate solutions to problems in the context of group support and direction.

Ethical Dilemmas in Group Work with Elders

Respecting Self-Determination

As mentioned earlier in this chapter, one of the biggest challenges facing group workers is how to get elders to participate in a group at all. Elders most in need of the socialization afforded by group participation may be those most reluctant to join any group effort. Schmidt (1994) suggested that resistance to join a group may be an elder's way of conserving personal energy, which he or she perceives to be already seriously depleted by physical illness or emotional stress. Other elders bypass groups specifically to avoid conflict with others, especially in institutional settings. Elders living in assisted living, congregate housing, or nursing homes are forced to coexist in ways not required of those who remain in their own homes. It may be much easier to stay clear of others whom the elder does not like or does not want to associate with. In institutional settings, group workers need to remind themselves that even after a group session is over, elders continue to interact with each other. Conflict that originates within the group may carry over to activities outside the group.

Other elders simply do not want to participate in a group. They may not like a structured interaction with either strangers or people they know well. They do not like sitting in a circle talking about feelings or sharing troubles. They are not interested in reviewing their lives or remembering past holidays or learning new skills. They do not care to make new friends or explore unresolved conflicts from earlier in life. As much as this realization might frustrate a gerontological social worker, elders reserve the right to make that decision. Groups exist to meet the needs of their elder members, not to advance the professional agendas of eager social workers. Respecting the dignity of elders means respecting their right to decline treatment. Forcing elders to attend group sessions, especially in institutional settings, regardless of the wishes of family or other staff is a clear ethical violation for a social worker.

Balancing Responsibilities to the Group and the Individual

When an elder proves to be highly disruptive to the group, a group leader may need to decide between the competing responsibility to the group as a whole and his or her responsibility to the individual as client. Every group struggles with the demands a "needy" member places on others in the group. An elder who monopolizes the leader's attention or is verbally or physically aggressive toward others can turn the group experience into a major disaster. While it seems a simple decision to ask the elder to leave the group, it is often exactly this type of group member who eventually benefits the most from the group experience. Acting out may be a subconscious attempt to get others to reject him or her, confirming personal fears that he or she is unlovable. If the group rejects the elder, his or her worst fears are confirmed. If the group accepts the elder but makes it clear that certain behavior will not be tolerated, the troubled elder may be able to develop the insight that changing specific behaviors will change people's attitudes toward him or her. It is the leader's responsibility to determine what damage or what benefit may be accrued by allowing disruptive members to stay in the group.

Respecting Confidentiality

One of the cardinal rules of group work is "what is said in the group, stays in the group." For elders who have never belonged to a group before and will be exposed to a menagerie of others' private experiences, resisting the temptation to talk about what has gone on in group will be a challenge. The importance of confidentiality must be emphasized throughout the group. Those who breach confidentiality need to be confronted before the integrity of the group is compromised.

In the abstract, it is easy to assure group members that their most personal thoughts and feelings will not be shared with anyone outside the group. Group members may be comforted by this promise and divulge information that threatens their own or others' welfare. Comments such as "one of these days, I am just going to take all my sleeping pills and never wake up" or "my son makes me so mad, someday I am going to blow him away" cannot be ignored. While a social worker is bound by confidentiality, he or she is also bound by a duty to protect the welfare of the client and others in the immediate environment who may be in danger from a client's actions. This can create a painful ethical dilemma for a social worker who does not want to be perceived by group members as a "snitch" but understands his or her professional responsibility to warn others of impending harm.

Intervening in Group Dynamics

The major assumption underlying group work is that once a sense of group cohesion has formed, the group will take on its own life through the magic of group dynamics. Under ideal circumstances, group members find strength and support in each other and assume responsibility for the direction of the group process. Group members become supportive healing agents for each other as the group leader fondly looks on. Resistant group members find their voice, overbearing elders miraculously wait patiently for their turn to make a contribution to the group, and everyone delights in the collective sense of "we-ness" that develops among members. Under real circumstances, group dynamics are not always so self-affirming for everyone. Destructive subgroups may develop that undermine the group leader. Particularly vulnerable elders may become scapegoats for more dominant group members. Feelings can be deeply hurt or dismissed by insensitive peers.

While the group leader may be deeply committed to the notion of a group that is run democratically with members making the vast majority of decisions about group process and procedures, on occasion it may be necessary to sacrifice the independent operation of the group for the sake of protecting a specific member. Groups that have taken a destructive turn can be a source of intense agitation for elders and turn into a "psychological lynch mob" (Schmidt, 1994, p. 378). The group leader may need to resolve the conflict within the group or dissolve the group if the destructive behavior continues. A group does not have a right to exist independent of its responsibilities to members.

Summary

Using a group approach to address the individual and collective challenges facing elders combines the therapeutic effect of group dynamics with the benefits of social interaction. In view of the limited professional social work resources in congregate settings, such as assisted or congregate-living centers, adult day health centers, and nursing homes, group work offers an efficient and effective way to reach a larger number of elders than is possible through individual intervention alone. This approach requires that accommodations be made for physical and sensory limitations elders may have and that elders be carefully assessed for their appropriateness for a group experience. Elders with severe cognitive limitations, disruptive or self-obsessed personalities, and acute emotional chaos following a life crisis may be more appropriately served in individual work.

A variety of groups can be adapted for use with elders. Reality orientation groups offer a structured approach to both orienting elders to their immediate environment and helping elders develop skills to reorient themselves if they become confused. As part of a total institutional approach to maintaining orientation, the reality orientation process shows promise in delaying additional memory loss among elders and reconnecting them to their environments. Remotivation group interventions are aimed at those elders who continue to have good orientation but have lost interest in present and future events. By stimulating their senses, developing social relationships, and learning new skills that build on existing competencies, elders can be revitalized to rejoin the mainstream of life.

Social and recreational groups derive their therapeutic benefit from the social interaction among elders in the context of enjoyment of new or familiar activities. The scope of social and recreational groups is virtually unlimited, but should appeal to the interests and abilities of the group. Support groups have a narrower focus and are geared to helping elders navigate life transitions, such as widowhood, the diagnosis of a chronic illness, or a change in living arrangements, within the supportive context of the group. Elders can learn to acknowledge negative feelings while developing new coping skills to manage the unfamiliar set of challenges created by life transitions.

Therapy groups are the last form of group intervention discussed in this chapter. Unlike reality orientation, remotivation, or social groups, which consciously avoid painful emotions and events, therapy groups focus on these sensitive issues. Elders who live with depression, anxiety, or other mental health problems often benefit from both the support offered by therapy groups and the power of the group problem-solving process. Members can learn new, more functional behaviors within the group setting that can be transferred to living situations outside the group.

Group work with elders from diverse racial, ethnic, and cultural groups requires workers to examine their own prejudices about these groups and engage in a cultural learning process that will better equip them to provide culturally sensitive services. In addition to respecting cultural diversity, group work with elders requires a social worker to be sensitive to the ethical challenges presented by respecting self-determination in elders, emphasizing the qualified nature of confidentiality in the group context, and balancing the needs of the individual with the needs of the group.

Check Out These Websites!

1. **www.fortnet.org/widownet** Widownet is an information and self-help resource for and by widows and widowers and is a good example of the growing number of chat lines and online support services available to elders. The site offers "cyber-support" for widowed elders with access to the internet with helpful suggestions about managing financial resources, finding books and other resources about topics of interest to widows and widowers, and locating support groups in their geographic areas.

2. **www.elderhostel.org** Elder Hostel is a nonprofit organization that develops and coordinates a wide variety of socioeducational experiences for elders who want to connect with other elders. Programs sponsored by Elder Hostel consist of one- to four-week programs throughout the United States, Canada, and many foreign countries that provide a travel experience with an educational component.

3. **www.sablier.com** Concepts du Sablier is a Canadian company that develops products for use in reality orientation, social, and recreational groups. This

website offers information on purchasing a variety of items—such as reality ori-entation boards and adaptive signs for use in institutions—that can be used by social workers, nurses, occupational therapists, and activities directors in geriatric settings.

4. www.aarp.org/griefandloss/onlineresources.html   Sponsored by the American Association of Retired Persons, this website offers links to a variety of online resources for elders struggling with grief and loss, including an online grief support group that meets three times a week.

References

Axelson, J. (1993). *Counseling and development in a multicultural society.* Pacific Grove, CA: Brooks Cole.

Burnside, I. (1994a). History and overview of group work. In I. Burnside & M. G. Schmidt (Eds.), *Working with older adults: Group process and technique* (pp. 24–38). Boston: Jones & Bartlett.

Burnside, I. (1994b). Support and self-help groups. In I. Burnside & M. G. Schmidt (Eds.), *Working with older adults: Group process and technique* (pp. 203–213). Boston: Jones & Bartlett.

Burnside, I., & Schmidt, M. G. (1994). *Working with older adults: Group process and technique.* Boston: Jones & Bartlett.

Capuzzi, D., Gross, D., & Friel, S. E. (1990). Group work with elders. *Generations* (Winter), 43–48.

Dennis, H. (1994). Remotivation groups. In I. Burnside & M. G. Schmidt (Eds.), *Working with older adults: Group process and technique* (pp. 153–162). Boston: Jones & Bartlett.

Dufour, M., & Fuller, R. K. (1995). Alcohol in the elderly. *Annual Review of Medicine, 46,* 123–132.

Gomberg, E. S. L., & Zucker, R. A. (1998). Substance use and abuse in old age. In I. H. Nordhus, G. R. VandenBox, R. S. Bera, & P. Fromholt (Eds.), *Clinical geropsychology* (pp. 189–204). Washington, DC: American Psychological Association.

Green, J. (1999). *Cultural awareness in the human services: A multi-ethnic approach.* Boston: Allyn and Bacon.

Kostyk, D., Fuchs, D., Tabisz, E., & Jacyk, W. R. (1993). Combining professional and self-help intervention: Collaboration in co-leadership. *Social Work with Groups, 16*(3), 111–123.

Lindesay, J. (1997). Suicide in later life. In I. J. Norman & S. J. Redfern (Eds.), *Health care for elderly people* (pp. 163–174). New York: Churchill Livingstone.

McMahon, R. (1988). The 24-hour reality orientation type of approach to the confused elderly: A minimum standard of care. *Journal of Advanced Nursing, 13,* 693–700.

Mosher-Ashley, P. M., & Barrett, P. W. (1997). *A life worth living: Practical strategies for reducing depression in older adults.* Baltimore, MD: Health Sciences Press.

Rose, S. (1991). Small group processes and interventions with the elderly. In P. K. H. Kim (Ed.), *Serving the elderly: Skills for practice* (pp. 167–186). New York: Aldine de Gruyter.

Scharlach, A. E. (1989). Social group work with the elderly: A role theory perspective. *Social Work with Groups, 12*(3), 33–46.

Schmidt, M. G. (1994). Ethical dilemmas in group work. In I. Burnside & M. G. Schmidt (Eds.), *Working with older adults: Group process and technique* (pp. 373–379). Boston: Jones & Bartlett.

Taulbee, L. (1986). Reality orientation and clinical practice. In I. Burnside (Ed.), *Working with the elderly: Group processes and techniques* (2nd ed., pp. 177–186). Boston: Jones & Bartlett.

Thomas, M. C., & Martin, V. (1992). Training counselors to facilitate the transitions of aging through group work. *Counselor Education and Supervision, 32,* 51–60.

Toseland, R. W. (1995). *Group work with the elderly and family caregivers.* New York: Springer.

Tross, S., & Blum, J. E. (1988). A review of group therapy with the older adult: Practice and research. In B. W. Maclennan, S. Saul, & M. B. Weiner (Eds.), *Group psychotherapies for the elderly* (pp. 3–32). Madison, CT: International Universities Press.

Weisman, C. B., & Schwartz, P. (1989). Worker expectations in group work with the frail elderly: Modifying the models for a better fit. *Social Work with Groups, 12*(3), 47–55.

Williams, E. M. (1994). Reality orientation groups. In I. Burnside & M. G. Schmidt (Eds.), *Working with older adults: Group process and technique* (pp. 139–152). Boston: Jones & Bartlett.

Woodrow, P. (1998). Clinical interventions for confusion and dementia 2: Reality orientation. *British Journal of Nursing, 7*(17), 1018–1020.

10

Spirituality and Social Work with Elders

Spirituality and Religion in Social Work Practice

The social work profession has historically had an approach-avoidance relationship with the issue of spirituality and its relevance to practice. Once seen as the domain of clergy and pastoral counselors, the concern about individuals' spiritual well-being and the role spirituality plays in mental health and social functioning have reemerged as legitimate professional foci. What roles do formal religious institutions play in the lives of clients? How do people find meaning in their lives? Is a spiritual crisis a mental health problem or a religious dilemma? Should social workers discuss spirituality with their clients openly or refer these clients to those who specialize in spiritual matters? This chapter addresses these questions particularly as they apply to social work with elders. Answering questions about life's meaning and purpose is among the most important tasks of this developmental period.

The discussion of spirituality and religion in the lives of older people is often approached within the context of helping elders prepare for dying and death. In this book, the separation of these topics is deliberate. Spirituality is not just about the business of preparing for death or reconciling with beliefs about an afterlife. Spirituality is about the business of living, finding meaning in life *now*, and cultivating ways in which to explore and express those beliefs. Spirituality is not a problem to be solved but a journey that both clients and professionals take in a variety of different ways.

Defining Spirituality and Religion

The terms *spirituality* and *religion* are often used interchangeably; however, their meanings are significantly different. While this chapter will discuss the importance of organized religion and its role as a social support system in the lives of elders, the discussion of elders' spirituality is the major focus. This emphasis on spirituality allows the practitioner to move beyond the confines of specific religious denominations to recognize the rich diversity of ways in which elders express the role of this force in their lives.

Spirituality.   Sherwood (1998) defined spirituality as the "search for transcendence, meaning, and connectedness beyond the self" (p. 81). Tolliver's (1997) notion of spirituality is conceptualized as "the renewable life force, the energy that enlivens the physical, and the space where human communion is possible" (p. 479). Bullis (1996) included the significance of "the immediacy of a higher power" as part of his definition of spirituality, which he sees as both "eclectic and inclusive" (p. 2). These definitions are a distillation of the dozens of definitions of spirituality but include the major factors common to most definitions: a transcendence beyond oneself, a search for meaning, and a sense of connectedness to others.

All human beings have a spiritual self, just as all humans have a biological, psychological, and social self, although people have quite different levels of awareness and development of their spiritual selves. For some people, transcendence beyond self is represented by a relationship with a single supreme being, such as God or another spiritual being. For others, transcendence is evident in nature and the cycle of the seasons. For others, the human community and the power of relationships with people represent both transcendence and connectedness as the force of spirituality. Regardless of its specific expression and interpretation, spirituality represents the means by which people derive meaning and purpose in their lives (Bullis, 1996; Canda, 1988).

Religion.   Religion is the formal institutionalized expression of spirituality characterized by "beliefs, ethical codes, and worship practices" (Joseph, 1988). Religious denominations espouse a basic set of principles about the existence of a supreme being, the existence (or lack of) an afterlife, how people should behave toward others, and the rituals important to the expression of faith in those principles. Persons can be spiritual without identifying with a specific religious denomination. It is also possible that persons can be active participants in a religion, but not be particularly spiritual.

Over 90 percent of people in the United States identify themselves as belonging to a particular religious denomination. In 1997, 58 percent of Americans classified themselves as Protestants, 26 percent as Catholics, and 2 percent as Jews, reflecting the influence of the Judeo-Christian tradition in this country. However, 6 percent identified themselves as Muslims, Hindus, Buddhists, or other denominations, and 8 percent indicated no religious preference, suggesting that, even within the strong religious tradition in this country, there is a great deal of diversity in religious affiliation (Princeton Religion Research Center, 1997).

The Social Work Profession's Approach–Avoidance Relationship with Spirituality

As mentioned in the opening paragraph of this chapter, the social work profession has historically had an approach-avoidance attitude toward spirituality. This conflicted attitude is the product of the historical context in which the profession emerged as well as a result of the evolution in social thought about spirituality itself during the twentieth century.

Early Ties to Charitable Organizations

The early history of the profession is inextricably tied to the notion of spirituality and religion as a formal institution. Religious and charitable organizations were the primary providers of social services in the United States until the twentieth century (Trattner, 1999). Providing services to widows, orphans, persons with disabilities, the elderly, and the unemployed was seen as an important part of organized religion's responsibility to society. The first social workers saw themselves as spiritually motivated to help others not only with material assistance but also with the spiritual support needed to achieve eternal salvation (Holland, 1989; Ortiz, 1991). Social work and charitable efforts shared many of the same goals: to preserve the dignity of the individual, to improve social functioning, and to protect society's most vulnerable populations—the fundamental values of the Judeo-Christian tradition. This was evident in the early efforts of charity organization societies to improve the moral character of the poor and immigrant populations and the settlement houses' focus on social and political reform.

The Influences of Empiricism and Freud

As social work sought to establish itself as a full-fledged profession in the early 1900s, attitudes changed about the appropriateness of intervening in the spiritual and moral fiber of clients. If social work was ever to gain professional integrity in the eyes of the public and other professions, it needed to distance itself from the association between receiving assistance and proselytizing, a common practice in sectarian agency services. At the same time service provision was moving away from the private and sectarian sector to the domain of the public sector, the social movement to separate the affairs of the state from the influence of organized religion was growing. This separation is fiercely maintained even today.

Social work education moved from the agency setting to the academic setting, requiring that social work educators make the profession's approach to assessment of client problems and the identification of appropriate interventions more rigorous (Canda, 1997). The emphasis in other professions, such as law and medicine, was moving toward empiricism—the process of gaining knowledge through making concrete observations about the cause and consequence of behavior (Canda, 1997; Graham, Kaiser, & Garrett, 1998). In order to influence an individual's behavior, the professional needed to be able to observe and quantify it. The focus on moral fiber and spiritual well-being did not fit into the profession's new interests in the scientific measurement and classification of human behavior.

The contributions of Sigmund Freud in the 1920s to the psychological knowledge base also had a profound influence on the profession's attempt to dissociate itself from organized charity and religion (Goldberg, 1996). Freud's work on the dynamics of the unconscious mind and the role of unresolved conflicts from early life experiences as an explanation for dysfunctional behavior attracted the social work profession as it searched for a theoretical foundation. Freud used his interpretation of the human experience to demystify the role and function of religion in humans' lives. He saw humans' creation of God as a revival of the forces that drive an infant to seek security and safety in a father-image. Religion was, according to Freud, an externalization of internal neurotic conflicts from childhood. As a result, Freud saw religion as a human weakness, not as a source of strength. He believed that human behavior was driven by the need to satisfy basic drives of hunger, sex, and aggression, not by the quest for meaning in life. Freud cited religion as the cause of some neurotic conflicts and rigid superegos, rather than considering its role as a coping mechanism. While he never clearly distinguished between spirituality and religion, his "pathologizing" of religion as a force in one's life implicitly included spirituality. His dismissal of the importance of the religious self was subtly assimilated into the social work profession's perspective on human behavior. The influence of empiricism as a mode of inquiry combined with the growing concern about separating church and state and Freud's ideas about religion effectively maintained the profession's distance from the issue of spirituality for over 50 years.

Social Work's Renewed Focus on Spirituality

Social work's renewed interest in spirituality began in the 1970s consistent with the changing paradigms of postmodern thinking. Postmodernism thrived in a radically changing social environment. The civil rights movement challenged social justifications for a racially segregated society. As more and more women sought college educations and found reproductive freedom with the development of safe and effective birth control, the traditional roles of wife and mother as the only valued roles for women were questioned. The ultimate right of the United States to interfere in the political upheavals in places such as Vietnam and Central America were contested. Traditional social norms about behavior and social roles were subject to intense scrutiny.

Postmodern social thought emphasizes the relative nature of the human experience. There is no single way of viewing the human experience and no single norm against which to ascertain truth. Rather, each individual has a unique view of his or her role and purpose in life. Social constructionism, discussed in Chapter 3, is an example of postmodern thinking. According to social constructionist theory, each individual defines his or her reality, basing subsequent behaviors on that reality. This important shift in social thought, in many respects, freed all people and the social work profession to explore and support the concept of diversity as a source of strength, not as a social anomaly. This shift in thinking helped social work and the other helping professions to "depathologize" religion as a force in people's lives, diminishing one of the last vestiges of Freud's antireligion stance (Jacobs, 1997). For some, a spiritual self is a critical component in defining the meaning of one's life and one's relationship with a supreme being, which may, or may not, include affiliation with a specific religious denomination. Regardless, postmodern thinking requires that the spiritual aspect of human perception be recognized if it constitutes part of a person's reality. The willingness to reconsider religion also facilitated the movement toward specifying the differences between religion as an institution and spirituality as a personality characteristic.

The Diagnostic and Statistic Manual IV (American Psychiatric Association, 1994), the handbook for classifying psychological and emotional disorders, now recognizes spiritual or religious problems, such as a loss of faith, questioning spiritual values, or emotional reactions to religious conversations, as legitimate mental health issues, not as an expression of mental illness (Bullis, 1996). Spirituality is considered a legitimate component of a comprehensive psychological assessment and calls on the social work profession to consider a person's faith development as an important part of psychosocial development (Jacobs, 1997).

The particular significance of spirituality and religion in the lives of elders was recognized in the formation of the National Interfaith Coalition on Aging (NICA) in 1975. NICA attested to the importance of the role of both organized religious institutions and private spiritual activity in an elder's attainment of spiritual well-being. Spiritual well-being is defined by NICA as "the affirmation of life in relationship with a [supreme being], self, community, and environment that nurtures and celebrates wholeness" (Blazer, 1991, p. 62). Moving the discussion of the importance of recognizing and utilizing an elder's spirituality from the private world of a limited number of helping professions to the forefront of service planning and delivery has helped to open discussion and awareness of this important part of an elder's functioning.

The development of postmodern thinking, a broadened concept of what constitutes spirituality, and depathologizing of spiritual issues has forced social work to reassess its role in exploring spirituality with clients. A critical discussion of the role of professional practice and client spirituality has begun to appear in the professional literature (Bullis, 1996; Canda, 1997; Jacobs, 1997; Sherwood, 1998; Wong, 1998).

The Relevance of Spirituality to Social Work with Elders

The return of professional interest in spirituality is particularly relevant to social work practice with elders. Addressing the spiritual well-being of an elder is a natural outgrowth of the profession's growing understanding of the complexities of human behavior (Jacobs, 1997). While empiricism serves an important role in the profession to hold social workers accountable for responsible practice and helps to identify what works and what does not work in practice, not all aspects of human behavior can be measured and quantified.

Naming Psychosocial Tasks as Spiritual

The components of spirituality (transcendence beyond oneself, a search for meaning, and a sense of connectedness to others) are, in many respects, the major psychosocial challenges elders face. The developmental task of establishing ego integrity versus ego despair as proposed by Erikson (1963) centers on an elder's ability to process all that has happened in his or her life and accept these life events as integral to life's meaning. Graham, Kaiser, and Garrett (1998) suggested that conflicts and problems often identified as psychosocial problems are actually spiritual issues and should be identified as such. For example, social isolation, the longing for a sense of connectedness to someone or something, is a common challenge for elders. This lack of connectedness can be defined as a spiritual concern as well as a psychosocial concern. Elders seek to maximize their own independence and ability to make choices versus becoming dependent on others—the quest for hope versus despair—a struggle that is both psychosocial and spiritual.

By naming a psychosocial challenge as a spiritual issue, the healing process has begun. Spiritual issues, unlike some psychosocial problems, cannot be reduced to the result of faulty thinking patterns or unresolved conflicts from earlier in life but are rather an expression of the basic need for people to connect with others or find meaning in their lives. Change happens for some people not when their personal pathology is corrected with talk therapy but when their spiritual needs are met by prayer, meditation, or joining a faith community. While not all social workers would uniformly agree with Graham and associates' (1998) contentions, reframing psychosocial problems as spiritual issues moves the profession toward considering a new range of interventions.

The Common Ground between Social Work and Spirituality

Social work and spirituality focus on the common interest in promoting self-respect, encouraging personal and social healing, and developing functional coping strategies, all of which are critical to healthy functioning in elders (Bullis, 1996). The powerful metaphor of change and growth as part of a journey is shared by both social work and spirituality, reinforcing a common perspective that a person's life satisfaction is contingent on moving from where they are to where they want to be. A focus on spirituality in social work practice with elders reaffirms the profession's commitment to preserving and respecting diversity through recognizing and valuing each individual's expression of spirituality.

There is no such thing as a fixed reality about the aging process or what it means to individuals. To understand how and why an elder behaves the way he or she does, it is important to understand how an elder defines reality for himself or herself within a spiritual context. Suffering may be understood by elders as a spiritual test by a greater power and as serving a greater purpose (Bullis, 1996). The losses and illnesses that often accompany the aging process may be viewed as an inevitable part of the total human experience rather than as punishment for sins or transgressions. If private prayer and devotion are sources of great comfort and serve as coping devices, elders will use them as such. Understanding an elder's spirituality helps the social worker understand the elder's view of the world and subsequent behavior.

Themes of Spirituality in Elders

Fischer (1993) identified five common themes that emerge in observing and describing the significance of spirituality in elders. The first of these themes is the importance to elders of embracing the present moment. This includes appreciating the preciousness of time and the importance of being truly present in the moment, "learning the art of being rather than doing" (p. 31). A second theme is finding meaning in past memories as part of constructing meaning in life, an important function of the life review process. In this process, elders often have the opportunity to confront their own limitations, a third theme in elders' descriptions of the importance of spirituality in their lives. After confronting one's limitations and accepting both the positive and negative aspects of one's life, an elder has the opportunity to seek reconciliation and forgiveness, Fischer's fourth theme. Having the opportunity to mend fences and revitalize estranged relationships may be a very important part of an elder's resolving inner conflicts from earlier in their lives. The final theme Fischer identified is that of "expanding the circle of one's love and compassion" (p. 33). As elders come to a better understanding of both their own life histories and the opportunities for service to others that still are available to them, many use the additional time in their later years to reach out to others through prayer or service.

Spiritual Development in Adults

A number of theories have been proposed about how people develop spirituality over the life course. Fowler (1991) described spiritual development in adulthood as a series of three stages. The indivuative-reflective stage occurs in early adulthood when young adults turn away from traditional sources of spiritual authority (traditionally organized religion) toward the development of an internal orientation about right and wrong. Reliance on one's own rational ideas about behavior and morals replaces an externally imposed code of behavior. As part of the process of establishing an adult identity, the young adult is deciding what behavioral standards he or she will follow and what relationship with a greater power exists.

These standards are often very rigid with little tolerance for attitudes and beliefs that differ.

By midlife, adults move into the phase of conjunctive faith, in which they are more accepting of paradox and ambiguity. They seek less to find definitive answers to the question "if there is an all-loving, all-good supreme being, why do bad things happen to people who believe?" Adults in this phase of development feel less need to rely on the strict conventions of logic and are more likely to accept things on faith, rather than reason. They become more tolerant of religions other than their own, recognizing the validity of diversity in belief systems. Fowler believed that most adults are fixed in these first two stages. A few rare individuals, such as Mother Theresa, Martin Luther King, Jr., and Mahatma Gandhi, move into what Fowler described as universalizing faith, the willingness to give up one's life to make spiritual values a reality on this earth.

Koenig (1990) described spiritual development as more of a continuum and less of a distinct set of developmental stages. The continuum ranges from a complete disregard for issues in spirituality and faith to what he termed "mature faith," in which one's spiritual beliefs are a major organizing principle in one's life. Mature faith occurs more frequently in elders who have a lifetime of spiritual experience and are intimately involved in answering the spiritual questions raised in the final developmental stage of life in preparation for dying and death. He sees the development of spirituality as a lifetime quest, but one that is heightened by the challenges and immediacies of old age.

The Effect of Religion and Spirituality on Elders

Elders who participate regularly in religious activities have been shown to have better physical and mental health, regardless of gender or racial or ethnic group membership (Koenig, 1990; Levin 1994; Musick, Koenig, Hays, & Cohen, 1998). Religion's positive effect on mental health can be attributed to a number of factors. The public aspect of religion, such as attendance at religious services and church membership, affords elders an opportunity to develop and maintain a social support system. Regular contact with a fellowship of others who share the same religious beliefs helps to counteract social isolation. Private forms of both religiosity and spirituality, such as prayer and meditation, can buffer the effects of stressors, such as illness, retirement, and widowhood (Ellison, 1994). Religious beliefs offer a cognitive framework for elders to accept painful events as part of the rhythm of life, not as the attempt of a supreme being to punish them. They also serve as valuable psychological resources to help elders process the painful emotions that accompany life events (White, 1998). In other words, religious practices and beliefs are powerful coping mechanisms to help elders survive negative life events—the precise reason recognizing spirituality as a life force is essential to sound social work practice (Sermabeikian, 1994). Both religion and spirituality can serve as a source of great comfort and encouragement when elders are faced with overwhelming challenges.

Koenig, Smiley, and Gonzales (1988) attributed this effect, among those who are deeply religious, to belief in a divine purpose for negative life events as well as faith in ultimate justice that makes sense of bad happenings. Religion and spirituality help elders maintain a sense of continuity and cohesion in their lives in the face of the changes that accompany the aging process (Wong, 1998). Early in life, one's personal worth is often associated with external accomplishments, such as work or social status. Spirituality helps elders work through a psychosocial transition to move indicators of personal worth to more internal accomplishments, such as life satisfaction and personal fulfillment. An elder's faith can help him or her to construct a meaning system that provides a feeling of personal value grounded in a relationship to a power greater than self (Marcoen, 1994).

Spirituality in the Lives of Women and Elders of Color

Women's Religiosity and Spirituality

Religion and spirituality may play a more significant role in the lives of women than those of men throughout the life cycle. McFadden (1995) found that women are more religious than men at any given time in their lives and that the influence of religion becomes more pronounced as women age. Women live longer and are more likely to live alone once they lose life partners, creating more solitude in the later years. This greater likelihood of solitude may facilitate a more introspective life and one that relies more heavily on the comfort afforded by spiritual and religious practices, such as prayer and meditation (Mull, Cox, & Sullivan, 1987; Zorn & Johnson, 1997). Church or synagogue membership is also an important source of social support for women and leads to greater participation in the social groups and activities sponsored by religious organizations (McFadden, 1995; Stolley & Koenig, 1997). As an older woman's social support system dwindles through death and illness, she may turn to church-related activities and friends as a way of revitalizing her social network.

Gilligan (1982) proposed that women experience spirituality as a life force in different ways from men, explaining its greater significance in their lives. Women's spirituality emphasizes a more interpersonal way of getting basic needs met, one of which is to reach out to others (in the institutional setting) and to a greater power (in the private setting). Women may define their own spirituality in terms of responsibility not only to self but also to others, emphasizing what Gilligan (1982) called "relational spirituality." Women see and experience their own spirituality in a context of others, not as a uniquely individual experience. Women's roles in childbearing and caregiving are in many ways unique spiritual experiences defined specifically by a relationship with another person.

Only recently has the long-standing tradition of referring to a supreme being as a male figure been challenged by both men and women. Male images are traditionally used to describe a supreme being as father—a caring, all-powerful force. In many religious organizations, such as the Roman Catholic Church, women have been denied access to positions of liturgical and doctrinal leadership. This lack of full access to the power structures of the church has required women to redefine both their participation in traditional religious organizations and their own personal relationships to a transcendent power (Hickson & Phelps, 1997). The growing movement in many religious denominations toward the use of inclusive language as well as the current discontent with women's exclusion from significant clerical roles in some denominations are indications that the redefinition of women's spirituality is, and will continue to be, a powerful force.

Elders of Color

Membership in a racial or ethnic group by itself does not determine religious practices or beliefs. Rather, it is the shared historical experience of oppression and discrimination that shapes the current social context in which elders of color live and influences the importance of the roles of both religious institutions and private religious activity in the lives of these elders (Maldonado, 1995). Organized religion serves a psychosocial as well as a spiritual role in the lives of many elders of color.

The buffering influence of religion and spirituality is particularly pronounced in the lives of elders of color, who have higher levels of religious participation than white elders (McFadden, 1995). A strong affiliation with a church has helped elders of color survive the stresses of lifelong discrimination and the hardships of poverty, as well as the psychological stresses of living as members of a minority population (Koenig, Cohen, & Blazer, 1992; Tripp-Reimer, Johnson, & Rios, 1995; Williams, 1994). Consideration of the role of spirituality both in the development of cultural identity and as a component in the healing practices of ethnic/cultural groups is essential to providing ethnically competent social services (Jacobs, 1997).

African American Elders.   The church has long been considered one of the most important and supportive social institutions in the African American community, serving both religious and nonreligious functions (Levin & Taylor, 1997; Stolley & Koenig, 1997). The ceremonial activities of traditional Baptist and Pentacostal religious services may actually provide a therapeutic function for its members (Levin & Taylor, 1997; Musick et al., 1998). The enlivening music, the energetic sermons, and the deep sense of communal worship actually make attendees feel good. Attending church services can provide a cathartic and intense social experience for elders who spend much of the week alone. For many African American elders, the hope and joy offered by the church help them to ward off the depression that accompanies physical illness and limited incomes. Ferraro and Koch (1994) observed that African American elders who attended church regularly have better physical health and lower levels of depression than those elders who do not attend church regularly.

Levin and Taylor (1997) found that African American elders pray more often, are more likely to identify with a religious denomination, and attend religious services more often than their white counterparts. They also participate in private religious activities, such as viewing religious programming or reading religious materials, more often than younger African Americans or white elders (Chatters & Taylor, 1989; Taylor & Chatters, 1991).

Churches in African American communities often provide direct services, such as food and clothing, to their members in times of financial hardship, especially when such instrumental support is not available from the public sector (Holmes & Holmes, 1995). Antonucci (1985) proposed that churches in all-ethnic communities offer their members an opportunity to help others when times are good in exchange for the expectation that they will be helped in times of need—a system of social credits. By maintaining an active membership in the church and assisting others throughout their lives, elders might realistically expect that as their needs increase with declining health and increasing social isolation, they will receive help in return.

Historically, the church in the black community has served as one of the few social institutions that African Americans have been able to control, direct, and lead in the face of systemic discrimination in other social institutions (Stolley & Koenig, 1997). For men and women denied positions of power and prestige in government, education, and business, the church remains an institution in which leadership needs can be met and a sense of mastery developed. While opportunities for advancement continue to improve outside the structure of the black church, the psychological significance of this remains important to African American elders.

Hispanic Elders.   Religious beliefs and practices as represented by organized religion are second only to families as the major source of emotional support for Hispanic elders (Cox, 1995; Delgado, 1996). The vast majority of Hispanic elders are members of the Roman Catholic Church, a reflection of the missionary work in their countries of origin, such as Central and South America. Attending worship services and prayer groups are the most frequently identified public religious activities in which Hispanic elders participate (Maldonado, 1995). Private religious activities include prayer and meditation, but are less likely to include reading the Bible, a noteworthy difference from African American elders (Maldonado, 1995).

A growing number of Hispanics are joining fundamentalist Protestant churches, such as Pentacostals, Seventh-Day Adventists, and Mormons. This move away from the traditional Roman Catholic Church is redefining the social and spiritual role organized religion plays in their lives (Maldonado, 1995). This is particularly relevant in the lives of elderly Puerto Ricans. Delgado (1996) found that fundamentalist churches, unlike traditional Roman Catholicism, make a conscious effort to retain Puerto Rican culture through preserving traditional religious celebrations and practices in addition to providing support for families in making the transition from Puerto Rico to the mainland United States. Ministers of predominately Puerto Rican congregations are often of Puerto Rican or other Hispanic origin and tend to be of the same socioeconomic class as parishioners, minimizing the social distance and eliminating the language barrier. Delgado also found that ministering to both the spiritual and physical needs of its members by providing educational and recreational activities helped church members view the church as psychologically more accessible than traditional Roman Catholic churches.

In this respect, fundamentalist churches in Hispanic communities serve many of the same functions as churches serve in African American communities (Delgado, 1996). Both have ministers indigenous to the community, provide major social and educational services, and bring a sense of cohesion to the community. Hispanic fundamentalist churches, however, are less likely to see their role as initiators of social action or consider themselves as providing opportunities for development of major leadership roles for members. Hispanic churches are also more likely to defer to the family in providing extensive material support to elderly members.

While church involvement actually increases over the life course for white elders, church involvement for Hispanics remains relatively stable, with significantly more women than men identifying with their religious faith (Ellison, 1995). This is not to say that Hispanic women are more or less spiritual than Hispanic men, but rather they are more visible participants in organized religion. Hispanic women may seek the social support provided by religious institutions, while Hispanic men obtain that support elsewhere, such as in social clubs or taverns (Stolley & Koenig, 1997). Hispanic elders who participate in both the liturgical and social activities of their churches and use the opportunity to maintain contact with family and friends appear to be more successful in managing both the emotional and social challenges of aging (Angel & Angel, 1992).

Asian American Elders.   Little research has been done on the role of religion and spirituality in the lives of Asian American elders due in part to their small numbers in the population. The religious traditions practiced by Asians in the United States include Hinduism, Buddhism, Islam, Sikhism, Jainism, and Shintoism, as well as various forms of Christianity. However, none of these religious traditions are unique to any specific Asian country. With the exception that most Filipinos are Catholic—reflecting the historical influence of Spain in the colonization of the Philippines—and most Thais are Buddhist, few generalizations can be drawn about a dominant religion among any Asian groups (Tweed, 1999). Among Asian elders, religious preference is a function of their country of origin, the circumstance surrounding their immigration (if immigrants), and their degree of assimilation into American culture. Traditional Eastern religions are quite different from mainline Judeo-Christian thinking in their beliefs about the existence of a supreme being, their beliefs and rituals surrounding the human connection to the spiritual world, and the way in which these beliefs influence daily life. It is likely that many of the religious and spiritual practices of this population are practiced privately rather than publicly. Their direct influence on Asian American elders remains largely unstudied.

Native American Elders.   The religious traditions of Native Americans are as diverse as the multitude of tribes throughout the country. Little formal research has been conducted to identify their religious practices and the role of religion and spirituality in the lives of older Native Americans. Specific tribes have developed unique religious and spiritual traditions based on their original means of sustenance, their language, and their geographical location (Gill, 1993). Tribes that were primarily agricultural developed rituals around the seasons and the crops they counted on to survive. Hunters are more likely to attribute spiritual powers to animals. Unlike other religious traditions, Native Americans do not have a written history or codification of religious beliefs, such as those found in the Bible or the Torah. Traditions have been passed down through storytelling and mythology. For many Native American tribes, the current cohort of elders is the last remaining connection to a rich, long tradition of unique spirituality.

The Native American population practiced a wide variety of native religions prior to any contact with white explorers. Therefore, the roots of Native American religious practices do not explicitly reflect the Judeo-Christian tradition, but rather are a unique blend of shamanic rituals and myths with an emphasis on harmony between humans and nature. Many Native American elders continue to practice some form of their native religion, which is actually less of a formal code of religious beliefs than it is a philosophy of life. Other elders have blended native beliefs with more traditional Christianity to form a unique form of religious practice (Maldonado, 1995). Traditional Christian rituals, such as weddings, liturgies, or funerals, may be conducted in the native language featuring native music and dress (Gill, 1993).

Native American culture is rich in spiritual language. Traditionally, Native American spirituality makes a strong connection between physical and mental illness and the spiritual world. Illness in either of these aspects of an individual's functioning may be seen as being caused by a "loss of soul" or by the presence of a malevolent object in the individual's body (Gill, 1993, p. 143). It is the role of a shaman to contact or visit the spiritual world to retrieve the soul or coax the offending object from the individual's body before either mind or body can be healed. This perspective may be particularly foreign to social workers trained in a traditional Judeo-Christian tradition. To uninformed practitioners, spiritual beliefs and rituals may be easily confused with dementia and thus diagnosed as pathology rather than as a valuable cultural support system.

Incorporating Spirituality into Social Work Practice with Elders

Precautions before Pursuing Spirituality

Spirituality and religion clearly play a very important role in the lives of many elders, providing the social work profession with an opportunity to incorporate a different set of intervention techniques in addressing the psychosocial problems of elders. The discussion of specific techniques, however, should be prefaced with three important precautions. First, although many elders find spirituality and religion a source of comfort and an important part of defining themselves, some elders do not. A social worker should never assume that elders are comfortable discussing this topic and exploring spirituality as a means of resolving emotional conflicts. Like younger groups in the population, a core group of elders find the general topic of religion and spirituality offensive and unwelcome. Clearly, it is not appropriate to attempt to use spirituality as a therapeutic force with elders who do not view religion or spirituality as important forces in their lives.

Second, incorporating spiritual techniques into one's professional practice should never, under any circumstance, involve proselytizing, preaching, or attempting to recruit elders into a religious group. The provision of help to elders should never be tied to the religious mission of an agency or organization. Professional social work recognized the dangers of this type of conditional assistance early in the twentieth century, and it remains unacceptable. Third, incorporating spiritual or religious techniques is not advised in cases in which clients suffer from severe mental illness, delusions, or hallucinations or have past histories of abuse by the clergy or other religious figures (Bullis, 1996). While for some elders spirituality and the existence of a supreme being are sources of comfort, elders who suffer from distorted thinking or post-traumatic stress may find a discussion of these images deeply disturbing. These precautions should be constant reminders to the social work practitioner to use the most astute professional judgment in determining the appropriateness of spiritual techniques in practice.

Self-Awareness and Spirituality

Social workers need to be deeply aware of the role that spirituality and religion play in their own lives. Do you see yourself as a spiritual person? Is organized religion important as a guiding force in your own life? How do you define your own spirituality? It is essential for you as the practitioner to be able to answer these questions for yourself before even considering using spirituality as a force in working with elders. Consider where you developed your attitudes about religion and spirituality and the role that your religious upbringing, if any, has played. Carefully assess where you are in your own spiritual development and where you would like to be. Determine how comfortable you are in discussing your own and others' spiritual concerns. Are issues in religion and spirituality compatible with the theoretical perspective you feel most comfortable using in social work practice? Developing your own comfort level with the language and images of religion and spirituality is necessary before you can use this force therapeutically in elders' lives.

The intention to incorporate spirituality into practice with elders requires that practitioners be able to view religion and spirituality as strengths in an elder's life, rather than as weaknesses. Social workers must be willing to respect the unique aspects of faith traditions dissimilar to their own. Social workers must also be able to both understand and accept a wide variety of personal values that at times will conflict with their most deeply cherished beliefs (Derezotes, 1995).

The lively and animated atmosphere in an African American church may be unsettling to a social worker more familiar with a quiet and pious worship environment. Non-Christian social workers may be bothered by an intense reverence for Jesus or the veneration of Mary, Jesus' mother. The rosary, the crucifix, and other religious objects may seem deeply superstitious to a non-Catholic. Ancestor worship and burning incense may seem particularly alien to social workers not familiar with Eastern religious traditions. Recognizing and supporting spirituality implies accepting it as it presents itself in unique ways in the lives of elders.

Learning about Religious Traditions and Practices

The social work profession is adamant about the importance of practitioners developing a strong knowledge base about the biological, psychological, and social components of human functioning before beginning to work with clients. The same applies to learning about the religious traditions and practices of the client groups with which practitioners will be working. Colleges and universities offer courses in comparative religions in which the traditional Judeo-Christian approach, most common in the United States, is contrasted with other religious traditions, such as Buddhism, Hinduism, or Taoism. Understanding the differences in basic religious principles in these faiths will provide an invaluable knowledge base to working with elders outside a practitioner's own faith tradition. Therefore, if you are working with a particular ethnic or religious group, you should find resource materials on these particular religions or attend a religious service to learn more about religious practices. If you have decided that spirituality and religion are important issues in the lives of your clients and you plan to incorporate some specific intervention techniques, ask clients directly about their religion. Most elders are proud of their religious tradition and would be happy to help you understand it better.

Spirituality as an Element in the Assessment Process

The assessment process with elders often includes questions about their religious affiliation or church membership as part of the process of identifying social support systems available to elders. Incorporating spiritual elements into the assessment process implies expanding both the older client's and the worker's understanding of the meaning of religious identification and the significance of spirituality in the elder's life. It moves beyond the question of "what" to the issue of "how and why."

Verbal and Nonverbal Indicators of Spirituality.   The most important tools you have to determine whether spirituality and religion are important in the lives of your clients and could be appropriately incorporated into an intervention plan are your ears and eyes. Listen carefully to the way an elder talks about not only current problems but also his or her life history. The language elders use in telling their life stories can be rich in spiritual metaphors, such as the description of life as a journey or a struggle for meaning. Phrases such as "It is God's will" or "The Lord will provide" are obvious indicators that the elder turns to spiritual and religious beliefs as a source of comfort and understanding. Elders who are active in religious organizations often speak of their pastors or rabbis as important figures in their lives. What elders say can also give the practitioner insight about elders who have deep unresolved conflicts about religion and spirituality. These conflicts may be exhibited in such statements as "Why does God let this happen to me?" or "Am I being punished for everything I have done in my life?" Observe whether elders have religious images, such as statues, crosses, or other religious artifacts, in their homes. A well-worn family Bible or a religious painting are often indicators that elders include some aspect of religion or spirituality in their daily lives.

The Spiritual Genogram and Time Line.   As part of exploring an elder's religious or spiritual upbringing, Bullis (1996) suggested the use of the spiritual genogram. An example of a spiritual genogram appears in Figure 10.1. A spiritual genogram is identical to the one constructed in depicting a family's genealogy to track the family history or, as it is used in family therapy, to identify intergenerational family patterns. Elders can use the genogram model to identify from whom they received religious training or assimilated messages about the importance of spirituality in their lives. It helps both the elder and the social worker to understand how religion is (or is not) an energy force that is nurtured in the elder's family.

The older woman whose spiritual genogram appears in Figure 10.1 is 70 years old and presents in counseling with deep concerns about her own spiritual well-being. She has a lifetime of unsatisfactory choices in spouses, being attracted to men of deep faith (a Baptist minister and an ex-priest) and simultaneously rejecting the notion of a supreme being. By tracing the sources of very mixed messages about formal religion, the notion of sin as punishment, and the notion of a just versus loving supreme being, the social worker can help this woman reexamine her own notion of religion and spirituality. This process can also help this elder gain a deeper insight into why she may have chosen the spouses she did and how to find less stressful and more rewarding relationships in the remaining years of her life.

Bullis (1996) also recommended the use of a spiritual time line, a linear depiction of the stages of spiritual growth and development of the elder over the life course. An example of a spiritual time line of a 68-year-old woman struggling with cancer appears in Figure 10.2. Writing from a first person perspective, the elder is able to think about her experiences both in a formal religious institution and as she places a supreme being in the context of her own life events. The themes of anger and confusion appear very early in her life and are reinforced by estrangement from her parents, rejection of her original religious upbringing, and tragic personal loss. As she faces the challenge of coping with a serious medical condition, she is struggling with guilt from her previous rejection of God and her intense awareness of the comfort she would feel from being reconciled with a

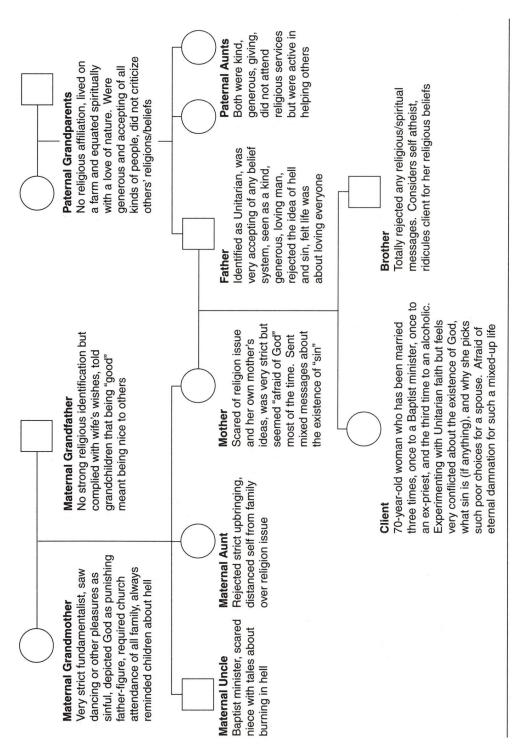

Maternal Grandmother
Very strict fundamentalist, saw dancing or other pleasures as sinful, depicted God as punishing father-figure, required church attendance of all family, always reminded children about hell

Maternal Grandfather
No strong religious identification but complied with wife's wishes, told grandchildren that being "good" meant being nice to others

Maternal Uncle
Baptist minister, scared niece with tales about burning in hell

Maternal Aunt
Rejected strict upbringing, distanced self from family over religion issue

Paternal Grandparents
No religious affiliation, lived on a farm and equated spiritually with a love of nature. Were generous and accepting of all kinds of people, did not criticize others' religions/beliefs

Paternal Aunts
Both were kind, generous, giving, did not attend religious services but were active in helping others

Father
Identified as Unitarian, was very accepting of any belief system, seen as a kind, generous, loving man, rejected the idea of hell and sin, felt life was about loving everyone

Mother
Scared of religion issue and her own mother's ideas, was very strict but seemed "afraid of God" most of the time. Sent mixed messages about the existence of "sin"

Brother
Totally rejected any religious/spiritual messages. Considers self atheist, ridicules client for her religious beliefs

Client
70-year-old woman who has been married three times, once to a Baptist minister, once to an ex-priest, and the third time to an alcoholic. Experimenting with Unitarian faith but feels very conflicted about the existence of God, what sin is (if anything), and why she picks such poor choices for a spouse. Afraid of eternal damnation for such a mixed-up life

FIGURE 10.1 *Example of a Spiritual Genogram*

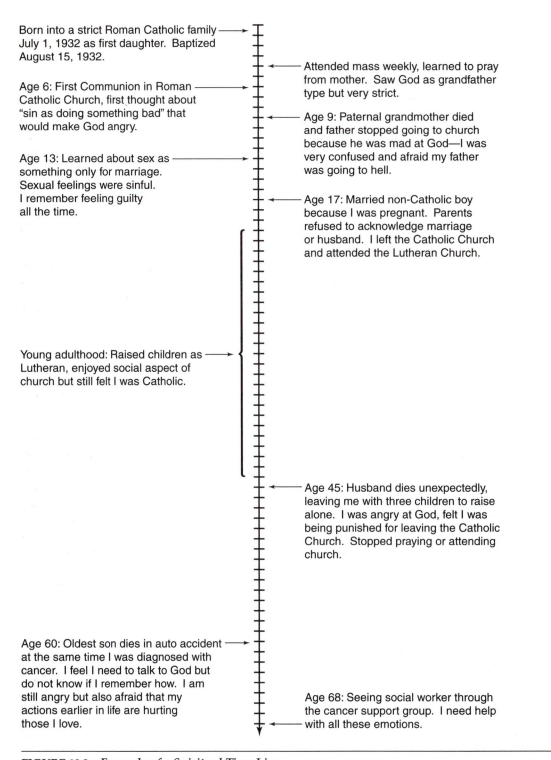

Born into a strict Roman Catholic family —→
July 1, 1932 as first daughter. Baptized
August 15, 1932.

←— Attended mass weekly, learned to pray
from mother. Saw God as grandfather
type but very strict.

Age 6: First Communion in Roman —→
Catholic Church, first thought about
"sin as doing something bad" that
would make God angry.

←— Age 9: Paternal grandmother died
and father stopped going to church
because he was mad at God—I was
very confused and afraid my father
was going to hell.

Age 13: Learned about sex as —→
something only for marriage.
Sexual feelings were sinful.
I remember feeling guilty
all the time.

←— Age 17: Married non-Catholic boy
because I was pregnant. Parents
refused to acknowledge marriage
or husband. I left the Catholic Church
and attended the Lutheran Church.

Young adulthood: Raised children as —→
Lutheran, enjoyed social aspect of
church but still felt I was Catholic.

←— Age 45: Husband dies unexpectedly,
leaving me with three children to raise
alone. I was angry at God, felt I was
being punished for leaving the Catholic
Church. Stopped praying or attending
church.

Age 60: Oldest son dies in auto accident —→
at the same time I was diagnosed with
cancer. I feel I need to talk to God but
do not know if I remember how. I am
still angry but also afraid that my
actions earlier in life are hurting
those I love.

Age 68: Seeing social worker through
the cancer support group. I need help
←— with all these emotions.

FIGURE 10.2 *Example of a Spiritual Time Line*

supreme being. By helping her develop an awareness of the lifelong struggle with her spiritual and religious experiences, the social worker can help her identify spiritual resources that can help her cope with the current health crisis.

This tool gives elders an opportunity to reflect on the ways in which spirituality and religion change over time depending on life events, psychosocial development, and the influence of social and environmental factors. It provides an opportunity for both the elder and the social worker to talk about what spirituality and religious beliefs mean at this point in life. Does life take on a new meaning as the elder thinks about the existence, or lack of, an afterlife? Is there unfinished business elders must attend to before they feel they have their "spiritual house" in order? Both the genogram and time line offer tools to visually depict these issues as part of the assessment process.

Spirituality and Social Work Intervention Techniques

Reconciling Spirituality with Other Theoretical Orientations.   One of the questions raised with social workers in the process of assessing their own spiritual development concerns whether or not they feel that spirituality and religion are compatible with their own professional theoretical orientations. Including spirituality as part of one's work with elders does not imply that spiritual techniques replace other methods of intervention but rather that spirituality serves as a supplement when working with elders for whom spirituality and religion are important aspects of their emotional well-being. Derezotes (1995) suggested that traditional social work techniques can be adapted to include spirituality. For example, practitioners most comfortable with a psychodynamic orientation in the therapeutic process can help a client gain insight into how past spiritual and religious experiences contribute to current inner conflicts. Those practitioners who employ cognitive-behavioral techniques may help elders replace thinking errors and subsequent dysfunctional behavior with new ways of thinking and acting that facilitate spiritual development. For those practitioners using a developmental perspective, the problems and crises that occur across the life course can be reframed as opportunities for clients' spiritual development. Psychodrama techniques can be used to help elders work through current spiritual experiences and take responsibility for current emotional challenges resulting from those experiences by those social workers who are most attracted to existential or humanistic approaches.

Including Spirituality in the Life Review Process.   The life review process, an important tool in helping elders process present and past emotional conflicts, was described in detail in Chapter 6. While the traditional life review process does not necessarily include spiritual development, the technique lends itself well to the inclusion of this topic as a natural part of the life review process (Wong, 1989). The very elements of spirituality, which include transcendence of self, the search for meaning, and the need to be connected with others, frequently emerge in the life review process. Some elders view the life review process as a way to find meaning in their later years, while others see it as an integral process of preparing for dying and death. The use of spiritual time lines or genograms can facilitate this process.

Using or Teaching Meditation.   Meditation is a classic example of a spiritual technique that may not necessarily require any formal religious affiliation. During meditation, elders are asked to clear their minds of all thoughts and concentrate on an image, word, or feeling that they find comforting or restful. Connecting a positive, relaxing word or phrase with progressive muscle relaxation is one of a variety of ways to harness spiritual energy to improve physical or emotional functioning.

Facilitating Elders' Participation in Religious Groups.   Participation in religious groups can take the form of participating as a member and gathering social and spiritual support from others. Many religious denominations sponsor groups specifically designed to be psychoeducational supports for elders and to develop and maintain social networks among its older members. Other religious groups for elders are more directed toward a meaningful service component. Wong (1989) suggested that in an attempt to achieve understanding of both transcendence beyond self and a connectedness to others as part of a spiritual journey that elders be encouraged to help others by volunteering through efforts organized by their local church or synagogue. These groups may be organized to help in providing hands-on care for infants with HIV/AIDS, foster grandparent programs, Habitat for Humanity, or other community service programs.

Working with Community Churches.   This chapter has already explored the significance of the church in a racial or ethnic community in its role as both spiritual leader and provider of social services. For agencies and social workers seeking to make a connection with specific ethnic communities, the local church can serve as a valuable inroad to accessing ethnic elders. Not only does working with a local church legitimize outreach efforts aimed at educating elders about available services but also it may offer a more convenient location for providing those services for elders with mobility or transportation limitations.

Developing Spiritual/Religious Opportunities in Institutions.   Elders living in congregate housing, nursing homes, or hospitals may be most isolated from access to religious services at the time when they are most likely to need the comfort of their faith. Social workers can play an important role in advocating for their older clients in these settings by encouraging institutions to provide opportunities for religious services or increasing an elder's access to clergy or chaplains. Ross (1997) also recommended that institutions consider the designation of a reflection room when a chapel is not available to accommodate elders who prefer more private worship practices.

How These Efforts Differ from
Pastoral Counseling or Spiritual Direction

Recognizing and utilizing religion and spirituality in social work practice with elders is not the same as engaging in pastoral counseling or spiritual direction. Social work's primary focus in working with elders is to enhance or restore social functioning through individual counseling, connecting elders to existing services, and mobilizing or developing supportive services in the elders' environment. Incorporating practice techniques that recognize and support an elder's spirituality serves to complement, not replace, these basic social work tasks.

While the tasks of social work and pastoral counseling or spiritual direction are compatible, they are not the same. Pastoral counseling focuses on assisting the elder to use religious faith to find hope during times of difficulty and stress. It is usually provided by a clergy member or trained pastoral counselor who works with the individual to find God in daily life. Pastoral counseling is often available to elders who are hospitalized, institutionalized, or have suffered a recent crisis, such as loss of a loved one. The content of pastoral counseling sessions is explicitly spiritual. It is based on the assumption that finding God in the midst of pain can be a source of healing and growth. Spiritual direction is different from pastoral counseling in that it can be described as "holy listening" (Guenther, 1992). An individual usually seeks out spiritual direction to help deepen his or her own spirituality and relationship with God. A spiritual director is seen as a companion on an individual's spiritual journey not specifically as an expert in spirituality or religion. While individuals may seek a spiritual director during a time of crisis, the focus of spiritual direction is not problem resolution but a heightened awareness of and sensitivity to the presence of God in one's life. Social workers may find these other spiritual professionals important adjuncts to social work with elders but should not assume the role of either pastoral counselor or spiritual director without specialized training.

Summary

Despite the social work profession's deliberate avoidance of issues in spirituality and religion through much of the twentieth century, the profession has developed a renewed interest in these aspects of elder functioning. Spirituality encompasses an individual's perception of transcendence beyond self, a search for meaning, and a sense of connectedness to others—all important social and emotional challenges associated with late life. Religion is more commonly identified as a formal institutional affiliation in which beliefs about a supreme being and standards for behavior are codified. While the terms *spirituality* and *religion* are often used interchangeably, they are not the same.

Formal religious institutions serve an important role in providing both emotional and instrumental support for many elders, particularly elders of color. Elders of color who are active in their local churches are more likely to have better physical and mental health than those elders who have no religious affiliation. Historically, churches have served as opportunities for persons of color to achieve social status and assume positions of leadership. While the opportunities for social and economic advancement outside the community church have improved for persons of color in all age groups, churches remain visible and influential forces in ethnic communities.

If spiritual and religious themes are important to elders and social workers are in touch with their own spirituality, spiritual and religious assessment can serve as a valuable component in a complete psychosocial assessment. The inclusion of this aspect of elder functioning offers the social worker an additional set of techniques to help in promoting better social and emotional functioning among elders. The need to find meaning and make the best use of this "third age" in their lives can serve as a powerful impetus to elders to embrace both private and public forms of worship. While it is not appropriate for social workers to assume the roles of pastoral counselors, proselytizers, or spiritual directors, they can serve an important role in facilitating an elder's connections with formal religious institutions or private spiritual activities.

Check Out These Websites!

1. www.aoa.dhhs.gov/aoa/dir/174.html   The National Interfaith Coalition on Aging offers additional information on its mission and services on this website. As the first organization established nationwide to address the importance of religion and spirituality in the lives of elders, NICA continues to work to coordinate the outreach and service efforts of a wide variety of religious denominations and organizations.

2. www.ubib.buffalo.edu/libraries/units/hsl/ref/guides/spir.htm   As part of web access to the library system at the University of Buffalo, this site offers a detailed bibliography of professional journal articles that address the connection between spirituality and healing. It draws primarily from medical and nursing literature, highlighting the extensive research done in this field in recent years.

3. www.pcusa.org/pcusa/ce/aamresou   This site provides an excellent annotated bibliography of selected resources on elder spirituality and older adult ministry. Although the site is sponsored by the Presbyterian Church (U.S.A.) Office of Adult Ministry, the bibliography is ecumenical, identifying resources to help elders of all faiths.

References

American Psychiatric Association. (1994). *Diagnostic and statistical manual of mental disorders* (4th ed.). Washington, DC: Author.
Angel, J. L., & Angel, R. J. (1992). Age at migration, social connections, and well-being among elderly Hispanics. *Journal of Aging and Health, 4,* 480–499.

Antonucci, T. C. (1985). Personal characteristics, social support, and social behavior. In R. H. Binstock & E. Shanas (Eds.), *Handbook of aging and the social sciences* (3rd ed., pp. 94–128). New York: Van Nostrand Reinhold.

Blazer, D. (1991). Spirituality and aging well. *Generations,* Winter, 61–65.

Bullis, R. K. (1996). *Spirituality in social work practice.* Washington, DC: Taylor and Frances.

Canda, E. (1988). Spirituality, religious diversity, and social work practice. *Social Casework, 69*(4), 238–247.

Canda, E. R. (1997). Spirituality. In *The encyclopedia of social work* (19th edition, 1997 supplement, pp. 299–309). Washington, DC: National Association of Social Workers.

Caraballo, E. R. (1990). *The role of the Pentecostal church as a service provider in the Puerto Rican community of Boston, Massachusetts: A case study.* Waltham, MA: Brandeis University.

Chatters, L. M., & Taylor, R. J. (1989). Age differences in religious participation among black adults. *Journal of Gerontology: Social Sciences, 44,* S183–S189.

Cox, H. (1995). *Fire from heaven: The rise of Pentecostal spirituality and the reshaping of religion in the twenty-first century.* Reading, MA: Addison-Wesley.

Delgado, M. (1996). Religion as a caregiving system for Puerto Rican elders with functional disabilities. *Journal of Gerontological Social Work, 26*(3/4), 129–144.

Derezotes, D. S. (1995). Spirituality and religiosity: Neglected factors in social work practice. *Arete, 20*(1), 1–15.

Derezotes, D. S., & Evans, K. E. (1995). Spirituality and religiousity in practice: In-depth interviews of social work practitioners. *Social Thought, 18*(1), 39–56.

Ellison, C. G. (1995). Race, religious involvement, and depression in a southeastern U.S. community. *Social Science and Medicine, 40,* 1561–1572.

Erikson, E. (1963). *Childhood and society* (2nd ed.). New York: Norton.

Ferraro, K. F., & Koch, J. R. (1994). Religion and health among black and white adults: Examining social support and consultation. *Journal for the Scientific Study of Religion, 33,* 362–375.

Fischer, K. (1993). Aging. In M. Downey (Ed.), *The new dictionary of Catholic spirituality* (pp. 31–33). Collegeville, MN: The Liturgical Press.

Fowler, J. W. (1991). *Weaving the new creation: Stages of faith and the public church.* San Francisco: Harper & Row.

Gill, S. D. (1993). Native American religions. In *Encyclopedia of the American religious experience: Studies of traditions and movements* (Vol. 1, pp. 137–151). New York: Scribners Sons.

Gilligan, C. (1982). *In a different voice: Psychological theory and women's development.* Cambridge, MA: Harvard University Press.

Goldberg, C. (1996). The privileged position of religion in the clinical dialogue. *Clinical Social Work Journal, 24*(2), 125–136.

Graham, M. A., Kaiser, T., & Garrett, K. J. (1998). Naming the spiritual: The hidden dimension of helping. *Social Thought, 18*(4), 49–61.

Guenther, M. (1992). *Holy listening: The art of spiritual direction.* Cambridge, MA: Cowley Publications.

Hickson, J., & Phelps, A. (1997). Women's spirituality: A proposed practice model. *Journal of Family Social Work, 2*(4), 43–57.

Holland, T. (1989). Values, faith, and professional practice. *Social Thought,* Winter, 28–40.

Holmes, E. R., & Holmes, L. D. (1995). *Other cultures, elder years.* Thousand Oaks, CA: Sage.

Jacobs, C. (1997). On spirituality and social work practice. *Smith College Studies in Social Work, 67*(2), 171–175.

Joseph, M. (1988). Religion and social work practice. *Social Casework, 69,* 443–452.

Koenig, H. G. (1990). Research on religion and mental health in later life: A review and commentary. *Journal of Geriatric Psychiatry, 23*(1), 23–53.

Koenig, H. G., Cohen, H. J., & Blazer, D. G. (1992). Religious coping and depression among elderly, hospitalized, medically ill men. *The American Journal of Psychiatry, 149,* 1693–1700.

Koenig, H. G., Smiley, M., & Gonzales, J. A. P. (1988). *Religion, health, and aging: A review and theoretical integration.* Westport, CT: Greenwood Press.

Levin, J. S. (1994). Religion and health: Is there an association, is it valid, and is it causal? *Social Science and Medicine, 38,* 1475–1482.

Levin, J. S., & Taylor, R. J. (1997). Age differences in patterns and correlates of the frequency of prayer. *The Gerontologist, 37*(1), 75–88.

Loewenberg, F. (1988). *Religion and social work practice in contemporary American society.* New York: Columbia University Press.

Maldonado, D. (1995). Religion and persons of color. In M. A. Kimble, S. H. McFadden, J. W. Ellor, & J. J. Seeber (Eds.), *Aging, spirituality, and religion: A handbook* (pp. 119–128). Minneapolis: Fortress Press.

Marcoen, A. (1994). Spirituality and personal well-being in old age. *Aging and Society, 14,* 521–536.

McFadden, S. H. (1995). Religion and well-being in aging persons in an aging society. *Journal of Social Issues, 51*(2), 161–175.

McFadden, S. H. (1996). Religion, spirituality, and aging. In J. E. Birren & K. W. Schaie (Eds.), *Handbook of the psychology of aging* (pp. 162–177). San Diego, CA: Academic Press.

Mull, C., Cox, C., & Sullivan, J. (1987). Religious role in the health and well-being of well elders. *Public Health Nursing, 4*(3), 151–159.

Musick, M. A., Koenig, H. G., Hays, J. C., & Cohen, H. J. (1998). Religious activity and depression among community-dwelling elderly persons with cancer: The moderating effect of race. *Journal of Gerontology: Social Sciences, 53B*(4), S218–S227.

Ortiz, L. (1991). Religious issues: The missing link in social work education. *Spirituality and Social Work Journal, 2*(2), 13–18.

Princeton Religion Research Center. (1997). *Religion in America: Annual report, 1997.* Princeton, NJ: Author.

Ross, L. A. (1997). Elderly patients' perceptions of their spiritual needs and care: A pilot study. *Journal of Advanced Nursing, 26,* 710–715.

Sermabeikian, P. (1994). Our clients, ourselves: The spiritual perspective and social work practice. *Social Work, 39*(2), 178–183.

Sherwood, D. A. (1998). Spiritual assessment as a normal part of social work practice: Power to help and power to harm. *Social Work and Christianity, 25*(2), 80–90.

Stolley, J. M., & Koenig, H. (1997). Religion/spirituality and health among elderly African Americans and Hispanics. *Journal of Psychosocial Nursing, 35*(11), 32–38.

Taylor, R. J., & Chatters, L. M. (1991). Non-organizational religious participation among elderly black adults. *Journal of Gerontology, 46,* S103–11.

Tolliver, W. F. (1997). Invoking the spirit: A model for incorporating the spiritual dimension of human functioning into social work practice. *Smith College Studies in Social Work, 67*(3), 477–486.

Trattner, W. I. (1999). *From poor law to welfare state: A history of social welfare in America.* New York: Free Press.

Tripp-Reimer, T., Johnson, R., & Rios, H. (1995). Cultural dimensions in gerontological nursing. In M. Stanley & P. F. Beare (Eds.), *Gerontological nursing* (pp. 28–36). Philadelphia: J. B. Lippincott.

Tweed, T. A. (1999). General Introduction. In T. A. Tweed & S. Prothero (Eds.), *Asian religions in America: A documentary history* (pp. 1–12). New York: Oxford University Press.

Williams, D. R. (1994). Measurement of religion. In J. S. Levin (Ed.), *Religion, aging, and health* (pp. 114–140). Thousand Oaks, CA: Sage.

White, V. K. (1998). Ethnic differences in the wellness of elderly persons. *Occupational Therapy in Health Care, 11*(3), 1–15.

Wong, P. T. P. (1989). Personal meaning and successful aging. *Canadian Psychology, 30*(3), 516–525.

Wong, P. T. P. (1998). Spirituality, meaning and successful aging. In P. T. P. Wong & P. S. Fry (Eds.), *The human quest for meaning: A handbook of psychological research and clinical applications* (pp. 359–394). Mahwah, NJ: Lawrence Erlbaum Associates.

Zorn, C. R., & Johnson, M. T. (1997). Religious well-being in non-instutitionalized elderly women. *Health Care for Women International, 18,* 209–217.

11

Social Work Practice with Elder Abuse and Neglect

Growing Concern about Elder Abuse and Neglect

While it is likely that elders have been mistreated throughout history, only recently have health and mental health providers and the legal system teamed up in an effort to heighten social awareness of the problem of elder abuse and neglect. Wolf and Pillemer (1989) referred to this as the "discovery of elder abuse and neglect," which has occurred in much the same way child abuse was uncovered as a significant social problem (p. 6). Although there has always been an awareness that children and elders were being physically, emotionally, or financially exploited by caregivers and family members, it is only since the last half of the twentieth century that efforts have been successful in criminalizing such abuse or neglect and holding the perpetrators legally liable for their actions.

A number of factors have heightened concern about the problem of elder abuse and neglect. As has been emphasized throughout this book, not only are the sheer numbers of elders growing but also they are becoming a larger percentage of the population. Their increased presence in society makes them a more visible population than ever before and one that yields significant political power (Johnson, 1995; Wolf & Pillemer, 1989). Society cannot ignore the problem of elder mistreatment when by 2030, one-fifth of the population will belong to this age group.

Perhaps, a more significant issue than the sheer numbers is society's willingness to intervene within the privacy of family boundaries. The women's movement challenged the notion that the family setting was a safe haven for women and children with the finding that a majority of all violence committed against women and children occurs within the domestic setting. This concern about the safety of family members has been extended to include elders (Wolf & Pillemer, 1989). Elders are vulnerable to abuse and neglect due to a greater likelihood of their suffering from physical and cognitive impairments and their need to rely on caregivers and family members for basic physical care.

In this chapter, the term *elder abuse* refers to intentional mistreatment inflicted on elders in the form of physical, emotional or psychological, sexual, or financial abuse or exploitation. Elder neglect encompasses both active and passive efforts in which elders fail to receive necessary care with that failure resulting in the deterioration of their physical, emotional, or psychological health. It is important to emphasize that neglect is not always intentional but does constitute unacceptable treatment of elders, regardless of intent. Self-neglect, a third category included in the general rubric of abuse and neglect, refers to an elder's inability to provide for his or her own physical care and well-being due to physical, psychiatric, or cognitive limitations. The investigation and prosecution of elder mistreatment and the provision of services to prevent future abuse or neglect are called adult protective services (APS).

This chapter will present what is known about the incidence of elder abuse and neglect and the variety of forms of elder mistreatment. The risk factors associated with being a victim of abuse as well as a perpetrator will be described, followed by a discussion of the evolving theoretical foundation that offers some understanding of why elder abuse occurs. Recommendations will be offered for identifying abuse and neglect and implementing intervention strategies. The chapter concludes with a discussion of the ethical dilemmas facing a social worker when a high-risk elder refuses intervention and protective services.

The Incidence of Elder Abuse and Neglect

Problems in Identifying Elder Abuse and Neglect

Accurately determining the number of elders who are abused or neglected is a very difficult undertaking. Unlike children who may be identified as abused or neglected by school personnel because they are required to attend school, elders may be much more socially isolated (Barnett, Miller-Perrin, & Perrin, 1997). If they are not expected to appear on a regular basis at work or church, their absence may not be noticed. The National Center on Elder Abuse (NCEA) estimates that only 16 percent of elder abuse cases are reported to adult protective services (APS) leaving over four-fifths of cases unreported (National Center on Elder Abuse, 1998).

The Problem of Substantiation.   Not only is the problem of elder abuse and neglect seriously underreported, but also less than one-half of reported cases are substantiated (National Center on Elder Abuse, 1998). This means that less than one-half of cases offered enough evidence to support a charge that an elder had been abused or neglected. This does not mean the elder was not abused or neglected but rather that the cases did not meet the state's requirements for physical evidence, testimony from the abused elder, or other documentation to pursue legal charges against an alleged abuser. Of those cases that are substantiated, many fewer cases result in actual legal prosecution. When a case of elder abuse or neglect is prosecuted and the perpetrator is convicted, he or she faces legal consequences that may include probation or imprisonment.

Lack of Uniform Definitions of Abuse/Neglect.   States use inconsistent definitions of what constitutes elder abuse and neglect (Goodrich, 1997). While physical injury is clearly a form of abuse, what constitutes emotional or psychological abuse may require a highly subjective judgment. Are ridicule and intimidation considered emotional abuse? Is failing to provide adequate companionship considered neglect? Should self-neglect be included in estimates of the problem? Often cases that meet the social work profession's criteria of abuse and neglect do not meet the legal criteria for either substantiation or prosecution. Meeting the legal criteria is imperative for prosecuting those who abuse or neglect elders. However, health and mental health professionals should not wait to meet legal criteria before taking steps to identify abuse and neglect and develop intervention solutions as part of a broader effort to provide services to vulnerable elders.

Mandated Reporting.   Finally, reporting of elder abuse and neglect is not mandated in every state in the United States as of 1997 (Administration on Aging, 1999). All fifty states have some form of legislation that authorizes the state to protect and provide services to vulnerable adults (as a result of age, physical, or mental state). However, seven states (Colorado, Illinois, New Jersey, New York, North Dakota, Pennsylvania, and Wisconsin) rely on voluntary reporting to identify cases of elder abuse and neglect. Seventy-five percent of states have authorized APS agencies that specifically address suspected abuse and neglect of elders with the remaining 25 percent relying on state units on aging to provide protective services. Policies and procedures regarding adult protective services vary dramatically among states making it difficult even to determine the number of cases that have been reported (Goodrich, 1997; National Center on Elder Abuse, 1998).

The Estimates of Abuse and Neglect.   Keeping in mind the limitations of determining the exact number of elders who are abused or neglected each year, the National Elder Abuse Incidence Study estimated that over 450,000 elders in non-institutional settings were abused or neglected during 1996 (National Center on Elder Abuse, 1998). When cases of self-neglect are included in estimates, the number rises to 551,000, an increase of 150 percent since 1986. Only a fraction of these cases are ever reported to APS, and fewer yet can be substantiated and prosecuted under states' current criteria. Some of this increase is due to improvements in reporting procedures and a heightened awareness of the problem. Yet, these estimates suggest that the problem of elder abuse and neglect is not an isolated incident, but a pervasive problem for an already vulnerable population.

The most common form of elder maltreatment that is reported and substantiated is neglect, which comprises almost one-half of all reported cases (National Center on Elder Abuse, 1998). Emotional or psychological abuse occurs in one-third of reported cases followed by financial or material exploitation occurring in 30 percent of all reported cases. Physical abuse is alleged in one-quarter of all reported cases. Abandonment and sexual abuse are reported far less frequently, comprising less than 5 percent of cases. These numbers, when added together, exceed 100 percent because of the frequency with which multiple forms of abuse or neglect occur in the same case.

What Constitutes Elder Abuse or Neglect?

While there are not uniform state legal definitions of what constitutes abuse or neglect, the 1987 Amendments to the Older Americans Act established the federal definitions of what constitutes maltreatment. Professional service providers in the area of adult protective services generally agree on a basic set of indicators that suggest an elder is being abused or neglected. The descriptions provided in this section are not intended to be exhaustive but provide the social work practitioner with an overview of what is considered abuse or neglect in each of the specific categories, reflecting the guidelines established by the amendments to the Older Americans Act.

Physical Abuse

Physical abuse is defined as the use of physical force against an elder that may result in bodily injury, the infliction of pain, or impairment (National Center on Elder Abuse, 1998; Quinn & Tomika, 1997). Hitting, punishing physically, pushing, shoving, shaking, slapping, burning, and pinching are included in this category. Inappropriate use of drugs, physical restraints, or force-feeding an elder are also considered in this category.

Symptoms of physical abuse include bruises, welts, burns, fractures, or other physical injuries that indicate intentional harm has been inflicted by another. Alleged abusers or elders themselves may attribute these injuries to falls or other mishaps. While it is often plausible that these injuries did occur due to circumstances other than physical abuse, the severity of the injury may appear to be inconsistent with the nature of the "accident." Social workers should be suspicious if the verbal reports from either elders or alleged abusers do not appear to corroborate with physical evidence.

In severe cases of physical abuse, alleged abusers may refuse to let others even visit the elder in an attempt to hide the abuse. Elders who have been physically abused often demonstrate fear of the perpetrator or appear to be very nervous or vigilant. While some elders will admit they have been hit or mistreated, many will not, out of fear of being sent to a nursing home if their only available caregiver is accused or prosecuted. They may also feel a need to protect the abuser out of a deep sense of family loyalty, believing that what happens within the family should remain "family business" (Quinn & Tomika, 1997).

Sexual abuse is considered by many as a subcategory of physical abuse, although it is also considered emotional or psychological abuse. Sexual abuse is a nonconsensual sexual behavior, including unwanted sexual touching, all types of sexual assault (including rape), sodomy, involuntary nudity, or sexually explicit photography. Signs of sexual abuse include bruises around breasts or genital areas, unexplained sexually transmitted diseases or infections, or abnormal genital or anal bleeding. Torn, stained or bloody underclothing may also be an indication that the elder has been sexually abused. Close attention to the signs of sexual abuse is particularly important when assessing elders with cognitive limitations who may not be totally aware of the abuse or have difficulty in accurately remembering facts and events. While sexual abuse constitutes less than 1 percent of all reported cases of elder maltreatment, it is perhaps one of the most difficult types of abuse to detect because of its intensely private nature (National Center on Elder Abuse, 1998). Health and mental health professionals should assess the nature of the relationship between an elder and any alleged abuser. Relationships that appear inappropriately and overtly sexual should raise concerns and require further investigation.

Emotional or Psychological Abuse

Emotional or psychological abuse of elders is much more difficult to detect because it does not provide the explicit empirical evidence usually associated with physical abuse. Identifying emotional or psychological abuse is a highly subjective process. What is considered abusive treatment to a health or mental health provider may be the reflection of a lifelong family history of conflictual communication patterns or the expression of anger by a frustrated caregiver, family member, or other person involved with the elder. Emotional or psychological abuse is generally considered to be the infliction of mental distress through nonverbal or verbal acts, including verbal assaults, threats, intimidation, or harassment (National Center on Elder Abuse, 1998). This may include infantilizing the elder or willful isolation of the elder from social contact with others as a means of punishment or control.

The most significant aspect of this type of abuse is its persistent pattern. Elders who are subject to emotional or psychological abuse are often continuously agitated or consistently withdrawn. Relationships with caregivers, family members, or other social contacts are often highly charged. Rather than occasionally losing one's temper and raising one's voice, a caregiver, family member, or social contact may adopt a hostile and aggressive tone in most interactions with the elder. The elder may respond in-kind with defensiveness and verbal aggression. When the emotional abuse continues for long periods of time, the elder may simply withdraw as a protective mechanism. Detecting emotional or psychological abuse requires a social worker's best use of professional intuition.

Financial Exploitation

The National Center on Elder Abuse has determined that approximately 30 percent of all reported cases of elder abuse involve some inappropriate use of an elder's financial resources, personal property, or other assets of value (1998). This includes unauthorized cashing of an elder's checks (personal, pension, or government benefits), forging an elder's signature on legal documents, misusing or stealing personal property, or forcing an elder to sign a legal document against his or her will or under deceptive circumstances. Financial exploitation also includes inappropriate execution of duties as a guardian or conservator of an elder's financial affairs. Extorting money from an elder in exchange for protection or care can also be considered within this category.

Detecting financial exploitation is difficult without access to an elder's financial records so it is not surprising that family members, attorneys, and banks are often the first to report financial exploitation of an elder. Abrupt changes in withdrawal patterns at banks, sudden changes in wills or other financial documents, and the disappearance of financial assets or personal property are often the first signs that an elder is being financially exploited (National Center on Elder Abuse, 1998; Quinn & Tomika, 1997). This type of elder mistreatment occurs within all socioeconomic classes. While wealthy elders may be bilked out of huge amounts of money or have valuable personal property disappear, it is just as likely that low-income elders may be extorted to pay family members or neighbors part of a meager monthly check.

Elders are particularly vulnerable to financial exploitation from home repair programs, investment schemes, or con games. Appealing to an elder's interest in maintaining the value of his or her home, a home maintenance salesperson can befriend an elder and quickly extract significant amounts of money for repairs that never get done. Well-meaning elders may be lured into a risky investment strategy hoping to reap enough money to secure their own future or leave more to their children only to find out that the investment advisor and the money have quickly disappeared. Even bright, savvy elders can be duped into get-rich-quick schemes by sophisticated con artists who prey on the trust of older people.

Neglect

Neglect falls into two major categories: active or passive neglect by others, usually caregivers or family members, and self-neglect, the failure on the part of an elder to provide for basic self-care and well-being.

Neglect by Others. Neglect is defined as active or passive failure to fulfill responsibility for the physical or emotional well-being of an elder. A caregiver, family member, or other social contact's failure to provide adequate food, shelter, clothing, medical care, and physical protection for an elder in his or her care is considered to be neglect. This may include the failure to pay for needed services to maintain an elder's physical well-being, including health care, basic homemaking services, or physical safety, particularly when someone has been designated to arrange for those services.

Signs of neglect include poor personal hygiene, untreated bed sores, poor hydration or malnutrition, and lack of appropriate supervision, indicating that basic daily care is not being provided. Elders suffering from neglect are often filthy, have soiled clothes or bedding, are found wandering unsupervised, or show indications that health conditions are not being attended to by health care providers. Sometimes it is just the elder who appears in such poor condition, while the general condition of other members of the household appears quite normal. Other times, elder neglect occurs within the context of extreme poverty in which the elder is one of a number of household members who are surviving in deplorable conditions. Unsafe or unsanitary living conditions, including decrepit housing, pest infestations, and lack of heat or running water, are considered evidence of neglect.

Self-Neglect. Self-neglect is a unique kind of elder mistreatment in which the elder appears to be incapable of providing adequate self-care and another caregiver has not been identified or asked to take responsibility for the elder. An elder may threaten his or her own physical well-being by failure to attend to personal hygiene, to provide adequate hydration or nutrition, or to take necessary medication. Elders who are found wandering without adequate supervision or engaging in careless use of fire may have a problem with self-neglect. Self-neglect is often a sign of cognitive or psychiatric impairment in which an elder is not capable of providing self-care and may have limited ability to understand the consequences of neglecting it. Elders who are mentally competent and aware of the consequences of self-neglect but consciously choose to engage in acts of self-neglect are not considered within this category of neglect. These elders will be discussed later in the chapter as part of the ethical dilemmas facing social workers when elders refuse intervention or protective services.

Indicators of self-neglect are similar to those of neglect but are not attributable to the failure of others to provide care when such care is explicitly or implicitly indicated. Through a process of increasing cognitive or physical limitations—often combined with social isolation—elders lose the ability to care for themselves. Family, friends, and neighbors may not even be cognizant of the elder's inability to care for himself or herself. Hospitals, neighbors, and police officers are the most frequent reporters of self-neglect according to the National Center on Elder Abuse (1998). What often begins as a progressive deterioration in an elder's ability to complete the activities of daily living, can result in a serious health problem or homelessness. It may remain largely invisible until it reaches crisis levels.

Risk Factors Associated with Elder Abuse and Neglect

Gender and Age

Women are at greater risk for abuse than men for several reasons (Miller & Dodder, 1988; Quinn & Tomika, 1997; National Center on Elder Abuse, 1998; Wolf & Pillemer, 1989). First, more women than men live to old age, thereby making them a greater proportion of the population of elders. Because they live longer, women are more likely to develop physical illness or cognitive impairments that place them in the context of being dependent on or cared for by others. Furthermore, women tend to lack the body strength to resist physical abuse from caregivers or others. This last situation, however, is not as dire as it initially would appear as the National Center on Elder Abuse indicates that women are more likely to experience emotional or psychological abuse and neglect as opposed to physical abuse.

The older the elder, the more likely he or she is to become the victim of any kind of abuse or neglect. The incidence of elder abuse begins to rise significantly for elders over the age of 75, reflecting the greater likelihood of cognitive and physical limitations that require dependence on others for meeting basic needs (National Center on Elder Abuse, 1998).

Health Status of the Elder

Elders with physical and cognitive limitations are more likely to be abused or neglected according to the National Center on Elder Abuse (1998). One-half of all reported cases of elder abuse and neglect involve elders who are unable to care for themselves physically. Mistreatment rates are even higher (60 percent) for elders who experience some level of confusion. It is particularly tragic that the most impaired elders—those who are very old and very frail—are at greatest risk for physical and emotional injury from those on whom they depend for meeting basic daily needs. The National Center on Elder Abuse determined an increased risk for abuse or neglect on the basis of *reported* cases.

Other studies have not observed a greater likelihood of mistreatment among elders with functional disabilities but concluded that, in some cases, abuse and neglect are not the product of an elder's dependence on a caregiver but rather the dependence of the abuser on the elder (Barnett, Miller-Perrin, & Perrin, 1997; Wolf & Pillemer, 1989). Ross (1991) clarified an important distinction in interpreting this contradictory evidence. She found that cognitively or psychiatrically impaired elders were more likely to be neglected than abused, while abuse of all kinds was more prevalent in elders who were not cognitively impaired but suffered from physical limitations (Ross, 1991). This finding suggests that the variation in mistreatment rates may be more the product of the kind of functional disability than the disability in general.

Socioeconomic Class

Lower-income elders appear to be more susceptible to being abused or neglected although socioeconomic class alone is not a solid predictor of the likelihood of maltreatment by family or caregivers (National Center on Elder Abuse, 1998). One explanation is that low-income families may attempt to provide care in lieu of hiring caretakers for longer periods of time than higher-income families, creating high levels of stress in addition to the demands of surviving on already limited incomes. Restricted incomes may limit the quality of any supplementary caregiving services, therefore increasing the risk of inadequate care.

Racial and Ethnic Group Membership

While belonging to a population of color is often associated with low income, race and ethnicity are not consistently associated with higher levels of abuse and neglect. The National Elder Abuse Incidence Study (1998) observed lower levels of reported abuse and neglect among American Indian, Asian, Pacific Islander, and Hispanic elders. However, there is not clear evidence that elders belonging to these populations actually experience less abuse and neglect, but rather the mistreatment is less likely to be identified and reported. Elders of color are more likely to rely on informal supports than white elders, which may keep the quality of their care out of public scrutiny (Gibson, 1989; Liu & Yu, 1985; Quinn & Tomika, 1997; Taylor & Chatters, 1986). Researchers also speculate that ethnic elders belonging to these groups are less likely to be aware of the existence of APS or be unable to access these services due to language or environmental barriers (Moon & Williams, 1993). A cultural hesitancy to go outside of the family for help or the shame associated with revealing abuse by other family members, especially within Asian American families, may force the elder to endure the abuse rather than threaten the family's integrity.

Certain risk factors have been identified with increased risk of elder abuse and neglect among American Indians. These include poverty, the fragmentation of nuclear families that often occurs when family members move off the reservation, and the stress that accompanies elders adapting to the dominant culture (Carson, 1995). These factors combined with alcohol abuse by both elders and their abusers may place American Indian elders at greater risk than is reflected in the limited statistics available (Chester, Robin, Koss, Lopez, & Goldman, 1994).

African American elders are disproportionately overrepresented within all categories of abuse and neglect, which would suggest that ethnicity does play some role in placing them at higher risk for maltreatment (National Center on Elder Abuse, 1998). The risk factors associated with a greater incidence of abuse or neglect for African American elders are poverty, poor health, and a heavy reliance on informal (unpaid) family support to provide caregiving services (Cazenave, 1983; Gibson, 1989; Griffin & Williams, 1992). There is not a predisposition to elder abuse and neglect in African American culture or any other cultural group; rather, the comorbidity of elder abuse with general social and economic stressors offers better insight as to why abuse and neglect may occur more frequently in this population.

Characteristics of Abusers

While there are certain elders who are at greater risk for abuse and neglect, there are also individuals who are more likely than others to be perpetrators of mistreatment—an important factor in identifying high-risk situations. Two-thirds of all perpetrators are family members, particularly adult children (Barnett, Miller-Perrin, & Perrin, 1997; National Center on Elder Abuse, 1998). Among those elders living with adult children, the likelihood of abuse or neglect increases. Family caregivers are most likely to experience firsthand the stresses and challenges of providing physical care for aging family members. While women, especially daughters and daughters-in-law, provide most of the direct caregiving services, perpetrators are more frequently adult sons (Pillemer & Finkelhor, 1988; National Center on Elder Abuse, 1998; Wolf & Pillemer, 1989).

Elder abuse and neglect occurs more frequently in the context of substance abuse by caregivers or co-residing adult family members (Greenberg, McKibben, & Raymond, 1990; Wolf & Pillemer, 1989). Alcohol and drugs may diminish inhibitions regarding the use of physical or psychological aggression or be an indicator of other psychological problems for the abuser. Substance abuse can be an expensive habit for abusers, which increases the likelihood of financial exploitation to support the habit or reliance on the income of the abused elder to purchase drugs and alcohol.

Elders and their caregivers, family members, or social contacts who are socially isolated show a greater incidence of abuse and neglect than those who maintain significant social contacts with friends, neighbors, and other family members (Barnett, Miller-Perrin, & Perrin, 1997; Bendik, 1992; Wolf & Pillemer, 1989). It is not entirely clear whether the abusive situation is caused by the social isolation or whether once abuse develops, the abuser begins to isolate himself or herself and the elder. Regardless, the hidden nature of much of the abuse and neglect of elders compounds the difficulty of detecting the mistreatment and providing intervention.

Understanding the Causes of Elder Maltreatment

A number of theoretical explanations have been proposed to help identify why elder abuse and neglect occur for some elders and not for others. While these theories do not excuse perpetrators from their abusive behavior, they do provide a greater insight into the complexities of family dynamics, intergenerational relationships, and the danger to elders wrought by the abuse of drugs and alcohol by family members, social contacts, and caregivers.

Social Learning Theory

Fulmer and O'Malley (1987) suggested that elder abuse is learned as part of a greater exposure to violence throughout an individual's life. Children who are physically or emotionally abused or witness violence in their families of origin as a means of conflict resolution may be less likely to develop norms that prohibit physical aggression. If children learn that hurting someone is not an acceptable means of showing their frustration, anger, or emotional hurt, they are less likely to demonstrate aggressive behavior. On the other hand, if children learn through observation that hitting or hurting someone is acceptable, physical aggression may become learned behavior. The basic tenet of social learning theory is that these children are more likely to grow up to abuse their own parents and grandparents as part of this learned behavior.

Social learning theory, however, is not consistently supported by observations of the interactions between abusers and abused elders. Wolf and Pillemer (1989) found "no association between physical punishment as a child and becoming an elder abuser later in life" (p. 71). These researchers admitted that exacting accurate information from both the abuser and the abused elder on this topic is difficult because of the strong social stigma against physical punishment. While a family life cycle of violence might be implicated in the perpetuation of violent behavior patterns later in life, researchers have not been able to identify a statistically significant relationship between childhood physical punishment and the abuse of an elder parent.

Social Exchange Theory

Social exchange theory proposes that relationships between people, organizations, or communities are characterized by a set of mutual expectations about what each can offer the other. Harmonious, cooperative relationships are more likely when one party believes the other party offers something to exchange in the relationships. Parents invest in their children not just out of parental affection but also with the expectation that children will make them happy, provide affection, or care for them in the future. While there may be little payback when children are very small, as they grow up children can be a source of tremendous support and joy. The parents' investment of time and affection is most often returned later in the child's life.

Social exchange theory proposes that elders suffering from physical and cognitive limitations have little to offer in the way of rewards in their relationship with adult children or other social contacts. The emotional and physical costs of interacting or caring for an elder may rarely be compensated by reciprocal behavior on the part of the elder (Wolf & Pillemer, 1989). This failure to recoup rewards for efforts expended results in frustration and disappointment on the part of caregivers, family members, or social contacts, and these may express themselves as abuse or neglect.

A variation of social exchange theory, dependency theory, suggests that an impaired elder's need for constant help and attention causes severe stress for the caregiver, who may react to the stress by striking out at the elder. Research in this area has contradictory findings. Reported cases of abuse and neglect appear to support the contention that functional disabilities increase the risk for abuse or neglect while other studies claim there is no strong statistical relationship (Barnett, Miller-Perrin, & Perrin, 1997; National Center on Elder Abuse, 1998; Wolf & Pillemer, 1989).

Psychopathology of the Abuser

Dependency.   Focusing on the dependency of the abuser on the abused elder offers more promise in understanding the dynamics of elder abuse and neglect. Studies have found that adult children who rely on elder parents for ongoing financial support well into adulthood are more likely to become abusive than adult children who have established their own independence (Finkelhor, 1983; Wolf & Pillemer, 1989; Quinn & Tomika, 1997). For example, a middle-aged son who has difficulty keeping a job due to lack of skills, alcohol or drug abuse, or mental health problems and lives with an elderly parent is at high risk for becoming an abuser. This prolonged dependency role does not conform with normal expectations of adulthood. The perceived lack of power over the individual's own life may exhibit itself in abuse of the elder parent out of frustration and a need to regain some degree of power (Finkelhor, 1983).

Alcoholism, Drug Abuse, and Mental Illness.   Alcoholism, drug abuse, and mental illness are associated with an escalation in family violence at all stages in the family life cycle, including the context of caring for an elder (Barnett, Miller-Perrin, & Perrin, 1997). Wolf and Pillemer (1989) found that 38 percent of the elder abusers they studied had a history of psychiatric illness and 39 percent admitted to problems with alcohol at some time in their adult lives. Caring for an elder with diminished functional abilities is stressful under the best circumstances, but when a caregiver, family member, or other social contact has diminished capacities due to alcohol or drug intoxication or is struggling with a mental illness, the results can be deadly.

Assessment of Elder Abuse, Neglect, and Self-Neglect

Reporting Abuse or Neglect

The investigation and substantiation of elder abuse and neglect is the primary focus of APS agencies, which employ social workers specifically trained to follow a strict protocol for investigating suspected mistreatment of elders. As previously mentioned, all 50 states have designated either an APS agency or a subunit of the state aging unit to carry out this task. The exact procedure for responding to allegations of abuse or neglect varies from state to state, and it is not the intent of this chapter to identify all the variations in the investigative procedure. Rather, this discussion assumes the social worker is not employed by an agency whose specific responsibility is to pursue abuse and neglect investigations, but rather is alerted to the possibility of abuse or neglect in the process of providing more general services to elders.

Becoming Aware of Suspected Abuse or Neglect.   Social workers can become aware of possible abuse, neglect, or self-neglect of elders in a number of different ways. Through direct involvement with elders in case management, the provision of psychological and social services, and contact with elders in senior centers, assisted-living centers, adult day health centers, or other settings, social workers may suspect that an elder is being abused or neglected either by others or themselves. In other circumstances, social workers employed by agencies that serve elders may receive a report of elder abuse from a concerned family member, friend, or neighbor. Hospital personnel, police officers, firefighters, utility workers, repair persons, and even postal carriers are also frequent reporters of suspected abuse and neglect of elders.

Clarifying the Social Worker's Role. It is essential for the social worker to clearly identify what his or her role is in relationship to the elder in any of these cases. If the social worker is not directly involved with the elder in question, it is imperative to facilitate a referral to the respective adult protective agency. Connecting the source of the referral with the local APS unit and preferably a specific contact person is imperative. Referring sources may need strong encouragement to follow through with a report and be aware of their responsibilities in making such an allegation. Most states offer reporters of suspected abuse immunity from legal prosecution should the report be unfounded, but require that referral sources identify themselves. Other states will pursue an anonymous report and do not require any identification. The local adult protective services office in your community is in the best position to advise you as to local and state laws regarding reporting procedures. It is important that social workers be keenly aware of the legal climate in which APS functions in their own communities. Alleged abuse or neglect of an elder is a serious accusation, and laws exist to protect the rights of both elders and alleged abusers in the process of investigating complaints.

Assessing an Elder for Abuse or Neglect

If a social worker is working directly or indirectly with an elder and suspects that elder is being abused or neglected, it is essential the worker contact the local agency responsible for APS immediately. Adult protective services workers are in the best position to determine if there is sufficient evidence to warrant a full-fledged investigation. Even if there is minimal evidence to substantiate a formal report, it is important for the social worker to identify high-risk situations in which preliminary interventions may prevent serious harm or injury to a vulnerable elder.

Quinn and Tomika (1997) recommended that the social worker inform elders that they are pursuing a suspicion of abuse or neglect. This gives the elder explicit permission to cooperate with the social worker in obtaining important information and to be aware of what is happening. Such openness carries some risk with it, however, and may lead to total noncooperation on the part of the elder. Remember, abuse and neglect occur within a context of fear and control. Elders fear what will happen to them if their caregivers, family members, or other social contacts are found to be abusive or neglectful. In particular, the emotional bond between an aging parent and adult children is very strong, and elders may feel an obligation to protect adult children at all costs, even at risk of their own well-being. It is deeply embarrassing for an elder to admit that one of his or her own children is guilty of mistreatment.

Direct Observations.   As emphasized throughout this book, the social worker must trust his or her own direct observations as part of the assessment process. Open your eyes and look! Open your ears and listen! Does the elder have bruises or injuries in various stages of healing? Does the elder make any attempt to hide those injuries? Is there any evidence of physical injuries that may have been inflicted by others and are not the direct result of a plausible accident? It is important to remember that elders bruise more easily than younger people due to physical changes in the thickness of the skin and the resiliency of blood vessels—changes associated with the biological aspects of aging discussed in Chapter 2.

Does the elder appear unusually withdrawn or frightened? Is he or she unusually vigilant or easily startled? Does the elder's emotional state change from calm to agitated when others are around? Does the elder seem to use a lot of self-degrading statements, such as "I am a bother to everyone" or "I am just a worthless old person"? These statements might be indicators of long-term emotional or psychological abuse in which an elder has internalized the disparaging remarks of the abuser. They may also be due to depression or anxiety, discussed earlier in this book. Direct observations are important but not sufficient by themselves to accurately determine whether behavioral disturbances are the result of abuse or neglect or are due to other socioemotional problems the elder may be experiencing.

What does the elder look like? Is his or her personal hygiene appropriate? Are clothes reasonably clean and in good repair? If incontinence is a problem for the elder, are incontinence products properly used so that the elder is dry and comfortable? Are appropriate toileting and bathing facilities available? Is the elder's immediate living space clean and free of waste and pests? These questions are very similar to those used in the general process of assessment, but in this case, the social worker is attempting to determine if deficits in any of these areas are due to the failure of caregivers, other social contacts, or the elders themselves to provide adequate care.

Functional Assessments.   If the social worker is working with an elder on a regular basis, he or she should be familiar with the elder's functional status and ability to perform both the activities of daily living and instrumental activities of daily living. Have there been any changes in the elder's ability to perform any of these activities that are not explained by declining physical or mental health status? How does the elder perform on the Mini-Mental Status Exam? Is he or she oriented to time, space, and person? Have there been recent changes in performance in this area?

How does the elder score on the Geriatric Depression Scale? Has there been a change in recent weeks or months in depressive mood? It is important to determine what the alcohol and drug use patterns are in the home if a social worker suspects abuse or neglect by a caregiver, family member, or other social contact. Does the elder drink alcohol to excess? Does the primary caretaker or do other residents of the home drink or use drugs on a regular basis?

If a social worker is involved with an elder or the elder's family on an on-going basis and notices significant changes in any of these areas, it is important for the social worker to pursue a reasonable explanation for the differences. A social worker may feel he or she knows an elder or an elder's family very well and would never suspect abuse or neglect. The hidden nature of abuse and neglect, however, necessitates the social worker's examining even a familiar situation from a different perspective.

Interview the Elder Alone. If a social worker is determining whether there is just cause for suspecting abuse or neglect, the social worker needs to interview the elder alone—without the alleged abuser present. The presence of an alleged abuser may prevent the elder from answering questions honestly out of fear of retaliation. Implicating an alleged abuser in front of another person may result in escalation. For many elders who are highly dependent on others (even those who are abusing or neglecting them), the prospect of losing their sole source of care and support is very frightening.

Quinn and Tomika (1997) recommended the social worker be very direct in asking the elder questions about circumstances that constitute abuse or neglect even if these are very sensitive questions. Ask the elder directly if he or she is being hit, beaten, slapped, or shoved. Ask if he or she has ever been left alone for long periods of time, tied to the bed, or locked in the room. Has money ever been taken from him or her? Has he or she ever been forced to sign over property or money against his or her will? Has medication, food, or medical care ever been withheld by a caregiver, family member, or other social contact? Has the elder been threatened by anyone?

If the elder has bruises or other injuries, what explanation does he or she give for the cause of the injury? Does the severity of the injury coincide with the explanation? Is there evidence that injuries were treated promptly? Is there evidence of over- or undermedication, poor nutrition, or dehydration? Does the elder defend the alleged abuser for providing substandard care? What does your intuition tell you about the relationship between the alleged abuser and the elder? Determining whether an elder has been abused or neglected depends on a careful blend of empirical observations that serve as direct evidence of such mistreatment and the honing of a social worker's professional intuition to more subtle clues about the way an elder is being treated. An elder has the right to be protected from abuse and neglect from others. An elder also has the right to deny such abuse or neglect exists, even if the social worker's professional intuition indicates otherwise.

If the social worker has strong evidence to suggest an elder is being abused or neglected either through direct observation of injuries or by the admission of the elder, it is imperative that a formal report be filed with the local APS unit or state unit on aging immediately. Most states *mandate* that social workers and other professional helpers report suspected abuse or neglect and offer professional immunity from prosecution should the abuse or neglect be unsubstantiated. If there is no direct evidence of abuse or neglect, but the elder is at high risk for mistreatment or the social worker suspects past or fears future abuse, it is important to consider what interventions may prevent future harm. Recommendations for designing these kinds of interventions will be discussed later in this chapter.

Interviewing the Alleged Abuser.   Interviewing the alleged abuser usually falls within the responsibilities of an APS worker, who is empowered by the state to question the alleged abuser in the course of an investigation. However, if a social worker has an ongoing relationship with an elder and the family, he or she may be asked to work with APS in gathering the information necessary for a complete investigation.

It is important to clarify the nature of the relationship between the alleged abuser and the elder. What kinds of care does the alleged abuser provide? What are the alleged abuser's and elder's expectation about the quantity and quality of that care? It is important to discuss with the alleged abuser the kinds of demands the elder places on him or her and to ask if he or she feels capable of providing such care. What does the elder need assistance with? Basic activities of daily living? Instrumental activities of daily living? Financial management? Or homemaking services? What other support services, if any, are being provided? It is often quite revealing to compare an elder's perception of the alleged abuser's responsibilities with the ideas about what he or she is being asked to do. Both parties can have very unrealistic ideas about these responsibilities.

Clarify who manages the financial assets of the elder. Who is responsible for paying bills, procuring prescriptions, and managing medical appointments? Is the alleged abuser under financial stress of his or her own? What are his or her expectations for compensation for caregiving duties?

Ask the alleged abuser about the difficulties he or she experiences in the process of providing care for the elder. How does he or she cope when the elder is uncooperative or exhibits frustrating behavior? What does he or she do to deescalate the inevitable conflict that arises in the caregiving situation? How does the alleged abuser describe his or her relationship with the elder? What other friends or neighbors visit the elder on a regular basis? These questions are important in constructing an accurate picture of the demands and stresses that face both the elder and the alleged abuser. It serves as a baseline for determining the accuracy of responses to more sensitive questions later in the interview.

If the elder shows evidence of physical injuries, clarify with the alleged abuser how the elder was hurt. Be sensitive to the corroboration between the elder's and the alleged abuser's explanation for such injuries. Was medical care for the injuries sought in a timely fashion? What reasons are given for any dehydration, malnutrition, or overmedication observed in the elder? Has the caregiver, family member, or other social contact ever yelled at the elder or threatened the elder with social isolation or withholding care? The reaction to the question is almost as important as the answer. Alleged abusers who become overtly hostile and uncooperative may be feeling very defensive when confronted with such sensitive questions.

According to Quinn and Tomika (1997), the following characteristics indicate a caregiver, family member, or other acquaintance is at particularly high risk for inflicting abuse or neglect:

- The individual has a history of drug or alcohol abuse or mental illness.
- Both the elder and the alleged abuser are alienated, depressed, or socially isolated.
- The alleged abuser is immature and generally dissatisfied with life.
- The alleged abuser has not assumed caregiving responsibilities voluntarily.
- The alleged abuser is financially dependent on the elder.
- The alleged abuser is overtly hostile toward the elder or shows little concern for the elder.
- The alleged abuser blames the elder for any alleged abuse or neglect.

These characteristics suggest that there is, or could be, a dysfunctional relationship between the alleged abuser and the elder, placing the elder at risk for harm.

Designing Interventions to Prevent Abuse or Neglect

Determining that elder abuse or neglect has occurred does not automatically imply that the elder will be removed from the immediate situation and placed elsewhere. Less than one-fifth of reported and substantiated cases of elder abuse result in removal and replacement of an elder (Cash & Valentine, 1987; National Center on Elder Abuse, 1998). However, if it is determined that an elder is at immediate risk for serious harm, APS agencies have access to short- and long-term facilities that can provide crisis care for the elder and pursue legal charges against the perpetrator. Adult protective service agency staff can advise social workers on the protocol for intervening in this type of crisis.

Protecting against Financial Abuse or Exploitation

If it has been determined that an elder is being financially exploited by a caregiver or other person, it is important to act quickly to protect the elder's assets. When an elder is no longer able to manage his or her own finances, it may be necessary to contact other family members to assume this responsibility, if they are willing. Determine who has legal rights and responsibilities to manage the elder's finances. Contact the responsible party to discuss what appears to be going on and solicit their help in stopping the financial abuse. If it is the designated payee or conservator who appears to be financially exploiting the elder, contact an attorney about what legal steps need to be taken to stop the payee from accessing the elder's financial resources until a full investigation has been completed.

Offering Supportive Counseling

One of the most important things elders in abusive and neglectful situations need is reassurance and support. While they may be relieved that someone knows of the abuse or neglect, they may also be very fearful about what will happen to them and to the abuser. They may automatically assume they will be sent to a nursing home or, if they live with a caregiver, be forced to leave a familiar, although dangerous, situation. They will be concerned about how they will pay for a different set of services. They may fear the abuse or neglect will escalate once it has been discovered. The social worker plays an important role in offering emotional support and helping the elder to understand what is happening and what will happen, to the best of the social worker's knowledge. It is important to work with the elder (if cognitively able) to develop an immediate plan of action that addresses the short-term solution to the abusive or neglectful situation while a long-term action plan is being developed.

If an elder remains in the care of an abuser or continues to have regular contact with a family member or friend who is suspected to be abusive, it may be helpful to work with the elder on assertiveness training. Helping elders to find their own voice to resist either physical or verbal aggression may help to redefine the power relationship between an elder and an abuser. Elders also need to know whom to contact to report any future incidents of abuse or neglect or to have a contact person who can help them make a report. Supportive counseling can help elders understand that they are not to blame for abuse or neglect and that they should not tolerate mistreatment from anyone, much less a family member.

Perpetrators may also need to help identify those areas in which the stress of caregiving has led to an abusive or neglectful situation. This may include training the perpetrator in managing anger and frustration with the elder or in conflict resolution, or helping the perpetrator identify and manage high-risk situations. The social worker may need to help the perpetrator give himself or herself permission to turn to others for support. Providing care for an elder on a daily basis can drain the energy and patience of even the most dedicated family members or other support figures. While abuse or neglect of an elder can never be excused or overlooked, the perpetrator is a victim as well in this situation.

Developing Support Services

Support for Alleged Abusers. In many cases of suspected elder abuse and neglect, caregivers, family members, or other social contacts are simply not able to provide the level of care required by the elder and need to be connected with support services to augment caregiving activities. The social worker plays an important role in helping alleged abusers identify their immediate needs and locate services in the community to help meet those needs. This involves not only identifying appropriate services, such as homemaking, home health care, or Meals-on-Wheels, but also determining how to pay for and arrange these services. Frequently, the caregiver, family member, or other social contact is simply not aware of the range of available services or is too embarrassed to seek outside assistance in caring for the elder.

Support services can also include respite care that allows a caregiver to take some time off from caregiving responsibilities. If a caregiver can regain some private time to meet his or her own personal and social needs, he or she may feel less resentful toward the elder. Respite care may be best provided by other family members, neighbors, or friends—natural support networks that may not be used as extensively as they could be. Caregiving for an elder should not be the sole responsibility of a single adult child when other family members can provide some assistance, but caregivers may need encouragement to approach these individuals. If other family members cannot provide direct support, they may be able to offer financial assistance so that these services can be purchased from community agencies.

Support for the Elder. A socially isolated elder is at greater risk for abuse and neglect than one who maintains relationships with family, friends, and neighbors. Arranging for a daily telephone call from friends or family or using a community calling service can open an important social lifeline to the outside world for an isolated elder. Some community agencies can arrange for social visits from staff or volunteers who are willing to visit with the elder, read to him or her, or provide general companionship. The regular presence of even one significant other may be reassuring to an elder who fears for his or her physical or emotional safety.

If the elder is suffering from serious depression or anxiety, it may be necessary to consult with health care providers about medication that can help alleviate the depression. Treating an elder's depression can significantly reduce the emotional drain an elder places on his or her caregiver as well as alleviate an elder's suffering. If the elder's physical and psychological condition permits, social activities outside the elder's home, such as senior center activities, concerts, or plays, can be arranged. Breaking the tedium of looking at the same four walls day in and day out, may play a significant role in improving the elder's emotional well-being, thereby alleviating stress for both the elder and those providing care or support for their care.

Modifying the Environment

The purpose of any environmental modification as a preventative measure in reducing the likelihood of abuse or neglect is to find the safest space possible that will maximize independent functioning for as along as possible. With enough supportive services and minor environmental modifications, elders are often able to stay in their current living situations, even when abuse or neglect is suspected. Other times, the needs of the elder may far exceed the ability of a caregiver or the elder to meet those needs and then it is necessary to make significant changes in the elder's living arrangement.

The Physical Environment.   Modifications in the elder's immediate living space may help alleviate the demands placed on caregivers, family members, or social contacts. Modified bathing facilities, such as assistive devices in a bathtub or a bench in a shower, can help improve an elder's personal hygiene by making it easier to maintain personal cleanliness. Stair lifts and handrails may allow an elder to be more mobile around the house, rather than be relegated to a single room for the entire day. Occupational therapists can be extremely effective in helping elders and their caregivers. For instance, they may modify eating utensils, toileting facilities, and other items to be more easily used by an elder with physical limitations.

Adult Day Health.   It may be necessary to help the elder and caregiver arrange for another living arrangement to prevent future harm to the elder. Adult day health services can provide a caregiver with important respite from caregiving responsibilities as well as provide the elder with an opportunity to interact with other elders and work on maintaining and developing self-care skills. Continuing to live with a caregiver or family member may work out if the elder attends adult day health during the daytime hours. This reduces the actual amount of time caregiver and elder spend together, reducing some of the stress and tension.

Assisted Living.   Assisted living or semi-independent living are other options if it is not advised that the elder remain in the current living situation. Assisted living requires a moderate degree of ability to perform the activities of daily living with support for some kinds of personal care, such as bathing and homemaking services. In assisted living, meals are usually served in a congregate setting, meeting an elder's need for adequate nutrition as well as social stimulation. For elders with more limited functioning, semi-independent living allows elders to maintain their living space, usually a bedroom, supplemented by supervision for medication regimes, physical therapy, or other support services intended to maintain the maximum amount of independent functioning possible.

Elder Abuse and Neglect in Nursing Homes

Unfortunately, when elders are removed from family caregiving situations and placed in nursing homes, they are not immune from abuse or neglect. Although less than 5 percent of the population over the age of 65 years reside in nursing homes, they represent the most physically and emotionally vulnerable group of elders. It is extremely difficult to ascertain accurate figures about the extent of mistreatment in nursing homes both because the abuse occurs outside the view of family and friends and because it may occur in covert forms. Medication of elders and the use of restraints, specifically with cognitively impaired elders, may be seen by nursing home personnel as the only means to manage an elder's behavior but may be interpreted as abusive by family members or professional helpers.

Meddaugh (1993) identified three covert forms of abuse that frequently occur in the nursing home setting. The first is the loss of personal choice over basic daily activities, such that an elder is forced to eat, bathe, and sleep on the basis of institutional rather than personal demands. The second form is isolation, whereby aggressive residents are excluded from social or recreational activities because their behavior does not conform to group standards. Rather than be included in group activities, such as current events groups or entertainment, difficult residents may be banished to their rooms or propped in front of the television. It may be easier simply to avoid a resident's unpredictable or disruptive behavior than attempt to address it. The third form is what Meddaugh (1993) referred to as "labeling" in which the label "good resident" or "bad resident" results in differential treatment. If a resident is identified as bad, staff may make less of an effort to determine why a resident is being hostile or aggressive and not attempt to resolve the difficulty. If a resident is labeled as good, staff may see difficult behavior as an anomaly and work with the resident to determine what can be done to eliminate the behavior. This differential treatment reinforces both residents' problematic behavior and the use of aggressive or isolating techniques to cope with it in the institutional setting. It can be argued that these three situations are not actual abuse but unfortunate by-products of institutional life. Regardless, they can be interpreted as abuse by the elder and the elder's family.

Pillemer and Moore (1989) found psychological abuse that included verbal aggression and social isolation to be the most common form of mistreatment of elders occurring in a nursing home. This type of abuse occurred most frequently when elders failed to cooperate with daily caregiving, such as feeding and bathing schedules. In an attempt to regain some degree of personal control over their daily schedules, elders may resist the attempts of others to fit care into the institution's schedule, resulting in a tempestuous relationship between the elder and the caregiver. Staff members who related to elders as "difficult children" were more likely to abuse the elders than those who were able to interpret the resistance as an adult's intention of reestablishing control over their lives.

Pillemer (1988) suggested that the type and degree of abuse or neglect occurring in the nursing home setting is a function of the relationship between the resident and staff. Difficult residents place a high demand on already overworked nursing staff, making them a challenge. Staff members whose personal lives are stressful and who have compromised coping abilities are less likely to exercise the self-restraint necessary to avoid either physical or psychological abuse when they interact with difficult residents. Staff in the nursing home setting may feel unsupported in view of their importance as caregivers, and their frustration may exhibit itself as poor care of residents. These factors do not excuse abusive behavior, but provide some insight into the complexities of abuse in these settings.

To prevent abuse in the nursing home setting, the administration should provide staff with adequate training in managing difficult behavior in elders, anger management, and conflict resolution. Helping staff members to determine the cause of the behavior that precipitates abuse of an elder is the most effective way to prevent mistreatment. Finding the precipitating event that elicits uncooperative or aggressive behavior on the part of the elder is the most important step in preventing the problematic behavior and the abusive response on the part of staff. For example, if an elder is particularly uncooperative around bath time, it is helpful to determine what specifically is causing the elder to act out. Does the resident become chilled when bathing, causing him or her to resist undressing for the bath? Is the resident afraid of being hurt while being lifted in and out of the tub? Is a shower a better way to help an elder feel more secure during bathing? What choices can the resident be given regarding the time of bathing that might help this seem a more personal choice? Are there any unresolved issues with the staff assigned to bathing an elder that get acted out during the process? What is going on that would explain why getting a bath is such a trauma for the elder?

Once elder abuse has been substantiated in the nursing home setting, it is the administration's responsibility to take the necessary actions to hold the employee accountable and show that efforts have been made to avoid future abuse or neglect. The social worker's role is to be alert to evidence that an elder is being abused or neglected, to use professional knowledge and training to identify those elders who are at high risk for abuse or neglect, and to offer suggestions to administrators on means to break the cycle of abuse and neglect. The social worker plays an important role in acting as an advocate for those elders who are especially vulnerable to abuse or neglect or those who are unable to act on their own behalf due to physical or cognitive limitations.

When an Elder Refuses Protective Services

One of the most difficult situations facing social workers in both APS and general services to elders occurs when an elder who has been abused or neglected refuses any type of intervention. It is painful to watch an abused or neglected elder choose to continue living in a situation that has proved to be dangerous to the elder's health and well-being. It is frustrating for a social worker who has identified support services that can improve the quality of life for an elder to present those options only to have the elder adamantly refuse any assistance. This is often the case when working with elders who are self-neglecting but refuse to leave unsafe living conditions or seek medical or psychological care that might improve their lives.

What Is the Ethical Dilemma?

Adult protective services workers do not need an elder's permission to report suspected abuse or neglect. In some states, they also do not need an elder's permission to initiate an investigation to determine whether suspected abuse or neglect can be substantiated. The right to proceed with an investigation is determined by state law, not by the interests or concerns of either an elder or APS worker. Identifying and prosecuting physical abuse or neglect of vulnerable adults is assumed within the purview of the state's legal responsibility to its citizens. These issues are matters of state law and should be clarified as they pertain to the state in which a social worker practices.

The state has the responsibility to offer an elder intervention services that will reduce the likelihood of future abuse, regardless of whether either elder or abuser has assisted in the investigation of alleged abuse. However, the elder is not required, under law, to accept these services. The ethical dilemma facing the social worker in this case is not whether adults have the legal right to choose a dangerous situation over one the social worker feels will offer more safety and security. Adults do have this right. While it may be personally and professionally uncomfortable for a social worker to watch an elder remain in an unsafe situation, the law in all states recognizes an adult's right to choose danger over safety, if he or she has not been deemed incompetent by a court of law (Ross, 1991). No matter how dangerous a situation an elder willingly places himself or herself in, the social worker cannot override what is considered the legal right of an adult to make decisions about his or her life.

The ethical dilemma facing social workers when an elder refuses services is how to determine if the elder is capable of making the decision to refuse services. Does the elder have the cognitive ability to actually make an informed choice? Is the elder fully aware of the potential consequences of the decision to refuse services—a decision that may place him or her in future danger? If there is no evidence that the elder's ability to make that choice is impaired, the elder's decision stands. If there is some question about the elder's decision-making ability, additional action may be necessary.

Determining Legal Competence

Determining an elder's competence to make his or her own decisions about services and managing his or her own life is a complicated process. A social worker cannot simply determine independently that an elder cannot make those decisions. In some cases, it is possible to elicit the assistance of family members, who voluntarily step forward and assume decision-making responsibilities. With a family member's assurance, an elder may feel more comfortable consenting to intervention services. The elder may simply need family support to fully realize that his or her life could improve substantially with more support.

It is necessary to involve the legal system when there are no family members or when family members are the perpetrators of abuse and neglect. It may be possible for the court to appoint a guardian for the elder, who is empowered to protect the best interests of the elder while taking responsibility for making decisions about caregiving, financial management, or the use of supportive services. In some cases, the elder may retain all legal rights to self-determine but need someone to be assigned as the designated payee for his or her income. There are varying degrees of court-appointed assistance that can provide an elder with help from concerned others without resorting to a legal declaration of incompetence.

These options vary by state and should be thoroughly explored before proceeding with more drastic decisions. Pursuing a legal declaration of an elder's incompetence should be a last resort in the social worker's attempt to protect an elder from future abuse and neglect.

Summary

Although reporting requirements and procedures have improved in the last 20 years, elder abuse and neglect continue to remain largely a hidden problem. It is estimated that less than one-fifth of all cases of elder mistreatment are ever reported and less than half of those cases are substantiated (National Center on Elder Abuse, 1998). Elder abuse can take the form of physical injury, emotional or psychological mistreatment, or inappropriate sexual contact with an elder. Misuse of an elder's financial resources is also considered abuse and is subject to prosecution under state laws. A far greater problem and one that is less visible than physical, psychological, or financial abuse is neglect—the passive or active failure to provide for an elder's basic needs.

Elderly women with physical or cognitive limitations with limited financial resources who reside with an adult family member are at highest risk for abuse or neglect. This risk increases when caregivers or co-residing family members have a history of alcohol or drug abuse, have a mental illness, or are financially dependent on the elder. It is apparent that the dynamics of elder abuse and neglect are highly contingent on the nature of the relationship between the elder and the abuser as well as on any psychopathology present in the abuser.

In designing interventions to prevent future harm to the elder, it is essential to work with both the elder and the abuser. Providing emotional support for both parties, connecting the household with supportive services to relieve the caregiver of some of the burdens of providing care, and making environmental modifications are important steps in addressing the original cause of the abuse and neglect. However, it remains the right of the elder, even in cases of severe abuse and neglect, to accept or refuse offered services once abuse or neglect has been ascertained to have occurred. This right is recognized and supported as part of a greater context of protecting the rights of adults to self-determine. If a social worker suspects that an elder is not competent to make that decision, it may be necessary to take formal legal steps to designate others to assume the responsibility for making that decision. Attempts to have an elder declared incompetent should be a choice of last resort and must be carefully monitored to protect an elder's right to choose.

Check Out These Websites! _____

1. www.gwjapan.com/NCEA Sponsored by the National Center on Elder Abuse, this site provides a variety of links to further information about elder abuse and neglect. It includes the full text of the National Elder Abuse Incidence Study quoted extensively in this chapter. The website addresses of the APS agencies in all states are available from this site for further information about the laws, reporting requirements, and locations of protective services in any state. Also accessible from this site is the Clearinghouse on Abuse and Neglect of the Elderly (CANE) located at the University of Delaware. CANE is the largest computerized collection of elder abuse resources and materials.

2. www.home.bc.rogers.wave.ca/jhawkey/1e6.htm   This website describes the problem of alcohol use and abuse as it exacerbates elderly abuse and neglect. It examines personal experiences of both perpetrators of abuse and elderly victims who have experienced this problem. It contains extensive references for further study on the problem of substance abuse and domestic violence.

3. www. ink.org/public/kein/bibs/bibindex.html   This site is sponsored by the Kansas Elder Law Center and deals specifically with the legal climate regarding elder abuse and neglect in the state of Kansas. However, it contains a comprehensive overview of the problem of elder abuse in institutional, family, and financial settings as well as an excellent set of legal references regarding substantiation of abuse and neglect and protection for elders under the law.

4. www.abanet.org/domvio/home/html   On this site, the American Bar Association offers immediate advice for all persons who feel they might be victims of domestic violence, including elder abuse. The site offers guidelines for doing safety planning as well as identifying teaching resources, providing legal research and analysis, and using multidisciplinary efforts to combat domestic violence.

References

Administration on Aging. (1999). *Elder abuse.* Washington, DC: Administration on Aging. Retrieved from the World Wide Web, November 16, 1999. Available at http://www.aoa.gov.

Barnett, O. W., Miller-Perrin, C. L., & Perrin, R. D. (1997). *Family violence across the life-span.* Thousand Oaks, CA: Sage.

Bendik, M. F. (1992). Reaching the breaking point: Dangers of mistreatment in elder caregiving situations. *Journal of Elder Abuse and Neglect, 4*(3), 39–59.

Carson, D. (1995). American Indian elder abuse: Risk and protective factors among the oldest Americans. *Journal of Elder Abuse and Neglect, 7*(1), 17–39.

Cash, T., & Valentine, D. (1987). A decade of adult protective services: Case characteristics. *Journal of Gerontological Social Work, 10*(3/4), 47–60.

Cazenave, N. (1983). Elder abuse and black Americans: Incidence, correlates, treatment and prevention. In J. Kosberg (Ed.), *Abuse and maltreatment of the elderly: Causes and interventions* (pp. 187–203). Boston: Wright.

Chester, B., Robin, R., Koss, M. P., Lopez, J., & Goldman, D. (1994). Grandmother dishonored: Violence against women by male partners in American Indian communities. *Violence and Victims, 9*(3), 249–258.

Finkelhor, D. (1983). Common features of family abuse. In D. Finkelhor, R. J. Gelles, G. Hotaling, & M. Strauss (Eds.), *The dark side of families: Current family violence research* (pp. 17–26). Beverly Hills, CA: Sage.

Fulmer, T. T., & O'Malley, T. A. (1987). *Inadequate care of the elderly.* New York: Springer.

Gibson, R. C. (1989). Minority aging research: Opportunities and challenges. *Journal of Gerontology Social Sciences, 44,* 52–53.

Goodrich, C. S. (1997). Results of a national survey of state protective services programs: Assessing risk and defining victim outcomes. *Journal of Elder Abuse and Neglect, 9*(1), 69–85.

Greenberg, J. R., McKibben, M., & Raymond, J. A. (1990). Dependent adult children and elder abuse. *Journal of Elder Abuse and Neglect, 2*(1–2), 73–86.

Griffin, L. W., & Williams, O. (1992). Abuse among African American elderly. *Journal of Family Violence, 7*(1), 19–35.

Johnson, I. M. (1995). Family members' perceptions of and attitudes toward elder abuse. *Families in Society: The Journal of Contemporary Human Services, 76*(2), 220–229.

Liu, W. T., & Yu, E. (1985). Asian/Pacific American elderly: Mortality differentials, health status, and use of health services. *Journal of Applied Gerontology, 4*(1), 35–64.

Meddaugh, D. I. (1993). Covert elder abuse in the nursing home. *Journal of Elder Abuse and Neglect, 5*(3), 21–37.

Miller, R., & Dodder, R. (1988). The abused-abuser dyad: Elder abuse in the state of Florida. In R. Filinson & S. Ingman (Eds.), *Elder abuse: Practice and policy* (pp. 166–178). New York: Human Sciences.

Moon, A., & Williams, O. (1993). Perceptions of elder abuse and help-seeking patterns among African-American, Caucasian-American, and Korean-American elderly women. *The Gerontologist, 33*(3), 386–395.

National Center on Elder Abuse. (1998). *National elder abuse incidence study.* Washington, DC: The American Public Human Services Association.

Pillemer, K. A. (1988). Maltreatment of patients in nursing homes: Overview and research agenda. *Journal of Health and Social Behavior, 29,* 227–238.

Pillemer, K. A., & Finkelhor, D. (1988). The prevalence of elder abuse: A random sample survey. *The Gerontologist, 28,* 51–57.

Pillemer, K. A., & Moore, C. (1989). Abuse of patients in nursing homes: Findings from a survey of staff. *The Gerontologist, 29,* 314–320.

Quinn, M. J., & Tomika, S. K. (1997). *Elder abuse and neglect: Causes, diagnoses and interventions strategies* (2nd ed.). New York: Springer.

Ross, J. W. (1991). Elder abuse. *Health and Social Work, 16*(4), 227–229.

Taylor, R., & Chatters, L. (1986). Patterns of informal support to elderly black adults: Family, friends, and church members. *Social Work, 31*(6), 432–438.

Wolf, R. S., & Pillemer, K. A. (1989). *Helping elder victims: The reality of elder abuse.* New York: Columbia University Press.

12

Working with Elders' Support Systems

Spouses, Partners, Families, and Caregivers

Elders' Support Systems

Much of this book has focused on working with elders as individuals, helping them face the challenges of the biopsychosocial changes that accompany the aging process. The day-to-day coping required to meet these challenges and the initiative needed to make changes when necessary remain primarily with the individual elder. However, elders function within a complex social system that can effectively help or hinder their ability to maintain a high quality of life and independent functioning. This chapter will focus on elders' support systems, their spouses, partners, families, and caregivers. These support systems serve as vital resources not only to elders but also to the gerontological social worker in providing comprehensive services to them.

Effectively mobilizing support systems requires the practitioner to "think family" (Neidhardt & Allen, 1993). "Thinking family" means seeing the elder as part of a complex system of multigenerational relationships that have had a profound influence on his or her life and serve as the primary source of interaction and support. Family roles, such as spouse or partner, parent, grandparent, aunt, uncle, or sibling, are important parts of elders' self-concepts, influencing elders' thinking even when the specific functions associated with those roles have ceased. Human beings are born into various family constellations, create their own versions of family in adulthood, and turn to whatever they perceive to be family as they grow older.

This chapter will begin with a focus on the couple dyad and some of the challenges facing older couples whether in traditional marriage relationships or as long-time partners in gay or lesbian relationships. Most likely the gerontological social worker will encounter couple relationship issues in the course of offering other support services to elders. With this in mind, it is important to explore the goals of offering supportive counseling to elder couples and examine specific interventions to help stabilize mature relationships. The importance of involving families in work with elders, including the use of "family meetings" in preserving an elder's connection to kin, will be discussed. The remainder of the chapter is devoted to family caregiving and social work's role in supporting caregivers.

Spouses and Partners

Three-fourths of men over the age of 65 live with a spouse compared to less than half of women of the same age (U.S. Bureau of the Census, 1996). This is due largely to the difference in life expectancies between the genders. Women are more likely to outlive their spouses, placing them at increasingly greater risk of living alone after age 65. By age 85, less than 10 percent of women are living with their husbands (Lugalia, 1997). These figures suggest that even though the number of married couples declines with advancing age, a reasonable number of older couples continue to live together well into old age and will face a set of unique challenges, including changing marital roles, retirement, and shifting dependency needs.

Gay and Lesbian Couples

While little research has specifically addressed the late-life challenges facing long-term gay and lesbian couples, the dynamics of growing older together and facing illness and disability in one's partner are very similar for straight and gay couples (Mackey, O'Brien, & Mackey, 1997). Older gay and lesbian couples often consider themselves married in every sense of the word; however, the legal and social system in the United States does not. As of the writing of this book, gay and lesbian couples do not have the rights straight couples have to make legal decisions for each other, transfer property, or share retirement benefits, except in the state of Vermont, which recognizes civil unions. Civil unions are not considered marriages but rather a sanctioned legal relationship between same-sex persons, which endows many of the same legal rights traditional married couples enjoy. The current cohort of older gay and lesbian couples may also be reluctant to openly disclose the nature of their relationship out of fear that they will be ridiculed or dismissed as significant others in their partners' lives.

Life partners are an essential part of gay or lesbian elders' support systems and need to be recognized for the importance they play in each others' lives. Social work as a profession is committed to respecting the life choices of people of all ages. While the legal system does not yet recognize the significance of gay or lesbian relationships, the social work profession does. Partners should be considered as significant as spouses and included in the consideration of any case planning.

Changing Marital Roles

Return to the Couple Dyad. For couples who have assumed traditional parenting roles, the financial and custodial activities associated with these roles usually begin to subside when the couples are in their fifties. Adult children complete formal education, begin their own families, and rely less and less on the material support of parents, as part of the normal family life cycle. Gradually, the couple returns to the original dyad of the early years of marriage (Wolinsky, 1990). Some couples maintain a healthy, vital relationship that thrives despite the demands of parenthood. They have managed to maintain emotional intimacy and a commitment to the relationship that exists separate from their parenting roles. For these couples, a household free of children is a welcome relief and a time to return to the joys of being a couple. For other couples, raising children has been the bond that has kept them together, often at the expense of their personal relationship. When the children are gone, they may be faced with living with a relative stranger. They know each other well as "Mom" or "Dad," but are less comfortable with being intimates. Couples who choose to stay together are faced with the prospect of redefining their partnership as more than the reciprocal responsibilities of parenthood.

Retirement. Workers in contemporary society have very mixed feelings about retirement. For some elders who have worked physically and intellectually demanding jobs their entire lives, retirement may be seen as a welcome relief from the pressures of the workplace. Finally, there is time to relax and do all the things that employment and family responsibilities precluded. It is seen as a time of both new beginnings and prolonged recreation. Others face retirement with great trepidation, seeing retirement as the end of the most productive and important part of life.

The decision to retire creates a new set of challenges for older couples (Weeks & Hof, 1995; Wolinksy, 1990). The most obvious is that of defining a lifestyle within limited financial resources. While there is more time for recreational activities, there is less income. For many individuals, the workplace is the primary source of social contact and interaction. Retirement requires individuals to find creative ways to replace the ongoing socialization with others. For yet others, retirement requires both men and women to redefine a self-image often closely aligned with occupational roles. Regardless of socioeconomic status, individuals can derive great personal satisfaction from being of service and knowing that what they have done throughout their lives is important. The role of being "retired" defines individuals in terms of what they *no longer do* rather than what they *are doing*. Finding meaningful activities to occupy leisure time can also be a great challenge for both men and women who have devoted most of their time and energy to work. A concern about money, the threat of social isolation, redefining self-image, and occupying unstructured time may create stresses for both the individual elder and the couple.

Shifting Dependency Roles.   While there may be the implicit understanding that spouses will take care of each other in the case of illness or disability, few couples are realistically prepared for the psychological and physical demands of caregiving for a spouse (Nichols, 1996). The reciprocal duties of caring for each other is seriously disrupted when one spouse needs special care. Shifting dependency needs can create anger and resentment on the part of the caregiver spouse despite the deep affection and commitment present in most long-lasting relationships. For example, an older man may need to assume meal preparation and housekeeping responsibilities if his wife becomes ill—tasks for which he may be totally unprepared. An older woman may need to take over the family finances when her husband develops Alzheimer's disease, challenging a lifetime of prescribed roles and responsibilities. Both situations require spouses to develop new skills and assume new tasks in the relationship, a source of great fear and uncertainty for couples who operated within a familiar framework of mutuality for many years.

The Goals of Supportive Interventions with Older Couples

The Context of Couples Work

Most of the couples work that social workers do with elders occurs within the context of providing other direct service, such as coordinating home health care services, supporting family caregivers, or involving case management. In this context, couples work is seen as part of a larger intervention effort with a focus broader than the couple's relationship. However, supporting or enhancing the ability of a husband and wife to provide support to one another and continue to work together in decision making and problem solving is essential to the overall success of any coordinated case plan.

It is important to emphasize that any couples counseling with elders should not focus on trying to undo or correct a lifetime of marital dysfunction. Research has found that older couples find the greatest threat to their relationship to come from outside forces rather than internal forces (Neidhart & Allen, 1993). It is important to help older couples work with the strengths that have enabled the relationship to survive this long rather than reconstruct relationship patterns the social worker considers more functional.

Little attention is given to older couples, straight or gay, in the couples counseling literature, suggesting both a hesitancy to work with older couples and a limited understanding of the psychosocial challenges facing this population

(Sandberg & Harper, 1999). As has been emphasized throughout this book, there is a subtle ageism that permeates the field of mental health counseling. Elders are seen as too old to change, with limited abilities to mobilize personal insight to change lifelong behavior patterns, or too ill or demented to be active participants in the therapeutic process (Weeks & Hof, 1995). There is also the dangerous assumption that couples that have stayed together for a long time have worked out their differences and simply learned to adjust to each other, thus having little need for supportive counseling to improve their relationship.

The current cohort of elders may also harbor negative attitudes about counseling that prevent them from seeking professional help with relationship problems. Marriage counseling may be seen as appropriate for "crazy" people or those couples with drug, alcohol, parenting, or infidelity issues. Couples who have been together for a long time can take justifiable pride in having "stuck it out" in the face of a lifetime of challenges and may be far less idealistic about the notion of marital bliss. However, in the face of an age-related crisis, such as a serious illness, traditional coping skills may be shattered, destabilizing even the most durable relationship.

Older couples have many of the same concerns as couples of all ages, including communication, the balance of power in the marriage, finances, and sexuality (Wolinsky, 1990). These issues are continuously renegotiated throughout the family life cycle. Elderly couples, however, are faced with an additional set of psychosocial challenges associated with the aging process.

Helping Older Couples Manage Loss

Helping older couples to manage loss without destabilizing their relationship is an important goal in supportive counseling. For example, a spouse may erroneously assume that once his or her spouse is no longer able to prepare meals or do the housekeeping that they will both end up in a nursing home. Rather than deprive the couple of each other's companionship and the security of living in their own home, helping the more able-bodied spouse to either learn new skills or access supportive services are ways to keep the couple together and still realistically deal with one member's loss of abilities. The same is also true for a spouse faced with managing money when the other spouse is no longer able to do so. Soliciting the help of an adult child or arranging for outside help with finances allows the couple to stay together but compensates for the loss of functioning.

An older couple may experience more subtle losses than those apparent in loss of physical or cognitive ability (Nichols, 1996). There is ample anecdotal evidence about the challenges an older couple faces when a husband retires and is home full time with a wife who has spent her life managing the responsibilities of homemaking. Too often the husband transfers his "executive and organizational abilities" to the home front, seeing a need to reorganize the kitchen or make unwelcome recommendations about how the wife could do her job more efficiently. The loss of meaningful responsibilities in the workplace creates intense stress for the wife, who may see the husband as an intruder on her work space in the home.

De-escalating the stress between the couple may involve helping them find creative ways to develop a new division of labor in the home.

Creating Opportunities for Mastery and Control

The process of managing losses without destabilizing the relationship is one part of the process of creating opportunities for mastery and control for the older couple—a significant factor in preventing the development of depression in elders (Sandberg & Harper, 1999; Weeks & Hof, 1995). For example, while an ill wife may not be able to prepare meals, she can still recommend meals or instruct the spouse in preparing them. An older husband may not be able to do simple maintenance around the house, but he can still be in charge of calling outside service providers and supervising the repair work. A couple that has always enjoyed gardening together may no longer be able to manage a large vegetable garden, but can transfer those interests to a smaller plot of flowers or an herb garden. Working with couples to identify and develop spheres of mastery and control can help couples to avoid marital stress by redefining ways in which they feel they can retain meaningful roles.

Maintaining Identity

Healthy couple relationships give each member an opportunity to define his or her own identity within the relationship through contributions to a shared life. When illness or disability take away a spouse's traditional role in the marriage, a spouse may feel some anxiety about maintaining this sense of identity. A husband who has always been the major breadwinner in a couple may become anxious during retirement, feeling that he no longer is making his contribution to the marriage. A wife who has always taken care of the home may become depressed when physical illness dictates she can no longer carry out those tasks and is failing in her contribution to the relationship. Couples may need continuous reassurance that their identities do remain the same in the relationship despite changing tasks and new ways to contribute to the union.

Therapeutic Interventions with Older Couples

Resource Mobilization

Sometimes what older couples need the most is information about resources. They are satisfied with their relationship and communication patterns but the demands of living on a limited income in the face of physical and cognitive limitations have exhausted their coping abilities. In this case, therapeutic work with couples means helping them clarify their needs and access the resources available to help them meet those needs. Couples may need assistance in identifying and mobilizing existing support networks and developing new ones (Wolinsky, 1990).

For elders who have always taken great pride in their ability to solve their own problems, the act of asking for help may represent a significant failure. Encouraging elders to seek assistance from families and professionals requires social workers to be extremely sensitive to the pain elders experience in the face of injured pride.

Elders may also need assistance in finding ways to balance their changing needs for dependence and independence (Weeks & Hof, 1995). When elders begin to show a need for supportive services, a well-intentioned but destructive tendency of helping professionals is to connect elders to more supportive services than they actually need. While this may make the elders' lives easier in the short run, it often deprives them of ways to maintain at least some level of self-sufficiency. For example, an older couple may have difficulty preparing their own lunch or dinner, but they may still be able to handle breakfast. Even the simple act of preparing breakfast can preserve the couples' feelings of independence and self-esteem. It is important to avoid the trap of creating learned helplessness when mobilizing resources for older couples.

Marital Life Review and Reminiscence

The process of marital life review is similar to the general process of life review described in Chapter 6, but focuses exclusively on the marital relationship (Arean, Perri, Nezu, Schein, Christopher, & Joseph, 1993; Hargrave, 1994; Wolinsky, 1990). The process focuses on helping the couple reminisce about how they met, what originally attracted them to each other, and memories about the early years of marriage. This can help elders rekindle old feelings about their decision to make a life together and remind them about what they found attractive in each other.

Couples are then asked to recount the early and middle years of their marriage, identifying the obstacles they faced and how they handled conflict and stress. As in individual life review, this process can help couples identify the ways in which they have supported each other throughout their married lives and remind couples of the variety of coping skills they have used in the past and can use again in the present. This is particularly helpful for couples who feel overwhelmed and inadequate facing the challenges of aging. They may have forgotten how they rallied to conquer obstacles successfully in the past. Recounting past events may also remind elders how they have renegotiated roles and responsibilities throughout their married lives and may need to do so again in the face of retirement, illness, or other loss.

One of the most important benefits of using marital life review with older couples is the opportunity for restorying, visiting past events with a new lens for interpreting their meaning. For example, an older couple may recount the time the husband was fired and put the family in serious jeopardy of losing the family home. While such an event can be remembered with both anger and embarrassment, something beneficial came out of that experience that a couple can identify, given the opportunity. Perhaps, it was that event that encouraged the husband to complete a college education or sent the wife into the labor force, events that ultimately helped the family achieve a more secure financial future. Although the couple would not see this event as a happy time in the marriage, being able to restory the event for its positive aspects mobilizes skills that can help the couple to reframe the current set of age-related challenges they face.

Marital life review may be instrumental in helping older couples identify and resolve conflicts from their past. Grudges and resentments can fester for a lifetime even among couples who express a high level of satisfaction with their relationship. Giving couples the opportunity to revisit old hurts and disappointments may also give them permission to finally let go and move ahead with their relationship. In the previous example of recounting a job loss, the wife may finally be able to say how angry she was about having to leave her children in the care of others to become the primary breadwinner for the family. Yet, in recounting her anger, she may also realize that returning to the labor force gave her the skills and confidence she needed to define herself as more than just a wife and mother, roles she enjoyed but did not feel challenged her intellectually. Seeing the positive consequences of a negative event from the perspective of 40 years later can be invaluable in helping her trade her anger for understanding.

Cognitive-Behavioral Approaches

Cognitive-behavioral approaches to couples work is designed to restructure a couple's negative thinking patterns and ultimately change dysfunctional behavior patterns (Moberg & Lazarus, 1990; Sandberg & Harper, 1999). Situations elicit thoughts that generate emotions that influence behavior. If the cognitive response to any given situation can be changed, the negative emotions and subsequent behavior can also be modified.

This can be particularly helpful in helping elders manage their reactions to loss. Nichols (1996) identified three kinds of losses facing elders: the loss of significant others, such as a spouse, friend, or family members; the loss of a significant aspect of self, such as one's health, bodily function, or role; and the loss of external objects, such as money or a home. After taking time to grieve these losses, many elders are able to accept them and not lose their self-esteem in the process. Other elders fixate on the loss and the resulting depression seriously compromises their ability to function. Cognitive-behavioral techniques can be used to help elders identify ways in which to compensate for losses and shift thinking to emphasize the resources an elder still possesses. For example, a retired attorney may be fixated on his boredom following retirement and feel he no longer has a productive role in society. His chronic unhappiness will affect couple's joint sense of well-being. While his wife continues to be involved in activities with the grandchildren and volunteer work with the church, the husband mopes around reminiscing about how exciting his life used to be. Cognitive-behavioral techniques can help the husband examine the negative thinking patterns that perpetuate his dissatisfaction. Rather than focus on what he used to do, he may need help in developing new responses to his feelings of being unproductive. A demanding law practice deprived him of the opportunity to spend time with family and friends, a situation he can now remedy. The same practice robbed him of the chance to provide pro-bono legal services to low-income clients, a dream he always had but never realized. He has these opportunities now in retirement. Reframing the retirement experience as an opportunity rather than a loss can help the individual move beyond self-indulgent pity. Cognitive restructuring recognizes the significance of losses, such as those represented by retirement, but helps an elder explore different behavioral responses that are more productive and fulfilling.

Communication Skills Training

Another technique that can be used to help older couples improve their relationship is communication skills training (Gotlib & Beach, 1995; Prince & Jacobsen, 1995). In long-lasting relationships, couples develop habitual ways of communicating with each other. As long as these patterns work, it is unlikely they will be changed. Couples learn to choose their battles, accommodate a spouse's moods, and interpret the meaning of subtle behavioral clues. However, changing roles or the onset of illness or disability may require significant changes in the way a couple must learn to communicate with each other.

For example, a husband may know that when his wife becomes uncommunicative and sullen, she is usually angry with him about something. He knows that eventually she will tell him what is wrong, but that it is best handled by letting her come to him in her own time. So he leaves her alone. In this situation, his wife is not angry with him. She is depressed about her physical health and worried about how they will manage to purchase the expensive medication she needs. She feels he is rejecting her because he does not seem to notice that something is wrong. She feels guilty talking to him about her concerns because money is tight and he seems preoccupied with his own issues. As a result, they rarely talk to each other, both harboring erroneous ideas about what the other is feeling and doing. This is a prime example of an older couple relying on familiar communication patterns applied to a new situation in their marriage. Communication skills training can help the couple to recognize situations as different and challenge their traditional ways of communicating and interpreting each other's behavior. The husband can no longer assume withdrawn moods are signs of his wife's anger but rather may signal depression or worry. The wife cannot assume the husband will magically interpret her silence as concern about money or her health when this behavior in their marriage was used traditionally to convey anger.

Traditional communication patterns may also be challenged when one of the members of the couple begins to experience the effects of sensory limitations, such as loss of sight or hearing or cognitive losses associated with dementia. For example, a husband may attribute a wife's poor housekeeping habits to a general lack of concern about cleanliness when in truth his wife can no longer see well enough to adequately perform these tasks. A wife may interpret the loud volume on the television as her husband's attempt to shut her out of his life when in reality his hearing is failing. Developing new communication techniques is especially important as spouses learn to live with the progressive deterioration inherent in Alzheimer's disease. In the middle and late stages of the disease as the individual loses the ability to interact with others, the spouse may become oblivious to the partner's feelings and make hurtful or destructive comments. Without professional help, it may take a spouse a long time to recognize this as a symptom of the disease rather than a problem in the relationship.

The Family Meeting

In addition to working with the couple dyad, an integral part of any work with elders involves the extended family and their role in providing both emotional and instrumental support. The specific challenges of working with family caregivers is covered in detail in the next section of this chapter but this section will address the use of the "family meeting" as a means of therapeutic intervention. The family meeting can serve both as a form of brief family work and as a forum for developing a coordinated service plan for elders and their families.

One such program currently in operation is the Facing Aging Concerns Together (F.A.C.T) program at Family Services in Seattle, Washington (Genevay, 1990). The program employs a one-time, intensive three-hour "family consultation," bringing together the elder, family members, concerned friends and neighbors, and a network of professionals, such as social workers and health care providers. The model is designed to encourage family members to take a more proactive role in planning for the needs of their elder family member, empowering family members to develop their own creative strategies for meeting an elder's needs. In addition, the program is aimed at helping family members recognize long-standing family conflicts and resentments and work toward resolving those conflicts in the process of helping an elder family member.

Goals of the Family Meeting

In the F.A.C.T program, four goals are targeted (Genevay, 1990). The first is to help the family get "unstuck"—moving beyond current obstacles to mobilizing the family on behalf of the elder. The second is to identify successful family coping skills and to develop new skills as needed. Helping the elder and family members to prioritize issues in the midst of conflicting demands is the third goal of the program. The fourth goal is helping families to move toward healing past hurts and grudges through a focus on developing an action plan for its elder member. These goals reflect a basic confidence in the ability of the elder and his or her family to find solutions to the challenges created by the aging process, with professional helpers acting as facilitators for mobilizing the family problem-solving process. This approach also recognizes the formidable influence of a lifetime of family dynamics as both a help and a hindrance. While families may be able to put their individual differences aside for the sake of determining care options for an elder member, the same crisis may bring unresolved conflicts to the surface. Both the functional and dysfunctional aspects of a family's functioning are addressed in this model.

The Content of Family Consultation Sessions

The family consultation (as it is called in the F.A.C.T. approach) covers six specific content areas. The most crucial content revolves around the current situation with an elder family member and a discussion of what decisions need to be made to protect the well-being of the elder. This discussion includes the direct participation of the elder. Rather than family members and the group facilitator talking about the elder as a third party, the elder assumes a decision-making role. It serves as a focal point for the development of an action plan, the ultimate goal of the family consultation. Addressing unfinished family business is a second content area of this approach. Helping the elder and the family member identify the past losses and how these losses have been processed in the family is intended to help uncover obstacles that may be hindering the decision-making process. During the discussion of losses and decision making, families often become aware of the existence of family rules and roles, those spoken and unspoken norms that influence what behavior is acceptable and what is not. It is not uncommon for adult family members to assume the childhood family roles when interacting with other members of the family, including that of caregiver, parentified child, rebel, scapegoat, or clown. The identification of family rules and roles often leads to a growing awareness of family communication styles and the division of labor within a family, the fourth and fifth content areas in the family consultation. Finally, the facilitator helps the family identify the skills (or lack of) a family uses in expressing conflictual emotions or other strong feelings that impede good family functioning.

The content of family consultations focuses first on the precipitating event of an elder needing supportive services but recognizes that impaired family dynamics may prevent the family from developing a mutually acceptable plan of action. Separating what are legitimate differences of opinion about what an elder family member needs and what family members are able to provide from a long history of family conflict prevents the two issues from becoming hopelessly enmeshed with each other.

The Role of the Facilitator

The facilitator plays a variety of roles in the family consultation process (Genevay, 1990). The exploration of family dynamics, communication patterns, and unresolved family conflicts requires the facilitator to function as a therapist or bereavement counselor. Managing conflict between family members also requires the facilitator to assume the roles of mediator and negotiator. Finally, facilitators need to have expertise in the area of the biopsychosocial changes associated with the aging process as well as in family dynamics. They also need to have broad knowledge of the array of community support services available to the elder and his or her family.

The ultimate goal of the family consultation is to have developed a preliminary action plan for meeting the needs of the elder family member. The brief family work component of the meeting is intended to address the obstacles getting in the way of moving from the recognition of a crisis situation of an elder to a mutually acceptable plan of action. Genevay (1990) admitted that some families have excellent decision-making abilities and spend limited time in redressing grievances and past conflicts. These families are able to move through the family dynamics portion of the meeting quickly and spend most of the family meeting identifying resources and engaging in active problem solving. Other families need more than one family consultation or need to receive long-term professional help for family problems. Regardless, the model offers an impressive way to maximize family involvement in decision making for an elder's care plan as well as an opportunity for families to improve familial relationships.

Caregivers as Support Systems for Elders

Despite a vast array of formal support services available to elders, three-quarters of all impaired elders rely solely on the caregiving assistance of friends and relatives using no formal services (Doty, 1986; Kane & Penrod, 1995; Tennstedt, 1999). There are over 22.4 million households in the United States with at least one caregiver who provides unpaid help to elders according to a 1996 nationwide survey (National Alliance for Caregivers and American Association for Retired Persons, 1997). These caregivers average 18 hours a week of assistance, with one-fifth of all caregivers providing more than 40 hours a week of care, the equivalent of a full-time job (National Alliance for Caregiving and American Association for Retired Persons, 1997). These activities range from instrumental support, such as assistance with transportation, grocery shopping, housekeeping, and managing finances, to personal assistance with the most basic activities of daily living. If the work of family caregivers were replaced with paid home care staff, the cost to the taxpayers is estimated to be $196 billion per year (Arno, Levine, & Memmott, 1999).

The demand for both formal and informal caregiving is expected to continue to rise as the number of elders in the population grows and longevity among elders with functional disabilities increases. Nearly one-quarter of all elders in the United States are functionally disabled or in need of some assistive services, and this number is expected to increase by 90 percent by the year 2040 (Tennstedt, 1999). The lower fertility rates of the baby boom generation, the geographical mobility of their children, and the growing numbers of women in the workforce suggest greater caregiving responsibilities will fall to a smaller number of available caregivers (Aldous, 1994). These demographic changes will have far-reaching implications for the development and delivery of formal services intended to replace the dwindling pool of informal helpers.

Gender as a Factor in Caregiving and Care Receiving

Women as Caregivers. The vast majority (72.5 percent) of caregivers are women, primarily spouses, daughters, or daughters-in-law (Merrill, 1997; National Alliance for Caregiving and American Association for Retired Persons, 1997). Often these caregivers work full-time jobs and are raising children in addition to their caregiving responsibilities. Women may be socialized to feel more responsible for the emotional and physical well-being of aging relatives, judging themselves according to an ethic of responsibility to others (Bould, 1997; Gilligan, 1982; Merrill, 1997). Women are also more likely to develop and maintain deep emotional bonds with aging parents so that their acceptance of caregiving responsibilities is as much the effect of affectional ties with aging parents as it is a subtle expectation by other family members (Bould, 1997).

Adult sons are more likely to become involved in caregiving activities when it is their father who needs assistance as opposed to their mother, presumably because of the intimate nature of personal care (Cohler, 1997; Merrill, 1997). However, men's involvement in caregiving more often involves coordinating formal services from the community rather than providing services directly to the elder (Cohler, 1997; Montgomery, 1992).

Care-Receivers. Older men are more likely to receive care from their spouses than from adult children, consistent with the fact that there is a greater likelihood older men will be married (Lugalia, 1997). Older wives are often the sole caregivers for their aging spouses, assuming responsibility not only for all of the homemaking tasks but also for the arduous tasks involved in providing personal care. Tennstedt (1999) found that services provided to men either by spouses or other female caregivers were often given on the basis of perceived need rather than functional ability. That is, older men were more likely to have meals prepared by someone else because they had no desire to learn how to cook rather than because they were not able to cook. The same appeared to be the case in other traditionally gender-linked activities, such as housekeeping and shopping.

Older women receive caregiving from adult children, particularly daughters, more often than from spouses. These adult children are more likely than spouses to expand the caregiving network (including formal services) to include two to four other caregivers (National Alliance for Caregiving and American Association for Retired Persons, 1997). This does not mean that older husbands do not provide care for their wives but that such an arrangement is less likely due to the fewer number of married women over age 65.

Caregiving among Racial and Ethnic Groups

The incidence of informal family caregiving increases among Asian American, African American, and Hispanic elders (National Alliance for Caregiving and American Association for Retired Persons, 1997). The greater number of informal caregivers is due to both culturally specific attitudes about caregiving and a greater likelihood that elders will reside with other family members prior to needing caregiving services (Choi, 1999).

Caregiving among Hispanic Elders.   Over one-quarter of all Hispanic households in the United States provide caregiving to an elderly family member (National Alliance for Caregiving and American Association for Retired Persons, 1997). Although there are significant differences between subgroups of the Hispanic population, the emphasis on the family unit crosses cultural and ethnic group boundaries. There is a strong expectation that elders will be cared for by family members should they become ill or disabled. Expectations are based on the cultural concept of reciprocity. The care one received as a child is to be repaid to older parents should they become disabled (Clark & Huttlinger, 1998). Clark and Huttlinger emphasized that as adult children of Hispanic elders become increasingly acculturated, an elder's expectations about reciprocal caregiving and an adult child's perception of those responsibilities will become increasingly dissonant. The availability and willingness of Hispanic family members to serve as caregivers will be restricted as employment and residential patterns continue to reflect that of their white counterparts.

Daughters are the primary caregivers for elders in all Hispanic groups due in part to traditional cultural roles for women in Hispanic culture (Circirelli, 1993; Delgado & Tennstedt, 1997; Noelker & Bass, 1994). Delgado and Tennstedt (1997) suggested that social service and health care agencies "have developed services, expertise, and comfort with female caregivers as the beneficiaries" (p. 125). Recently, there has been renewed interest in developing caregiver support services for sons who comprise a significant, but relatively invisible, segment of the Hispanic caregiving population (Delgado & Tennstedt, 1997; Dwyer & Coward, 1991; Dwyer & Seccombe, 1991).

Caregiving among African American Elders.   Almost 30 percent of African American households provide caregiving for an elder member (National Alliance for Caregiving and American Association for Retired Persons, 1997). The strong kinship system of both blood relatives and fictive kin is one of the most important social supports to African American elders (Cox, 1995). While blood relatives are more likely to provide long-term instrumental support, friends and church members are important sources of socioemotional and short-term support (Cox, 1995; Taylor & Chatters, 1986).

Despite high levels of caregiving within African American families, Johnson and Barer (1990) found low-income African American adult children were often unable to provide instrumental support despite deep affectionate ties with parents. The demands of living on limited incomes and the devastating effects of drugs and alcohol on the low-income African American community created distractions for adult children that interfered with the time and resources needed for caregiving. In such cases, African American elders turned to formal delivery systems both out of necessity and specifically to avoid further burdening their children.

The Stresses of Caregiving

Sources of Stress in Caregiving

Lack of Reciprocity in Relationships.   One of the sources of stress in caregiving relationships regardless of the dementia status of the elder is the lack of a reciprocal relationship between caregiver and care-receiver (Call, Finch, Huck, & Kane, 1999). In normal family relationships, family members provide mutual, intergenerational support. For example, an adult child may help an elder with transportation or shopping with the expectation the elder will provide child care for his or her children. When an elder becomes ill or disabled and begins to rely on adult children or other caregivers, the mutuality of this relationship is disrupted. Adult children find themselves providing care with little expectation that the elder will be able to reciprocate. For elders with dementia, even responding with affection and gratitude toward their caregivers becomes difficult (Mittleman, Ferris, Steinberg, Shulman, Mackell, Ambinder, & Cohen, 1993).

Spousal caregivers for persons with Alzheimer's disease experience dramatic changes in the nature of the marital relationship as the disease progresses (Call et al., 1999; Cummings, 1996). In the middle and later stages of Alzheimer's disease, caregiving elders lose the support and affection once present in the relationship. The personal attraction that maintains the relationship disappears as the impaired spouse is less capable of responding to his or her partner. A lifetime of mutuality can quickly become a one-sided situation.

Social Isolation.   Spousal caregivers, especially women who are the sole caregivers of their husbands, often become socially isolated, a high-risk factor for the development of both mental and physical health problems (Moen, Robison, Dempler-McClain, 1995; Williamson & Schutz, 1993). It becomes difficult to leave the house without respite care. Elders with late stage dementia are often uncommunicative, forcing their caregivers to live in silence as well. Over half of caregivers to elders (regardless of whether or not the elder has dementia) report they have significantly less time for family and friends or have had to give up vacations, hobbies, and other important sources of socialization (National Alliance for Caregiving and the Alzheimer's Association, 1999). Even those caregivers who have support systems are restricted from accessing them because of the demands of caregiving.

Dynamics of the Adult Child/Parent Relationship.   Caring for an older parent may revive long-standing problems in the relationship between adult children and their parents exacerbating an already demanding situation (Adamson, Feinauer, Lund, & Caserta, 1992). Cox and Dooley (1996) identified the quality of the relationship between caregiver and care-receiver as one of the most important determinants of the perception of stress associated with the caregiving arrangement. Adult children (or spouses) who have an open and mutually affectionate relationship with the care-receiver prior to the illness or disability are less likely to experience emotional stress or to consider the caregiving responsibilities to be a burden (Cox & Dooley, 1996).

The ability to individuate oneself from parents and establish a healthy level of emotional and instrumental independence is part of the developmental challenge associated with adolescence and young adulthood (Erikson, 1963). Adult children who remain emotionally or financially dependent on parents well into adulthood have great difficulty with assuming caregiving responsibilities (Rabin, Bressler, & Prager, 1993). Psychologically they find it difficult to accept the reality that parents now depend on them rather than being the ultimate source of support and comfort for them. Blenkner (1965) proposed that achieving "filial" maturity is an important challenge in achieving true adulthood. Filial maturity requires that adult children be able to see a parent as an individual with assets and faults that go beyond their role as caregivers of their children. When adult children have not achieved filial maturity or subconsciously cannot accept the reality that parents may need their assistance, caregiving can be perceived as a serious burden on the adult child.

Characteristics of the Care-Receiver. The degree of disability of the care-receiver is a crucial determinant of which caregivers experience the greatest amount of stress. When caregivers providing care for elders with dementia are compared with caregivers to elders who do not have dementia, the differences are striking. Caregivers to elders with dementia are more likely to report significant restrictions on personal time, a greater incidence of mental and physical illness, greater strains on other family relationships, and greater need to adjust employment than other caregivers (Adamson et al., 1992; Tennstedt, 1999). This stress is directly related to the challenges required to manage the disturbing behaviors that often accompany Alzheimer's disease and other dementia, such as wandering, hitting, or verbal abuse (Braithwaite, 1996; Tennstedt, 1999).

Caregivers of elders who are depressed experience greater stress than caregivers of elders who are not depressed (Adamson et al., 1992). It is not surprising that watching a loved one withdraw into the lonely world of depression would elicit a deep emotional response on the part of the caregiver. A caregiver's psychological reaction to the depressed elder's sadness, lethargy, and loss of interest in most activities that accompanies depression appears to spill over onto the family of the caregiver as well, creating tensions in the marital and familial relationships of the caregiver (Adamson et al., 1992).

Elders who cannot accept care even in the face of disability as well as those elders who relinquish their independence too quickly increase a caregiver's perception of stress (Cox & Dooley, 1996). Caregivers and care-receivers are more satisfied with the caregiving relationship when there is a balance between too little and too much care. Elders who consciously work to maintain even limited functional abilities and cultivate a positive attitude are less likely to become depressed and are perceived as less of a burden than those who do not (Cox & Dooley, 1996).

Depression among Caregivers

The most common psychological consequence of caregiving is depression (Braithwaite, 1996; Brody, 1990; Cox, 1995; Rosenthal, Sulman, & Marshall, 1993; Williamson & Schulz, 1993). Among caregivers for elders with dementia, depression rates have been found to be as high as 43 to 52 percent, nearly three times the rates observed in non-caregivers of the same age (Gallagher, Rose, Lovett, & Thompson, 1989; Tennstedt, 1999; Toseland & Rossiter, 1996). Even among caregivers to elders who do not have dementia, depression rates are twice those of non-caregiving counterparts (National Alliance for Caregiving and the Alzheimer's Association, 1999). Depression results from the caregivers' sense of burden, social isolation, and self-blame that they are not doing all they could be for the care-receiver, combined with physical and emotional exhaustion.

The incidence of depression appears to be higher among white caregivers than among caregivers of color (Tennstedt, 1999). Caregivers of color may be better adjusted to caregiving as an expected responsibility that accompanies adulthood, seeing those tasks as an obligation or expectation rather than as a burden (Cox, 1995; Henrichsen & Ramirez, 1992; Richardson & Sistler, 1999). This group of caregivers expresses a greater level of satisfaction and considers caring for an older relative to be less of an intrusion on their personal lives than their white counterparts do (Henrichsen & Ramirez, 1992). African American caregivers have often developed more extensive kinship networks than white caregivers, giving them access to a greater number of informal helpers (Chatters & Taylor, 1989; Chatters, Taylor, & Jackson, 1985, 1986).

When depression was observed in Hispanic and African American caregivers, it was most often associated with a caregiver's feelings of inadequacy or incompetence in the role of caregiver, rather than because of the restrictions on personal time (Cox, 1995). These caregivers felt they could be doing a better job if they had more time or more financial resources to bring to the caregiving situation. It is dangerous to assume that ethnicity by itself is a buffer against the stresses of caregiving. Some of the differences observed may well be the result of a failure to use culturally sensitive measures to determine if caregivers are depressed. Caregivers of color are more likely to express depression somatically than emotionally by developing health problems not seen as directly related to the demands of caregiving (Cox, 1995).

Moderators of Caregiver Stress

A substantial number of caregivers report minimal negative effects associated with caregiving and describe their caregiving experience in very positive terms (McKinlay, Crawford, & Tennstedt, 1995; National Alliance for Caregiving and the Alzheimer's Association, 1999). Caregiving may provide adult children or spouses a deeply rewarding sense of purpose. The services provided to a loved one can be a source of great pride, even in previously stormy relationships. The opportunity to resolve lifelong conflicts or unfinished business can be a cathartic experience for both caregiver and care-receiver.

Emotional Support.   Those caregivers who do not report caregiving as a stressful experience have found successful ways to moderate the effects of stress on both their personal lives and their relationship with the care-receiver. Caregivers who have support systems, including spouses, partners, or friends, experience lower levels of stress. Two-thirds of respondents in the National Alliance for Caregiving and American Association for Retired Persons Survey (1997) cited talking with friends or relatives as an important way to cope with the caregiving experience, while less than 16 percent relied on professional mental health counseling. Maintaining a close connection to intimates and family members appears to buffer the frustrations and demands of being a caregiver more effectively than the support afforded by professional counseling.

Instrumental Support.   In addition to using family and friends, caregivers who expressed lower levels of stress seemed better able to identify those situations in which caregiving responsibilities exceeded their abilities and to ask for help in those situations (Szabo & Strang, 1999; Tennstedt, 1999). Using adult day health services or occasional respite care offered caregivers the opportunity to prevent stress from reaching crisis levels, avoiding the endangerment of the health and well-being of both caregiver and care-receiver. The instrumental support offered by either family members or formal caregiving services created a sense of control in caregivers that mediated feelings of being overburdened and overwhelmed.

Other Moderating Factors.   Prayer was identified by three-quarters of all caregivers in the National Alliance for Caregiving/American Association for Retired Persons Study (1997) as a coping strategy. As presented in Chapter 10, recognizing and mobilizing strategies that appeal to an elder's spirituality may also be important to the caregivers of those elders. Another third of caregivers identified exercise or hobbies as activities that helped their mental and physical health—good examples of protecting their personal time in the face of caregiving responsibilities. Any activity that allows a caregiver to disengage from the intensity of the caregiving responsibilities for even a brief time appears helpful.

Social Work Interventions with Caregivers

Caregiver Support Groups

Caregiving for an elder as a friend, family member, or spouse can be a rewarding but extremely challenging responsibility. Not only is the actual work of providing care physically and emotionally difficult, caregivers face the additional risk of becoming socially isolated as caregiving demands more and more of their time. Caregiver support groups offer members an opportunity to talk with others about the stresses involved in caregiving and to learn new ways to manage its multiple demands.

The Goals of a Caregiver Support Group.   The primary purpose of caregiver support groups is to sustain the caregiver, offering both emotional support and concrete suggestions for making caregiving tasks more efficient and rewarding. What caregivers often need is for others to acknowledge that mixed feelings about the caregiving role are legitimate. While a caregiver may be very willing to assume the daily tasks of personal care, housekeeping, and financial management for an elder, he or she may also be haunted by guilt about neglecting their own families and by feelings of inadequacy about the job they are doing. Support groups can help its members normalize these feelings and find ways to acknowledge and express them. Novices to the caregiving experience may be totally overwhelmed and not know where to begin to learn about resources or learn personal care skills. Support groups can help a new caregiver sift through the barrage of new demands on their time and regain control of their lives.

Support groups can also assist the caregiver in preventing, managing, or minimizing the problematic behaviors of care-receivers. Mittleman and associates (1993) found that when caregivers had a better understanding of the disruptive behaviors associated with dementia and learned ways to manage those behaviors in the caregiver situation, the care-receiver not only received better care but also was less likely to be institutionalized.

Group Membership.   The common bond between members of caregiver support groups is the caregiver experience. However, the challenges facing caregivers of elders with dementia appear to be more stressful, and it may be more beneficial to group members to share caregiving responsibilities for similar kinds of care-receivers (Adamson et al., 1992; Tennstedt, 1999). Elders without dementia can still communicate with caregivers and remain active participants in their own caregiving, even with severe physical disabilities. Care-receivers actually feel better about the caregiving experience when they can maintain as much independence as possible and feel they can show their gratitude to caregivers (Cox & Dooley, 1996). On the contrary, elders in the middle and late stages of dementia have often lost the ability to communicate much other than basic needs making caregiving a less mutually interactive experience. The realities of caring for these two groups will be very different. Developing different groups for each set of caregivers may be a more effective way of addressing their unique needs. The support system developed within the caregiver group may serve as a valuable resource to members after the termination of the group experience.

Caregiver groups should also be sensitive to the specific cultural concerns of caregivers (Cox, 1995). Caregivers of color may find it too uncomfortable to talk about family problems outside of their racial or ethnic group, especially if there are unique cultural expectations and traditions. When elder parents are immigrants or deeply influenced by traditional norms of filial obligation, adult children may be embarrassed to discuss their feelings with others, who they feel could not understand. Culturally specific groups are also recommended for caregivers and their families who prefer to speak in their native languages. The time and effort required to translate back and forth between English and another language can seriously discourage a group member from fully participating in the support group.

Support Group Activities.   Support groups can be organized around specific topics, such as time management, personal care skills, resolving conflict, or accessing formal resources to supplement informal caregiving. These groups are primarily psychoeducational, offering a combination of personal emotional support and specific information of use to caregivers. Other support groups are less structured, focusing on group members' needs to talk about the trials and tribulations of caregiving. This approach appeals to caregivers who feel in command of the practical realities of caregiving but still struggle with emotional chaos associated with caring for an elder. Regardless of the exact focus of a caregiver support group, it is essential that group members be given adequate time to talk to each other, to have the opportunity to gain the support and empathy of others who share their experience.

Role of the Leader.   The leader of a caregiver support group assumes a variety of roles. The leader serves in an educational capacity particularly when caregivers need information about the course of conditions, such as Alzheimer's disease, a stroke, or heart disease. Caregivers may have unrealistic ideas about how little or how much improvement they can expect in the care-receiver's condition. Newly designated caregivers are often very eager for more information about exactly what they and the care-receiver will face in the future. The group leader also serves as both a broker and advocate for members of the group. Group members often have difficulty accessing formal support services or in coordinating the various aspects of caregiving. The group leader can intervene on behalf of group members either through directly working with other support services or empowering the group member to be more assertive in procuring those services.

The most important role for the group leader is that of supporter and, when necessary, counselor. Sharing the frustrations of caregiving often exposes lifelong conflicts between the caregiver and care-receiver that need to be addressed early in the caregiving experience. Caring for an elder parent who was an abusive parent or is highly critical and demanding is extremely stressful. Helping caregivers recognize interpersonal problems that are compounding the complexities of the caregiving relationship can help members to resolve those issues before they endanger the well-being of both caregiver and care-receiver.

Improving the Caregiver/Care-Receiver Relationship

Caregivers who have long-standing conflicts with the care-receiver may benefit from individual counseling aimed at improving the relationship. This can include couples work, discussed earlier in this chapter, as well as supportive counseling for the adult child whose conflicts with an aging parent are frustrating the caregiving experience.

The Spousal or Partner Relationship. The changing roles and expectations of spousal or partner relationships were discussed earlier in this chapter but have particular relevance when one member of the couple becomes the caregiver for the other. The resulting imbalance in the relationship and the sociobehavioral changes that accompany conditions such as Alzheimer's disease or a stroke can create serious problems in long lasting relationships (Flosheim & Herr, 1990). Mittleman and associates (1993) observed that the strength of the affectionate attachment between members of a couple did not change even in advanced cases of dementia but rather caregivers were confused and frightened about how the disease had changed their spouses. Supportive counseling with the caregiver and care-receiver, if possible, can help to identify how the relationship has changed, what remains the same, and how each member must adapt to those changes to maintain the stability of the relationship.

Child/Parent Relationships. Among adult child caregivers, the quality of the relationship between child and parent is one of the most important predictors of stress in the caregiving relationship (Adamson et al., 1992; Cox & Dooley, 1996; Tennstedt, 1999). This quality is affected by the adult child's ability to achieve "filial maturity" and a healthy level of emotional and instrumental independence. For adult children who have not individuated from their parents or who have become emotionally estranged as adults, individual or family counseling may be indicated. Working on the quality of the child/parent relationship has the benefits of improving the caregiving experience for both parties and helping adult children and parents resolve lifelong conflicts while they still have the opportunity. Adult children may need permission from a social worker to admit to this unfinished business. When the concerns of care-receiver seem tantamount, the social worker may need to help the adult child articulate the emotional obstacles that are affecting the quality of the relationship.

Promoting Self-Care for the Caregiver

The social worker can be instrumental in encouraging caregivers to take care of themselves. The stress caregivers experience in the caregiving relationship is a major theme in this chapter. In the process of providing top quality care to an impaired elder, caregivers often neglect their own well-being. Depression, physical illness, and strained family relationships have been identified as all too common problems among caregivers. Caregivers may feel guilty even voicing their need for some personal time or asking others to provide respite care for the care-receiver.

Caregivers who can realistically assess their abilities to provide caregiving services and ask for help when they need it are much more likely to feel a sense of control and mastery over the caregiving situation, an important factor in a

FIGURE 12.1   *Ten Tips for Family Caregivers*

- Choose to take charge of your life, and don't let your loved one's illness or disability always take center stage.
- Remember to be good to yourself. Love, honor, and value yourself. You're doing a very hard job and you deserve some quality time, just for you.
- Watch out for signs of depression and don't delay in getting professional help when you need it.
- When people offer to help, accept the offer and suggest specific things that they can do.
- Educate yourself about your loved one's condition. Information is empowering.
- There's a difference between caring and doing. Be open to technologies and ideas that promote your loved one's independence.
- Trust your instincts. Most of the time they'll lead you in the right direction.
- Grieve for your losses and then allow yourself to dream new dreams.
- Stand up for your rights as a caregiver and a citizen.
- Seek support from other caregivers. There is great strength in knowing you are not alone.

Source: Reprinted from "Ten Tips for Family Caregivers" with permission of the National Family Caregivers Association, Kensington, MD, the nation's only organization for all family caregivers. 1-800-896-3650; www.nfcacares.org.

caregiver's perception of personal well-being (Szabo & Strang, 1999). In addition to the ability to identify personal resources and mobilize other caregiver support, a sense of control includes a willingness and ability to anticipate future demands on the caregiving relationship and to take corrective action to prevent the caregiving situation from spiraling out of control. Caregivers who do not become martyred to the cause of caregiving have learned how to maintain their own personal sense of well-being.

The process of self-care is more than just taking time to pray, exercise, or spend time away from the care-receiver. It is also a frame of mind that the social worker can help the caregiver develop. It means placing one's caregiving responsibilities within a larger context of one's life, being receptive to help from others, and feeling good about one's performance as a caregiver. While it is the professional responsibility of the social worker to offer praise and support to the caregiver, the caregiver must also be willing to accept and internalize the positive feedback. The National Family Caregivers Association has developed a list of tips for family caregivers which appears in Figure 12.1. These tips illustrate the importance of a caregiver's adopting both a sense of personal empowerment about the caregiving experience and continuously engaging in positive self-talk.

Summary

Family and friends are among the most important support systems available to an elder who is facing the daily challenges of living with a disability or illness. For spouses and partners who have raised children together, the aging process brings a need to redefine the couple relationship in terms of a personal relationship rather than through the lens of seeing one's life partner as primarily a parent. Retirement challenges couples not only to find ways to live within limited financial means but also to find mutually satisfying ways to occupy a newly available cache of leisure time. As couples move into middle and late old age, they may also face changing dependency needs in which one member will become a caregiver for another, a challenge to a lifetime of prescribed roles and responsibilities. The challenge to the social worker includes helping older couples manage loss, create opportunities to develop new spheres of mastery and control, and maintain personal identity in the face of changing cognitive and physical abilities. Through marital life review, communication skills training, and cognitive-behavioral techniques, couples can find new ways to relate to each other with the goal of making the later years of marriage among the most satisfying.

The family meeting is one technique for helping families not only to address the long-term care decisions that must be made for an aging family member but also to recognize and resolve lifelong family conflicts that endanger good family functioning. For many family members, this decision-making process will involve assuming the role of a family caregiver, one of the most difficult (and oftentimes rewarding) tasks a family will ever face. The creation of family caregiver support groups, the provision of supportive counseling that focuses on the relationship between the caregiver and care-receiver, and the promotion of caregiver self-care are offered as social work interventions to help relieve the stress inherent in many caregiving relationships.

Check Out These Websites!

1. www.caregivers.com   This site is a helpful place to begin for new caregivers as well as professionals who need to find access to information about financing caregiving services, linking with on-line caregiver support groups, purchasing products helpful in providing personal care to elders, and a variety of other topics. The site also provides links to the personal stories of family caregivers who have found ways to balance the personal demands of caregiving for an elder with raising a family of their own.

2. www.nfcacares.org   Sponsored by the National Family Caregivers Association (NFCA), this site is directed to family caregivers rather than to a professional audience. The site provides tips for family caregivers, news and information about financing caregiving, and details about joining NFCA. The organization has a positive and empowering approach to supporting family caregivers and can be a powerful on-line support for caregivers.

3. www.tcaging.org   This site is sponsored by the Metropolitan Area Agency on Aging of Minneapolis/St. Paul, MN. It offers numerous pages directed at helping caregivers: preparation for the caregiving experience, long-distance caregiving, and an on-line pep talk for caregivers about taking care of themselves. The site offers links to other useful sites on caregiving.

4. www.aoa.dhhs.gov/caregivers/FamCare.html   A detailed description of the National Alliance for Caregiving and American Association for Retired Persons 1997 study is available at this site in the text of a paper by Sharon Tennstedt entitled "Family Caregiving in an Aging Society." The paper includes the tabular results of the survey as well as an extensive bibliography on the subject of family caregiving.

References

Adamson, D., Feinauer, L., Lund, D., & Caserta, M. (1992). Factors affecting marital happiness of caregivers of the elderly in multigenerational families. *The American Journal of Family Therapy, 20*(1), 62–70.

Aldous, J. (1994). Someone to watch over me: Family responsibilities and their realization across family lives. In E. Kahana, D. Biegel, & M. Wykle (Eds.), *Family caregiving across the lifespan* (pp. 42–68). Thousand Oaks, CA: Sage.

Arean, P. A., Perri, M. G., Nezu, A. M., Schein, R. L., Christopher, F., & Joseph, T. X. (1993). Comparative effectiveness of social problem-solving therapy and reminiscence therapy as treatments for depression in older adults. *Journal of Consulting and Clinical Psychology, 61*(6), 1003–1010.

Arno, P. S., Levine, C., & Memmott, M. M. (1999). The economic value of informal caregiving. *Health Affairs, 18*(2), 182–188.

Blenkner, M. (1965). Social work and family relationships in later life with some thoughts on filial maturity. In E. Shanas & G. Streib (Eds.), *Social structure and the family: Generational relations* (pp. 40–59). Englewood Cliffs, NJ: Prentice-Hall.

Bould, S. (1997). Women and caregivers for the elderly. In J. M. Coyle (Ed.), *Handbook on women and aging* (pp. 430–442). Westport, CT: Greenwood Press.

Braithwaite, V. (1996). Understanding stress in informal caregiving. *Research on Aging 18*(2), 139–174.

Brody, E. M. (1990). *Women in the middle: Their parent-care years.* New York: Springer.

Call, K. T., Finch, M. A., Huck, S. M., & Kane, R. A. (1999). Caregiver burden from a social exchange perspective: Caring for older people after hospital discharge. *Journal of Marriage and the Family, 61,* 688–699.

Chatters, L. M., & Taylor, R. J. (1989). Age differences in religious participation among black adults. *Journal of Gerontology: Social Sciences, 44,* S183–S189.

Chatters, L. M., Taylor, R. J., & Jackson, J. S. (1985). Size and composition of the informal helper networks of elderly blacks. *Journal of Gerontology, 40,* 605–614.

Chatters, L. M., Taylor, R. J., & Jackson, J. S. (1986). Aged blacks' choice for an informal helper network. *Journal of Gerontology, 41,* 94–100.

Choi, N. G. (1999). Living arrangements and household compositions of elderly couples and singles: A comparison of Hispanics and blacks. *Journal of Gerontological Social Work, 31*(1/2), 41–61.

Circirelli, V. G. (1993). Attachment and obligation as daughters' motives for caregiving behavior and subsequent effect on subjective burden. *Psychology and Aging, 8,* 144–155.

Clark, M., & Huttlinger, K. (1998). Elder care among Mexican American families. *Clinical Nursing Research, 7*(1), 64–81.

Cohler, B. J. (1997). Fathers, daughters, and caregiving perspectives from psychoanalysis and life-course social science. In J. M. Coyle (Ed.), *Handbook on women and aging* (pp. 443–464). Westport, CT: Greenwood Press.

Cox, C. (1995). Meeting the mental health needs of the caregiver: The impact of Alzheimer's disease on Hispanic and African American families. In D. K. Padgett (Ed.), *Handbook of ethnicity, aging, and mental health* (pp. 265–283). Westport, CT: Greenwood Press.

Cox, E. O., & Dooley, A. C. (1996). Care-receivers' perception of their role in the care process. *Journal of Gerontological Social Work, 26*(1/2), 133–152.

Cummings, S. M. (1996). Spousal caregivers of early stage Alzheimer's patients: A psychoeducational support group model. *Journal of Gerontological Social Work, 26*(3/4), 83–98.

Delgado, M., & Tennstedt, S. (1997). Puerto Rican sons as primary caregivers of elderly parents. *Social Work, 42*(2), 125–134.

Doty, P. (1986). Family care of the elderly: The role of public policy. *Milbank Memorial Fund Quarterly, 64*, 34–75.

Dwyer, J. W., & Coward, R. T. (1991). A multivariate comparison of the involvement of adult sons versus daughters in the care of impaired parents. *Journal of Gerontology, 46*, S259–S269.

Dwyer, J. W., & Seecombe, K. (1991). Elder care as family labor: The influence of gender and family position. *Journal of Family Issues, 12*, 229–247.

Erikson, E. (1963). *Childhood and society* (2nd ed.). New York: Norton.

Flosheim, M. J., & Herr, J. J. (1990). Family counseling with elders. *Generations, 14*(1), 40–42.

Gallagher, D., Rose, J., Lovett, S., & Thompson, L. W. (1989). Prevalance of depression in family caregivers. *The Gerontologist, 29*(4), 449–456.

Genevay, B. (1990). A summit conference model of brief therapy. *Generations, 14*(1), 58–60.

Gilligan, C. (1982). *In a different voice: Psychological theory and women's development.* Cambridge, MA: Harvard University Press.

Gotlib, I. H., & Beach, S. R. H. (1995). A marital/family discord model of depression: Implications for therapeutic intervention. In N. S. Jacobson & A. S. Gurman (Eds.), *Clinical handbook of couple therapy* (pp. 411–436). New York: Guilford.

Hargrave, T. D. (1994). Using video life review with older adults. *Journal of Family Therapy, 16*, 259–268.

Henrichsen, G. A., & Ramirez, M. (1992). Black and white dementia caregivers: A comparison of their adaptation, adjustment, and service utilization. *The Gerontologist, 32*, 375–381.

Johnson, C., & Barer, B. (1990). Family networks among older inner-city African Americans. *The Gerontologist, 30*, 726–733.

Kane, R. A., & Penrod, J. D. (1995). *Family caregiving in an aging society: Policy perspectives.* Thousand Oaks, CA: Sage.

Lugalia, T. A. (1997). *Marital status and living arrangements: March 1997.* U.S. Bureau of the Census, Series P20–506. Washington, DC: U.S. Government Printing Office.

Mackey, R. A., O'Brien, B. A., & Mackey, E. F. (1997). *Gay and lesbian couples: Voices from lasting relationships.* Westport, CT: Praeger.

McKinlay, J. B., Crawford, S., & Tennstedt, S. (1995). The everyday impacts of providing care to dependent elders and their consequences for the care recipients. *Journal of Aging and Health, 7*(4), 497–528.

Merrill, D. M. (1997). *Caring for elderly parents: Juggling work, family, and caregiving in middle- and working-class families.* Westport, CT: Auburn House.

Mittleman, M. S., Ferris, S. H., Steinberg, G., Shulman, E., Mackell, J. A., Ambinder, A., & Cohen, J. (1993). An intervention that delays institutionalization of Alzheimer's disease patients: Treatment of spouse caregivers. *The Gerontologist, 33*(6), 730–740.

Moberg, P. J., & Lazarus, L. W. (1990). Psychotherapy of depression in the elderly. *Psychiatric Annals, 20*(2), 92–96.

Moen, P., Robison, J., & Dempler-McClain, D. (1995). Caregiving and women's well- being: A life course approach. *Journal of Health and Social Behavior, 36*, 259–273.

Montgomery, R. (1992). Gender differences in patterns of child-parent caregiving relationships. In J. Dwyer & R. Coward (Eds.), *Gender, families, and elder care* (pp. 65–83). Newbury Park, CA: Sage.

National Alliance for Caregiving and the Alzheimer's Association. (1999). *Who cares? Families caring for persons with Alzheimer's disease.* Bethesda, MD: Author.

National Alliance for Caregiving and American Association for Retired Persons. (1997). *Family caregiving in the U.S.: Findings from a national survey.* Bethesda, MD: Author.

National Family Caregivers Association. (1999). *Ten tips for family caregivers.* Kensington, MD: National Family Caregivers Association. Available at http://www. nfcacares.org/tentipsf.html.

Neidhardt, E. R., & Allen, J. A. (1993). *Family therapy with the elderly.* Newbury Park, CA: Sage.

Nichols, W. C. (1996). *Treating people in families: An integrative framework.* New York: Guilford.

Noelker, L. S., & Bass, D. M. (1994). Relationships between the frail elderly's informal and formal helpers. In E. Kahana, D. E. Biegel, & M. L. Wykle (Eds.), *Family caregiving across the lifespan* (pp. 356–381). Thousand Oaks, CA: Sage.

Prince, S. E., & Jacobsen, N. S. (1995). Couple and family therapy for depression. In E. E. Beckham & W. R. Leber (Eds.), *Handbook of depression* (2nd ed., pp. 404–424). New York: Guilford.

Rabin, C., Bressler, Y., & Prager, E. (1993). Caregiver burden and personal authority: Differentiation and connection in care for an elder parent. *American Journal of Family Therapy, 21*(1), 27–39.

Richardson, R. C., & Sistler, A. B. (1999). The well-being of elderly black caregivers and noncaregivers: A preliminary study. *Journal of Gerontological Social Work, 31*(1/2), 109–117.

Rosenthal, C. J., Sulman, J., & Marshall, V. W. (1993). Depressive symptoms in family caregivers of long-stay patients. *The Gerontologist, 33*(2), 249–257.

Sandberg, J. G., & Harper, J. M. (1999). Depression in mature marriages: Impact and implications for marital therapy. *Journal of Marital and Family Therapy, 25*(3), 393–406.

Szabo, V., & Strang, V. R. (1999). Experiencing control in caregiving. *Journal of Nursing Scholarship, 31*(1), 71–75.

Taylor, R., & Chatters, L. (1986). Patterns of informal support to elderly black adults: Family, friends, and church members. *Social Work, 32*, 432–438.

Tennstedt, S. (1999). *Family caregiving in an aging society.* Paper presented at the U. S. Administration on Aging Symposium: Longevity in the New American Century, Baltimore, MD, March 29, 1999. Available at http://aoa.dhhs.gov/caregivers/FamCare.html.

Toseland, R. W., & Rossiter, C. M. (1996). Social work practice with family caregivers of frail older persons. In M. J. Holosko & M. D. Feit (Eds.), *Social work practice with the elderly* (2nd ed., pp. 299–320). Toronto: Canadian Scholars Press.

U.S. Bureau of the Census. (1996). *Projections of the number of households and families in the United States: 1995–2010* by Jennifer C. Day, Current Population Reports, P25–1129. Washington, DC: U.S. Government Printing Office.

Weeks, G. R., & Hof, L. (1995). *Integrative solutions: Treating common problems in couples therapy.* New York: Brunner/Mazel.

Williamson, G. M., & Schulz, R. (1993). Coping with specific stressors in Alzheimer's caregiving. *The Gerontologist, 33*(6), 747–755.

Wolinsky, M. A. (1990). *A heart of wisdom: Marital counseling with older and elderly couples.* New York: Brunner/Mazel.

13

Dying, Bereavement, and Advance Directives

Death and Dying as Part of Gerontological Social Work

Coming face-to-face with the reality of dying and bereavement is an unescapable part of social work with elders and one of the most challenging for both novice and experienced professionals. Losing a client to death or helping an elder or family cope with the loss of a loved one is a constant reminder of the way death will touch everyone's life, if not now, then certainly in the future. Few will be spared the pain of losing a parent, spouse or partner, or perhaps even a child. Death anxiety was discussed in Chapter 1 as one of the significant challenges of working with elders. A social worker's fear of his or her own death or that of a loved one can create debilitating levels of discomfort and many times discourages social workers from even considering social work with elders.

This chapter explores the process of dying and bereavement. It begins with a description of the physical, psychosocial, and spiritual needs of elders who are dying. Once death occurs, the social worker plays an important role in facilitating the process of bereavement, the period of grief and mourning that follows for those who have lost a loved one. Within this context, the hospice movement is discussed as a thoughtful and humane approach to death with dignity not only for elders but also for dying persons of all ages. Advance directives, written instructions to others about an elder's wishes for end-of-life treatment decisions, are presented in the next section of the chapter as one means to empower elders in affecting the quality of life. The chapter concludes with a frank discussion of the ethical challenges that face the social worker in dealing with death, including the controversies about the allocation of scarce health care resources to frail elders and the issue of physician-assisted suicide. The role of the social worker in dying and bereavement is highlighted throughout the chapter, including the importance of self-care for the social worker confronting these issues.

The Process of Dying

The Meaning of Death to Elders

While an individual elder's reaction to his or her own impending death or that of a loved one is just as painful and disconcerting as death is to one of any age, there are indications that elders experience far less denial about the reality of death than other age groups. The developmental task of achieving ego integrity versus ego despair associated with old age requires accepting one's life as important and meaningful as one moves closer to death, according to Erikson (1963). As elders face the biopsychosocial challenges of aging, they inevitably think about their own death. They become acutely aware of the passage of time as their children grow up and start their own families, friends and family members die, and they confront the limitations of declining physical health. The privately or professionally directed process of life review is intended to help elders address unfinished business and find ways to make peace with themselves about their lives. Death does not come as a surprise to elders. Most have thought about it for a long time.

Unfortunately, when elders most want to talk about death and their feelings about it, professionals and family members are more likely to brush aside their concerns with well-meaning (but destructive) comments such as "you have a long time ahead of you" or "you will probably live to be 100!" With many sensitive emotional issues dealt with in the social work profession, such as family violence, substance abuse, or mental illness, the professional often needs to prod the client to address the issues. With issues surrounding death and dying, often the elder wants to talk about it and the helping professional may resist (Chirchin, Ferster, & Gordon, 1994).

Elders may be less fearful of death for two reasons. First, elders are able to approach their own death from the perspective of having lived much of the developmental life span (Cook & Oltjenbruns, 1998; Kalish, 1985). They have had the opportunities and challenges of all of the life stages from childhood through adulthood. They have had the chance to fall in love, raise a family, or pursue a career. Anticipating death does not mean centering on a life cut short before it had a chance to develop. Second, adults become increasingly more socialized to death as they grow older (Kalish, 1985; Steeves & Kahn, 1999). Elders have watched others their own age die or have buried family and friends. As they become more familiar with death, they are more likely to accept it as a natural part of the life cycle. It needs to be emphasized here that accepting death is not synonymous with becoming immune to its devastating emotional consequences, but rather accepting the reality that death is no longer something that only happens to others.

Some elders may actual welcome death rather than fear it (Silverman & Klass, 1996). Those elders who face chronic health problems or who have lost their spouses or partners may feel that quantity of life is no gift without quality. Battling physical limitations or struggling with loneliness may deplete an elder's energy for life. While these elders may never consider ending their own lives, they may wish that death would come sooner rather than later. Even among elders who are not depressed or ill, there may be a common feeling of "I am ready to go anytime." They may be deeply satisfied with their lives and remain actively engaged in social activities but feel psychologically prepared to die.

The Needs of Dying Elders

Physical Needs.   While elders may or may not be better prepared for the inevitability of death, a fear of prolonged physical discomfort or pain is perhaps the most frightening part of anticipating death. Dying persons need to know that everything is being done to manage pain (Cook & Oltjenbruns, 1998; Olson, 1997). It is only since the advent of the hospice movement (to be discussed later in this chapter) that the importance of managing a dying person's pain has been directly and publicly addressed. Society's fears about promoting drug addiction by administering too much pain medication seems particularly ironic when a person suffers from a terminal condition.

Despite adjustments they have made to the physical changes accompanying the aging process, dying elders continue to be concerned about body image and the way others view them (Cook & Oltjenbruns, 1998; Olson, 1997). One of the important aspects of promoting death with dignity is to help an elder maintain good personal hygiene and an acceptable appearance for as long as possible. Elders feel better when they have clean bodies and clothes and are not worried about offending others with their appearance.

Emotional and Psychological Needs.   The emotional and psychological needs of the dying elder are as important as physical needs. They need to maintain some sense of mastery and control over their lives for as long as possible (Cook & Oltjenbruns, 1998). This can be accomplished by including the elder in end-of-life treatment choices through advance directives or in decision making about their daily care, if they are physically and cognitively capable of participating. Decisions as simple as what to eat or wear or what items they want to have by their bedside can be important ways for elders to retain even a small sense of independence and continuing involvement in their care.

Dying elders need an opportunity to talk about their impending death in an atmosphere that is safe and accepting of the wide array of emotions they may be feeling. Accepting the reality of dying is a process of grieving in which the elder may feel sadness, anger, resentment, fear, or panic (Bowlby, 1980; Freeman & Ward, 1998; Steeves & Kahn, 1999). In essence, an elder is grieving the loss of life and opportunities, separation from loved ones, and the loss of power over life events in much the same way that others will grieve for him or her after death. Elders may engage in a process of life review and reminiscence that helps them to find meaning in their lives in their final days. This life review may prompt elders to want the chance to "settle emotional accounts" with family or friends with whom they have unfinished business.

Elders also need time to adjust to the reality that they are dying—a process that usually involves a number of stages of acceptance (Bowlby, 1980; Kubler-

Ross, 1969; Pattison, 1977). Initially, dying persons are shocked or numbed by the news of a terminal diagnosis, followed by a period of emotional confusion before reaching a true realization of what it means to them to be dying. However, not all persons go through identifiable stages, and there is no evidence that going through a series of stages is inherently necessary to come to a healthy acceptance of death (Worden, 1991). Individuals may also vacillate between stages or work through them in a different sequence. Stage theories of grief and their limitations are discussed later in this chapter.

Social Needs.   Dying elders need to remain connected to family and friends despite the mutual social withdrawal that often characterizes the dying process. Friends and family may be uncomfortable with the dying person and withdraw as part of the process of preparing for grief. Elders may feel less and less like being around others due to the ravages of an illness or their own grieving process. When parties withdraw from each other, both are robbed of the importance of maintaining mutual social support. Elders need to see their children, grandchildren, nieces, and nephews as reminders that a part of them will live on in the next generation.

Elders who remain physically and cognitively able often benefit from support groups of other dying persons, who are experiencing the same fears and concerns. In Chapter 9, the important benefits of group membership for elders was discussed in detail, and the positive attributes of socialization may be particularly important to elders as they face death.

Spiritual Needs.   Even if they have not been deeply religious or spiritual throughout their lives, death is often a time when elders want to put their spiritual houses in order through prayer, meditation, or spiritual counseling. Access to a spiritual advisor of their choice can be a great source of comfort to elders and their families. Struggling with the meaning of life, even in its final days, is an important part of reaching a true acceptance of death.

The Role of the Social Worker in the Dying Process

Providing Emotional Support

A social worker's most apparent role for elders and their families in the dying process is to provide emotional support. Elders and family members need to be able to talk openly about the range of feelings that accompany the growing realization that someone is dying. These emotions can be frightening and intense. For example, it is not uncommon for a relative of a dying person to become extremely angry at the dying person, blaming him or her for not seeking medical treatment earlier or for persisting in self-destructive behavior, such as heavy smoking or drinking. This intense anger may seem incongruous with the sadness and deep affection a family member really feels for a dying elder. Elders may also lash out at family caregivers, which may seem alarmingly ungrateful. The emotional roller coaster that accompanies the dying process is unpredictable and disconcerting to both an elder and the family support system.

Elders and their family members need to be given permission to talk about death. At times, family members may have difficulty even saying the word much less discussing it openly with the elder who is dying. A mutual avoidance of a direct discussion of death can deprive both parties of important emotional business that needs to be addressed while there is still time.

Advocating on Behalf of the Elder and Family

A dying elder and his or her family may be too emotionally distraught to play an active role in advocating on their own behalf with health care providers. Social workers can play an important role in representing the family to other professionals and being more assertive in making sure that health care providers are sensitive to and understand the needs of the elder and family members. For example, if a family would like to pursue hospice arrangements, but the physician has not yet suggested it, it may be necessary to bring the issue to the attention of health care providers as well as to empower the family to bring it up even if the physician does not. Family members or the elder may be hesitant to question the course of treatment out of deference to the physician. While social workers need to respect the professional expertise of health care providers, elders and their families have the right to input regarding treatment decisions when possible.

Providing Information

Another important part of advocating for elders and family members is helping them gain access to information about the medical condition, treatment options, advance directives, hospice care, and support services. Social workers play an important complementary role to health care providers in helping elders and family members obtain this information. Health care providers are not unwilling to help but may be too busy to take the time to make sure elders and family members truly understand the information. In the midst of the emotional stress associated with the dying process, family members may be too totally overwhelmed to even know where to start. The social worker can be helpful in organizing what it is the family needs to know and in breaking down the overwhelming challenges into more manageable tasks. For example, if a family is considering hospice care, the social worker can provide the family with information regarding local hospice care organizations and detailing the preliminary steps in selecting this option. Likewise, if elders or a family need more detailed information about the terminal illness, the social worker can obtain simple, comprehensible information in pamphlets or brochures from the hospital or reliable sources on the internet to help the family begin to get a better understanding. Social workers should not take the place of health care providers in providing medical information, but can help families access information they need.

Self-Care for the Social Worker

Working with dying elders and their families is one of the most difficult challenges facing social workers, especially for novice professionals (Kirschberg, Neimeyer, & James, 1998). While the social worker can be helpful to the elder and family members in providing emotional support, advocating on their behalf, and providing information, no intervention techniques will actually prevent the death from occurring. Working with terminal illness on a daily basis activates one's own death anxiety and creates tremendous stress on the physical and emotional well-being of a helping professional (Kirschberg et al., 1998). It is essential that the social worker be sensitive to those indicators that the stress is becoming problematic and take measures to alleviate it before it causes physical damage or professional burnout.

Olson (1997) found that helping professionals, including nurses and social workers, who survived and thrived in working with dying patients and their families were those with a specific set of attitudes. She found those professionals who were realistic about their ability to influence the quality of life for dying patients and were grounded in a solid sense of their place in the natural world were most capable of balancing the demands of their jobs with their own emotional and physical well-being. Dying is an unpleasant but natural part of the life span. Knowing that one has provided emotional support within reasonable limits to elders and families facing death and accepting the limitations of both modern medicine and the human body to overcome illness helped these professionals to accept and process death within healthy boundaries.

Social workers working with dying and bereaved persons need to address their own personal stress. Olson (1997) emphasized the importance to social workers of maintaining their own personal physical health through adequate nutrition and exercise. Aerobics, tennis, jogging, vigorous walking, or other sports can help to relieve stress and build physical stamina, an important component of emotional stamina. Learning and using progressive muscle relaxation or getting a massage will help relieve the physical tension that develops in the course of handling stressful emotional and psychological experiences. It is important for professionals to develop their own support systems both to help process difficult emotions when necessary and to provide opportunities to talk about something other than death or dying.

Marshall and Kasman (1980) suggested professionals working with dying and bereaved persons develop their own decompression routine, a ritual in which they consciously take physical and emotional leave of their work situation. This can include a period of relaxation or meditation, a brisk walk, listening to particular music that allows the worker to disengage from thoughts of death and dying, or any other ritual that symbolizes leaving the stresses of death work behind.

Hospice workers in all professions have learned that even the most well-adjusted, experienced, seasoned professional occasionally needs time away from constant exposure to death, known as death saturation. For nurses, this has often meant switching to another unit for several weeks or months to take a break from hospice. For social workers, this may mean working with elders and their families in other aspects of gerontological social work, not so closely related to death and dying. Regardless, it is important for the social worker to know when it is time to take a break from the demands of working with terminal elder clients.

Bereavement and Grief

The long-term period in which elders and their families must learn to cope with the loss of a significant other in their lives is known as bereavement. While in bereavement, individuals process deep feelings of sadness, abandonment, or loneliness—the experience of grief. The behaviors associated with socially and culturally sanctioned rituals—beginning with funeral and burial arrangements and ending when an individual has reorganized his or her life, processed grief, and reengaged in the mainstream of life—constitute mourning.

Manifestations of Grief

Psychological and Emotional Characteristics. People who are grieving are acutely aware that what they are feeling is different from anything they have ever felt before both in its intensity and in the chaotic nature of their mood swings, leading many to believe that they are losing their minds (Schuchter & Zisook, 1993). They express a wide variety of emotions including shock, denial, sadness, anger, guilt, confusion, and depression (Freeman & Ward, 1998; Lund, Caserta, & Dimond, 1993). They may feel chronically indecisive or confused about what they should be doing. All of these symptoms are indicative of the depth of the emotional shock people suffer upon the death of a loved one. The enormity of the loss may be too overwhelming to process immediately or too painful to grasp. Grieving persons often express a difficulty with thinking clearly or trusting their own judgment. They often feel like they are on an emotional roller coaster, feeling sad at one moment and angry a few minutes later. Yet, others do not feel anything immediately, describing themselves as feeling "dead inside."

A common response for grieving persons is to have either auditory or visual experiences with the deceased. They may hear the deceased person's voice or feel they are seeing the deceased in a crowd or a room in the house. These visions may be triggered by familiar stimuli, such as hearing a car door slam about the time the deceased used to return home from work or by smelling the perfume of the deceased on personal belongings, or they may have no apparent stimulus. Some grieving persons find these experiences extremely unsettling and worry they are going crazy while others find such experiences with the deceased a source of great comfort and solace. The social worker should not dismiss these experiences as necessarily pathological, but rather explore with the elder what meaning these experiences have for him or her in the process of grieving.

Somatic Characteristics. During grief, people have distinct physical as well as emotional responses to grief. Disturbed sleep patterns, including insomnia or excessive sleepiness, are common (Reynolds et al., 1993). Grieving persons often crave sleep but are not able to stay asleep, being awakened by dreams or nightmares about the loved one. The inability to obtain restful sleep can result in a person's feeling fatigued or physically weak all the time, draining him or her of vital energy (National Hospice Organization, 1996). Disrupted sleep patterns may be accompanied by difficulty breathing or a feeling of chronic shortness of breath, exacerbating the feeling of fatigue (Cook & Oltjenbruns, 1998; Lindemann, 1944).

Some grieving persons experience the same physical symptoms exhibited by the deceased during the dying process or develop other illnesses. For example, the survivor of a person who has died of cancer may begin to worry that he or she has cancer and feel pain in the same location. This may be particularly problematic for elders who have a tendency to somatize depression rather than express it openly. There is some scientific evidence that grief suppresses the immune system, making grieving persons more susceptible to developing real physical illnesses although there is no evidence that this has a long-term effect (Irwin & Pike, 1993; Kim & Jacobs, 1993). While physical illness is more prevalent among grieving persons, it is most likely due to the combination of lack of sleep, depressed appetite, and the cumulative effect of emotional exhaustion.

Behavioral Manifestation.   Behaviorally, persons express grief by crying, withdrawing from social interactions (or overdependence on others), hostility, restlessness, and a loss of interest in social relationships or activities. These symptoms are very similar to those shown in depression, as discussed in Chapter 5. For this reason, it is very important in developing interventions for elders to make a clear distinction between symptoms associated with a serious depression and those that are manifestations of bereavement. A diagnosis of major depression is traditionally not applied to elders who have had significant losses within the preceding two years, in recognition that the symptoms are more likely indicative of bereavement.

Recently widowed elders and those experiencing the death of any loved one are always advised to delay making any major changes in their lives during the first year following the death. It takes time for a bereaved person to settle down emotionally and to reorganize his or her life. There is a strong temptation to immediately sell the family home, move far away, or do something drastic as a panicked effort to alleviate the pain of grief. Because judgment may be temporarily impaired immediately following a significant other's death, drastic and expensive moves are not recommended.

Stage Theories of Grief

Kubler-Ross's (1969) stages of grief, suppositions about a sequence of feelings and behaviors that can be observed as individuals move through the bereavement process, are perhaps the best known of popular stage theories of grief. A description of Elisabeth Kubler-Ross's stage theory appears in Figure 13.1.

FIGURE 13.1 *Kubler-Ross's Stages in the Progression of Dying*

Elisabeth Kubler-Ross is perhaps best known for her work in identifying the stages that persons go through in both accepting their own inevitable death or that of others. These stages include:

1. *Denial.* A sense of shock and numbness about the news of a death or impending death in which people often psychologically reject the idea with expressions such as "I do not believe it!" or "This cannot be happening to me!"
2. *Anger.* When the numbness wears off, dying persons or their families may respond with a deep feeling of anger. This anger may be directed at a supreme being, medical personnel, or at the dying person. "Why is God punishing me?" or "Those doctors should have found this illness sooner!" are examples of the anger felt at this stage.
3. *Bargaining.* Bargaining is characterized by the proposal of a series of "deals" with God, others, or oneself. For example, a person who promises to be a better parent or grandparent or spouse in exchange for a few more years of life is engaged in bargaining. "God, if you let me live, I will dedicate my life to caring for needy children" or "Just let me live to see my granddaughter's wedding" are typical bargaining statements.
4. *Depression.* When it becomes apparent that anger and bargaining are not going to change the inevitability of death, persons often become depressed. Death has become real, and individuals are forced to struggle with what that means. People often become very despondent or withdrawn, typical of the clinical symptoms of depression.
5. *Acceptance.* Acceptance occurs when an individual or those grieving a loss reach a level of "quiet expectation" about death (pp. 112–113). They do not become hopeless or resigned to the death, but do not struggle to fight the inevitable.

Source: Adapted from Kubler-Ross, 1969.

Bowlby's Stage Theory of Grief. Another popular stage theory was proposed by Bowlby (1980). Based on attachment theory, Bowlby suggested that humans have an instinctive need to form attachments with others and when death separates humans from the object of their attachment, a distinct set of behaviors are exhibited. In the first stage of bereavement, individuals are in shock or numbed to the point of not actually feeling much other than bewilderment and confusion. They are unable to understand the meaning and significance of the loss. In the second stage, an individual experiences a deep sense of yearning to reconnect with the deceased and may become preoccupied with belongings or photographs of the deceased. Memories of the loved one become the central focus of much of the bereaved's thought patterns both during the day and in dreams. When the bereaved fully realizes that the loved one is gone, he or she moves into a period of disorganization or despair characterized by apathy, deep sadness, anger, resentment, or despair. In this period, the bereaved is forced to confront the reality of the loss of the object of attachment. Bowlby's fourth stage is reorganization in which bereaved individuals must redefine their sense of self and reassess their life situation. It is time to learn new roles and acquire new skills necessary to live without the deceased.

Limitations of Stage Theories.   In reality, it is rare that persons move predictably between these stages or that it is even possible to distinguish which stage a grieving person is in at any time (Cook & Oltjenbruns, 1998). People may show signs of being in more than one stage at a time or move back and forth between stages almost randomly. There is no clear evidence that individuals need to experience every stage to reach a healthy resolution of their grief (Worden, 1991). The benefit of presenting stage theories is that they give the helping professional a better picture of the fluid and highly individualized nature of the grieving process. As stated earlier, bereavement is a process, not an event. Stage theories are important in developing an understanding that elements of denial and shock, deep feelings of anger or depression, and a conscious struggle to redefine and reorganize one's life are essential parts of this process, regardless of the order in which they occur.

The Continuing Bonds Theory.   As an alternative to stage theories about the process of bereavement, Silverman and Klass (1996) offered the theory of continuing bonds. They suggested that the bereavement process is one of continuous negotiating and renegotiating the meaning of the loss over a period of time rather than a process of resolving the loss. For example, immediately following the death of her husband, a widow may feel her life has lost its meaning and central focus, leaving her confused about what she is supposed to do. As she becomes more accustomed to getting through the days and weeks without her husband, turning her focus to other social outlets and activities, the initial intensity of the loss subsides somewhat. She may continue to miss her husband deeply but has filled some of the lonely hours with activities with other widows and family members. She is going through a process of negotiating and renegotiating the loss as she adjusts to her life as a widow. While the loss is never totally resolved, the form and function of grief changes over time.

Factors Affecting the Grieving Process

Gender.   Women have been found to be able to grieve and move through the bereavement process more effectively than men (Cook & Oltjenbruns, 1998; Hill, Lund, & Packard, 1996). This is due in part to the fact that women traditionally have more highly developed social systems than men. These offer them both a supportive environment for sharing the deep feelings associated with grief and wider opportunities to participate in social activities that help move them back into the social mainstream.

In many marriages, women are more likely than men to manage the social relationships for the couple (Campbell & Silverman, 1996). When a man is widowed, he may find his primary social network consists of other married couples, a situation with which he may feel extremely uncomfortable (Bryne & Raphael, 1997). Men also have a more difficult time with grief because of societal messages about the outward expression of emotion and the expectation that men need to stay in control of both emotions and the situation (Staudacher, 1991). Widowed men have a greater likelihood of dying shortly after their spouses due to the intense physical and emotional toll the death takes on them (Stroebe & Stroebe, 1993).

Women may make a more rapid adjustment to becoming widows because they have psychologically rehearsed the role. It is a fact that women are more likely to become widowed as opposed to men. The reality of watching other women struggle with widowhood gives women the opportunity to consider their own situation. The conscious or subconscious expectation that one day a woman will have to handle the finances or dispose of a lifetime of possessions accumulated as part of a couple may encourage a woman to think about the consequences of losing a spouse long before it happens.

Cultural Context.   The process of mourning takes place within a sociocultural context that prescribes or at least condones many specific rituals for acknowledging the death of a significant other and the expression of emotions and appropriate behavior (Cook & Oltjenbruns, 1998). While these cultural traditions differ dramatically between specific ethnic and racial groups, just the existence of an expected set of behaviors and even an acceptable time frame for the process of mourning help give a grieving person permission to engage in the mourning process. These cultural traditions may center around beliefs regarding the meaning of death and the existence of (or lack of) an afterlife. If cultures embrace death as a transition to an afterlife in which one is reunited with all the loved ones from one's life on earth, then death has both its joyful and sorrowful aspects. Cultural and religious expectations may also direct the bereaved in terms of making specific decisions about the funeral and burial. Funeral rites in the Catholic, Protestant, Jewish, or Muslim faiths are strongly ritualized by the guiding principles of the faith. If cultural traditions include the active involvement of many others in the community, a grieving person and family can call on a wide social network for both instrumental and emotional support in the days and months following a death.

A classic example of such cultural traditions are the traditional mourning rituals often observed in the Jewish faith (Cytron, 1993; Getzel, 1995). These rituals serve a joint purpose: to honor the dead and comfort the grieving family and friends. *Shiva* is a period of seven days following the burial of a loved one in which family and friends are expected to engage in deep and emotional mourning. During the last few days of shiva, friends are expected to visit the family to share their grief and provide emotional and instrumental support. The responsibilities for meal preparation and other domestic activities are assumed by friends and extended family members to give the bereaved an opportunity to engage in the necessary emotional tasks of grieving. The bereaved are not expected to make important decisions or to get over their grief quickly. In the immediate year following a death, the bereaved are expected to refrain from many sources of entertainment and social activities, a recognition that self-sacrifice is part of one's reflective activities following the death. The traditional mourning period lasts for one year. Following the anniversary of the death, the bereaved are expected to return to the mainstream of life. The highly ritualized activities of mourning are not as prevalent among Jewish families as they once were; however, the prescriptions for social support, the recognition of a reasonable length of time in which a bereaved person can focus solely on grieving, and the expectation following a year that it is time for the bereaved to rejoin life and move ahead reflect a healthy understanding of bereavement as a process, involving both individual and communal responses.

Ambiguous Loss.   The process of grieving is also affected by what Boss (1990) called "ambiguous loss." A death occurring in a fire or plane crash when the body is never recovered is an example of ambiguous loss. The deceased is not physically there but remains present psychologically. Likewise, when an elder is in the last stages of Alzheimer's disease and has long since lost all cognitive abilities, he or she may be physically present but psychologically absent, another form of ambiguous loss. This type of loss makes it difficult to really grasp the meaning of death. It is challenging to move ahead with the bereavement process when there is not clear evidence that the dying or deceased is really gone.

Anticipatory Grief.   Caregivers of elders with Alzheimer's disease frequently engage in what is called anticipatory grief, a sense of withdrawal and disengagement from the dying person before the person actually dies (Lindemann, 1944; Walker, Pomeroy, McNeil, & Franklin, 1994). Caregiver grief occurs at each stage of Alzheimer's disease as the elder loses functional abilities (Ponder & Pomeroy, 1996). Grieving occurs when an elder can no longer care for himself or herself and becomes increasing dependent on the caregiver. Grieving occurs when the elder is no longer able to recognize loved ones and the caregiver is providing care for an elder who has become a stranger. Caregiver grief, therefore, waxes and wanes through each specific loss, forcing the caregiver to "recycle again and again through the grief experience" (Ponder & Pomeroy, 1996, p. 15).

Having grieved individual losses through the course of Alzheimer's disease or any other disease in which essential human functioning gradually disappears, does not preclude additional grieving once the individual actually dies. Caregivers who engage in anticipatory grief often develop a kind of ambivalence toward the elder (Walker et al., 1994). At a time when the elder requires the greatest care, a caregiver may be less emotionally invested in the caregiving process, a painful process of "holding on, letting go, and drawing closer" all at the same time (Rando, 1986, p. 24).

Social Support Networks.   One of the most important factors affecting the course of the grieving process is the existence of social support networks for the bereaved (Prigerson, 1993; Sprang, McNeil, & Wright, 1993; Willert, Beckwith,

Holm, & Beckwith, 1995). The existence of friends and family who are able to comfort the bereaved and ease the loneliness following the death of a loved one greatly facilitates the process of bereavement. For elders, social support is particularly important. Elders need to be surrounded by others who will listen to them, give them permission to fully experience the frightening but normal range of emotions associated with the death, and provide instrumental and emotional assistance during bereavement. The emotional support provided by a helping professional, while helpful in many cases, cannot substitute for the social support of family and friends.

Emotional Well-Being and Coping Strategies. The grieving process is also affected by the elder's emotional well-being and ability to mobilize previously successful strategies. Elders who are emotionally frail and have trouble handling any kind of change may have more difficulty in successfully negotiating the grieving process (Worden, 1991). Elders who have been basically satisfied with their lives and express a moderate to high level of personal happiness prior to a death are those most likely to be able to grieve successfully and eventually rejoin the mainstream of life (Cook & Oltjenbruns, 1998). Elders susceptible to depression, anxiety, or having lifelong mental health problems may find the process of resolving grief to be extraordinarily difficult.

Complicated Grief

Despite its many challenges and the inevitable emotional pain associated with the grieving process, the majority of elders emotionally survive the loss of a loved one and after grieving can psychologically restructure a significant loss and achieve a good adjustment to a life without the loved one without professional intervention (Costa, Zonderman, & McCrae, 1991; Murrell, Himmelfarb, & Phifer, 1995). However, those who are unable to work through bereavement and find themselves "stuck" in the grieving process present a greater challenge to gerontological social workers.

Incomplete or unresolved bereavement is called complicated grief. Complicated grief is characterized by prolonged mourning and sadness that creates self-destructive or dysfunctional behavior in the bereaved. For example, the anger frequently seen during the grieving process becomes intensified over time rather than subsiding. Persons experiencing complicated grief often engage in substance abuse as a means to numb or dissipate painful emotions. Grieving persons may become overwhelmed with guilt feelings, convinced there was something they could have done to prevent the loved one's death. The difference between complicated and normal grief is the duration and intensity of emotional reactions. Normal grief reactions become exaggerated and present obstacles to resolving the grief.

The symptoms of complicated grief according to the *Diagnostic and Statistical Manual of Mental Disorders (DSM-IV)* (American Psychiatric Association, 1994) include:

1. A pronounced guilt about a wide range of things, many of which have nothing to do with the deceased
2. A preoccupation with death other than wishing one had died with the deceased
3. Recurring and intense beliefs about survivor worthlessness
4. Psychomotor retardation
5. Prolonged and serious functional impairment
6. Persistent hallucinations of the deceased beyond imagining the voice or sight of the deceased

Worden (1991) identified three conditions that increase the likelihood that the normal grieving process will evolve into complicated grief. First are losses referred to as "unspeakable," such as those due to suicide, AIDS, or other conditions in which it is presumed people hastened their own death by certain high-risk behaviors. The cause of death in some circumstances reflects poorly on the bereaved. Second are those deaths that are socially negated, such as a miscarriage or the death of someone with whom the bereaved has a disenfranchised relationship—an extramarital affair, a former spouse, or a homosexual lover (Kamerman, 1993; Rando, 1993). In these cases, there is little social recognition of the importance of an emotional attachment because it may fall outside socially sanctioned relationships. Worden (1991) identified persons who grieve without any social support network as the third high-risk group for developing complicated grief. No one knows (or cares) that they are grieving. Life goes on with no apparent recognition of the significance of the loss. Included among this group are elderly couples with no children and few friends who lose a spouse or partner. With few connections to the outside world, a widowed elder may truly be all alone with his or her grief.

Hospice Care

The Philosophy of Hospice Care

One of the approaches to caring for the dying of all ages dedicated to meeting their physical, psychosocial, and spiritual needs is the hospice movement. Hospice care is based on the philosophy that death should be neither hastened nor postponed but rather treated as a normal event in the life course. It is focused on providing palliative care rather than seeking treatment for a terminal condition. Maintaining the dignity of the dying patient through aggressive management of pain and discomfort while allowing the patient to remain in a familiar environment surrounded by family and friends characterizes the essence of the hospice movement.

The Guiding Principles of Hospice Care. Four principles guide the hospice movement's approach to providing care for the terminally ill (Rhymes, 1990):

1. The patient and family are the primary unit of care. Dying persons and their support systems both have special needs during the dying process.
2. Care is provided by an interdisciplinary team including physical, mental, and spiritual health care providers in recognition of the entire spectrum of biopsychosocial and spiritual needs.
3. Pain and symptom control are paramount. Death with dignity means that dying persons have the right to receive medication and services that will do all that is possible to alleviate pain and suffering.
4. Bereavement follow-up is provided as support to family members after the patient's death. Emotional and social support is important not only during the dying process but in the aftermath as families struggle with reorganizing their lives following the death of a loved one.

Hospice Care Services

Hospice care can be provided within a special unit within a hospital or nursing home, in a separate facility, or more commonly through care to the dying person in his or her own home. Family members often continue to be the primary caregivers for the dying person, but are connected to a resource network that assists with the caregiving process. Physicians, nurses, health care aides, social workers, and spiritual advisors are all involved in providing professional services to both the patient and family members.

Volunteers are an important component of the hospice care system. Volunteers may provide homemaking services, respite care, or visitation to support the family caregiver in caring for a dying patient. It is the philosophy of hospice care that providing an important support network for the dying patient and the family helps prevent the dangerous isolation both may experience in the last days and weeks of the dying process.

Pain and Symptom Control.   One of the most important aspects of hospice care is the attention given to controlling the pain and uncomfortable symptoms associated with terminal illness. Pain management strategies are medically supervised to insure responsible use of potent pain-relieving medications. They emphasize the importance of finding suitable dosages to minimize physical discomfort without rendering the patient totally incoherent. Medication is often supplemented by many of the alternative therapeutic approaches to relieving physical and emotional discomfort discussed in Chapter 7, including music, art, pet, or drama therapy. Massage and exercise are often used to relieve the physical stress facing both the dying patient and family caregivers. The goal of pain and symptom management is to find a combination of medication and other techniques to minimize the dying patient's discomfort.

Insurance Coverage.   Medicare—the federal health insurance program for persons who are elderly, disabled, or blind—covers the cost of hospice care for elders although small co-payments may be required in some instances. Medical

Assistance pays for hospice care in 80 percent of states (as of 2000). Many private insurance programs also cover the cost of hospice, which is considered a much more cost-effective alternative to prolonged hospital or institutional care for terminal patients. For elders who are not covered by any of these programs, hospice care organizations can often help them secure additional financial support from private contributions and foundation funds. Its broad coverage under public and private insurance programs and its humane approach to death with dignity make hospice care an attractive choice for dying elders and their families.

Bereavement Follow-Up.   Hospice care is committed to providing follow-up services to grieving family members after the death of a loved one. Traditionally, assistance with the mechanics of making funeral and burial arrangements, disposing of a deceased's personal effects, and on-going grief counseling are considered as part of the follow-up services, which may be provided for a year or more. The program recognizes that although caring for a dying loved one is difficult, processing the grief following the death also requires social and professional support.

Social Work Interventions with Bereaved Elders

It is a temptation in all fields of social work to want to take away another's pain when that person is facing a difficult emotional challenge. Part of what draws individuals to the social work profession is a deep compassion for the suffering of others, and watching another human being wrestle with deep sadness, confusion, or anger is extremely difficult. However, grieving needs to take its course.

The Tasks of the Mourning Process

Freeman and Ward (1998) identified five specific tasks associated with the mourning process that need to be accomplished before a bereaved person has successfully resolved the grief associated with the death of a significant other. These are not to be confused with stages of grief but rather represent an action-oriented perspective on what bereaved persons need to do, not exclusively what they need to feel. They represent a compilation of the work of several clinicians and researchers in the field of bereavement.

Experience the Reality of the Death.   A bereaved person needs to experience the reality of the death and be able to express that reality to others (Lindemann, 1944; Parkes, 1992; Worden, 1991). He or she needs to be able to say definitively, "My wife (husband, partner, family member) died" to self and to others. For some elders, this may mean touching the deceased body or spending time alone with the deceased before the body is rushed off for funeral and burial arrangements. For other elders who are in shock or denial immediately following the death, the true realization may come days or weeks later when the activity associated with the funeral subsides and he or she needs to face an empty house.

Tolerate the Emotional Pain.   Mourning elders need to experience the emotional pain, anger, resentment, confusion, or other emotions associated with the loss of a significant other (Schuchter & Zisook, 1993; Worden, 1991). At times well-intentioned family members ask physicians for tranquilizers to help elders get through the funeral and the time immediately following the death. As uncomfortable as family members may be watching an elder struggle with the sadness, it is a necessary step in the grieving process. The social worker and family members can be helpful in encouraging the elder to take care of himself or herself physically and emotionally, but trying to truncate the emotional parts of the process is unwise. An inability to experience and express difficult emotions contributes to the development of complicated grief.

Convert Present to Past.   During the process of mourning as the bereaved reorganizes his or her life around the absence of the deceased, the relationship between the bereaved and the deceased is transformed from a relationship in the present to a relationship of memory (Parkes, 1992; Rando, 1993). This is why it is extremely important that bereaved elders have ample opportunity to talk about the deceased and share memories. As elders talk about their loved ones, they often make a conscious or unconscious transition from speaking of the deceased in the present tense to remembering the deceased in the past tense. "We are" becomes "we were" signifying the elder is moving along with this task.

Develop a New Sense of Identity.   Part of the process of reorganizing life in the absence of the deceased involves the bereaved beginning to see himself or herself in a new light. As the bereaved takes on new activities or develops new relationships that were not part of the shared life with the deceased, he or she will develop a strengthened sense of personal, individual identity (Lindemann, 1944; Parkes, 1992; Ruskay, 1996). For example, a recent widow may find she needs to find employment following the death of her spouse to meet the financial demands of supporting herself. Her new identity as a worker strengthens her sense of individuality. A recent widower may find he has to learn how to cook, shop for groceries, or do laundry, creating a sense of independence and mastery he did not have before. Actively seeking new and fulfilling roles following another's death is an important part of active grief work.

Relate the Loss to a Context of Meaning.   The last task identified by Freeman and Ward (1998) is that of relating the experience of loss through the death of a loved one to a greater context of meaning. It is the philosophical and spiritual answer to the question of "why" the loved one died leaving the bereaved alone. Accepting that a supreme being has not singled out the bereaved for punishment and suffering by causing a loved one's death or that the deceased did not willfully abandon the deceased helps move the bereaved into a real acceptance of the death.

While the major tasks of mourning must be accomplished by the bereaved, there are a number of ways in which the social worker can help facilitate this process and offer the grieving elder opportunities to be an active participant in grief work.

Providing Information

The Grieving Process.   Elders and their families need information about the grieving process and what to expect as they process a significant loss. They may wonder how long the painful emotions will last and what they can do to get over their bereavement more quickly. Serving as an educator, the social worker can help the elder and his or her family to see bereavement as a process—a long-term series of adjustments in lifestyle and attitudes that are normal and necessary. Understanding the phases of the grief process can help the bereaved to be aware of unusual or troubling emotions that they may mistakenly identify as mental illness. Family members may be concerned that their elder relative "should be over this by now" or "need to get on with life" when, in fact, an elder is actually actively involved in the tasks of mourning.

Funeral and Burial Arrangements.   Elders and their families may also need concrete information on funeral and burial arrangements, executing a will, transferring property, or other important events that accompany the death of a family member. Bern-Klug, Ekerdt, and Wilkinson (1999) suggested that social workers play an important role helping families understand the complexities of funeral-related decisions. Decisions for funeral and burial arrangements must be made in a relatively short time, are very expensive, and require a social etiquette few people are familiar with unless they have made these arrangements before. At a time when an elder or the family is still in shock from the death, they are asked to make some of the most difficult (and irreversible) decisions they will ever make. The social worker can play an important role in providing families the information they need to decide about funeral arrangements, personalize the funeral ritual to reflect their personal preferences, and understand their role in the process rather than deferring these decisions entirely to the discretion of the funeral director (Bern-Klug et al., 1999).

Support Services.   Elders and their families also need access to information regarding support services that can help an elder reorganize his or her life following the death of a loved one. These support services can include individual or family counseling, homemaking services, budgeting and financial management services, home repair and maintenance, or social and recreational activities.

Accessing Support Groups

Bereavement.   Most bereaved persons need a private period of adjustment immediately following a death during which support groups may not prove helpful (Caserta & Lund, 1993). However, when an individual is ready and if he or she is interested, support groups can help facilitate the grieving process. Support groups, composed of a number of persons who are all somewhere in the grieving process, help to legitimize and normalize the disturbing array of emotions associated with grief (Scharlach & Fuller-Thompson, 1994; Thompson, 1996). By joining self-help groups, elders can learn new coping skills from others who are surviving a similar loss, develop new social relationships, and receive support from others who really do have an appreciation for the bereaved's thoughts and feelings (Hill, Lund, & Packard, 1996). It is easy for grieving persons to dismiss the supportive comments of others because they are convinced no one could know how they feel. While it is true that no one ever really knows what another is feeling, a group of others who have lost loved ones are a much more credible source of support.

For individuals engaged in anticipatory grief or experiencing complicated grief, therapy groups may be more appropriate than self-help groups. A trained therapist may be in a better position to help identify pathological reactions to grief that need professional intervention and support. Complicated grief does not necessarily subside with the passage of time and may require specific therapeutic interventions, such as the cognitive-behavioral techniques described in Chapter 6 (Hill et al., 1996).

Skills Training. In addition to self-help groups designed to help the bereaved process emotional responses, skills training groups are another beneficial type of support group. Skills training groups are focused on bereaved elders to develop the specific skills they need to reorganize their lives in the absence of the deceased (Hill et al., 1996). This may include teaching homemaking skills to widowers who have always relied on their spouses to take care of domestic chores or teaching basic budgeting skills to the widowed spouse who has never handled the finances in the relationship. It may include skills as simple as planning meals or doing laundry or skills as complicated as managing investments and disposing of real estate. It is not necessarily the complexity of the skill but the importance of giving elders the opportunity to begin the process of gaining mastery over an environment in which they feel overwhelmed. It is an active effort to address grief work in a way that gives elders a sense of power over the activities of daily life.

Facilitating or Recommending Family Counseling

While the elder's individual process of grieving has been the focus of this part of the chapter, family members may also need professional assistance in the grieving process. The death of a family member often throws the family into an emotional chaos that affects all of its members. Each member of a family has had a unique relationship with the deceased. Family members who had "unfinished business" or a conflictual relationship with the deceased may need additional work to avoid the development of complicated grief. Short-term focused work, such as the family meeting described in Chapter 12, may help all family members to move along in the bereavement process.

Advance Directives

Although elders and their families have little control over the exact circumstance surrounding a death, efforts within the past decade have helped to empower elders to make important decisions regarding their wishes for end-of-life treatment. These are decisions that can prolong or shorten the dying process. As a result of the passage of the Patient Self-Determination Act of 1990, hospitals and other health care institutions receiving Medicare or Medical Assistance funds are required to inform patients of their rights to make decisions about the medical care they wish to receive should their illness become life-threatening. The legislation grew out of the growing controversy about a patient's rights to refuse extraordinary means of treatment that sustained the length of life but did little to improve its quality. For example, should the family of a brain-damaged individual have the right to discontinue a respirator when there is no hope that the patient will recover the ability to breath on his or her own? Should people be allowed to refuse hydration and nutrition to hasten death when there is no hope for recovery? The legislation was written to answer questions about the obligation of both the patient and medical personnel to sustain life indefinitely in cases of terminal illness. The purpose of such legislation was to support patient self-determination and autonomy as well as to give people an opportunity to designate another responsible party to make decisions on their behalf should they become incapacitated.

The ultimate result of this legislation has been the development of advance directives—written instructions by the individual to health care providers and family members about end-of-life decisions. Advance directives are completed while an individual is still able to let others know what they want, rather than waiting until the individual is too ill to provide input. There are two primary forms of advance directive, the living will and the durable power of attorney for health care.

Living Wills

A living will is a written document that states what the patient does or does not want in medical treatment should he or she become incapacitated. It does not empower another person to make the decision on the patient's behalf but simply makes the patient's general wishes known to guide medical decision making. The right to accept or refuse treatment as proscribed in the living will is protected by constitutional and common law in every state in the United States, although there is not presently any legal assurance that living wills can be legally enforced (Williams, 1991). However, states regulate when living wills go into effect and whether they can be enforced in cases where an illness has not been determined to be terminal. Although an attorney is not needed to draft a living will, the acceptable form for living wills are state specific (Partnership for Caring, 2000). An example of a living will (specific to the state of Massachusetts) appears in Figure 13.2.

FIGURE 13.2   *Partnership for Caring Living Will (for Massachusetts Only)*

I, _____, being of sound mind, make this statement as a directive to be followed if I become permanently unable to participate in decisions regarding my medical care. These instructions reflect my firm and settled commitment to decline medical treatment under the circumstances indicated below:

I direct my attending physician to withhold or withdraw treatment that merely prolongs my dying, if I should be in an **incurable or irreversible mental or physical condition with no reasonable expectation of recovery,** including but not limited to: (a) **a terminal condition;** (b) **permanently unconscious condition;** or (c) **a minimally conscious condition in which I am permanently unable to make decisions or express my wishes.**

I direct that treatment be limited to measures to keep me comfortable and to relieve pain, including any pain that might occur by withholding or withdrawing treatment.

While I understand that I am not legally required to be specific about future treatments, **if I am in the condition(s) described above I feel especially strongly about the following forms of treatment:** (cross out statements that do not reflect your wishes):

I do not want cardiac resuscitation.
I do not want mechanical respiration.
I do not want tube feeding.
I do not want antibiotics.
However, I do want **maximum pain relief,** even if it may hasten my death.
Other directions (insert personal instructions):

These directions express my legal right to refuse treatment under federal and state law. I intend my instructions to be carried out unless I have revoked them in a new writing or by clearly indicating that I have changed my mind.

Signed _____   Date _____

Address _____

_____

I declare the person who signed this document appeared to execute the living will willingly and free from duress. He or she signed (or asked another to sign for him or her) this document in my presence.

Witness _____

Address _____

_____

Witness _____

Address _____

_____

Source: Reprinted by permission of Partnership for Caring, 1035 30th Street, NW, Washington, DC 20007. 800-989-9455.

The Durable Power of Attorney for Health Care

The Durable Power of Attorney for Health Care (DPAHC), also known as a health care proxy or medical power of attorney, is a legal document that designates another person to make decisions about health care when a patient becomes incapacitated. In some states, persons designated as health care proxies may also make decisions about health care any time the individual is unable to speak for themselves, even if the illness is not considered terminal. A DPAHC is usually drawn up by an attorney, witnessed and dated like any other legal document. The exact form of a DPAHC is regulated by state law and anyone considering one should consult the legal statutes in their own state. While living wills may or may not be legally enforceable, a DPAHC is recognized as a legal document (Williams, 1991).

In most states, a DPAHC does not enumerate the exact medical treatments an individual does or does not want. It is important, therefore, that people carefully communicate their wishes to a designated health care proxy. Elders, unfortunately, frequently assume that family members will know what they would want and complete a DPAHC but fail to give the health care proxy an adequate idea about their wishes for end-of-life decisions (Bailly & DePoy, 1995). As difficult as this discussion may be for elders and family members, it is essential in fulfilling the original intent of advance directives. Social work can be instrumental in starting the discussion between family members, the elder, and the health care provider so that the wishes of the elder can be honored. It is the ideal to have both a living will and a DPAHC to clearly communicate one's wishes about treatment decisions. In cases where both documents exist, the DPAHC takes precedence over a living will (Williams, 1991).

The Controversy Surrounding Advance Directives

Variation in State Laws.   While advance directives have been in effect in the United States for over a decade, they still remain controversial. State laws vary significantly around the specific procedure, content, and process for drafting and executing living wills and DPAHCs. The commitment to the importance of allowing patients self-determination in end-of-life decisions has progressed faster than the legal structure needed to enforce it (Rothchild, 1998). These issues will no doubt be worked out in the nation's court system.

Burden on Family Members.   Advance directives move the difficult decision making about medical treatment from the physician to the patient's family, perceived by many family members to be an unfair burden (Rothchild, 1998). If a family member has been designated as a health care proxy and has never discussed an elder's preferences for life-sustaining treatment, he or she is in an unusually difficult situation. Family members may be emotionally paralyzed in the face of making a life and death decision about a loved one's care.

Sustaining Life at Whose Expense?   Some opponents of advance directives argue that the wishes of a patient may actually disenfranchise families by requesting an expensive life-sustaining treatment that takes important financial resources away from other family members. For example, long-term sub-acute care for a co-matose elder may deplete an extended family's finances that are invested in a home or designated for higher education.

Unforseen Circumstances.   Finally, neither a living will nor a DPAHC provides sufficient detail to cover every possible contingency in health care provision, making their interpretation in the clinical setting extremely difficult. While patients may be adamant about not being placed on a ventilator or wanting a feeding tube, hydration and nutrition issues need to be specifically delineated in a DPAHC or hospitals may be required legally to continue to nourish a comatose patient through intravenous feeding (Rothchild, 1998). The more the detail that can be provided in writing by individuals before they become incapacitated, the greater the likelihood their wishes will be honored when the document is implemented.

Racial, Ethnic, and Religious Variations in Advance Directives.   Advance directives are not accepted or considered moral by some ethnic, racial, or religious groups. Despite the professional's enthusiasm for the importance of self-determination and patient's rights, it is important to be sensitive to the values of these individuals. Rothchild (1998) and Klessig (1992) found that African American and Hispanic families were more likely to want life-sustaining treatments than their white counterparts due in part to a distrust of white treatment teams. The suggestion that an individual of color might refuse treatment rather than extend life indefinitely was seen as a racial/ethnic issue rather than a medical one.

Limited research has been done on Asian American attitudes toward advance directives. In one of the few studies of its kind, Klessig (1992) found Chinese Americans' basic philosophy included the right to chose death over the burden of continuing life support systems. Terminating life support to reduce the prolonged suffering of the patient and family is considered an act of compassion.

Caralis, Davis, Wright, and Marcial (1993) emphasized that certain religious groups take a more fatalistic yet accepting view of death, such as pious Muslims who would see interfering with the process of dying as morally unacceptable. Klessig (1992) found that Iranian families did not recognize the right to die even in circumstances where an individual was in chronic pain. Suffering was seen as a way to show faith and place trust in Allah. Other religious groups may object to advance directives as a form of passive suicide. It is essential that both the health care and social work profession respect an elder's personal and religious values when advanced directives are discussed.

Ethical Dilemmas in Death and Dying

With the development of technological advances that can prolong life much longer than ever before, medicine is now facing a new set of ethical quandaries regarding what role, if any, it should play in either extending or shortening life. In some cases, life can be prolonged almost indefinitely but at the expense of quality for both a patient and the family. In other cases, individuals want to be able to make the decision to hasten death through passive or active means to avoid reaching the point where they are suffering the inevitable consequences of a serious condition or are incapable of making that decision. This section of the chapter explores two ethical dilemmas that face the medical profession, elders in the final stages of life, and their families. Even though the ultimate decisions regarding the allocation of scarce resources to frail elders and physician-assisted suicide remain with physicians and patients' families, it is important for social workers providing services to elders and their families to be familiar with the ethical dilemmas posed by these issues.

The Allocation of Scarce Resources to Frail Elders

One of the incentives behind the development of advance directives is to give elders and their families choices about what they do or do not want in medical treatment during the last stages of a terminal illness. Rather than relying strictly on the judgment of the physician, advance directives give dying individuals the opportunity to decide for themselves whether they want extraordinary means employed to prolong their lives regardless of the cost and availability of resources. While the use of advance directives has complicated clinical decisions for physicians in some cases, it has simplified them in many others. The physician no longer has to balance the benefit of prolonging a dying elder's life with the cost of scarce medical resources that might better be allocated to a younger person. In cases where elders have not completed advance directives, this difficult ethical dilemma continues to challenge the medical profession and the families of the terminally ill.

The Case for Limiting Medical Resources to Frail Elders. While few medical ethicists would ever want to be put in the position of deciding who gets scarce medical resources and who deserves to live and who does not, a number of arguments support limiting the provision of expensive medical resources to frail, dying elders. Harris (1996) proposed the "fair innings" position in which the human life span is seen as a series of innings, similar to a baseball game. If elders have had a reasonable number of innings (a life of reasonable length), out of fairness to younger persons, these elders should have limited access to expensive and scarce medical resources. This position is echoed in Callahan (1996) who argued that there is a natural life span connected to a series of life events, such as raising a family, engaging in a career, or enjoying friends and social activities. While medicine should have the prevention of premature death and suffering as its foremost goals, the profession is not morally obligated to extend life beyond what can be reasonably expected. In his words, "The indefinite extension of life combined with an insatiable ambition to improve the health of the elderly is a recipe for monomania and bottomless spending. It fails to accept aging and death as a part of the human condition. It fails to present to younger generations a model of wise stewardship" (Callahan, 1996, p. 442).

Callahan suggested that the medical profession and the government, as the representative of collective social actions, have an obligation to help people live out a natural life span but are not obligated to extend life beyond that point. He further suggested government has the responsibility of supporting and encouraging only that medical research that supports sustaining a natural life span, but not efforts aimed at an indefinite extension of human life. Callahan (1996) and others (Daniels, 1996; Harris, 1996; Lockwood, 1996) represent a growing sentiment among ethicists and physicians that medical resources are not a right of frail elders but part of a greater communal resource for patients of all ages. While this position may be economically and philosophically compelling, it should raise serious questions among physicians and social workers about the assumptions that would guide the decision to withhold life-sustaining medical technology. What is the ethically correct number of "fair innings"? How many years and what life events comprise a "natural life span?" Does medicine, or any other group, have the ultimate truth in making these decisions?

The Case against Limiting Medical Resources to Frail Elders. The case against limiting medical resources to frail elders emphasizes that the decision to withhold life-sustaining treatments based on the age of the patient (when not directed otherwise in an advance directive) is beyond the moral boundaries of medicine and ethics (Veatch, 1996). Medicine cannot stand in judgment of the worth of another's life based on any objective or subjective criteria. Human life retains its inherent sacredness and value by its sheer existence, not on the basis of how valuable any given life is considered by others.

Scitovsky and Capron (1996) stated that argument about the economics of life-sustaining treatment for frail elders is only speculative and that it is impossible to determine that resources committed to treating frail elders are wasteful. The failure to show strong economic evidence that excessive resources are being spent on frail elders combined with a deep concern about the morality of relegating these kinds of decisions led these authors to conclude the following:

> Until medical prognostic powers improve substantially and ethical and legal standards emerge to allay fears that any failure to "do everything possible" for these patients would send the country sliding into the abyss of active euthanasia, medical treatment will continue to be provided that possibly wastes resources and that may harm, rather than help some patients. (Scitovsky & Capron, 1996, p. 427)

In the course of working with dying elders and their families, no doubt social workers will witness this ethical dilemma in action. While it is easy to understand how a family would want everything possible done to prolong the life of an elder, it is also realistic to struggle with the question: How many medical resources can be spent on a single frail elder and who is obligated to pay for the services? It is a convincing argument that medical resources might be better spent on younger patients who hold the promise of a longer life and have yet to make their contributions to the world. Yet, how can families decide to forego treatment of a beloved elder in favor of a hypothetical younger person who is not real to them? This quandary represents one of the most difficult ethical dilemmas facing both medicine and the helping professions.

Physician-Assisted Suicide

Physician-assisted suicide (PAS) is one of the most controversial issues facing both the medical and legal systems in the United States. For the purpose of this discussion, PAS is defined as the active effort on the part of a physician to provide a person with the means to take his or her own life. While advance directives allow an individual to reject some forms of life-sustaining treatment, they do not permit that individual to legally request assistance from a physician to initiate the dying process.

Two-thirds of the public and a majority of physicians in this country support physician-assisted suicide as a legitimate right in cases in which a patient is suffering from an incurable and debilitating disease (Bachman et al., 1996; Blendon, Szalay, & Knox, 1992; Cohen et al., 1994). However, in 1997, the U.S. Supreme Court rejected physician-assisted suicide as a right under the U.S. Constitution but left the decision to allow or forbid PAS to state legislatures (*Vacco* v. *Quill*, 117 S Ct 2293, 1997; *Washington* v. *Glucksberg*, 117 S Ct 2258, 1997). As of 2000, the state of Oregon is the only state to have legalized PAS under strictly controlled conditions directed by very specific guidelines. Even if PAS becomes legal in every state, its legal availability should not be confused with the ethical dilemma that remains concerning morality of physicians' taking an active role in assisting suicide. In addition to the physicians' role, many persons are not in favor of any encouragement or moral acceptance of an individual's right to take his or her own life under any circumstance. The morality or immorality of taking one's own life will not be discussed here, but rather that moral dilemma posed by the involvement of physicians and other health care professionals in facilitating suicide.

The Case for Physician-Assisted Suicide.   The most common argument in favor of PAS is that it is a compassionate and humane response to the suffering of a patient whose quality of life is seriously compromised by a debilitating illness (Clark, 1997). If medicine cannot cure an illness or provide treatment that will prevent suffering, PAS is a "compassionate response to a medical failure" (Brody, 1997, p. 149). In other words, if medicine cannot help people live with dignity, it can help people die with dignity. Families and friends can be spared the emotional agony of watching a loved one suffer as both physical and cognitive abilities deteriorate.

The importance of respecting an individual's right to self-determination is another common reason for supporting an individual's decision to take his or her own life with the help of a physician or other health care professional (Byock, 1997; Clark, 1997). This position considers the decision to take one's own life, especially when one is suffering from a devastating illness, to be the individual's, not society's, ultimate decision. As people have a right to determine the course of their lives, they have a concomitant right to determine the circumstances surrounding their death under these circumstances.

Carpenter (1993) suggested that an elder's decision to commit suicide could be considered an ethical and rational decision. If an elder is facing a debilitating illness, feels that life has been long and meaningful, and does not want to impose a lengthy and expensive illness on family members, the decision to take one's life may fall within the parameters of an ethical decision based on the ethos of self-determination. While the social work profession respects and supports an individual's right to self-determination, the issue of physician-assisted suicide is not specifically identified in the National Association of Social Workers Code of Ethics.

The Case against Physician-Assisted Suicide.   The argument against PAS focuses on two elements: the immorality of suicide itself and the inappropriateness of obtaining assistance from a physician for the purpose of taking one's life. Some opponents of PAS consider suicide to be morally and ethically wrong under any circumstances, including those in which a person is suffering from a debilitating, painful illness (Clark, 1997). The circumstances surrounding the decision do not negate the immorality of the act. Therefore, PAS should not be allowed in any case. Many religious faiths support this perspective, identifying suicide as sin against God.

The second component of the argument against PAS centers on the inappropriateness of involving physicians whose role is to protect and maintain life in an individual's actions to end life (Byock, 1997). It is unreasonable for society to ask medicine to participate in and condone the deliberate taking of a human life, while at the same time expecting medicine to devote itself to saving lives. Callahan (1998) opposed PAS on the basis of the ideology of control—that medicine has no right to assume the goals of mastering life and death. He did not see the act of a physician assisting another to take his or her own life as morally justifiable under the rubric of self-determination. Asking a physician to assist in taking the life of an individual does not just involve the individual; it involves the physician as a second party. A life cannot be terminated by the actions of an individual alone; rather, such action requires a physician—whose primary responsibility is to do all that is possible to preserve life—to be an active participant in taking the life of another. Callahan (1998) believes this presents a precarious ethical dilemma for physicians.

Difficult decisions about allocating expensive health care resources to frail elders and the continuing debate about the legality and morality of physician-assisted suicide are two very challenging ethical dilemmas facing social workers in the field of aging. There is no uniform agreement in the profession of social work to support or reject either side of these ethical dilemmas. It is important that social workers consider these issues very carefully and determine how both personal and professional values influence their own ethical stances on these end-of-life decisions.

Summary

Facing issues in dying and bereavement is one of the most difficult challenges facing social workers in the field of aging. Yet, as a normal part of the life span, social workers will be called on to provide support services to elders and their families both during the process of dying and in the extended period of bereavement. One of the most promising options available to elders and their families is the hospice movement, dedicated to preserving the dignity of the dying patient through an extensive network of support services provided by an interdisciplinary team along with aggressive management of pain and discomfort.

Advance directives offer elders an opportunity to take an active part in making decisions about end-of-life decisions regarding the extent and kind of treatment they wish to receive when death is inevitable. The combination of a living will, which details specific wishes about life-sustaining treatment, and a durable power of attorney for health care, in which a health proxy can be designated, offer elders the best chance of knowing their wishes will be respected as they near death.

The ability of the medical profession to lengthen or shorten life poses two very difficult ethical dilemmas for physicians. Elders and families will struggle with hard decisions about employing desperate means to sustain life for even a few more days versus withholding extraordinary treatment and letting death take its course. As an important support system for elders and families, a social worker will be witness to agonizing decisions that both families and physicians must make. Another option, physician-assisted suicide presents a new set of challenges. The legality of PAS will be decided in the court system but the morality of this decision must be decided by the individual who is considering requesting physician assistance to take life. Social workers working with terminally ill patients, adults with severe disabilities, and elders with chronic, debilitating illnesses will face this issue at some time in their professional practice.

Check Out These Websites!

1. www.partnershipincaring.org   Partnership in Caring is an organization devoted to public education about the use of living wills and durable powers of attorney for health care. At this website, you can download the appropriate forms for all 50 of the states in the United States. The site also provides links to other legal and social organizations promoting the responsible use of advance directives.

2. www.hospicenet.org   This website, sponsored by Hospice Net, provides extensive information for dying persons, their families, and professionals who are working with them. Topics include general information about the hospice movement, advance directives, pain and symptom management, and helpful information about the grieving process.

3. **www.growthhouse.org**   Located in San Francisco, Growth House, Inc. is an organization specifically geared to providing information and referral services for professionals working with death and dying issues. The site offers information and links to other sites covering death, dying, bereavement, and resources helpful in making end-of-life decisions. Chat rooms, an online bookstore, and access to professional forums concerning these issues are also available.

4. **www.about.com/health/dying/msub42.htm**   About.com offers a network of sites compiled by specific experts. The site deals with the topics of death, dying, and the concerns of caregivers of dying persons. It offers specific suggestions to family caregivers about preventing burnout, processing difficult emotions, and reducing caregiver stress.

References

American Psychiatric Association. (1994). *The diagnostic and statistical manual of mental disorders (DSM IV)* (5th ed.). Washington, DC: American Psychiatric Association.

Bachman, J. G., Alcser, K. H., Doukas, D. J., Lichtenstein, R. L., Coming, A. D., & Brody, H. (1996). Attitudes of Michigan physicians and public toward legalizing physician-assisted suicide and voluntary euthanasia. *New England Journal of Medicine, 334,* 303–309.

Bailly, D. J., & DePoy, E. (1995). Older people's responses to education about advance directives. *Health and Social Work, 20*(3), 223–228.

Bern-Klug, M., Ekerdt, D. J., & Wilkinson, D. S. (1999). What families know about funeral-related costs: Implications for social work practice. *Health and Social Work, 24*(2), 128–137.

Blendon, R. J., Szalay, V. S., & Knox, R. (1992). Should physicians aid their patients in dying? The public perspective. *Journal of the American Medical Association, 267,* 2658–2662.

Boss, P. (1990). *Family stress management.* Beverly Hills, CA: Sage.

Bowlby, J. (1980). *Attachment and loss (Vol. 3): Loss, sadness, and depression.* New York: Basic Books.

Brody, H. (1997). Assisting in patient suicides is an acceptable practice for physicians. In R. F. Weir (Ed.), *Physician-assisted suicide* (pp. 136–151). Bloomington, IN: Indiana University Press.

Byock, I. R. (1997). Physician-assisted suicide is not an acceptable practice for physicians. In R. F. Weir (Ed.), *Physician-assisted suicide* (pp. 107–135). Bloomington, IN: Indiana University Press.

Byrne, G. J. A., & Raphael, B. (1997). The psychological symptoms of conjugal bereavement in elderly men over the first 13 months. *International Journal of Geriatric Psychiatry, 12,* 241–251.

Callahan, D. (1996). Limiting health care for the old. In T. L. Beauchamp & R. M. Veatch (Eds.), *Ethical issues in death and dying* (pp. 441–443). Upper Saddle River, NJ: Prentice Hall.

Callahan, D. (1998). Physician-assisted suicide: Moral questions. In M. D. Steinberg & S. J. Youngner (Eds.), *End-of-life decisions: A psychosocial perspective* (pp. 283–297). Washington, DC: American Psychiatric Press.

Campbell, S., & Silverman, P. R. (1996). *Widower: When men are left alone.* Amityville, NY: Baywood.

Caralis, P. V., Davis, B., Wright, K., & Marcial, E. (1993). The influence of ethnicity and race on attitudes toward advance directives, life prolonging treatments, and euthanasia. *Journal of Clinical Ethics, 4,* 155–165.

Carpenter, B. D. (1993). A review and new look at ethical suicide in advanced age. *The Gerontologist, 33*(3), 359–365.

Caserta, M. S., & Lund, D. A. (1993). Intrapersonal resources and the effectiveness of self-help groups for bereaved older adults. *The Gerontologist, 33,* 619–629.

Chirchin, E. R., Ferster, L., & Gordon, N. (1994). Planning for the end of life with the home care client. *Journal of Gerontological Social Work, 22*(1/2), 147–158.

Clark, N. (1997). *The politics of physician-assisted suicide.* New York: Garland.

Cohen, J. S., Fihn, S. D., Boyko, E. J., Jonsen, A. R., & Wood, R. W. (1994). Attitudes toward assisted suicide and euthanasia among physicians in Washington state. *New England Journal of Medicine, 331,* 89–94.

Cook, A. S., & Oltjenbruns, K. A. (1998). *Dying and grieving: Life span and family perspectives.* Fort Worth, TX: Harcourt Brace.

Costa, P. T., Zonderman, A. B., & McCrae, R. R. (1991). Personality, defense, coping, and adaptation in older adulthood. In E. M. Cummings, A. L. Green, & K. Karraker (Eds.), *Life-span developmental psychology: Perspectives on stress and coping* (pp. 227–293). Hillsdale, NJ: Lawrence Erlbaum.

Cytron, B. (1993). To honor the dead, to comfort the mourners: Traditions in Judaism. In D. P. Irish, K. F. Lundquist, & V. J. Nelsen (Eds.), *Ethnic variations in dying, death, and grief: Diversity in universality* (pp. 113–124). Washington, DC: Taylor and Francis.

Daniels, N. (1996). A life span approach to health care. In T. L. Beauchamp & R. M. Veatch (Eds.), *Ethical issues in death and dying* (pp. 444–446). Upper Saddle River, NJ: Prentice-Hall.

Erikson, E. (1963). *Childhood and society* (2nd ed.). New York: Norton.

Freeman, S. J., & Ward, S. (1998). Death and bereavement: What counselors should know. *Journal of Mental Health Counseling, 20*(3), 216–226.

Getzel, G. S. (1995). Judaism and death: Practice and implications. In J. Parry & A. S. Ryan (Eds.), *A cross-cultural look at death, dying and religion* (pp. 18–31). Chicago: Nelson-Hall.

Harris, J. (1996). The value of life. In T. L. Beauchamp & R. M. Veatch (Eds.), *Ethical issues in death and dying* (pp. 435–440). Upper Saddle River, NJ: Prentice-Hall.

Hill, R. D., Lund, D., & Packard, T. (1996). Bereavement. In J. I. Sheikh (Ed.), *Treating the elderly* (pp. 45–74). San Francisco: Jossey-Bass.

Irwin, M., & Pike, J. (1993). Bereavement, depressive symptoms, and immune function. In M. S. Stroebe, W. Stroebe, & R. O. Hansson (Eds.), *Handbook of bereavement: Theory, research, and intervention* (pp. 160–174). New York: Cambridge University Press.

Kalish, R. A. (1985). Death and dying in a social context. In R. H. Binstock & E. Shanas (Eds.), *Handbook of aging and the social sciences* (2nd ed., pp. 149–170). New York: Van Nostrand.

Kamerman, J. (1993). Latent functions of enfranchising the disenfranchised griever. *Death Studies, 17,* 281–287.

Kim, K., & Jacobs, S. (1993). Neuroendocrine changes following bereavement. In M. S. Stroebe, W. Stroebe, & R. O. Hansson (Eds.), *Handbook of bereavement: Theory, research, and intervention* (pp. 143–159). New York: Cambridge University Press.

Kirschberg, T. M., Neimeyer, R. A., & James, R. K. (1998). Beginning counselors' death concerns and empathic responses to client situations involving death and grief. *Death Studies, 22,* 99–120.

Klessig, J. (1992). The effect of values and culture on life-support decisions. *The Western Journal of Medicine, 157*(3), 316–321.

Kubler-Ross, E. (1969). *On death and dying.* New York: Macmillan.

Lindemann, E. (1944). The symptomatology and management of acute grief. *The American Journal of Psychiatry, 101,* 141–148.

Lockwood, M. (1996). Quality of life and resource allocation. In T. L. Beauchamp & R. M. Veatch (Eds.), *Ethical issues in death and dying* (pp. 429–434). Upper Saddle River, NJ: Prentice-Hall.

Lund, D. A., Caserta, M., & Dimond, M. (1993). The course of spousal bereavement in later life. In M. S. Strobe, W. Strobe, & R. O. Hansson (Eds.), *Handbook of bereavement: Theory, research, and intervention* (pp. 240–254). New York: Cambridge University Press.

Marshall, R. E., & Kasman, C. (1980). Burnout in the neonatal intensive care unit. *Pediatrics, 65*(6), 1161–1165.

Murrell, S. A., Himmelfarb, S., & Phifer, J. F. (1995). Effects of bereavement/loss and pre-event status on subsequent physical health in older adults. In J. Henricks (Ed.), *Health and health care utilization in later life* (pp. 159–177). Amityville, NY: Baywood Press.

National Hospice Organization. (1996). *A guide to grief.* Arlington, VA: National Hospice Organization.

Olson, M. (1997). *Healing the dying.* Albany, NY: Delmar.

Parkes, C. M. (1992). Bereavement and mental health in the elderly. *Reviews in Clinical Gerontology (UK), 2,* 45–51.

Partnership for Caring. (2000). *Advance directives and health care proxies.* Retrieved from the World Wide Web, June 19, 2000. Available at http://www.partnershipforcaring.org.

Pattison, E. M. (1977). *The experience of dying.* Englewood Cliffs, NJ: Prentice-Hall.

Ponder, R. J., & Pomeroy, E. C. (1996). The grief of caregivers: How pervasive is it? *Journal of Gerontological Social Work, 27*(1/2), 3–21.

Prigerson, H. G. (1993). Protective psychosocial factors in depression among spousally bereaved elders. *American Journal of Geriatric Psychiatry, 1,* 296–309.

Rando, T. (1986). A comprehensive analysis of anticipatory grief: Perspectives, processes, promises, and problems. In T. A. Rando (Ed.), *Loss and anticipatory grief* (pp. 3–37). Lexington, MA: Lexington Books.

Rando, T. (1993). The increasing prevalence of complicated mourning: The onslaught is just beginning. *Omega, 26*(1), 43–59.

Reynolds, C. F., Hoch, C. C., Buysse, D. J., Houck, P. R., Schlernitzaur, M., Pasternak, R. E., Frank, E., Masumdar, S., & Kupfer, D. J. (1993). Sleep after spousal bereavement: A study in recovery from stress. *Biological Psychiatry, 34,* 791–797.

Rhymes, J. (1990). Hospice care in America. *Journal of the American Medical Association, 264,* 369–372.

Rothchild, E. (1998). Family dynamics in decisions to withhold or withdraw treatment. In M. D. Steinberg & S. J. Youngner (Eds.), *End-of-life decisions: A psychosocial perspective* (pp. 77–107). Washington, DC: American Psychiatric Press.

Ruskay, S. (1996). Saying hello again: A new approach to bereavement counseling. *Hospice Journal, 11,* 5–14.

Scharlach, A. E., & Fuller-Thompson, E. (1994). Coping strategies following the death of an elderly parent. *Journal of Gerontological Social Work, 21*(3/4), 85–100.

Schuchter, S. R., & Zisook, S. (1993). The course of normal grief. In M. S. Stroebe, W. Stroebe, & R. O. Hansson (Eds.), *Handbook of bereavement: Theory, research, and intervention* (pp. 160–186). New York: Cambridge University Press.

Scitovsky, A. A., & Capron, A. M. (1996). Medical care at the end of life: The interaction of economics and ethics. In T. L. Beauchamp & R. M. Veatch (Eds.), *Ethical issues in death and dying* (pp. 422–428). Upper Saddle River, NJ: Prentice-Hall.

Silverman, P., & Klass, D. (1996). Introduction: What's the problem? In D. Klass, P. Silverman, & S. Nickman (Eds.), *Continuing bonds: New understandings of grief* (pp. 3–27). Washington, DC: Taylor and Francis.

Sprang, M. V., McNeil, J. S., & Wright, R. (1993). Grief among surviving family members of homicide victims: A causal approach. *Omega, 26*(2), 145–160.

Staudacher, C. (1991). *Men and grief.* Oakland, CA: New Harbinger.

Steeves, R. H., & Kahn, D. L. (1999). Coping with death: Grief and bereavement in elderly persons. In E. Swanson & T. Tripp-Reimer (Eds.), *Life transitions in the older adult: Issues for nurses and other health professionals* (pp. 89–109). New York: Springer.

Stroebe, M. S., & Stroebe, W. (1993). The morality of bereavement: A review. In M. S. Stroebe, W. Stroebe, & R. O. Hansson (Eds.), *Handbook of bereavement: Theory, research, and intervention* (pp. 175–195). New York: Cambridge University Press.

Thompson, S. (1996). Living with loss: A bereavement support group. *Groupwork, 9*(1), 5–14.

Veatch, R. M. (1996). How age should matter: Justice as the basis for limiting care to the elderly. In T. L. Beauchamp & R. M. Veatch (Eds.), *Ethical issues in death and dying* (pp. 447–456). Upper Saddle River, NJ: Prentice-Hall.

Walker, R. J., Pomeroy, E. C., McNeil, J. S., & Franklin, C. (1994). Anticipatory grief and Alzheimer's disease: Strategies for intervention. *Journal of Gerontological Social Work, 22*(3/4), 21–39.

Willert, M. G., Beckwith, B. E., Holm, J. E., & Beckwith, S. K. (1995). A preliminary study of the impact of terminal illness on spouses' social support and coping strategies. *Hospice Journal, 10*(4), 35–48.

Williams, P. G. (1991). *The living will and durable power of attorney for health care book.* Oak Park, IL: P. Gaines.

Worden, J. W. (1991). *Grief counseling and grief therapy: A handbook for the mental health practitioner* (2nd ed.). New York: Springer.

Index

Diabetes, 37
Diagnostic workup, definition of, 79–80
Diet and "successful" aging, 53–54
Digestive system, changes in, 35
Disability and health status, 6–7
Disengagement theory and elders, 69–70
Diversity among elderly, 1–2
    and group dynamics, 231–232
Drama as therapeutic activity, 179–185
Drug misuse and dependency, 208–213
    illegal drugs, 208–209
    prescription drugs, 209–211
    treatment, 211–213
Drug therapy for depression and anxiety, 163–164
Drug toxicity and dementia, 116–117, 118
Durable Power of Attorney for Health Care
    (DPAHC), 348
Dysthymic disorders, 106 (*see also* Depression)

Economic well-being and health status, 6–7
Elders, definition of, 1
Elders' choice of goals for intervention, 21, 140–
    141, 143
Electroconvulsive therapy (ECT), 165
Emotional abuse, definition of, 279 (*see also* Abuse
    and neglect of elders)
Emotional and cognitive problems, 105–137
    anxiety disorders, 128–134
    delirium, 120–122, 125–126, 127
    dementia, 113–120, 124–125, 127
    depression, 106–113, 122, 123, 127
Emotional needs of dying elders, 329–330
Emotional support to elders, 98
    by social worker to dying elders, 330–331
Emotional well-being, assessment of, 94–96
Employment of elderly, 6
Empowerment as goal of intervention,
    139–141, 143
End-of-life decisions, 15, 19
Endocrine and reproductive systems, changes in,
    37–38, 41
Environment of elder:
    adaptations to, 42–43
    assessment of , 100–102
    and intellectual functioning, 63
Estrogen levels, 36–37
Ethical dilemmas in death and dying, 349–353
Ethnicity and depression, 109–110
Exercise, 32
    and "successful" aging, 54–55

Facing Aging Concerns Together (F.A.C.T.)
    program, 310
Family counseling for bereaved, 345

Family histories:
    and alcoholism, 198–199
    and depression, 106–107
Family meetings, 310–312
Fear of death, 328–329
Feminist theory of aging, 72
Financial exploitation of elderly, 279–280, 291–292
Financial resources of elderly, assessment of, 100
Free radical theory, 27–28
Freud, Sigmund, psychological influences of, 254
Funeral and burial arrangements, 344

Gastrointestinal system, changes in, 35, 41
Gay and lesbian couples, 302–303
Gender and depression, 107
Generalized Anxiety Disorder (GAD), 129–130
Genetic programming theory of aging, 27
Genetics and depression, 106–107
Genogram, 266, 267
Geriatric Depression Scale (GDS), 94, 110, 111, 160
Goals of elders for change/intervention, 21, 140–
    141, 143
Graying of hair, 30
Grief:
    factors affecting process, 336–339
    manifestations of, 333–334
    mourning process, 342–343
    stage theories of, 334–336
Group work with elders, 13, 225–250
    cultural issues, 230–232
    ethical dilemmas, 245–247
    process, 232–233
    reality orientation groups, 234–236
    remotivation groups, 236–239
    social/recreational groups, 239–240
    support groups, 240–242
    therapy groups, 13, 242–245

Hamilton Anxiety Rating Scale (HARS), 132
Health care proxy, 348
Health status and poverty, 6–7
Hearing loss, 39–40, 41, 88, 89
Heart disease, 32–33
Height, changes in, 33
Heterogeneity of elder population, 83–84
High blood pressure, 33
HIV/AIDS and elders, 47–52
    people of color, 50
    vulnerability of elders, 48–50
Home of elder:
    condition of, 100–102
    as setting for assessment, 85
Home health care agencies and social worker, 11
Hormonal changes, 37–38